W0016618

International Education for the Millennium:

Toward Access, Equity, and Quality

International Education for the Millennium

Toward Access, Equity, and Quality

edited by

BENJAMIN PIPER
SARAH DRYDEN-PETERSON
YOUNG-SUK KIM

Harvard Educational Review
Reprint Series No. 42

Library of Congress Control Number 2005937618

ISBN 0-916690-46-6

13-digit ISBN 978-0-916690-46-5

Published by the Harvard Educational Review,
an imprint of the Harvard Education Publishing Group

Harvard Educational Review
8 Story Street
Cambridge, MA 02138

Cover Design: Anne Carter

The typeface used in this book is Adobe Garamond.

Printed in Canada

FOR OUR FAMILIES, WHO INSPIRE US;
AND FOR THE SAMUELS OF THE WORLD, WHO DRIVE US.

Contents

Foreword

MARLAINE E. LOCKHEED

1990 was a turning point in the dialogue around education within the international community, as consensus was reached that education is not only an important determinant of development, but that the quality of education — as measured by student learning observed in classrooms — matters. It was determined that research that looks inside the "black box" of schools can provide vital evidence about how to improve the quality of education in developing countries and, furthermore, that research by educators on how to improve the quality of education can take its place alongside research by economists on how education improves development. This awareness emerged through the publication of a World Bank policy paper on improving primary education and at a meeting of donors in Jomtien, Thailand. I was fortunate to be part of both activities, and to observe how research findings can be used to inform policy. Fifteen years later, education research still has a role to play in the formulation of policy that addresses the new challenges facing education in developing countries.

Arguments in favor of expanding education have been based on three main beliefs regarding the consequences of education: that an educated population is healthier and more productive than an uneducated one, that knowledge is essential for modern societies to function, and that schools play an essential role in building social cohesion and national integration. Over the past three decades, evidence regarding the positive effects of education on social and economic progress has burgeoned.

First, it is now widely agreed that high-quality, equitable education is a driving force for development. Education leads to broad economic and social benefits for individuals and for society: higher productivity and economic growth, lower infant- and child-mortality rates, and better health (Birdsall, Levine, & Ibrahim, 2005; Hanushek & Kimko, 2000). The education of girls and women, in particular, has become recognized as an essential step in improving child health and mortality rates (Herz & Sperling, 2004; Hill & King, 1995; Klasan, 1999; Shultz, 1993) and for reducing fertility (Lloyd, Kaufman, & Hewett, 2000).

Second, education promotes the knowledge economies that are the hallmark of modern society. National measures of "knowledge" that include both education and communication technologies have been found to be significant determinants of long-term economic growth (Chen & Dahlman, 2004). Knowledge economies benefit from both domestic innovation, such as new patents and technological adaptation of foreign innovations to local circumstances. Knowledge economies also benefit from information and communication infrastructures that provide avenues for information exchange, even to remote and rural communities, directly connecting them to markets.

Third, education leads to greater social cohesion. As Heyneman (2000) notes, "The principal task of public schooling, properly organized and delivered, has traditionally been to create harmony within a nation of divergent peoples" (p. 177). Such harmony not only improves the quality of life for individuals, but also benefits society at large through improved cooperation and trade (Putnam, 1993). Inclusive education that reaches ethnic and language minorities and other excluded groups is essential not only to provide education for all, but also to build this social cohesion.

The international community has long achieved near consensus about the importance of equitable access to education, beginning with the Universal Declaration of Human Rights in 1948, which recognized compulsory elementary education as a universal entitlement (United Nations, 1948). Other international declarations followed: the Convention on the Elimination of All Forms of Discrimination against Women called for "no discrimination in the extent of educational provision for women and men" (United Nations, 1979, Part III, Article 10.a-h); the Convention on the Rights of the Child reaffirmed the right of every child to free and compulsory primary education (United Nations, 1989, Article 28.1.a); the Jomtien World Declaration on Education For All called for basic education "to be provided to all children, youth and adults" (World Conference on Education for All, 1990, Article III.1); the Dakar Framework for Action focused on remediating inequities caused by poverty (World Education Forum, 2000); and the Millennium Development Goals (United Nations, 2000), which established timetables for eliminating gender inequities in education. Despite these international commitments, it is estimated that over 100 million children remain out of school, of which the majority are girls and ethnic or language-minority children. Providing them access is important, but access alone is not enough.

Quality counts, and for children enrolled in school in many developing countries, the quality of education is shockingly poor. The 1990 Jomtien Declaration recognized this and introduced something new to the international dialogue, a call for quality in education: "Whether or not expanded educational opportunities will translate into meaningful development . . . depends ultimately on whether people actually learn as a result of these opportunities" (World Conference on Education for All, 1990, Article III.1). In 1990, there was little concrete evidence about what and how much children learned in schools in developing countries, although despair regarding the poor quality of education was widespread. However, as I wrote in one of the World Bank's contributions to Jomtien, there were

> enormous difficulties in demonstrating that educational quality, as indicated by children's learning, is unsatisfactory. Cross-national evidence of children's learning is limited to a few studies, and evidence of change in learning is virtually nonexistent. (Lockheed & Verspoor, 1991, p. xvi)

Only fourteen low- and lower-middle-income countries had participated in any of those few cross-national studies of learning between 1970 and 1983. One consequence of this lack of research was that despite much agreement about the poor quality of education, little evidence was available to document the claim or to recommend mechanisms for change. Change began in 1990 and, with international support and national commitments, the number of countries participating in international studies of achievement had increased nearly five-fold by 2005, including multi-country international studies of learning carried out in countries of Africa, Asia, Eastern Europe, and Latin America, under the auspices of such groups as the Southern Africa Consortium for the Monitoring of Education Quality, the International Association for the Evaluation of Educational Achievement, the Organisation for Economic Co-operation and Development (OECD), and the Latin American Laboratory for Evaluating the Quality of Education.

The new availability of rigorous cross-national measures of learning allowed for an explosion of new research on the determinants and consequences of learning in developing countries. In the mid-1990s, research examined correlates of learning achievement: instructional inputs such as textbooks, teacher knowledge, teaching practices, management focused on learning, and strategies for greater inclusion (Fuller & Clark, 1996; Levin & Lockheed, 1997). More recently, economists have begun using measures of achievement to estimate the effects of education quality on economic growth and to document the weak performance of school systems in some developing countries (Hanushek & Kimko, 2000; Pritchett, 2004).

Much of this research was designed to inform education policy and practice internationally. This research has been summarized in documents of such multilateral organizations as the World Bank, UNESCO, and the Inter-American Development Bank, and by various bilateral donors (e.g., Bruns, Mingat & Rakotomalala, 2003; UNESCO, 2004; Wolff, Schiefelbein, & Schiefelbein, 2002). The foundation for these documents is research on international education, carried out increasingly by scholars from the developing countries. In 1990, the share of education research carried out by developing country researchers was miniscule (see, for example, Lockheed & Verspoor, 1991). Today, the evidence for what works in schools in developing countries is being generated by researchers in developing countries working alone, in partnership with colleagues in other developing countries, or in partnership with colleagues from more developed countries.

As rigorous research on education quality continues to expand, new research is needed to guide strategies and policies for improving education. With the challenge of primary school access met in the majority of countries and significant progress being made on the challenge of equity, the challenge of how to improve the quality of education remains substantial in many developing countries (Baker & LeTendre, 2005). There is much consensus about what good schools look like and how they operate, but little agreement about the best ways to create these good schools. New studies are exploring methods for delivering services to the poor (World Bank, 2004), including how to ensure that schools have the instructional materials, teachers, and management they need for improved teaching and learning. International education research is guiding policy decisions at the national and local levels. For example, new research supports placing greater authority and responsibility in the hands of local communities and schools. In 1990, most education systems worldwide were managed centrally by ministries of education, and only in a few federal systems were education systems controlled by subnational units. Research found that central delivery systems led to inequitable and poor-quality systems. Today, as a result of these research findings, decentralized education systems are common, with responsibility devolved to local schools and communities. At the same time, another increasingly popular strategy depends on centralized programs that boost student attendance by providing "conditional cash transfers" to poor families who send their children to school regularly. These sorts of subsidies were rare in 1990. But, today, because of carefully designed evaluations that documented the success of cash subsidies on the educational outcomes of children, such cash transfer programs are operating successfully in Bangladesh, Brazil, Chile, Honduras, Mexico, and Nicaragua (Morley & Coady, 2003).

International research has shed light on many past challenges of educational development, but newly emerging challenges will require as much or more attention as the earlier ones. These challenges affect not only the ability of countries to provide a good quality education for all, but also the ability of education systems to contribute to social and economic development. Some of these new challenges are:

- *Armed conflict.* In 1990, reconstruction was a word seldom associated with education systems. Today, schools in as many as forty countries have been destroyed or are threatened by war and civil disorder, and millions of child refugees lack access to any form of education. Others receive education under the auspices of the United Nations High Commissioner for Refugees, which is sorely stretched to provide all that is required.
- *Natural disasters.* Further destruction of the physical infrastructure of education has come from hurricanes and flooding, as in Indonesia, Thailand, and Guatemala. Poorly constructed schools also have been destroyed by earthquakes in Iran, Pakistan, and India. How will the education system respond? By rebuilding in vulnerable areas? By providing alternative education to children displaced from their own communities? By expanding education provision in less vulnerable areas?
- *Communicable diseases.* In 1990, the international community recognized that children's ability to learn was affected by parasites, chronic malnutrition, micronutrient deficiencies, and such communicable diseases as measles and malaria. Today, in addition to these, HIV/AIDS has orphaned a million children in Africa alone, while at the same time eroding the quality of their schools, with entire cohorts of teachers having vanished, victims of the disease. These shifts create acute policy problems.
- *Urbanization.* In 1990, the vast majority of children who were out of school lived in rural areas. Today, with urbanization growing dramatically, high percentages of children not in school live in cities and mega-cities. While access issues related to distance have declined, those related to urban poverty and the high cost of school construction in urban areas have increased. Again, educational research in developing countries must address these trends.

- *Technology and the Internet.* In 1990, few education systems could access global knowledge, and the Internet was unheard of in the poorest countries. Today, community learning centers bring the world to the remotest locations, but equity in access remains a challenge. For example, in 1999, fewer than half of eighth grade students in Indonesia, Iran, Morocco, South Africa, Tunisia, Turkey, or the Slovak Republic attended schools that had computers (Mullis et al., 2000).
- *Content of the curriculum.* In 1990, little evidence was available regarding the not-so-hidden messages in school textbooks that promoted discrimination against women, ethnic minorities, and people from other countries. Today, scholars of international education have documented how, in some countries, textbooks contribute to ethnic, gender, and cultural intolerance. Active strategies that deal with these curricula and hidden curriculum problems remain critical for those interested in international education.

It remains for the next generation of scholars of international education to address these challenges. There is reason for optimism in this regard. These new scholars are increasingly international and have had life experiences that inform their work. They are also more broadly and rigorously trained, bringing both quantitative and qualitative research methods to guide their investigations. And they are more adept at translating their research results into policy documents that are accessible to non-researchers. As a consequence, significant progress should be made in moving toward high-quality education for all.

References

Baker, D., & LeTendre, G. (2005). *National differences, global similarities: World culture and the future of schooling.* Stanford, CA: Stanford University Press.

Birdsall, N., Levine, R., & Ibrahim, A. (Eds.). (2005). *Towards universal primary education: Investments, incentives and institutions.* Sterling, VA: Stylus.

Bruns, B., Mingat, A., & Rakotomalala, R. (2003). *A chance for every child: Achieving universal primary education by 2015.* Washington, DC: World Bank.

Chen, D. H. C., & Dahlman, C. J. (2004, August). *Knowledge and development: A cross-section approach* (Working Paper Series 3366). Washington, DC: World Bank.

Fuller, B., & Clark, P. (1996). Raising school effects while ignoring culture? Local conditions and the influence of classroom tools, rules and pedagogy. *Review of Educational Research, 64,* 119–158.

Hanushek, E., & Kimko, D. (2000). Schooling, labor force quality and the growth of nations. *Journal of Economic Literature, 90,* 1184–1208.

Herz, B., & Sperling, G. B. (2004). *What works in girls' education: Evidence and policies from the developing world.* Washington, DC: Council on Foreign Relations.

Heyneman, S. P. (2000). From the party/state to multiethnic democracy: Education and social cohesion in Europe and central Asia. *Educational Evaluation and Policy Analysis, 22,* 173–192

Hill, M. A., & King, E. (1995). Women's education and economic well-being. *Feminist Economics, 1,* 21–46.

Klasan, S. (1999). *Does gender inequality reduce growth and development: Evidence from cross-country regressions* (World Bank Policy Research Report on Gender and Development, Working Paper 7). Washington DC: World Bank.

Levin, H. M., & Lockheed, M. E. (Eds.). (1997). *Effective schools in developing countries.* Washington, DC: Falmer Press.

Lloyd, C. B., Kaufman, C. E., & Hewett, P. (2000). The spread of primary schooling in sub-Sarahan Africa: Implications for fertility change. *Population and Development Review, 26,* 483–515.

Lockheed, M. E., & Verspoor, A. (1991). *Improving primary education in developing countries.* New York: Oxford University Press.

Morley, S., & Coady, D. (2003). *From social assistance to social development: Targeted education subsidies in developing countries.* Washington, DC: Center for Global Development and International Food Policy Research Institute.

Mullis, I. V. S., Martin, M. O., Gonzalez, E. J., Gregory, K. D., Garden, R. A., O'Connor, K. M., et al. (2000). *TIMSS 1999 International mathematics report: Finding from IEA's Repeat of the Third International Mathematics and Science Study at the Eighth Grade.* Boston: Boston College, Lynch School of Education.

Postlethwaite, T. N., & Ross, K. (1992). *Effective schools in reading: Implications for educational planners.* The Hague: International Association for the Evaluation of Educational Achievement

Pritchett, L. (2004, April). *Towards a new consensus for addressing the global challenge of the lack of education.* Copenhagen Consensus Challenge Paper.

Putnam, R. D. (1993). *Making democracy work: Civic tradition in modern Italy.* Princeton, NJ: Princeton University Press.

Shultz, T. P. (1993). Returns to women's schooling. In E. King, & A. Hill (Eds.), *Women's education in developing countries: Barriers, benefits and policy* (pp. 51–99). Baltimore: Johns Hopkins University Press.

UNESCO. (2004). *Education for All: The quality imperative.* Paris: Author.

United Nations. (1948). *Universal declaration of human rights.* New York: Author.

United Nations. (1979). *Convention on the elimination of all forms of discrimination against women.* New York: Author.

United Nations. (1989). *Convention on the rights of the child.* New York: Author.

United Nations. (2000). *Millennium Development Goals.* New York: Author.

Wolff, L., Schiefelbein, E., & Schiefelbein, P. (2000). *Primary education in Latin America: The unfinished agenda.* Washington, DC: Inter-American Development Bank.

World Bank. (2004). *World development report: Making services work for poor people.* Washington, DC: Author.

World Conference on Education for All. (1990). *World declaration on Education for All.* Jomtien, Thailand: Author.

World Conference on Education for All. (1990). *Meeting basic learning needs: A vision for the 1990s.* New York: Interagency Commission for World Conference on Education for All.

World Education Forum. (2000). *Dakar framework for action.* Dakar, Senegal: Author.

International Education for the Millennium: Toward Access, Equity, and Quality

INTRODUCTION

Samuel is ten years old. He talks about school in the way most parents in the United States wish their children would: he loves it. The problem is that school has been a rare experience for Samuel. He lives in Kampala, Uganda, and, even under universal primary education, primary schools charge user fees, or tuition. His family does not have enough money to pay for food, let alone for education for Samuel and his siblings. Samuel's access to school is barred in part because of who he is and in part because of where he lives. Samuel is a refugee from the Democratic Republic of Congo and, like nearly half a million of his fellow countrymen (United Nations High Commissioner for Refugees [UNHCR], 2004), he has fled armed conflict and now lives in exile in Kampala.

Like many others who have been marginalized due to ethnicity or poverty, displaced people — who number over 44.5 million worldwide (Global Internally Displaced Person Project, 2005; UNHCR, 2004) — do not have equitable access to schools. Rapid urbanization around the world, which has reached 5 percent per annum on the African continent (Harsch, 2001; Ogbu & Ikiara, 1995; Simone, 2003), also contributes to growing inequity in terms of who goes to school and who, like Samuel, does not. While a community-organized and -supported school allowed Samuel to be in school for two years, it has since closed, and Samuel now sits at home with eyes that speak of a lost hope. "What makes me most sad," Samuel says, "is to see my friends go to school in the morning, but not me."

Since the 1990 and 2000 Education For All (EFA) conferences in Jomtien, Thailand, and Dakar, Senegal, respectively, United Nations (UN) agencies and national ministries of education have led efforts to improve children's access to and the equity of primary education. These initiatives have inspired great increases in the number of children enrolled in primary school but have left out children like Samuel. Indeed, the UN Educational, Scientific, and Cultural Organization (UNESCO, 2004) reports that there are more than 100 million children still not in school. Like Samuel, most of these children live in countries in sub-Saharan Africa, Asia, and Central and South America — countries collectively known as the global South. The global South

1

includes the majority of our world: 157 of the 184 recognized states. These countries face some of the greatest global challenges of our time: poverty, hunger, disease, environmental degradation, human rights abuses, and ethnic conflicts.

In 2002, UN Secretary General Kofi Annan commissioned the Millennium Project to develop an action plan to address these challenges. One of the eight Millennium Development Goals (MDGs) calls for a dramatic increase in educational access while ensuring equity for those disadvantaged by national and regional power structures. The title of this book — *International Education for the Millennium: Toward Access, Equity, and Quality* — reflects these goals, which have become the most relevant benchmarks for measuring educational progress. The millions of children that Samuel represents speak to the book's timeliness and urgency. Indeed, the UN recently released a progress report on the MDGs, indicating that many countries in sub-Saharan Africa and some countries in other parts of the global South are unlikely to reach these goals by the 2015 target date (UNESCO, 2004). The responsibility to act on this crisis in education is one we must all share, regardless of where we live.

Educational opportunities are not finite, but in many parts of the world they are limited. Great educational inequities exist within the United States, for example, where most of our readers live. But the largest educational disparities exist between wealthy countries like the United States and the global South, and within the global South itself. As part of an interconnected, globalized world, we cannot afford — economically, socially, environmentally — to stand by and watch the potential of generations of children go to waste. The *Harvard Educational Review* sees the fight against this inequity in education as a cornerstone of its mission. The focus of this book, education development in countries of the global South, is an attempt to address these disparities in a forward-looking way. Research in the field of education, in which our journal specializes, has much to contribute to effective policy and practice designed to move toward educational access, equity, and quality for *all* children.

This book highlights three components of education development: access, equity, and quality. While the Dakar EFA Framework for Action set a precedent for this division, our use of these components in understanding education development differs in important ways. First, the central focus of EFA is access, a lens through which equity and quality are evaluated (UNESCO, 2004). This focus, however, limits the potential for educational development to meet the goals outlined above. We argue instead that the three components cannot be separated one from the other, or prioritized. Second, the three components of EFA have often been presented as a linear progression. From this perspective, the first obstacle Samuel faces is obtaining a free seat in a classroom (access); the second obstacle is his difficulty in obtaining that seat due to ethnicity, language spoken at home, gender, rural or urban location, or regional differences (equity); and the third obstacle is whether Samuel's teacher has adequate training and his school sufficient supplies (quality). While access, equity, and quality often do occur sequentially, our understanding of these terms does not depend on linearity. Indeed, in many Southern countries, working directly for quality — and thereby eschewing forms of access that lend themselves to inequity and low quality — may prove critical to achieving all three components of education development.

Access

The sharp gains in worldwide educational access achieved postindependence in much of the global South slowed, or even reversed completely, as a result of the neoliberal international macroeconomic policies of the World Bank and the International Monetary Fund in the 1980s. However, as mentioned above, EFA has galvanized the international community and Southern governments to tackle the problem of access, and we have entered the new millennium with many encouraging developments. In Ethiopia, for example, access rates leapt from 24 percent in 1993 to 65 percent in 2003 (Ethiopian Ministry of Education, 2003), nearly a threefold increase in ten years.[1] However, despite a general trend of increase in access to primary education, the authors of this volume emphasize significant caveats to the notion that universal access has been achieved. Recent evaluations of progress toward the MDGs note that eight out of ten children who are not in school live in sub-Saharan Africa, South Asia, and Southeast Asia (UNESCO, 2004). India has the largest number of children not in school, as well as the greatest numbers of illiterate adults (Dréze & Sen, 2002). The move toward universal access to education has indeed been unequal across the globe: Although education access has generally increased, access rates in sub-Saharan Africa, South Asia, and Southeast Asia have leveled off well below 100 percent.

In seeking to address persistent impediments to access, the implementation of universal primary education comes into question. Although a rhetoric of universal access exists in countries such as Uganda and Kenya, ancillary fees preclude many children living in poverty from enrolling in school or continuing their education (Amutabi, 2003; Mukudi, 2004). In Uganda, for example, Samuel does not have the money to pay for items that are prerequisites for taking up a seat in a classroom: textbooks, pencils, paper, and a uniform. These material impediments to universal access could be overcome with increased educational expenditures. Many Southern governments, however, already spend 20 percent of their total budgets on education (Colclough, 1991; Samoff, 2003), and these expenditures are unlikely to increase as an absolute percentage. As a result, many Southern countries will only be able to overcome the material constraints encountered by children like Samuel when the country's relative wealth increases. Ironically, this increase is likely to occur only with the increased human capital that results from an educated population. Furthermore, some scholars argue that while the provision of school buildings, teachers, and some materials provides the incentives necessary to achieve 90 percent access, harnessing the last 10 percent is more difficult (Samoff, 2003). This final push requires efforts to deal with demand-side constraints, particularly the economic production lost to families when their children attend school (Colclough, 1991). The *Progresa* program in Mexico addresses this problem by granting vouchers that make up for the loss of labor to families that enroll their children in school (Schultz, 2001).

To achieve truly universal access to education, this type of innovative scheme that addresses existing economic and social conditions is essential. In the long run, however, only giving attention to eradicating poverty and to development focused on raising the relative wealth of Southern countries (Sachs, 2005) will make sustainable, universal access to education a reality. China is a powerful example of this connection between increased access and economic growth; indeed, China's recent economic boom was preceded by significant increases in educational access over the preceding decades. To accomplish the goal of access, Northern and Southern governments alike must do more than sign declarations and EFA action plans. They must contribute material and technical resources to help end poverty and to make school attendance an economic reality, for both families and nations.

Equity

Access and equity are intertwined. The field of international education often measures equity by disaggregating access rates to determine whether any ethnic, language, socioeconomic, or gender groups have been overlooked by the education system. For example, the language of instruction can limit the ability of a group of children to benefit from education (Bamgbose, 1991; Brock-Utne & Holmarsdottir, 2004; Wagaw, 1999). Recognizing this barrier to equity, South African and Ethiopian policies now allow for the use of the mother tongue, local languages, and indigenous languages in primary education, thus promoting equity in access to the content of teaching. Despite these encouraging policy shifts, questions still remain about educational equity for children who are still language minorities, even in schools that teach in local languages.

Indeed, efforts are needed to ensure that equity does not come at the cost of access. This paradox is particularly evident in the example of gender parity. In many parts of the global South, girls are underrepresented in schools; this inequity has significant consequences for individuals and for society, as Stromquist and Stefanos point out in this volume. UNICEF, UNESCO, the UN Girls Education Initiative, the Forum for African Women Educationalists, bilateral donors, international nongovernmental organizations, and especially local community organizations have worked to increase the educational opportunities of girls. However, these successful efforts have had the effect of transforming the broader term "equity" into one that means "gender parity." With equity defined in this limited manner, access to education for ethnic and language minorities, for example, has been largely ignored.

The search for equity in education has in large part been directed by local community organizations, which create and maintain schools to serve hard-to-reach students (Bray, 1999; USAID, 2001). A community-based school was the only educational possibility for Samuel in his situation of displacement, for example. The need for local solutions in creating educational equity is echoed multiple times in this volume, by Freire, Mahshi, Vacarro, and the volunteers of Reach Out. These chapters present stories of local communities working for educational equity for their children. While celebrating these efforts, we cannot ignore the inadequacy and inequitable nature of state education systems. Emphasizing the responsibilities of the state and of the international community is critical to long-term equity in education.

Finally, we pose the need to look beyond national borders in examining equity. Although the extent of globalization's impact on much of the world's population remains largely unknown, individual economic agents are certainly in competition across borders. While many scholars have for years eschewed the use of national-level data, arguing that they mask dramatic inequities, micro-level comparisons across borders provide important insight into equity. We write from Cambridge, Massachusetts, where the average per-pupil expenditure in 2004 was U.S. $16,116 (Massachusetts Department of Education, 2005). In Uganda, around U.S. $19 would have been spent on Samuel's education in 2001 (Uganda Ministry of Education and Sports, 2003). Different economic systems aside, this immense disparity is evidence of the significant hurdles that remain to achieving real equity in international education.

Quality

At this point in the debate about education development in countries of the global South, a central question must be addressed: Access and equity to what end? In many countries, increased education access — and equity of that access — often does not afford real educational opportunities. In this volume, Vavrus shows that without systemic planning that affords real change, education can be a duplicitous act: It appeases populations that should be organizing for a drastic overhaul of government systems. In addition, the focus on primary education in the South is not sufficient if a graduate is to compete in an increasingly globalized market. The attention paid to primary education has allowed many countries to hide paltry secondary and tertiary enrollment rates. The result is often a near universally primary-educated population but a continually stratified society based on education level.

A paradigm shift in the evaluation of access and equity is necessary, such that the classroom becomes paramount. The definition of quality must depend on equitable access to well-trained teachers engaged in high-quality pedagogy in sufficiently equipped classrooms. Evidence from around the world shows that access and equity are not enough to ensure educational progress: Even with equal access, girls, ethnic minorities, language minorities, and indigenous populations struggle to read and write at high rates (Brenzinger, 1997; Reimers & Schmelkes, 2002; Sutton, 1998).

The recent focus on quality that has begun to replace and refine earlier discussions on access and equity in international education is encouraging (UNESCO, 2004). However, quality has only recently begun to receive attention in EFA documents, and the academic literature on this topic is in its infancy. This volume makes a number of contributions to this nascent conversation. Reimers and Mahshi, for example, make the argument that the quality of education depends on teachers. Since more than 90 percent of education budgets in the South are teacher salaries, this focus on the teaching force is well justified and provides a solid base for forward-looking strategies aimed at promoting universal quality (Farrell & Oliveira, 1993). Indeed, the prevailing World Bank model of the student learning process is incomplete. It focuses largely on inputs (i.e., books, school infrastructure, school governance, pencils, and uniforms) and outputs (i.e., student learning measured by end of grade and end of school tests), while neglecting the very place where these inputs and outputs intersect: the classroom.

In the endeavor to expand the role of teachers in increasing education quality, many Southern countries have implemented preservice and in-service training that focuses on active learning or student-centered instruction (Ackers & Hardman, 2001; Brodie, Lelliot, & Davis, 2002; Cuban, 1993; Gidey, 2002). This pedagogical strategy trains teachers to utilize group work, encourage questions from students, make engaging use of teaching aids, and allow real dialogue in the classroom. There is some evidence that where these strategies have tapped into local realities relevant to students, some success with respect to student achievement has been achieved (Croft, 2002; O'Sullivan, 2002). However, in some contexts the active learning methodology has proven difficult to implement, perhaps because the strategies are very different from how teachers themselves were taught or because they require extra work on behalf of already overtaxed teachers (Brodie et al., 2002; Clarke, 2003; Dyer & Choksi, 2004).

Although teacher practice is difficult to change (Cuban, 1993), it is by far the most important element of education development. And while getting the substance of the reform right will prove a continual challenge, there is real evidence that this effort will be worthwhile. In various contexts, rigorous research has shown that increasing the skill level of teachers, decreasing class size to manageable levels, providing basic materials, and offering sustained teacher training and incentive structures for continued professional learning will result in better teachers, higher student achievement, and high-quality education (Angrist & Lavy, 2001; Hanushek, Kain, & Rivkin, 2004; Jacob & Lefgren, 2005; Mullens, Murnane, & Willett, 1996). Samuel deserves no less.

Taken together, the collection of new and reprinted articles in this volume offers a comparative view of education development in countries of the global South. Each article differs in the issues it addresses, the strategies it explores, and the geographic setting. In many cases, however, these issues and strategies will be relevant to other situations throughout the world. Such our hope for this book. Indeed, each author has forward-looking commentary to offer on the critical goals of access, equity, and quality that we have outlined here.

We have divided the book into three sections with the aim of allowing readers to investigate the entire continuum of the education development process. Part One, Frameworks and Theoretical Perspectives on International Education, presents theoretical conceptions of educational development that can be used as tools in thinking about educational change. Part Two, Transitions and Reform in International Education, explores the formation of education policy and methods of educational reform in light of national and local realities. The book concludes with Part Three, Community Solutions for Educational Change, which explores the critical role communities play in closing gaps in formal education systems and in pushing for large-scale change. While we present these sections in a sequential order, as the format of a printed book requires, we do not suggest that the processes themselves are linear. Like access, equity, and quality, theory, policy, and action interact continuously. As many of the authors suggest, it is through these interactions that real change for Samuel and millions of children in similar situations can occur.

Benjamin Piper, Sarah Dryden-Peterson, Young-Suk Kim

Note

1. These are net primary enrollment rates.

References

Ackers, J., & Hardman, F. (2001). Classroom interaction in Kenyan primary schools. *Compare, 31,* 245–261.

Amutabi, M. N. (2003). Political interference in the running of education in post-independence Kenya: A critical retrospection. *International Journal of Educational Development, 23,* 127–144.

Angrist, J., & Lavy, V. (2001). Does teacher training affect pupil learning? Evidence from matched comparisons in Jerusalem public schools. *Journal of Labor Economics, 19,* 343–369.

Bamgbose, A. (1991). *Language and the nation: The language question in sub-Saharan Africa.* Edinburgh: Edinburgh University Press.

Bloor, T., & Tamrat, W. (1996). Multilingualism and education: The case of Ethiopia. *Journal of Multilingual and Multicultural Development, 17,* 321–338.

Bray, M. (1999). Control of education: Issues and tensions in centralization and decentralization. In R. F. Arnove & C. A. Torres (Eds.), *Comparative education: The dialectic of the global and the local* (pp. 207–232). Lanham, MD: Rowman & Littlefield.

Brenzinger, M. (1997). An evaluative account of Ethiopia's new language policy. In M. Putz (Ed.), *Language choices: Conditions, constraints, and consequences* (pp. 207–221). Amsterdam: John Benjamins.

Brock-Utne, B., & Holmarsdottir, H. B. (2004). Language policies and practices in Tanzania and South Africa: Problems and challenges. *International Journal of Educational Development, 24,* 67–83.

Brodie, K., Lelliot, A., & Davis, H. (2002). Forms and substance in learner-centred teaching: Teachers' take-up from an in-service programme in South Africa. *Teaching and Teacher Education, 18,* 541–559.

Clarke, P. (2003). Culture and classroom reform: The case of the District Primary Education Project, India. *Comparative Education, 39,* 27–44.

Colclough, C. (1991). Who should learn to pay? An assessment of neo-liberal approaches to education policy. In C. Colclough & J. Manor (Eds.), *States or markets? Neo-liberalism and the development policy debate* (pp. 197–213). Oxford, England: Clarendon Press.

Croft, A. (2002). Singing under a tree: Does oral culture help lower primary teachers be learner-centred. *International Journal of Educational Development, 22,* 321–337.

Cuban, L. (1993). *How teachers taught.* New York: Teachers College Press.

Dréze, J., & Sen, A. (2002). *India: Development and participation* (2nd ed.). New York: Oxford University Press.

Dyer, C., & Choksi, A. (2002). Democratizing teacher education research in India. *Comparative Education, 38,* 337–351.

Ethiopian Ministry of Education. (2003). *Indicators of the Ethiopian education system.* Addis Ababa: Author.

Farrell, J., & Oliveira, J. (1993). *Teachers in developing countries: Improving effectiveness and managing costs.* Washington, DC: World Bank.

Gidey, M. (2002, March 6). *Preparing more and better teachers: A new vision of teacher development in Ethiopia.* Paper presented at the annual meeting of the Comparative International Education Society, Orlando, FL. (ERIC Document Reproduction Service No. ED 470507)

Global Internally Displaced Person Project. (2005). *Internal displacement: Global overview of trends and developments in 2004.* Geneva: Author.

Hanushek, E., Kain, J., & Rivkin, S. (2004). *Teachers, schools, academic achievement* (NBER Working Paper No. 6691). Cambridge, MA: National Bureau of Economic Research.

Harsch, E. (2001). African cities under strain: Initiatives to improve housing, services, security and governance. *Africa Recovery, 15,* 1–9.

Jacob, B. A., & Lefgren, L. (2002). *The impact of teacher training on student achievement: Quasi-experimental evidence from school reform efforts in Chicago* (NBER Working Paper No. 8916). Cambridge, MA: National Bureau of Economic Research.

Massachusetts Department of Education Office of School Finance. (2005, August). *Per pupil expenditures.* Retrieved December 19, 2005, from http://finance1.doe.mass.edu/statistics/pp04.xls

Mukudi, E. (2004). Education for all: A framework for addressing the persisting illusion for the Kenyan context. *International Journal of Educational Development, 24,* 231–240.

Mullens, J. E., Murnane, R. J., & Willett, J. B. (1996). The contribution of training and subject matter knowledge to teaching effectiveness: A multilevel analysis of longitudinal evidence from Belize. *Comparative Education Review, 40,* 139–157.

Lockheed, M., & Verspoor, A. (1991). *Improving primary education in developing countries.* Washington, DC: World Bank.

Ogbu, O., & Ikiara, G. (1995). The crisis of urbanisation in sub-Saharan Africa. *Courier, 149,* 52–59.

O'Sullivan, M. (2002). Reform implementation and the realities within which teachers work: A Namibian case study. *Compare, 32,* 219–237.

Reimers, F., & Schmelkes, S. (2002). *Education policy and equity in Chile.* Unpublished report.

Sachs, J. (2005). *The end of poverty: Economic possibilities for our time.* New York: Penguin Press.

Samoff, J. (2003, November 3). *EFA in Africa: Tracks, delays and derailments.* Paper presented at the Harvard Graduate School of Education, Cambridge, MA.

Schultz, T. P. (2001). *School subsidies for the poor: Evaluating the Mexican Progresa poverty program* (Economic Growth Center Discussion Paper No. 834). New Haven, CT: Economic Growth Center.

Simone, A. M. (2003, June 4). *Moving towards uncertainty: Migration and the turbulence of African life.* Paper presented at the Conference on African Migration in Comparative Perspective, Johannesburg, South Africa.

Sutton, M. (1998). Girls' educational access and attainment. In N. P. Stromquist (Ed.), *Women in the third world. An encyclopedia of contemporary issues* (pp. 381–396). New York: Garland.

Uganda Ministry of Education and Sports. (2003). *ADEA country case study.* Kampala: Uganda Ministry of Education and Sports. Retrieved December 18, 2005, from http://www.education.go.ug/adea_country_case_study.htm

United Nations Educational, Scientific, and Cultural Organization. (2004). *EFA global monitoring report: The quality imperative.* Paris: Author.

United Nations Educational, Scientific, and Cultural Organization. (2005). *Education: Primary education.* Paris: Author. Retrieved December 20, 2005, from http://portal.unesco.org/education

United Nations High Commissioner for Refugees. (2004). *2004 global refugee trends: Overview of refugee populations, new arrivals, durable solutions, asylum-seekers and other persons of concern to UNHCR.* Geneva: Author, Population Data Unit.

United States Agency for International Development. (2001). *Overview of USAID basic education programs in sub-Saharan Africa III* (Sustainable Development Publication Series Technical Paper No. 106). Washington, DC: Author.

Wagaw, T. (1999). Conflict of ethnic identity and the language of education policy in contemporary Ethiopia. *Northeast African Studies, 6,* 75–88.

The Editors would like to thank Douglas Clayton, Dody Riggs, Laura Clos, Jeffrey Perkins, and the Editorial Board of the *Harvard Educational Review* for their hard work and wise guidance.

PART ONE

Frameworks and
Theoretical Perspectives
on International Education

PART ONE

Introduction

In recent years, international education as a field has grown and shifted in exciting ways. The Education For All conference held in Jomtien, Thailand, was an important marker for education in the developing world, as countries from the Northern and Southern Hemispheres came together and agreed to work to increase access to education for all of the world's children. The Millennium Development Goals, approved by 189 United Nation member countries, reaffirmed the worldwide educational community's commitment to that task. However, at the beginning of the new millennium, many challenges remain, among them the elusive task of achieving equity in access to and quality of education in all nations.

The best tools at our disposal in the quest for increased educational access, equity, and quality are the theories and frameworks that help us to understand the educational milieus of countries in the global South. In order to recognize the appropriateness of employing methods and programs that have been successful in one context in another, we draw on theories about the cross-cultural nature of such programs. To evaluate the success of programs and reforms, we employ frameworks to measure that success. To ensure that education will be a means to achieve liberty and freedom, we seek to understand how and why education has frequently been used as a weapon for control. This section presents such theories and frameworks and a broad historical overview of the field of comparative and international education. We hope that, seen through a theoretical lens, research and policy can become more effective at improving the educational systems of Southern countries.

In "Comparative and International Education: A Journey toward Equality and Equity," Nelly Stromquist summarizes the shifting understanding of the field of Comparative and International Education (CIE). She provides an overview of historical trends in theory, research methods, and central findings over recent decades. Stromquist begins by differentiating and synthesizing the two separate yet closely connected fields of comparative education and international education. She discusses shifting themes and theories in CIE: studies on student achievement, modernism, dependency, critical studies, postmodernism, poststructuralism, and postcolonialism. She also discusses the changing role of education in society, the various types of learning outside of formal schools, the role of multicultural education, gender studies, and the impact of globalization on various dimensions of education. Stromquist delineates and foreshadows current trends in education, which are discussed in more detail in other chapters in the book. These include the unprecedented role of financial and transnational institutions and nongovernmental organizations (NGOs) in today's education systems, the proliferation of research sponsored by multilateral and bilateral institutions, and the Education For All and Millennium Development Goals movements. Stromquist is able to combine this broad history with a theoretical synopsis, while maintaining a theme of hope of achieving educational equity and quality through the collective actions of stakeholders.

Two contributions from Paulo Freire, a pillar of educational development and the father of critical pedagogy, have shaped the way that scholars and practitioners in the field of international education view their work. In these seminal articles, "The Adult Literacy Process as Cultural Action for Freedom" and "Cultural Action and Conscientization," Freire provides a synopsis of critical pedagogy. He defines the adult literacy process not only as decoding written symbols or depositing knowledge, but as "cultural action for freedom," a process that occurs through authentic dialogue between learners and teachers. Criticizing "traditional" education, which he suggests has been a means of reproducing the existing social structure, Freire argues that learning and teaching are political acts that should facilitate students' achievement of freedom. Thus, literacy acquisition empowers learners to be aware and critical of the culture of power in which individuals live. Constant engagement with the problematization of learners' existential situations helps learners transform their realities. Freire also elaborates on the concept of conscientization, a process through which one analyzes and becomes aware of the power of the sociocultural reality. Freire presents the philosophical basis and the social context that led him to develop his view. Through this discussion of the historical conditions and transitions in Latin America in the 1960s, he explains the emergence of levels of consciousness that transformed the "mute" masses into agent of political and historical change in the Third World.

In "No Longer Overlooked and Undervalued? The Evolving Dynamics of Endogenous Educational Research in Sub-Saharan Africa," Richard Maclure questions Africa's dependence on Northern researchers for education research in this region. Maclure demonstrates two primary approaches to research in sub-Saharan Africa. The first is called the donor-control approach, which is characterized by a hierarchical framework in which the needs and perspectives of multilateral and bilateral institutions are paramount. The second, the praxis-oriented approach, is more organic; it includes an understanding that for education research to have an influence on policymaking, policymakers and other stakeholders must have active and empowering roles in the creation and formulation of that research. He focuses on the latter approach by providing an overview of two prominent African educational research networks: the Educational Research Network of West and Central Africa and the Association for the Development of Education in Africa. He argues that the praxis-oriented approach strives to stimulate and strengthen the links between endogenous critical inquiry in research and educational policy formulation and implementation by expanding research networks. Maclure demonstrates that the two networks have uncovered many studies on a wide range of topics, promoted a research model aimed to influence policymaking, and disseminated research findings through publications and conferences. Despite these efforts to build endogenous research capacity and to communicate research findings in order to influence policymaking, Maclure notes that problems remain, primarily due to endogenous scholars' isolation from the international research community and weak infrastructure in the region. Maclure reminds us of the hard work required to achieve "symbiosis between research, reflection, and action."

The chapters in this section present a critical framework for understanding and examining dynamic changes in educational research across Southern countries. They provide a synopsis of the evolution of conceptualizations of international education, research, and analytical methodologies; a prognosis for successfully dealing with the remaining challenges in educational research in sub-Saharan Africa; and the tools to examine critically the current state of international education. This section encourages readers to think about the intellectual history of the field, and about the remaining gaps and issues involved in achieving educational access, equity, and quality.

Comparative and
International Education:
A Journey toward Equality and Equity

NELLY P. STROMQUIST

Comparative and international education is a field characterized by wide and constant borrowing of theories, concepts, and research methods from the social sciences. While some see this multidisciplinarity as cause for alarm, others consider it a source of intellectual wealth. Given the multiple disciplines, perspectives, and events that attract the attention of comparative and international education (CIE hereafter), it is difficult to present a consensual view of contributions, progress, and challenges to date. In examining the trajectory of CIE over several decades, I lean on my professional experience, a review of the major journals in the field, and my five years as associate editor for the *Comparative Education Review*. Even so, I make no claims that my account is the most complete or most accurate. Since education systems are intended to have positive effects on society both by providing essential skills and by promoting social mobility and inclusion of all citizens, this review focuses on the issues of equality and equity in the comparative education context.

In 1969, two distinct groups of professionals joined to form the Comparative and International Education Society. In general, comparative education emphasizes the understanding of the dynamics of educational change and seeks to detect patterns of change across countries. International education concentrates primarily on developing countries and endeavors to gear education to the improvement and building of nation-states. CIE is found in university courses and programs and in academic journals, as well as in negotiations between and within states for purposes of policy-making. The ideas and preferences of CIE professionals are played out in various spaces: economists prevail in government and international transactions; in universities, there is a more balanced array of sociologists, political scientists, and, increasingly, anthropologists; in civil society — particularly nongovernmental organizations (NGOs), trade unions, and religious groups — one finds adult educators.

In our recent history, the world has witnessed a second world war, the enactment of the UN Universal Declaration of Human Rights (1948), pervasive conflict along

Harvard Educational Review Vol. 75 No. 1 Spring 2005, 89–111

15

political ideologies in the Cold War, and the formal demise of colonialism. It has also seen several conventions in favor of political, economic, and social rights (particularly the 1979 Convention on the Elimination of All Forms of Discrimination Against Women and the 1989 Convention on the Rights of the Child); numerous global agreements on issues ranging from gender equality to protection of the environment; and increasing tensions along economic and religious lines. During those decades, CIE professionals have shifted their views and priorities, moving from strong reliance on the power of education to shape society and promote development to recognition that education is one force among many — one that is sometimes exploited politically to promise more than it can deliver. In the 1960s, themes included modernization, development, and social transformation; by the 1980s, concerns were more circumscribed, emphasizing basic needs, income generation, and employment (Kelly, 1987). Salient CIE themes at the beginning of the twenty-first century include globalization, gender in education, education in development, and equality in education (Cook, Hite, & Epstein, 2004).

CIE for Prediction or for Understanding?

In the early days of comparative education — the 1960s — there was a firm expectation that the field would develop its own research tools and theories in order to identify regularities characterizing educational systems in the world. Inspired by the significant methodological contributions of the social sciences during World War II, comparative educators such as Bereday (1964) and Noah and Eckstein (1968) guided the quest toward laws governing educational systems. At the same time there were those, notably Holmes (1965) and King (1968), who were less certain about finding regularities through decontextualized and ahistorical knowledge of education. Today the latter perspective is more prevalent, as it is now considered fruitless to search for a general theory of education to explain change and persistence, although it is recognized that conflict is always present in educational decisions and even processes (Behrman, 2003; Bray, 2003; Carnoy & Samoff, 1990; Farrell, 1988).

   In the 1960s and 1970s, the Ford Foundation provided support to several American universities to create international education programs. This support played a decisive role in incorporating the social sciences in the design of curricula for educational programs and financed the training of a large cadre of American and international graduate students as comparative educators. Over time, CIE has shifted from a predominantly equilibrium/functionalist paradigm (based on assumptions of widespread social consensus) to more emphasis on neo-Marxist/conflict theoretical frameworks (more attentive to questions of power differences and domination). According to Crossley and Jarvis (2000), CIE now increasingly recognizes the cultural dimension of education, particularly its efforts to understand distinctions and similarities between cultures in the western and eastern parts of the world. Models focusing on modernization, world systems, and globalization are in common usage, while critical sociological, postmodernist, and feminist paradigms are increasingly present. The field continues to give limited attention to historical and philosophical aspects of education, and to the interaction between education and mass media.

At present, international comparisons coexist with within-nation studies. Large-scale, cross-national studies are expensive and tend to be limited in number, the best known being those conducted by the International Association for the Evaluation of Educational Achievement (IEA) and by the Organization for Economic Cooperation and Development (OECD). A review of publications in three major CIE journals over forty years (Rust, Soumare, Pescador, & Shibuya, 1999) found that fewer than one-third of the articles were based on research designs that explicitly compared two or more countries. Two main foci have characterized comparative studies. Some have focused on student performance, and others have sought to explain the functioning and impact of education systems.

Student Achievement Studies

From 1967 to 2004, IEA had conducted more than twenty cross-national studies focusing on school curricula. The rich information collected in the national studies and the background information gathered for each student benefited the study of educational policy in the context of overall social and economic policy (Husen, 1987). In addition, their multivariate analysis enabled education researchers to disentangle larger social influences and home background from factors operating in the school. The IEA studies have contributed powerful conceptualizations of the education system, covering not only a wide range of inputs and important outcomes, but also making us aware of promising elements in the processes of teaching and learning. IEA studies introduced the distinction between the official, the implemented, and the attained curriculum, a framework that permeates all IEA studies.

Given the complex nature of the learning experience, the quantitative studies provide limited explanation for variation in individual achievement. The Six-Subject Survey (1970), which employed over 500 independent variables, accounted for only 45 percent of the between-student variance for any one school population in a country. Some differences, however, have been detected between developed and developing countries. Major determinants of student achievement in developing countries include the availability of trained teachers, books, and basic infrastructure, such as electricity and water (Velez, Schiefelbein, & Valenzuela, 1993). According to Cronbach (as cited in Riddell, 1989), the majority of studies of educational achievement have produced "false conclusions" because of the "misapplication of a single-level model to a reality that is clearly hierarchical" (p. 484).

In recent years, a new set of quantitative studies has emerged, of which the best known are the Programme for International Student Assessment (PISA) investigations organized by OECD. These studies follow conceptualizations of school impact similar to those used by IEA, but differ in their data collection and analysis. IEA uses intact classrooms, and thus analyzes data by grade, whereas PISA gathers and analyzes data by student age. Moreover, PISA studies do not engage in multilevel analysis of schooling effects.

Recent cross-national studies have incorporated a greater number of countries, including developing countries. Their findings in general show that students from developed countries do much better than those from developing countries; students in urban areas have higher achievement than those in rural regions; and those in private schools perform better than those in public schools (e.g., PASEC, 2002; PIRLS, 2001; PISA, 2000, 2003; TIMSS, 1995; TIMSS-R, 1999). These findings confirm what one would expect, and perhaps reflect the substantial differences in public investment across countries, in the education and economic conditions of teachers, and in school infrastructure within countries. Few studies compare educational achievement between countries within specific developing regions. In one of the few studies of particular interest, Casassus, Froemel, Palafox, and Cusato (1998) compared thirteen Latin American countries in primary school language and mathematics achievement. The researchers found that Cuba surpassed all other countries in both subjects by between 1.5 and 2 standard deviations. Explanations for this extraordinary performance have not been investigated; Silvestre (2004) argues that the synergistic array of particular conditions in Cuban society, including health, housing, and sustained educational investments, account for the results.

Critical Theory Studies

In stark contrast to cross-national quantitative surveys of student achievement, critical theory studies employ qualitative approaches attentive to history and to cultural and political transactions. Bourdieu and Passeron's work (translated into English in 1977) on cultural reproduction and the role of the school in legitimating the dominant cultural capital has helped to present schooling as a terrain far from neutral to all social groups. The extension of Bourdieu's thought by Bowles and Gintis (1976) to the economic reproduction function of schooling further created awareness of the way schools work. Their "correspondence theory" argued that the hierarchically structured patterns of values, norms, and skills that characterized the workforce and the dynamics of class interaction under capitalism were mirrored in the dynamics of daily classroom transactions.

Critical theoreticians such as Gramsci, Freire, and Habermas have shaped the debate of international and comparative education. Gramsci (1992, 1994), exploring the efficacy of persuasion over coercion and the role of education in the establishment of a hegemonic view, has helped us understand the persistence of subordinate social groups in all areas of society. Gramsci's work brought to CIE important, accessible concepts such as hegemony and counterhegemony, the "organic intellectual," and a revitalized civil society. Freire is another important contributor, whose writings were first introduced to North American audiences in the *Harvard Educational Review* in 1970. His *Pedagogy of the Oppressed*, first published in 1970, has sold more than 750,000 copies worldwide and is one of the most broadly read books in education. Freire's work underscores the political nature of education and calls for processes, notably "conscientization" — a deliberate examination of our economic and political environment — as a prerequisite to envisaging how knowledge can serve to eliminate oppression and create a just society. The Frankfurt School further unveiled traditional power relationships and the ideology that supported them by highlighting the importance of cultural and literacy forms in the creation of social representations. Habermas (1984), the contemporary heir of the Frankfurt School, reinforced the emancipatory potential of dialogue inherent in communicative action while defending the value of modernity and reason.

More directly linked to schooling, work by Willis (1977) represented a turning point in the development of resistance theories, which explained how individuals confronted their oppression and how they sometimes ended up reproducing what they sought to question. Subsequent work by Giroux (1983) questioned reproduction theory for downplaying the importance of human agency and resistance, and argued instead that schools are "contested terrains" marked not only by structural and ideological contradictions but also by collective student resistance. From Giroux (1989) we have learned that pockets of resistance in schools can serve as models for new forms of learning and social relations, and that efforts toward democracy can take place in and through teachers who act as transformative intellectuals. These teachers engage in activities such as discussing collective struggles "in which suffering was shaped and contested" and identifying "the material and ideological preconditions" that must be in place to create effective schools (pp. 99, 101).

Dependency theory, which maintains that the development of industrialized countries is predicated on the exploitation of the less developed regions of the world, was first applied in Latin America to explain developing countries' failure to attain the economic growth that modernity promised. This theory was first applied to CIE by Carnoy in 1974. The extension of dependency to education focused on the exportation of cultural models from industrialized countries to the periphery, showing that what was promoted by hegemonic countries' national systems did not often favor the particular needs and situations of the Third World. Altbach and Kelly's (1984) analysis of education in former colonized countries was among the first to document the existence of differentiated educational systems within a country. Their research found that in former colonies there were two distinct education systems, both controlled by the colonizing country and aimed at different populations.

CIE has seen frequent attacks on modernity, a notion largely taken for granted under both functionalist and conflict paradigms. Disappointed by the unfulfilled promise of industrialization, urbanization, and economic growth, several social scientists — including such CIE researchers as Rust (1991), Masemann and Welch (1997), and Paulston (1999) — have moved toward the explanatory frameworks afforded by postmodernity, neocolonial theories, and poststructuralism. CIE researchers have borrowed heavily from Foucault; his discussions of the symbiosis between power and knowledge (1977), the transactional nature of power and its manifestations at multiple levels (1980) have been invaluable to analyses of education among subordinated groups.

The Role of Education *Beginning*

Over the years, CIE has seen drastic shifts in the definition of "national development," from an emphasis on economic growth to a concern for redistribution of assets and opportunity, with implications for the diminution of inequalities, including poverty. Freire (1970) introduced a modified view of development that embraced material and spiritual dimensions in which he defined education as the practice of freedom. Sen (1999) further expanded the definition of development by including the notion of "capabilities," specifically, what individuals are able to do in areas that are essential to improving the quality of their lives. Economic analyses of the contribution of education, which was deemed consequently essential to the formation of human capital (Schultz, 1961, 1970), propelled attention to the field. Harbison and Myers' 1964 economic study, based on seventy-four countries, supported the conclusion that human resources were an essential ingredient to modernization. A study of sociopsychological variables in six developing countries led Inkeles and Smith (1974) to conclude that schooling is the most powerful factor in making individuals modern (which the two authors defined as people who favor rationality, are open to new experiences, defy superstition, and assume control of their lives through planning), and that education was a more powerful tool to develop modern attitudes than were work in modern industrial factories and the mass media.

From 1945 to 1981, 105 new states joined the United Nations. The independence of African countries spurred attention to education expansion, leading to studies that sought to explain how educational systems function and expand. Work by Archer (1979) focusing on European systems, found that structural characteristics (centralized vs. decentralized) generated different dynamics in the form and pace of educational change. Collins (1979) found that mass education resulted from competition among status groups for social dominance. Others, including Boli, Ramirez, and Meyer (1985), contended that global diffusion of democratic values is at work and that the gradual adoption of these values creates modern polities that reflect collective religious, political, and economic preferences.

Following World War II, many hoped that educational institutions would create economic growth and good citizenship, but subsequent disappointments led to more modest assessments of the potential of education. This was captured by Weiler (1978), who argued that the field had moved from the age of innocence to the age of skepticism. Today, the lack of correlation between educational levels and economic growth in some regions of the world, particularly Latin America and Africa, reveals the critical importance of factors other than education in economic and social development. Moreover, the lack of correlation between income distribution and educational levels suggests that formal schooling — which has become increasingly segmented by social class — is not fostering the empathy and respect for the "other" that is necessary for a fair social contract.

Equality/Diversity

Equality of opportunity is generally considered one of the most enduring educational issues. It is at the heart of the notion of education as a means for mobility in societies that consider themselves meritocratic. The first shock about the conditions of a disadvantaged group came with Myrdal's (1944) study on the "American dilemma." This report underscored the contradictions between a country's professed commitment to human rights and the oppression of Black people. Myrdal's recognition of "white supremacy" ignited new understanding and gave strength to studies of racism and schooling not only in the United States, but also in the rest of the world, particularly South Africa and several Latin American countries with indigenous populations. The U.S. Supreme Court's desegregation decision in *Brown v. Board of Education of Topeka, Kansas* (1954) opened wide debate over education in both industrialized and developing countries.

The 1966 Coleman Report in the United States and the 1967 Plowden Report in the United Kingdom investigated students' achievement across different schools. Both reports showed the salience of family conditions in successful student learning, but found that schools also did contribute to cognitive gains. About the same time, Illich (1971) issued his debate-provoking challenge to "deschool" society, rejecting the claim that education behaved as a "great equalizer" and asserting instead that it served to manipulate individuals into a highly consumerist society. *Harvard Educational Review* produced a special issue on equal educational opportunity in 1968. In it, Coleman (1968) addressed the complexities inherent in the definition of educational equality, ranging from differences in inputs, processes, and racial composition of schools, to differences in outcomes for individuals of equal and unequal backgrounds.

Substantial differences still exist in understanding the causes of educational (and social) inequalities and therefore in the nature of the solution. At one end we have educators and politicians who envision a within-the-school set of changes, including better trained teachers, more and better educational materials, and adequate infrastructure. At the other end we have many social scientists who think that solving inequality necessitates interventions in society as a whole, including areas of health, employment, and housing. The two proposals are not mutually exclusive; in practice, however, most measures to combat inequality have concentrated on schools and have been piecemeal.

International education has seen the implementation of a number of compensatory and remedial measures in the industrialized world. Ethnic minorities in the United States — who exhibit the greatest incidence of poverty — have benefited from compensatory education programs. With increased immigration, ethnic segregation in schooling has also emerged in Europe. In response, countries such as the U.K., France, Belgium, and the Netherlands have set up compensatory educational programs, though the teaching support and the additional materials provided by these programs have not been able to erase the disadvantages suffered by minority children. Consequently, this part of the world has seen a shift toward other interventions: preschool and early school education, greater reliance on school-community and school-parent relations, promotion of integrated services, and an emphasis on the transition from school to work (Driessen, 2001).

In developing countries, where disadvantages are even stronger for the poor and minorities, few interventions have been enacted. While the disparities in educational achievement and attainment between urban and rural areas are sizable, practically no developing country has a rural public policy. Two programs that are exceptions are PROGRESA (now called *Oportunidades*) in Mexico, which seeks to provide rural children with nutrition, health, and education stipends, and the District Primary Education program in India, which prioritizes scheduled castes and scheduled tribes (legally classified and protected groups of disadvantaged people) and supplies them with resources to improve student access and retention, teacher training, and instructional aids. Neither program has been able to affect student achievement but they have increased enrollment and retention.

Another way of serving the disadvantaged has been through the provision of school content that recognizes their cultural identity and teaches non-U.S. minorities to respect the "other." Multicultural education is considered an offshoot of the civil rights movement. It developed in the United States and the U.K. as a government response to the increasing number of people from minority cultures (Banks, Banks, & Banks, 1989), and spread to the European Community in the 1980s. It continues to take two different approaches: One concentrates on the acceptance and tolerance of cultural diversity, the other questions cultural assumptions and stereotypes and locates them in a terrain shaped by asymmetric power relations. This second approach calls for antiracist, antisexist, and other antidiscriminatory perspectives in education; not surprisingly, this approach is applied much less frequently than the first.

Multicultural education has had its detractors, including those who hold that teaching minority cultures strengthens prejudice, separatism, and even racism (Schlesinger, 1992). In countries with sizable ethnic populations, such as Guatemala, Bolivia, and Peru, the need for "multicultural" and "intercultural" education (the latter term implying greater two-way communication between cultures) is recognized, but adequate programs do not exist. Bilingual and intercultural education reflect the very political nature of education. What emerges in reality are not tangible struggles between ethnic groups and government, but "unresolved" issues regarding teaching in native languages or the comprehensive training of teachers to address the characteristics and needs of diverse student populations. There is a dearth of studies that focus on the school experiences of children of subordinate social classes and ethnicities.

Gender in Education

The 1970s' women's movement triggered analyses of schools and classrooms that examined the role of teachers' expectations and practices in the creation of masculinity and femininity norms, and the type of knowledge provided by formal education. The women's movement, and the gender and feminist theories that followed, also brought a more sober look into what seemed to be an end in itself: access to schooling. With the adoption of the concept of gender in the 1980s, studies have been more sensitive to the construction of gender ideologies and practices affecting women and men simultaneously, although asymmetrically. Many works have influenced the understanding of gender in international education. Salient among them is Connell's work (1987) showing the intertwined nature of gender, power, and politics. Empirical and conceptual work by Pateman (1988), Kelly and Elliott (1982), Arnot and Weiler (1993), Blackmore and Kenway (1993), Weiner and Arnot (1987), and Stromquist (1991) demonstrated the gendered nature of the state and its social institutions, documented the myriad ways the formal and hidden curricula shaped women's conceptions of self, and advanced the debate toward a critical feminist approach.

Significant reference to women in CIE can be detected as early as 1979, when the *Harvard Educational Review* produced a special issue on women and education.

Other special issues appeared in the *Comparative Education Review* in 1982 (and later in 2004) and *Comparative Education* in 1987. The understanding of women's education has moved from a focus on gender differences to describing difficult conditions experienced by female students, to identifying the variables that accounted for differential access and attainment (years of schooling) between boys and girls, and most recently to documenting the patterns and causes of masculinity in schools. Legislation such as the Civil Rights Act of 1964 and Title IX of the Higher Education Amendments of 1972 — both in the United States — expanded the definition of women's rights in education. Notable among them was the removal of discrimination in access to higher education programs, scholarships, employment, and sports, and the redefinition of sexual harassment as sexual discrimination.

Current gender studies are now more aware of the impact of culture, the state, the labor market, and the family on educational outcomes of women and men at all levels of education. Because research on gender issues is poorly funded, limited cross-national studies exist on this crucial topic. The most common type of study has been content analysis of textbooks. Many have documented the tendency of textbooks to present women in biased ways, primarily as mothers, homemakers, and caregivers, with limited roles as professionals. Textbooks and curricular content have improved in several countries, both developed and developing. However, it is still the case that references to women decline as grades become more advanced and that women's professional roles are presented in narrower ranges than those of men. Pre- and in-service training of teachers in gender issues remains sporadic and reaches only a small minority of teachers. Currently, in the midst of the HIV/AIDS epidemic, many sex education programs in developing countries present sexual relations as sinful and dangerous and thus advise abstinence, despite the fact that sexual behavior is increasingly prevalent among adolescents. In countries with high mortality rates in general, almost 40 percent of the deaths among females between the ages of fifteen and twenty-nine are due to this epidemic; another 20 percent of female deaths are due to maternal conditions (pregnancy and delivery complications, and abortions; Lloyd, 2005). Since HIV/AIDS affects youths in great proportions and kills both parents and teachers, it unleashes challenges for what schools should do for new generations of students.

Most policymakers, including the Vatican, would accept today that women's education is important. But there are still some who believe that what is needed is simply that women accommodate to family and outside work by becoming professionals while continuing to engage in domestic management. It is insidious to maintain that professional women can be successful while completely absorbing family care and related duties. Tead (1947) noted that there was an increasing number of women in higher education in the United States but added that the "psychological and social success of the home requires that each college woman will assume her share and take her part in local civic affairs, to the infinite toning up of the quality of health, recreation, art, education, and worship of her community" (p. 160). More than fifty-five years later, the Vatican similarly welcomed women's higher levels of education while denying that sex differences are "mere effects of historical and cultural conditioning" and observing that there is an "irreplaceable role of women in all aspects of family and social life involving human relationships and caring for others" (Vatican, 2004). The educational system's inability to question ideologies of women's and men's work and the gendered power relations in the private sphere exists across all levels of education, from primary to tertiary education.

A number of studies in industrialized countries have found that schools and classrooms are very much involved in producing masculinity and femininity through teacher practices and attitudes, and various forms of peer transactions (Connell, 1995; Mac an Ghaill, 1994). Such studies are much less frequent in developing countries, but the few that exist indicate a similar pattern. In recent IEA and PISA studies, researchers have noticed a slight superiority of girls in reading achievement. There are no studies that explain why girls are doing better than boys in reading while they continue to perform less well in math and science. A possible and partial explanation might be that in societies where women are delegated to domestic spheres, reading may be a source of vicarious living. The stagnation of boys' enrollment in sub-Saharan African countries and the weaker performance of boys in reading in the international comparisons has prompted claims by governments and some donor agencies that the women's movement has gone "too far" and that efforts must be taken to help male students.

As reflection on gender and education has progressed, it has revealed a clear intersection of gender with other forms of social disadvantage, such as class, ethnicity, and race. A challenge to both research and policy at present is how to address this persistent confluence of social markers. Yet it is evident that girls' enrollment and attainment rates on aggregate are increasing faster than those of boys (Lloyd, 2005). There is no solid explanation for this, since governments have not engaged in policies focusing on the situation of girls, except for a handful of countries in Africa. The reasons might lie elsewhere: more educated parents who seek more schooling for all their children, smaller families that diminish the need for child care, and increasing urbanization that brings schools into greater proximity and facilitates access to domestic technologies.

Before 1980 the field did not closely investigate women, family, or the relationships among education, health, and nutrition. Today, however, we realize that it would be incomplete to carry out an educational analysis if it did not acknowledge the differential experiences and consequences of schooling for men and women. We have gained considerable understanding of both the reproductive and transformative possibilities of schooling. In international development, there has been a transition from a women-in-development focus (WID) to a gender-and-development framework (GAD). Unfortunately, the educational initiatives under GAD, although stronger in conceptual argumentation, have remained weak and fragmented in terms of societal interventions to modify gender relations.

Nonformal Education and Informal Learning

While it has been common knowledge that learning occurs in venues beyond schooling, Coombs and Ahmed (1974) brought the concept of nonformal education to CIE. This concept was accompanied by a more systematic look at the potential of alternative forms of education for youths and adults to provide useful knowledge and training outside the strictures of formal educational systems and without leading to formal degrees.

Nonformal education — defined as that offered primarily to youth and adults outside the strictures and conventions of formal schooling, such as workshops on family nutrition or in union organizing (Coombs & Ahmed, 1974) — is still far from being accepted as having equal value to formal education. Some educational researchers (e.g., Bock & Papagiannis, 1983) see it as technical and vocational education that creates second-class citizens. Other researchers, particularly in Latin America (Arnove, 1994; Schugurensky, 2003; Torres, 1990), see education for adults outside the school as providing critical learning about one's society, including knowledge of a contested nature. This approach, often called popular education, received substantial support in the ideas of Gramsci, Freire, and liberation theology. Gramsci's (1992, 1994) notion of "the organic intellectual" brought new understanding to the role of adult educator. His notion of education as political and politics as essentially educational also helped revolutionize previously technocratic and instrumental views of adult education. Freire's (1970) questioning of "banking education," which concentrates on conveying information to individuals rather than incorporating their experience and prior knowledge in their learning process, and the need for ongoing dialogue through cultural circles also modified pedagogical practices with adults.

Foley (1999, 2004) has contributed significantly to adult education. Using the concept of informal learning, he has transformed the old concept of political socialization to focus on the learning that occurs through struggle and transformative action. Informal learning — that which occurs through engagement in various political and cultural actions — is helping individuals, both men and women, to acquire knowledge and skills through participation in organizations that seek change or that question changes that have been made without the people's consent.

Adult illiteracy in the world has diminished in percentages but has remained rather stable in absolute numbers. Two-thirds of illiterates are women, a proportion that has proven extremely tenacious. The large number of youth and adult illiterates — estimated to be close to 900 million people — constitute a population that can be served only through nonformal education. The United Nations Educational, Scientific, and Cultural Organization, the international body in charge of education, has been found to foster forms of adult education that offer remedial rather than transformative literacy (Jones, 1990). Few countries give sufficient attention to the condition of rural education; in fact, it is difficult to identify a country today that has a rural education policy.

Much popular education work (the version of nonformal education in many developing countries) has been carried out by NGOs and community-based organizations, which are small groups that function informally at the neighborhood level. Popular education practices and philosophies prevail in many parts of the developing world. For example, South Africans benefited greatly from this mode of education in their struggle against apartheid. Adult education today, in its traditional and popular education forms, is still not properly acknowledged by CIE, in either research or academic training. Much of the existing literature on the subject is in languages other than English and is not published in academic journals.

Globalization and Its Impact

Through scholarly work, journalistic accounts, and recent events, the concept of globalization has pierced our consciousness in indelible ways. Northern scholars and institutions — those located in the industrialized countries — perceive globalization primarily as a set of technological discoveries that have compressed time and space, leading to the integration of economies and societies through flows of goods, finance, information, and labor. From the perspective of southern scholars and activists — those inhabiting the less developed regions of the world — globalization has economic and political features that perpetuate and even exacerbate disadvantages faced by less industrialized countries.

Tikly (2001) and other northern scholars assert that cultural hybridization is leading to new individual and group identities. Other accounts, particularly outside education, present a different picture, one in which political forces continue to shape the world but have taken on new forms. Robinson (2004), working with the notion of the transnational state (TNS), which he conceives as "a particular constellation of class forces and relations bound up with capitalist globalization" (p. 100), holds that this apparatus is multilayered and multicentered. The TNS is said to link institutions informally but effectively with distinct gradations of "state-ness." These supranational organizations are economic and political, formal and informal. The economic forms include the International Monetary Fund, the World Bank, the World Trade Organization (WTO), and the regional development banks. The political forms include the Group of Eight, OECD, the European Union, the United Nations, the Association of Southeast Asian Nations, the North American Free Trade Agreement, and others.

Today, 300 transnational companies own one-fourth of the productive assets of the world (Korten, 2001). In shaping the nature of the economy, these transnational organizations and firms introduce new demands and roles for education. While contemporary society is portrayed as the "knowledge society" — and it is evident that people with higher levels of education command higher salaries and standard of living — it is also clear that the economic system produces individuals who will occupy the lower ranks. This dynamic requires an education system that favors competition and inculcates among "losers" the notion that merit alone determines life chances.

As society has become globalized, there have been substantial changes in postsecondary education. This portion of the education sector has expanded greatly, through both conventional (based on physical student and teacher presence) forms of education and distance (particularly Internet-based) education. As more individuals earn technical, vocational, and professional degrees, society gains greater amounts of information and knowledge. Yet, the expansion of postsecondary education has occurred through great doses of diversification, in this case the sprouting of numerous institutions of varied quality and social recognition. Governance under a competitive ethos is changing the university toward a managerial and entrepreneurial organization, as documented by Slaughter and Leslie's (1997) comparative study. Similar changes are being reported in universities throughout the developing world. Altbach (1987) highlighted the crucial role of higher education, which he termed "the most important intellectual institution with widespread impact on culture, politics, and ideology" (p. 2). Much for-profit expansion of universities is occurring through distance education. While there were large open universities in Indonesia and Thailand before the presence of globalizing forces, English-speaking universities from the United Kingdom, the United States, Australia, New Zealand, and India have now entered the education market, creating possibilities for democratization as well as social exclusion that are not fully understood. Orfield (1992), reviewing ten years of policy debate in the United States (1980–1989), found that the research shows "a direct relationship between income and college attendance and that higher tuition produces declining participation" (p. 362). Today, with the increasing impact of economic and technological globalization on postsecondary education access, curricula, objectives, governance, and the changing structure of the labor market and economy in general, higher education has become a crucial topic for CIE study.

Many feminists (Blackmore, 2000; Kenway & Kelly, 2000; Stromquist, 2002) find that with globalization we are experiencing the reconfiguration of all forms of oppression. Since globalization is characterized by an uneven distribution of power, it is far from certain that the reality of globalization matches the "global citizenship" discourse, by which a transnational sense of purpose and obligation is developing. Interdependency characterized by denser relations in politics, economics, communications, and the environment is emerging, but it is less evident that transnationalism — defined as a position that seeks the common good and thus the reduction of all types of inequality across nation-states — may prevail. Vilas (2004) holds that a global capitalism — one without nationality and without ties to states, territories, and national markets — lacks empirical validity.

New Educational Actors

In recent decades, abetted by globalization forces, significant players other than nation-states have emerged. On the one hand, international finance agencies and transnational organizations are assuming greater presence and power than ever before in educational decisionmaking circles. On the other hand, NGOs are attaining greater responsibilities in the provision of education.

Financial and Transnational Institutions

The World Bank (WB) attained visibility in CIE with its 1980 *Education Policy Paper*, which some of its staff called "a modern Bible on educational development" (Psacharopoulos, 1981, p. 141). Since then, other reports have followed, notably *Education in Sub-Saharan Africa* (1988), *Higher Education: The Lessons of Experience* (1994), and *Priorities and Strategies in Education* (1995). Typically, WB policy papers and reports present a strong defense of formal schooling, arguing that the human capital developed by schooling not only alleviates poverty but also contributes to growth in national productivity and income. WB research focuses on identifying what works in education and skirts any discussion of political and economic issues affecting equality and equity in education, except perhaps for its recent consideration of corruption as a development issue. Similar positions and reports have been produced by the Inter-American, the Asian, and the African Development banks, re-gional banks with significant influence of their own.

The WB gives priority to education issues dealing with efficiency, equality, ac-countability, decentralization, user fees, privatization, and related forms of parental choice. The efficiency orientation in WB policy, however, usually boils down to pri-vatization as a means to avoid what is seen as inherent waste in low student retention, low achievement, and high dropout rates due to the monopoly held by public schools. Equality is often mentioned, yet the clearest treatment by the WB is its rec-ommendation that the middle and upper social classes pay for their own higher edu-cation. Psacharopoulos (see, e.g., 1986) suggested using incentives to create private schools and to provide credits/loans so that people could invest in education. His perspective is quite prescient in WB literature and programs. A WB publication that has had a significant impact in developing countries is *Improving Primary Education in Developing Countries* by Lockheed and Verspoor (1991). The WB's position that the economic situation in Africa had deteriorated due to shortages of educated man-power or deficiencies in educational quality has been questioned by CIE scholars, no-tably Foster (1998), who maintains that although there are inefficiencies in its educa-tional systems, the region is substantially more affected by the depressed commodity prices and the heavy interest burden on its external debts.

The World Bank prefers to conduct its own research, which is almost exclusively quantitative. With more than 1,200 researchers on staff, the WB has become a major actor in education, influencing policies in both developing countries and former communist countries. Bilateral agencies, even those that defend more humanistic de-velopment models, generally defer to WB positions.

Two other organizations that have a major impact on educational decisions in the international arena are the OECD and the United Nations Development Program (UNDP). The OECD is notable for its various studies focusing on student achieve-ment, while the UNDP garners much attention for its annual *Human Development Report*. The report has introduced two indices that are frequently used by various ed-ucational ministries and agencies: the Human Development Index (in existence since 1990 and available for 162 countries by 2001) and the Gender Empowerment Mea-sure (since 1995), both of which consider levels of education and literacy rates. These indices have provided metrics that enable countries to track their performance over time and to do so in comparison with similar nations. UNDP now also produces reports for specific countries.

Social Movements

Social movements crystallized in the form of NGOs have multiplied in recent de-cades as a response to economic and social hardships invoking numerous issues: ac-cess to land, gender equality, apartheid, privatization of basic services, domestic vio-lence, HIV/AIDS, neoliberal policies, hunger, and others. NGOs' work in education takes two forms: 1) a type of adult education that tends to be both critical of the sta-tus quo and proactive, and thus focused on social transformation, particularly gender and ethnic change, and 2) a more incipient but rapidly expanding form that seeks to provide formal schooling to rural children who are not being served by government schools, mainly in sub-Saharan Africa and South Asia.

Successful examples from the U.S. civil rights movement, women's rights movements, and ecological movements throughout the world have provided constant inspiration and support to progressive NGOs. Many of the educational programs, especially those centered on women's advancement, work to empower participants, something not attempted by most formal education programs (Stromquist, in press).

CIE research does not cover this very important set of actors. For instance, it is not following to any significant degree the educational role of social movements involving indigenous people, particularly in Latin America, where strong networks are developing the capacity to convene regional conferences. These groups are examining themes such as autonomy and territory, diversity and plurinationality, rights of people and nations, militarization (a reference to current events to fight the drug traffic in the Amazon), and the role of women in the construction of a plurinational state.

Public Policies in Education

Two different models of public policy are used to characterize nations: the socialist egalitarian model in communist countries and the liberal competitive model in capitalist countries. Today we see a movement toward convergence, with the liberal capitalist model prevailing, in which schools are organized for competition — trying to outperform one another in student performance — rather than equity. Developing countries now tend to invest little in education, as large proportions of the national budgets are allocated to pay the external debt (UNDP, 1999). Ironically, at a moment of state retrenchment, official discourse related to government policies abounds. We know relatively little about policy formulation and subsequent implementation in developing countries. Many governments subscribe to global agreements to expand the educational supply and quality but then do little to reach those objectives. One explanation might be the essentially distributive nature of educational policy, a process that seldom requires a significant redistribution of wealth and thus does not threaten powerful domestic groups. Most policy analyses concentrate on the policy itself and give limited consideration to the historical and political context in which the policy functions. An exception to this is the work by Carnoy and Samoff (1990) that produced a state-centered political perspective in its comparative study of national systems of education. Hannum's (1999) work on China has also been of interest because of its identification of radical changes in educational policies, even within a socialist regime.

Many educational policies today resemble one another. Innovations frequently involve decentralization, accountability, parental choice, and privatization. This convergence appears for several reasons, including the fast spread of information and thus the "contagion effect," and the powerful leverage wielded by multilateral and bilateral aid agencies. Developing countries' need for additional resources through loans or grants makes them vulnerable to the technical advice of these agencies; consequently, "external players seek to shape the policy-related judgments and decisions made within the normal operation of decision-making in sovereign states" (Jones,

1990, p. 43). The diffusion of policies has also been explained by the fact that supranational organizations are staffed by transnational functionaries who work with their transnational counterparts in the transformed national states (Robinson, 2004).

Two major global policies have affected education since 1990. The Education for All (EFA) policies endorsed by most national governments seek to ensure access to basic education for all, reduce gender disparities at all levels of education, and eliminate illiteracy. The Millennium Development Goals, unanimously agreed upon by the United Nations in 2000, were in part an attempt to rescue the EFA goals and set the year 2015 as their ultimate attainment date. Though widely accepted, few national education plans have so far designed interventions to meet these goals, much less allocated resources to specific ends.

Increasingly, accountability policies mandate testing to determine how schools are performing and how quality could be elevated. In an article entitled "Testomania," Sorokin (1955), one of the greatest sociologists of his time, questioned the scientific nature of tests, calling them "a new form of the old beliefs in revealing omens, paper-pen magical operations, or vocal incantations dressed in modern scientific garb" (p. 213). Contemporary critics maintain that testing now functions as an instrument that reflects the cultural capital students possess before coming to school and registers the value added by the school only in modest ways. Test scores are usually reported by school, with little statistical control for differences in inputs and student background, which perpetuates a belief in the beneficial results of the private school and the "low quality" of public schools. Experts on the production of tests have remarked that test items designed to guide the teaching/learning process require different features from those designed to compare schools.

Decentralization policies are widespread. They range from the state level to the municipal level to the school level. Decentralization offers the promise of release from the bureaucratic and financial control of central ministries, and the possibility of adapting curricula to meet local cultures and needs. However, when enacted, these policies have been characterized by the simple transfer of miniscule budgets to local levels, along with a lack of training for these new administrative responsibilities. This leaves decentralization susceptible to failure. Although no studies have been conducted to date on the impact of decentralization on equality, there is reason to believe that the subordination of women and ethnic groups may not be ameliorated through decentralization, as antagonisms and authoritarian practices are sometimes stronger at the community level than at national levels.

In recent years we have seen intensified debate on schools as quasi-markets: public financing to ensure that all have access to basic education, private financing to ensure free school choice. The UN Universal Declaration of Human Rights enacted in 1948 (Article 26) declares education a basic human right and recognizes the obligation of the state to provide free and compulsory elementary education. It also gives parents "a prior right to choose the kind of education that shall be given to their children," a right reiterated in the International Covenant on Economic, Social, and Cultural Rights (1966). Arguments favoring the creation of charter schools and the use of school vouchers that ensure the transfer of public funding primarily to private institutions originated in the United States in 1955. They received attention in the developing world in the 1990s, primarily due to endorsement by the World Bank. However, there has been only limited adoption of the voucher model, primarily because it requires a complex system of administration and monitoring. Society faces a serious dilemma. Parental choice is part of essential freedom. Yet, in selecting private schools for their children, parents — especially those who have greater levels of income and wealth — contribute to what has become an unstoppable phenomenon: the segmentation of the educational system into the public and private. Given the persistent criticism of public schools, privatization is gaining favor among parents who seek to provide their children a more competitive position in society and the economy.

Recent consideration of public policies highlights the need to move into second-generation reforms to make the structural reforms that have existed since the late 1980s effective. Unlike those in the past, the new measures would not avoid public regulation but would instead pursue "sensible legislation" so that government will function efficiently and engage in clear rules for taxation, adjudication of service, electoral reforms, and changes in tariff structures to complement unskilled labor (Naím, 1994; Navia & Velasco, 2003). What constitutes a major analytical contribution of second-generation reforms is the sober realization that they offer low political visibility and are not appealing to politicians seeking short-terms results. These reforms are also likely to counter the interests of highly organized and vocal groups, ranging from teachers and judicial unions to the upper echelons of public bureaucracy, state and local governments, owners and managers of private monopolies, and the medical establishment. However, the heterogeneity of these groups may provide space for maneuvering and negotiating common agreements.

Conclusions

In its path toward equality, CIE has seen a few watershed moments, most of which have come from outside education in the form of judicial decisions, social movements, or neoliberal policies imposed by international institutions. Some events have accelerated the consideration of equality and its attainment, particularly for women. Others are broadening the separation between social classes and reducing the possibilities of good quality public education schooling for ethnic and rural populations.

CIE theories and research methods have developed greater precision and complexity over time. However, the influence of CIE is determined not only by its intellectual value but also by the proximity of its practitioners to the circles of power. Those wielding influence are not academics but rather the staff members of international organizations and their transnational counterparts who subscribe to dominant, market-oriented development models that are not substantiated by empirical research.

Are educational systems in developing countries improving over time? Pertinent cross-national comparisons are relatively recent. They show that students in developing countries attain much lower scores than those in the industrialized nations. It is also clear, however, that public investment in education in developing countries tends to be low. Are minorities doing better today than in earlier decades? Their educational access has been expanding, but primary school completion rates and learning achievement remain low. Studies from Mexico, Brazil, and India show that ethnic minorities and castes have not been able to significantly improve their disadvantaged status in educational attainment. Are women registering improved access and performance compared to men? By and large they are, even in sub-Saharan African countries where educational access has stagnated in the last decade. However, attitudes about gender have changed only marginally, as the women/motherhood nexus prevails. According to UNDP statistics, people live longer, healthier lives, are more educated, and have higher incomes than thirty years ago (2001). This is true on the *aggregate*, but the world is becoming polarized by region, by social class, and by rural/urban residence, with the income gap between the richest 10 percent and the poorest 10 percent of most countries increasing in most instances.

Our future looms imperfect and with enormous challenges. We face three distinct paths: 1) to witness and document the progressive privatization of education and the parallel deterioration of its public counterpart with no particular value judgment; 2) to respond through greater research on the impact of current state retrenchment on equality and equity policies and educational rights, while asserting a position vis-à-vis the emerging reality; or 3) to go beyond research and establish alliances among academics, progressive educators, and activists of all generations to shape an educational world responsive to justice and solidarity. What will we choose? Comparative educators cannot remain indifferent to growing global inequalities in the economy, political power, and education. We must respond through collective action and span diverse communities within and between the north and south. The path of exclusive engagement in research activities will only contribute to CIE's decline.

References

Altbach, P. (1987). *Higher education in the Third World: Themes and variations.* New York: Advent Books.

Altbach, P., & Kelly, G. (Eds.). (1984). *Education and the colonial experience.* New Brunswick, NJ: Transaction Books.

Archer, M. (1979). *Social origins of educational systems.* London: Sage.

Arnot, M., & Weiler, K. (Eds.). (1993). *Feminism and social justice in education: International perspectives.* London: Falmer Press.

Arnove, R. (1994). *Education as contested terrain: Nicaragua, 1979–1993.* Boulder, CO: Westview.

Banks, J., Banks, C., & Banks, M. (Eds.). (1989). *Multicultural education: Issues and perspectives.* Boston: Allyn & Bacon.

Behrman, E. (2003). The political economy of educational reform in Australia, England and Wales, and the United States. In R. Arnove & C. Torres (Eds.), *Comparative education: The dialectic of the global and the local* (2nd ed., pp. 252–291). Lanham, MD: Rowman & Littlefield.

Bereday, G. (1964). *Comparative methods in education.* New York: Holt, Rinehart and Winston.

Blackmore, J. (2000). "Hanging onto the edge": An Australian case study of women, universities, and globalization. In N. Stromquist & K. Monkman (Eds.), *Globalization and education: Integration and contestation across cultures* (pp. 333–352). Lanham, MD: Rowman & Littlefield.

Blackmore, J., & Kenway, J. (Eds.). (1993). *Gender matters in educational administration and policy: A feminist introduction.* London: Falmer Press.

Bock, J., & Papagiannis, G. (1983). *Nonformal education and national development: A critical assessment of policy, research, and practice.* New York: Praeger.

Boli, J., Ramirez, F., & Meyer, J. (1985). Explaining the origins and expansion of mass education. *Comparative Education Review, 29,* 145–170.

Bourdieu, P. & Passeron, J. C. (1977). *Reproduction in education, society and culture.* London: Sage.

Bowles, S., & Gintis, H. (1976). *Schooling in capitalist America: Educational reform and the contradictions of economic life.* New York: Basic Books.

Bray, M. (2003). Control of education: Issues and tensions in centralization and decentralization. In R. Arnove & C. Torres (Eds.), *Comparative education: The dialectic of the global and the local* (2nd ed., pp. 204–228). Lanham, MD: Rowman & Littlefield.

Carnoy, M. (1974). *Education as cultural imperialism.* New York: D. McKay.

Carnoy, M., & Samoff, J. (Eds.). (1990). *Education and social transformation in the Third World.* Princeton, NJ: Princeton University Press.

Casassus, J., Froemel, J. E., Palafox, J. C., & Cusato, S. (1998). *Primer estudio internacional comparativo sobre lenguaje, matemáticas y factores asociados en tercer y cuarto grado.* Santiago, Chile: Oficina Regional de Educacion para America Latina y El Caribe.

Coleman, J. S. (1968). The concept of equality of educational opportunity. *Harvard Educational Review, 38,* 7–22.

Collins, R. (1979). *The credential society: A historical sociology of education and stratification.* New York: Academic Press.

Connell, R. (1987). *Gender and power: Society, the person and sexual politics.* Sydney, Australia: Allen & Unwin.

Connell, R. (1995). *Masculinities: Knowledge, power and social change.* Cambridge, Eng.: Polity Press.

Cook, B., Hite, S., & Epstein, E. (2004). Discerning trends, contours, and boundaries in comparative education: A survey of comparativists and their literature. *Comparative Education Review, 48,* 123–149.

Coombs, P., with Ahmed, M. (1974). *Attacking rural poverty: How nonformal education can help.* Baltimore: Johns Hopkins University Press.

Crossley, M., & Jarvis, P. (Eds.). (2000). Comparative education for the twenty-first century [Special issue]. *Comparative Education, 36*(3).

Driessen, G. (2001). The limits of educational policy and practice? The case of ethnic minorities in The Netherlands. *Comparative Education, 36,* 7–20.

Farrell, J. (1988). *The national unified school in Allende's Chile.* Vancouver: University of British Columbia Press.

Foley, G. (1999). *Learning in social action: A contribution to understanding informal education.* London: ZED.

Foley, G. (Ed.). (2004). *Dimensions of adult learning: Adult education and training in a global era.* Maidenhead, Eng.: Open University Press.

Foster, P. (1989). Some hard choices to be made. *Comparative Education Review, 33,* 104–110.

Foucault, M. (1977). *Discipline and punish.* London: Tavistock.

Foucault, M. (1980). *Power/knowledge: Selected interviews and other writings, 1972–1977.* New York: Pantheon.

Freire, P. (1970). *Pedagogy of the oppressed.* New York: Herder and Herder.

Giroux, H. (1983). *Theory and resistance in education: A pedagogy for the opposition.* Exeter, NH: Heinemann.

Giroux, H. (1989). *Schooling for democracy: Critical pedagogy in the modern age.* New York: Routledge.

Gramsci, A. (1992). *Prison notebooks.* New York: Columbia University Press.

Gramsci, A. (1994). *Letters from prison.* New York: Columbia University Press.

Habermas, J. (1984). *The theory of communicative action.* Boston: Beacon Press.

Hannum, E. (1999). Political change and the urban-rural gap in basic education in China, 1949–1990. *Comparative Education Review, 43,* 193–211.

Harbison, F., & Myers, C. (1964). *Education, manpower, and economic growth: Strategies of human resource development.* New York: McGraw-Hill.

Holmes, B. (1965). *Problems in education: A comparative approach.* London: Routledge & Kegan Paul.

Husen, T. (1987). Policy impact of IEA research. *Comparative Education Review, 31,* 29–46.

Illich, I. (1971). *Deschooling society.* New York: Harrow Books.

Inkeles, A., & Smith, D. (1974). *Becoming modern: Individual change in six developing countries.* Cambridge, MA: Harvard University Press.

Jones, P. (1990). UNESCO and the politics of global literacy. *Comparative Education Review, 34,* 41–60.

Kelly, G. (1987). Comparative education and the problem of change: An agenda for the 1980s. *Comparative Education Review, 31,* 477–489.

Kelly, G., & Elliott, C. (Eds.). (1982). *Women's education in the third world. Comparative perspectives.* Albany: State University of New York Press.

Kenway, J., & Kelly, P. (2000) Local/global labor markets and the restructuring of gender, schooling, and work. In N. Stromquist & K. Monkman (Eds.), *Globalization and education: Integration and contestation across cultures* (pp. 173–195). Lanham, MD: Rowman & Littlefield.

King, E. (1968). *Comparative studies and educational decisions.* Indianapolis: Bobbs-Merrill.

Korten, D. (2001). *When corporations rule the world* (2nd ed.). Bloomfield, CT: Kumarian Press.

Lloyd, C. (Ed.). (2005). *Growing up global: Transitions to adulthood in developing countries.* Washington, DC: National Academy Press.

Lockheed, M., & Verspoor, A. (1991). *Improving primary education in developing countries.* New York: Oxford University Press.

Mac an Ghaill, M. (1994). *The making of men: Masculinities, sexualities and schooling.* Buckingham, Eng.: Open University Press.

Masemann, V., & Welch, A. (1997). *Tradition, modernity and postmodernity in comparative education.* Amsterdam: Kluwer.

Myrdal, G. (1944). *An American dilemma: The Negro problem and modern democracy.* New York: Harper & Row.

Naím, M. (1994). Latin America: The second stage of reform. *Journal of Democracy, 5,* 32–48.

Navia, P., & Velasco, A. (2003). The politics of "second-generation reforms." In P.-P. Kuczynski & J. Williamson (Eds.), *After the Washington consensus: Restarting growth and reform in Latin America* (pp. 265–303). Washington, DC: Institute for International Economics.

Noah, H., & Eckstein, M. (1968). *Toward a science of comparative education.* New York: Macmillan.

Orfield. G. (1992). Money, equity, and college access. *Harvard Educational Review, 62,* 337–372.

Pateman, C. (1988). *The sexual contract.* Stanford, CA: Stanford University Press.

Paulston, R. (1999). Mapping comparative education after postmodernity. *Comparative Education Review, 43,* 438–463.

Psacharopoulos, G. (1981). The World Bank in the world of education: Some policy changes and some remnants. *Comparative Education Review, 17,* 141–146.

Psacharopoulos, G. (1986). The planning of education: Where do we stand? *Comparative Education Review, 30,* 560–573.

Riddell, A. (1989). An alternative approach to the study of school effectiveness in Third World countries. *Comparative Education Review, 33,* 481–497.

Robinson, W. (2004). *A theory of global capitalism: Production, class, and state in a transnational world.* Baltimore: Johns Hopkins University Press.

Rust, V. (1991). Postmodernism and its comparative education implications. *Comparative Education Review, 35,* 610–626.

Rust, V., Soumaré, A., Pescador, O., & Shibuya, M. (1999). Research strategies in comparative education. *Comparative Education Review, 43,* 86–109.

Schlesinger, A. M. J. (1992). *The disuniting of America.* New York: Norton.

Schugurensky, D. (2003). Two decades of neoliberalism in Latin America: Implications for adult education. In S. Ball, G. Fischman, & S. Gvirtz (Eds.), *Crisis and hope: The educational hopscotch of Latin America.* New York: RoutledgeFalmer.

Schultz, T. (1961). Investment in human capital. *American Economic Review, 1,* 1–17.

Schultz, T. (1970). *Investment in human capital: The role of education and of research.* New York: Free Press.

Sen, A. (1999). *Development as freedom.* New York: Knoff.

Silvestre, M. (2004). El LLECE y Cuba. Retrieved May 6, 2004, from Comunidad Educativa@ gruposyahoo.com.arg.

Slaughter, S., & Leslie, L. (1997). *Academic capitalism: Politics, policies, and the entrepreneurial university.* Baltimore: Johns Hopkins University Press.

Sorokin, P. (1955). Testomania. *Harvard Educational Review, 25*, 199–213.

Stromquist, N. (Ed.). (1991). *Women and education in Latin America.* Boulder: CO: Lynne Rienner.

Stromquist, N. (2002). *Education in a globalized world: The connectivity of economic power, technology, and knowledge.* Lanham, MD: Rowman & Littlefield.

Stromquist, N. (in press). *Organizaciones feministas y la transformación social en América Latina.* Lima: Ediciones Flora Tristan/Manuela Ramos.

Tead, O. (1947). Women's higher education — past, present, and future. *Harvard Educational Review, 18*, 151–161.

Tikly, L. (2001). Globalisation and education in the postcolonial world: Towards a conceptual framework. *Comparative Education, 37*, 151–171.

Torres, C. (1990). *The politics of nonformal education in Latin America.* New York: Praeger.

United Nations Development Programme. (1999). *Human development report.* New York: Author.

Vatican. (2004). *Letter to bishops of the Catholic church on the collaboration of men and women in church and in the world.* Rome: Vatican. Retrieved July 2, 2004, from http://www. vaticanva/roman_curia/congregations/cfaith/documents.

Velez, E., Schiefelbein, E., & Valenzuela, J. (1993). *Factors affecting achievement in primary school: A review of the literature for Latin America and the Caribbean.* Washington, DC: World Bank, Human Resources Division.

Vilas, C. (2004). *Entre la desigualdad y la globalización: La calidad de nuestras democracias*. Retrieved September 9, 2004, from http://www.universidadabierta.edu.mx/SerEst/MCP/Processos%20Electorales%20III_archive.

Weiler, H. (1978). Education and development: From the age of innocence to the age of scepticism, *Comparative Education, 14*, 179–198.

Weiner, G., & Arnot, M. (1987). *Gender under scrutiny: New inquiries in education.* London: Open University Press.

Willis, P. (1977). *Learning to labour: How working class kids get working class jobs.* Farnborough, Eng.: Saxon House.

World Bank. (1988). *Education in sub-Saharan Africa: Policies for adjustment, revitalization and expansion.* Washington, DC: Author.

World Bank. (1994). *Higher education: The lessons of experience.* Washington, DC: Author.

World Bank. (1995). *Priorities and strategies for education: A World Bank review.* Washington, DC: Author.

The Adult Literacy Process as Cultural Action for Freedom

PAULO FREIRE

Every Educational Practice Implies a Concept of Man and the World

Experience teaches us not to assume that the obvious is clearly understood. So it is with the truism with which we begin: All educational practice implies a theoretical stance on the educator's part. This stance in turn implies — sometimes more, sometimes less explicitly — an interpretation of man and the world. It could not be otherwise. The process of men's orientation in the world involves not just the association of sense images, as for animals. It involves, above all, thought-language; that is, the possibility of the act of knowing through his praxis, by which man transforms reality. For man, this process of orientation in the world can be understood neither as a purely subjective event, nor as an objective or mechanistic one, but only as an event in which subjectivity and objectivity are united. Orientation in the world, so understood, places the question of the purposes of action at the level of critical perception of reality.

If, for animals, orientation in the world means adaptation to the world, for man it means humanizing the world by transforming it. For animals there is no historical sense, no options or values in their orientation in the world; for man there is both a historical and a value dimension. Men have the sense of "project," in contrast to the instinctive routines of animals.

The action of men without objectives, whether the objectives are right or wrong, mythical or demythologized, naive or critical, is not praxis, though it may be orientation in the world. And not being praxis, it is action ignorant both of its own process and of its aim. The interrelation of the awareness of aim and of process is the basis for planning action, which implies methods, objectives, and value options.

Teaching adults to read and write must be seen, analyzed, and understood in this way. The critical analyst will discover in the methods and texts used by educators and students practical value options that betray a philosophy of man, well or poorly outlined, coherent or incoherent. Only someone with a mechanistic mentality, which Marx would call "grossly materialistic," could reduce adult literacy learning to a

Harvard Educational Review Vol. 40   No. 2   May 1970, 205–225

purely technical action. Such a naive approach would be incapable of perceiving that technique itself as an instrument of men in their orientation in the world is not neutral.

We shall try, however, to prove by analysis the self-evidence of our statement. Let us consider the case of primers used as the basic texts for teaching adults to read and write. Let us further propose two distinct types: a poorly done primer and a good one, according to the genre's own criteria. Let us even suppose that the author of the good primer based the selection of its generative words[1] on a prior knowledge of which words have the greatest resonance for the learner (a practice not commonly found, though it does exist).

Doubtlessly, such an author is already far beyond the colleague who composes his primer with words he himself chooses in his own library. Both authors, however, are identical in a fundamental way. In each case they themselves decompose the given generative words and from the syllables create new words. With these words, in turn, the authors form simple sentences and, little by little, small stories, the so-called reading lessons.

Let us say that the author of the second primer, going one step further, suggests that the teachers who use it initiate discussions about one or another word, sentence, or text with their students.

Considering either of these hypothetical cases we may legitimately conclude that there is an implicit concept of man in the primer's method and content, whether it is recognized by the authors or not. This concept can be reconstructed from various angles. We begin with the fact, inherent in the idea and use of the primer, that it is the teacher who chooses the words and proposes them to the learner. Insofar as the primer is the mediating object between the teacher and students, and the students are to be "filled" with words the teachers have chosen, one can easily detect a first important dimension of the image of man that begins to emerge here. It is the profile of a man whose consciousness is "spatialized," and must be "filled" or "fed" in order to know. This same conception led Sartre, criticizing the notion that "to know is to eat," to exclaim: "*O philosophie alimentaire!*"[2]

This "digestive" concept of knowledge, so common in current educational practice, is found very clearly in the primer.[3] Illiterates are considered "undernourished," not in the literal sense in which many of them really are, but because they lack the "bread of the spirit." Consistent with the concept of knowledge as food, illiteracy is conceived of as a "poison herb," intoxicating and debilitating persons who cannot read or write. Thus, much is said about the "eradication" of illiteracy to cure the disease.[4] In this way, deprived of their character as linguistic signs constitutive of man's thought-language, words are transformed into mere "deposits of vocabulary" — the bread of the spirit that the illiterates are to "eat" and "digest."

This "nutritionist" view of knowledge perhaps also explains the humanitarian character of certain Latin American adult literacy campaigns. If millions of men are illiterate, "starving for letters," "thirsty for words," the word must be *brought* to them to save them from "hunger" and "thirst." The word, according to the naturalistic concept of consciousness implicit in the primer, must be "deposited," not born of the creative effort of the learners. As understood in this concept, man is a passive being, the object of the process of learning to read and write, and not its subject. As object his task is to "study" the so-called reading lessons, which in fact are almost completely alienating and alienated, having so little, if anything, to do with the student's socio-cultural reality.[5]

It would be a truly interesting study to analyze the reading texts being used in private or official adult literacy campaigns in rural and urban Latin America. It would not be unusual to find among such texts sentences and readings like the following random samples:[6]

> *A asa é da ave* — "The wing is of the bird."
> *Eva viu a uva* — "Eva saw the grape."
> *O galo canta* — "The cock crows."
> *O cachorro ladra* — "The dog barks."
> *Maria gosta dos animais* — "Mary likes animals."
> *João cuida das arvores* — "John takes care of the trees."
> *O pai de Carlinhos se chama Antonio. Carlinhos é um bom menino, bem comportado e estudioso* — "Charles's father's name is Antonio. Charles is a good, well-behaved, and studious boy."
> *Ada deu o dedo ao urubu? Duvido, Ada deu o dedo a arara. . . .*[7]
> *Se você trabalha com martelo e prego, tenha cuidado para nao furar o dedo.* — "If you hammer a nail, be careful not to smash your finger."[8]

* * * * *

Peter did not know how to read. Peter was ashamed. One day, Peter went to school and registered for a night course. Peter's teacher was very good. Peter knows how to read now. Look at Peter's face. [These lessons are generally illustrated.] Peter is smiling. He is a happy man. He already has a good job. Everyone ought to follow his example.

In saying that Peter is smiling because he knows how to read, that he is happy because he now has a good job, and that he is an example for all to follow, the authors establish a relationship between knowing how to read and getting good jobs that, in fact, cannot be borne out. This naiveté reveals, at least, a failure to perceive the structure not only of illiteracy, but of social phenomena in general. Such an approach may admit that these phenomena exist, but it cannot perceive their relationship to the structure of the society in which they are found. It is as if these phenomena were mythical, above and beyond concrete situations, or the results of the intrinsic inferiority of a certain class of men. Unable to grasp contemporary illiteracy as a typical manifestation of the "culture of silence," directly related to underdeveloped structures, this approach cannot offer an objective, critical response to the challenge of illiteracy. Merely teaching men to read and write does not work miracles; if there are not enough jobs for men able to work, teaching more men to read and write will not create them.

One of these readers presents among its lessons the following two texts on consecutive pages without relating them. The first is about May 1st, the Labor Day holiday, on which workers commemorate their struggles. It does not say how or where these are commemorated, or what the nature of the historical conflict was. The main theme of the second lesson is *holidays*. It says that "on these days people ought to go to the beach to swim and sunbathe . . ." Therefore, if May 1st is a holiday, and if on holidays people should go to the beach, the conclusion is that the workers should go swimming on Labor Day, instead of meeting with their unions in the public squares to discuss their problems.

Analysis of these texts reveals, then, a simplistic vision of men, of their world, of the relationship between the two, and of the literacy process that unfolds in that world.

A asa é da ave, Eva viu a uva, o galo canta, and *o cachorro late* are linguistic contexts that, when mechanically memorized and repeated, are deprived of their authentic dimension as thought-language in dynamic interplay with reality. Thus impoverished, they are not authentic expressions of the world.

Their authors do not recognize in the poor classes the ability to know and even create the texts that would express their own thought-language at the level of their perception of the world. The authors repeat with the texts what they do with the words, that is, they introduce them into the learners' consciousness as if it were empty space — once more, the "digestive" concept of knowledge.

Still more, the a-structural perception of illiteracy revealed in these texts exposes the other false view of illiterates as marginal men.[9] Those who consider them marginal must, nevertheless, recognize the existence of a reality to which they are marginal — not only physical space, but historical, social, cultural, and economic realities — that is, the structural dimension of reality. In this way, illiterates have to be recognized as beings "outside of," "marginal to" something, since it is impossible to be marginal to nothing. But being "outside of" or "marginal to" necessarily implies a movement of the one said to be marginal from the center, where he was, to the periphery. This movement, which is an action, presupposes in turn not only an agent but also his reasons. Admitting the existence of men "outside of" or "marginal to" structural reality, it seems legitimate to ask: Who is the author of this movement from the center of the structure to its margin? Do so-called marginal men, among them the illiterates, make the decision to move out to the periphery of society? If so, marginality is an option with all that it involves: hunger, sickness, rickets, pain, mental deficiencies, living death, crime, promiscuity, despair, the impossibility of being. In fact, however, it is difficult to accept that 40 percent of Brazil's population, almost 90 percent of Haiti's, 60 percent of Bolivia's, about 40 percent of Peru's, more than 30 percent of Mexico's and Venezuela's, and about 70 percent of Guatemala's would have made the tragic *choice* of their own marginality as illiterates.[10] If, then, marginality is not by choice, marginal man has been expelled from and kept outside of the social system and is therefore the object of violence.

In fact, however, the social structure as a whole does not "expel," nor is marginal man a "being outside of." He is, on the contrary, a "being inside of," within the social structure, and in a dependent relationship to those whom we call falsely autonomous beings, inauthentic beings-for-themselves.

A less rigorous approach, one more simplistic, less critical, more technicist, would say that it was unnecessary to reflect about what it would consider unimportant questions such as illiteracy and teaching adults to read and write. Such an approach might even add that the discussion of the concept of marginality is an unnecessary academic exercise. In fact, however, it is not so. In accepting the illiterate as a person who exists on the fringe of society, we are led to envision him as a sort of "sick man," for whom literacy would be the "medicine" to cure him, enabling him to "return" to the "healthy" structure from which he has become separated. Educators would be benevolent counselors, scouring the outskirts of the city for the stubborn illiterates, runaways from the good life, to restore them to the forsaken bosom of happiness by giving them the gift of the word.

In the light of such a concept — unfortunately, all too widespread — literacy programs can never be efforts toward freedom; they will never question the very reality that deprives men of the right to speak up — not only illiterates, but all those who are treated as objects in a dependent relationship. These men, illiterate or not, are, in fact, not marginal. What we said before bears repeating: They are not "beings outside of"; they are "beings for another." Therefore the solution to their problem is not to become "beings inside of," but men freeing themselves; for in reality they are not marginal to the structure, but oppressed men within it. Alienated men, they cannot overcome their dependency by "incorporation" into the very structure responsible for their dependency. There is no other road to humanization — theirs as well as everyone else's — but authentic transformation of the dehumanizing structure.

From this last point of view, the illiterate is no longer a person living on the fringe of society, a marginal man, but rather a representative of the dominated strata of society, in conscious or unconscious opposition to those who, in the same structure, treat him as a thing. Thus, also, teaching men to read and write is no longer an inconsequential matter of *ba, be, bi, bo, bu,* of memorizing an alienated word, but a difficult apprenticeship in naming the world.[11]

In the first hypothesis, interpreting illiterates as men marginal to society, the literacy process reinforces the mythification of reality by keeping it opaque and by dulling the "empty consciousness" of the learner with innumerable alienating words and phrases. By contrast, in the second hypothesis — interpreting illiterates as men oppressed within the system — the literacy process, as cultural action for freedom, is an act of knowing in which the learner assumes the role of knowing subject in dialogue with the educator. For this very reason, it is a courageous endeavor to demythologize reality, a process through which men who had previously been submerged in reality begin to emerge in order to re-insert themselves into it with critical awareness.

Therefore the educator must strive for ever greater clarity as to what, at times without his conscious knowledge, illuminates the path of his action. Only in this way will he truly be able to assume the role of one of the subjects of this action and remain consistent in the process.

The Adult Literacy Process as an Act of Knowing

To be an act of knowing, the adult literacy process demands among teachers and students a relationship of authentic dialogue. True dialogue unites subjects together in the cognition of a knowable object that mediates between them.

If learning to read and write is to constitute an act of knowing, the learners must assume from the beginning the role of creative subjects. It is not a matter of memorizing and repeating given syllables, words, and phrases, but rather of reflecting critically on the process of reading and writing itself, and on the profound significance of language.

Insofar as language is impossible without thought, and language and thought are impossible without the world to which they refer, the human word is more than mere vocabulary — it is word-and-action. The cognitive dimensions of the literacy process must include the relationships of men with their world. These relationships are the source of the dialectic between the products men achieve in transforming the world and the conditioning that these products in turn exercise on men.

Learning to read and write ought to be an opportunity for men to know what *speaking the word* really means: a human act implying reflection and action. As such it is a primordial human right and not the privilege of a few.[12] Speaking the word is not a true act if it is not at the same time associated with the right of self-expression and world-expression, of creating and re-creating, of deciding and choosing and ultimately participating in society's historical process.

In the culture of silence the masses are "mute," that is, they are prohibited from creatively taking part in the transformations of their society and therefore prohibited from being. Even if they can occasionally read and write because they were "taught" in humanitarian — but not humanist — literacy campaigns, they are nevertheless alienated from the power responsible for their silence.

Illiterates know they are concrete men. They know that they do things. What they do not know in the culture of silence — in which they are ambiguous, dual beings — is that men's actions as such are transforming, creative, and re-creative. Overcome by the myths of this culture, including the myth of their own "natural inferiority," they do not know that *their* action upon the world is also transforming. Prevented from having a "structural perception" of the facts involving them, they do not know that they cannot "have a voice," that is, that they cannot exercise the right to participate consciously in the socio-historical transformation of their society, because their work does not belong to them.

It could be said (and we would agree) that it is not possible to recognize all this apart from praxis, that is, apart from reflection and action, and that to attempt it would be pure idealism. But it is also true that action upon an object must be critically analyzed in order to understand both the object itself and the understanding one has of it. The act of knowing involves a dialectical movement that goes from action to reflection and from reflection upon action to a new action. For the learner to know what he did not know before, he must engage in an authentic process of abstraction by means of which he can reflect on the action-object whole, or, more generally, on forms of orientation in the world. In this process of abstraction, situations representative of how the learner orients himself in the world are proposed to him as the objects of his critique.

As an event calling forth the critical reflection of both the learners and educators, the literacy process must relate *speaking the word* to *transforming reality*, and to man's role in this transformation. Perceiving the significance of that relationship is indispensable for those learning to read and write if we are really committed to liberation. Such a perception will lead the learners to recognize a much greater right than that of being literate. They will ultimately recognize that, as men, they have the right to have a voice.

On the other hand, as an act of knowing, learning to read and write presupposes not only a theory of knowing but a method that corresponds to the theory.

We recognize the indisputable unity between subjectivity and objectivity in the act of knowing. Reality is never just simply the objective datum, the concrete fact, but is also men's perception of it. Once again, this is not a subjectivistic or idealistic affirmation, as it might seem. On the contrary, subjectivism and idealism come into play when the subjective-objective unity is broken.[13]

The adult literacy process as an act of knowing implies the existence of two interrelated contexts. One is the context of authentic dialogue between learners and educators as equally knowing subjects. This is what schools should be — the theoretical context of dialogue. The second is the real, concrete context of facts, the social reality in which men exist.[14]

In the theoretical context of dialogue, the facts presented by the real or concrete context are critically analyzed. This analysis involves the exercise of abstraction, through which, by means of representations of concrete reality, we seek knowledge of that reality. The instrument for this abstraction in our methodology is codification,[15] or representation of the existential situations of the learners.

Codification, on the one hand, mediates between the concrete and theoretical contexts (of reality). On the other hand, as knowable object, it mediates between the knowing subjects, educators and learners, who seek in dialogue to unveil the "action-object wholes."

This type of linguistic discourse must be "read" by anyone who tries to interpret it, even when purely pictorial. As such, it presents what Chomsky calls "surface structure" and "deep structure."

The "surface structure" of codification makes the "action-object whole" explicit in a purely taxonomic form. The first stage of decodification[16] — or reading — is descriptive. At this stage, the "readers" — or decodifiers — focus on the relationship between the categories constituting the codification. This preliminary focus on the surface structure is followed by problematizing the codified situation. This leads the learner to the second and fundamental stage of decodification, the comprehension of the codification's "deep structure." By understanding the codification's "deep structure" the learner can then understand the dialectic that exists between the categories presented in the "surface structure," as well as the unity between the "surface" and "deep" structures.

In our method, the codification initially takes the form of a photograph or sketch that represents a real existent, or an existent constructed by the learners. When this representation is projected as a slide, the learners effect an operation basic to the act of knowing: they gain distance from the knowable object. This experience of distance is undergone as well by the educators, so that educators and learners together can reflect critically on the knowable object that mediates between them. The aim of decodification is to arrive at the critical level of knowing, beginning with the learner's experience of the situation in the "real context."

Whereas the codified representation is the knowable object mediating between knowing subjects, decodification — dissolving the codification into its constituent elements — is the operation by which the knowing subjects perceive relationships between the codification's elements and other facts presented by the real context — relationships that were formerly unperceived. Codification represents a given dimension of reality as individuals live it, and this dimension is proposed for their analysis in a context other than that in which they live it. Codification thus transforms what was a way of life in the real context into "objectum" in the theoretical context. The learners, rather than receive information about this or that fact, analyze aspects of their own existential experience represented in the codification.

Existential experience is a whole. In illuminating one of its angles and perceiving the inter-relation of that angle with others, the learners tend to replace a fragmented vision of reality with a total vision. From the point of view of a theory of knowledge, this means that the dynamic between codification of existential situations and decodification involves the learners in a constant re-construction of their former "ad-miration" of reality.

We do not use the concept "ad-miration" here in the usual way, or in its ethical or esthetic sense, but with a special philosophical connotation.

To "ad-mire" is to objectify the "not-I." It is a dialectical operation that characterizes man as man, differentiating him from the animal. It is directly associated with the creative dimension of his language. To "ad-mire" implies that man stands over against his "not-I" in order to understand it. For this reason, there is no act of knowing without "ad-miration" of the object to be known. If the act of knowing is a dynamic act — and no knowledge is ever complete — then in order to know, man not only "ad-mires" the object, but must always be "re-ad-miring" his former "ad-miration." When we "re-ad-mire" our former "ad-miration" (always an "ad-miration *of*") we are simultaneously "ad-miring" the act of "ad-miring" and the object "ad-mired," so that we can overcome the errors we made in our former "ad-miration." This "re-ad-miration" leads us to a perception of an anterior perception.

In the process of decodifying representations of their existential situations and perceiving former perceptions, the learners gradually, hesitatingly, and timorously place in doubt the opinion they held of reality and replace it with a more and more critical knowledge thereof.

Let us suppose that we were to present to groups from among the dominated classes codifications that portray their imitation of the dominators' cultural models — a natural tendency of the oppressed consciousness at a given moment.[17] The dominated persons would perhaps, in self-defense, deny the truth of the codification. As they deepened their analysis, however, they would begin to perceive that their apparent imitation of the dominators' models is a result of their interiorization of these models and, above all, of the myths of the "superiority" of the dominant classes that cause the dominated to feel inferior. What in fact is pure interiorization appears in a naive analysis to be imitation. At bottom, when the dominated classes reproduce the dominators' style of life, it is because the dominators live "within" the dominated. The dominated can eject the dominators only by getting distance from them and objectifying them. Only then can they recognize them as their antithesis.[18]

To the extent, however, that interiorization of the dominators' values is not only an individual phenomenon, but a social and cultural one, ejection must be achieved by a type of cultural action in which culture negates culture. That is, culture, as an interiorized product that in turn conditions men's subsequent acts, must become the object of men's knowledge so that they can perceive its conditioning power. Cultural action occurs at the level of superstructure. It can only be understood by what Althusser calls "the dialectic of overdetermination."[19] This analytic tool prevents us from falling into mechanistic explanations or, what is worse, mechanistic action. An understanding of it precludes surprise that cultural myths remain after the infrastructure is transformed, even by revolution.

When the creation of a new culture is appropriate but impeded by interiorized cultural "residue," this residue, these myths, must be expelled by means of culture. Cultural action and cultural revolution, at different stages, constitute the modes of this expulsion.

The learners must discover the reasons behind many of their attitudes toward cultural reality and thus confront cultural reality in a new way. "Re-ad-miration" of their former "ad-miration" is necessary in order to bring this about. The learners' capacity for critical knowing — well beyond mere opinion — is established in the process of unveiling their relationships with the historical-cultural world *in* and *with* which they exist.

We do not mean to suggest that critical knowledge of man-world relationships arises as a verbal knowledge outside of praxis. Praxis is involved in the concrete situations that are codified for critical analysis. To analyze the codification in its "deep structure" is, for this very reason, to reconstruct the former praxis and to become capable of a new and different praxis. The relationship between the *theoretical context*, in which codified representations of objective facts are analyzed, and the *concrete context*, where these facts occur, has to be made real.

Such education must have the character of commitment. It implies a movement from the *concrete context* that provides objective facts, to the *theoretical context* where these facts are analyzed in depth, and back to the *concrete context* where men experiment with new forms of praxis.

It might seem as if some of our statements defend the principle that, whatever the level of the learners, they ought to reconstruct the process of human knowing in absolute terms. In fact, when we consider adult literacy learning or education in general as an act of knowing, we are advocating a synthesis between the educator's maximally systematized knowing and the learners' minimally systematized knowing — a synthesis achieved in dialogue. The educator's role is to propose problems about the codified existential situations in order to help the learners arrive at a more and more critical view of their reality. The educator's responsibility as conceived by this philosophy is thus greater in every way than that of his colleague whose duty is to transmit information that the learners memorize. Such an educator can simply repeat what he has read, and often misunderstood, since education for him does not mean an act of knowing.

The first type of educator, on the contrary, is a knowing subject, face to face with other knowing subjects. He can never be a mere memorizer, but rather a person constantly readjusting his knowledge, who calls forth knowledge from his students. For him, education is a pedagogy of knowing. The educator whose approach is mere memorization is anti-dialogic; his act of transmitting knowledge is inalterable. For the educator who experiences the act of knowing together with his students, in contrast, dialogue is the seal of the act of knowing. He is aware, however, that not all dialogue is in itself the mark of a relationship of true knowledge.

Socratic intellectualism — which mistook the definition of the concept for knowledge of the thing defined and this knowledge as virtue — did not constitute a true pedagogy of knowing, even though it was dialogic. Plato's theory of dialogue failed to go beyond the Socratic theory of the definition as knowledge, even though for Plato one of the necessary conditions for knowing was that man be capable of a *prise de conscience*, and though the passage from *doxa* to *logos* was indispensable for man to achieve truth. For Plato, the prise de conscience did not refer to what man knew or did not know or knew badly about his dialectical relationship with the world; it was concerned rather with what man once knew and forgot at birth. To know was to remember or recollect forgotten knowledge. The apprehension of both doxa and logos, and the overcoming of doxa by logos occurred not in the man-world relationship, but in the effort to remember or rediscover a forgotten logos.

For dialogue to be a method of true knowledge, the knowing subjects must approach reality scientifically in order to seek the dialectical connections that explain the form of reality. Thus, to know is not to remember something previously known and now forgotten. Nor can doxa be overcome by logos apart from the dialectical relationship of man with his world, apart from men's reflective action upon the world.

To be an act of knowing, then, the adult literacy process must engage the learners in the constant problematizing of their existential situations. This problematizing employs "generative words" chosen by specialized educators in a preliminary investigation of what we call the "minimal linguistic universe" of the future learners. The words are chosen (a) for their pragmatic value, that is, as linguistic signs that command a common understanding in a region or area of the same city or country (in the United States, for instance, the word *soul* has a special significance in black areas that it does not have among whites), and (b) for their phonetic difficulties that will gradually be presented to those learning to read and write. Finally, it is important that the first generative word be tri-syllabic. When it is divided into its syllables, each one constituting a syllabic family, the learners can experiment with various syllabic combinations even at first sight of the word.

Having chosen seventeen generative words,[20] the next step is to codify seventeen existential situations familiar to the learners. The generative words are then worked into the situations one by one in the order of their increasing phonetic difficulty. As we have already emphasized, these codifications are knowable objects that mediate between the knowing subjects, educator-learners, learner-educators. Their act of knowing is elaborated in the *círculo de cultura* (cultural discussion group) that functions as the theoretical context.

In Brazil, before analyzing the learners' existential situations and the generative words contained in them, we proposed the codified theme of man-world relationships in general.[21] In Chile, at the suggestion of Chilean educators, this important dimension was discussed concurrently with learning to read and write. What is important is that the person learning words be concomitantly engaged in a critical analysis of the social framework in which men exist. For example, the word *favela* in Rio de Janeiro, Brazil, and the word *callampa* in Chile, represent, each with its own nuances, the same social, economic, and cultural reality of the vast numbers of slum dwellers in those countries. If favela and callampa are used as generative words for the people of Brazilian and Chilean slums, the codifications will have to represent slum situations.

There are many people who consider slum dwellers marginal, intrinsically wicked and inferior. To such people we recommend the profitable experience of discussing the slum situation with slum dwellers themselves. As some of these critics are often simply mistaken, it is possible that they may rectify their mythical clichés and assume a more scientific attitude. They may avoid saying that the illiteracy, alcoholism, and crime of the slum, its sickness, infant mortality, learning deficiencies, and poor hygiene reveal the "inferior nature" of its inhabitants. They may even end up realizing that if intrinsic evil exists it is part of the structures, and that it is the structures that need to be transformed.

It should be pointed out that the Third World as a whole, and more in some parts than in others, suffers from the same misunderstanding from certain sectors of the so-called metropolitan societies. They see the Third World as the incarnation of evil, the primitive, the devil, sin and sloth — in sum, as historically unviable without the director societies. Such a manichean attitude is at the source of the impulse to "save" the "demon-possessed" Third World, "educating it" and "correcting its thinking" according to the director societies' own criteria.

The expansionist interests of the director societies are implicit in such notions. These societies can never relate to the Third World as partners, since partnership presupposed equals, no matter how different the equal parties may be, and can never be established between parties antagonistic to each other.

Thus, "salvation" of the Third World by the director societies can only mean its domination, whereas in its legitimate aspiration to independence lies its utopian vision: to save the director societies in the very act of freeing itself.

In this sense, the pedagogy that we defend, conceived in a significant area of the Third World, is itself a utopian pedagogy. By this very fact it is full of hope, for to be utopian is not to be merely idealistic or impractical, but rather to engage in denunciation and annunciation. Our pedagogy cannot do without a vision of man and of the world. It formulates a scientific humanist conception that finds its expression in a dialogical praxis in which the teachers and learners together, in the act of analyzing a dehumanizing reality, denounce it while announcing its transformation in the name of the liberation of man.

For this very reason, denunciation and annunciation in this utopian pedagogy are not meant to be empty words, but a historic commitment. Denunciation of a dehumanizing situation today increasingly demands precise scientific understanding of that situation. Likewise, the annunciation of its transformation increasingly requires a theory of transforming action. However, neither act by itself implies the transformation of the denounced reality or the establishment of that which is announced.

Rather, as a moment in a historical process, the announced reality is already present in the act of denunciation and annunciation.[22]

That is why the utopian character of our educational theory and practice is as permanent as education itself, which, for us, is cultural action. Its thrust toward denunciation and annunciation cannot be exhausted when the reality denounced today cedes its place tomorrow to the reality previously announced in the denunciation. When education is no longer utopian, that is, when it no longer embodies the dramatic unity of denunciation and annunciation, it is either because the future has no more meaning for men, or because men are afraid to risk living the future as creative overcoming of the present, which has become old.

The more likely explanation is generally the latter. That is why some people today study all the possibilities that the future contains, in order to "domesticate" it and keep it in line with the present, which is what they intend to maintain. If there is any anguish in director societies hidden beneath the cover of their cold technology, it springs from their desperate determination that their metropolitan status be preserved in the future. Among the things that the Third World may learn from the metropolitan societies there is this that is fundamental: not to replicate those societies when its current utopian becomes actual fact.

When we defend such a conception of education — realistic precisely to the extent that it is utopian — that is, to the extent that it denounced what in fact is, and finds therefore between denunciation and its realization the time of its praxis — we are attempting to formulate a type of education that corresponds to the specifically human mode of being, which is historical.

There is no annunciation without denunciation, just as every denunciation generates annunciation. Without the latter, hope is impossible. In an authentic utopian vision, however, hoping does not mean folding one's arms and waiting. Waiting is only possible when one, filled with hope, seeks through reflective action to achieve that announced future that is being born within the denunciation.

That is why there is no genuine hope in those who intend to make the future repeat their present, nor in those who see the future as something predetermined. Both have a "domesticated" notion of history: the former because they want to stop time; the latter because they are certain about a future they already "know." Utopian hope, on the contrary, is engagement full of risk. That is why the dominators, who merely denounce those who denounce them, and who have nothing to announce but the preservation of the status quo, can never be utopian nor, for that matter, prophetic.[23]

A utopian pedagogy of denunciation and annunciation such as ours will have to be an act of knowing the denounced reality at the level of alphabetization and post-alphabetization, which are in each case cultural action. That is why there is such emphasis on the continual problematization of the learners' existential situations as represented in the codified images. The longer the problematization proceeds, and the more the subjects enter into the "essence" of the problematized object, the more they are able to unveil this essence. The more they unveil it, the more their awakening consciousness deepens, thus leading to the "conscientization" of the situation by the poor classes. Their critical self-insertion into reality, that is, their conscientization, makes the transformation of their state of apathy into the utopian state of *denunciation* and *annunciation* a viable project.

One must not think, however, that learning to read and write precedes conscientization, or vice-versa. Conscientization occurs simultaneously with the literacy or post-literacy process. It must be so. In our educational method, the word is not something static or disconnected from men's existential experience, but a dimension of their thought-language about the world. That is why, when they participate critically in analyzing the first generative words linked with their existential experience, when they focus on the syllabic families that result from that analysis, when they perceive the mechanism of the syllabic combinations of their language, the learners finally discover, in the various possibilities of combination, their own words. Little by little, as these possibilities multiply, the learners, through mastery of new generative words, expand both their vocabulary and their capacity for expression by the development of their creative imagination.[24]

In some areas in Chile undergoing agrarian reform, the peasants participating in the literacy programs wrote words with their tools on the dirt roads where they were working. They composed the words from the syllabic combinations they were learning. "These men are sowers of the word," said María Edi Ferreira, a sociologist from the Santiago team working at the Institute of Training and Research in Agrarian Reform. Indeed, they were not only sowing words, but discussing ideas, and coming to understand their role in the world better and better.

We asked one of these "sowers of words," finishing the first level of literacy classes, why he hadn't learned to read and write before the agrarian reform.

"Before the agrarian reform, my friend," he said, "I didn't even think. Neither did my friends."

"Why?" we asked.

"Because it wasn't possible. We lived under orders. We only had to carry out orders. We had nothing to say," he replied emphatically.

The simple answer of this peasant is a very clear analysis of "the culture of silence." In the culture of silence, to exist is only to live. The body carries out orders from above. Thinking is difficult, speaking the word, forbidden.

"When all this land belonged to one *latifundio*," said another man in the same conversation, "there was no reason to read and write. We weren't responsible for anything. The boss gave the orders and we obeyed. Why read and write? Now it's a different story. Take me, for example. In the *asentamiento*,[25] I am responsible not only for my work like all the other men, but also for tool repairs. When I started I couldn't read, but I soon realized that I needed to read and write. You can't imagine what it was like to go to Santiago to buy parts. I couldn't get orientated. I was afraid of everything — afraid of the big city, of buying the wrong thing, of being cheated. Now it's all different."

Observe how precisely this peasant described his former experience as an illiterate: his mistrust, his magical (though logical) fear of the world, his timidity. And observe the sense of security with which he repeats, "Now it's all different."

"What did you feel, my friend," we asked another "sower of words" on a different occasion, "when you were able to write and read your first word?"

"I was happy because I discovered I could make words speak," he replied.

Dario Salas reports,[26] "In our conversations with peasants we were struck by the images they used to express their interest and satisfaction about becoming literate.

For example, 'Before we were blind, now the veil has fallen from our eyes'; 'I came only to learn how to sign my name. I never believed I would be able to read, too, at my age'; 'Before, letters seemed like little puppets. Today they say something to me, and I can make them talk.'"

"It is touching," continues Salas, "to observe the delight of the peasants as the world of words opens to them. Sometimes they would say, 'We're so tired our heads ache, but we don't want to leave here without learning to read and write.'"27

The following words were taped during research on "generative themes."28 They are an illiterate's decodification of a codified existential situation:

> You see a house there, sad, as if it were abandoned. When you see a house with a child in it, it seems happier. It gives more joy and peace to people passing by. The father of the family arrives home from work exhausted, worried, bitter, and his little boy comes to meet him with a big hug, because a little boy is not stiff like a big person. The father already begins to be happier just from seeing his children. Then he really enjoys himself. He is moved by his son's wanting to please him. The father becomes more peaceful, and forgets his problems.

Note once again the simplicity of expression, both profound and elegant, in the peasant's language. These are the people considered absolutely ignorant by the proponents of the "digestive" concept of literacy.

In 1968, an Uruguayan team published a small book, *You Live as You Can* (*Se Vive como se Puede*), whose contents are taken from the tape recordings of literacy classes for urban dwellers. Its first edition of three thousand copies was sold out in Montevideo in fifteen days, as was the second edition. The following is an excerpt from this book:

THE COLOR OF WATER

> Water? Water? What is water used for?
> "Yes, yes, we saw it (in the picture)"
> "Oh, my native village, so far away . . ."
> "Do you remember that village?"
> "The stream where I grew up, called Dead Friar . . . you know, I grew up there, a childhood moving from one place to another . . . the color of the water brings back good memories, beautiful memories."
> "What is the water used for?"
> "It is used for washing. We used it to wash clothes, and the animals in the fields used to go there to drink, and we washed ourselves there, too."
> "Did you also use the water for drinking?"
> "Yes, when we were at the stream and had no other water to drink, we drank from the stream. I remember once in 1945 a plague of locusts came from somewhere, and we had to fish them out of the water. . . . I was small, but I remember taking out the locusts like this, with my two hands — and I had no others. And I remember how hot the water was when there was a drought and the stream was almost dry . . . the water was dirty, muddy, and hot, with all kinds of things in it. But we had to drink it or die of thirst."

The whole book is like this, pleasant in style, with great strength of expression of the world of its authors, those anonymous people, "sowers of words," seeking to emerge from "the culture of silence."

Yes, these ought to be the reading texts for people learning to read and write, and not "Eva saw the grape," "The bird's wing," "If you hammer a nail, be careful not to hit your fingers." Intellectualist prejudices and above all class prejudices are responsible for the naive and unfounded notions that the people cannot write their own texts, or that a tape of their conversations is valueless since their conversations are impoverished of meaning. Comparing what the "sowers of words" said in the above references with what is generally written by specialist authors of reading lessons, we are convinced that only someone with very pronounced lack of taste or a lamentable scientific incompetency would choose the specialists' texts.

Imagine a book written entirely in this simple, poetic, free, language of the people, a book on which interdisciplinary teams would collaborate in the spirit of true dialogue. The role of the teams would be to elaborate specialized sections of the book in problematic terms. For example, a section on linguistics would deal simply, though not simplistically, with questions fundamental to the learners' critical understanding of language. Let me emphasize again that since one of the important aspects of adult literacy work is the development of the capacity for expression, the section on linguistics would present themes for the learners to discuss, ranging from the increase of vocabulary to questions about communication — including the study of synonyms and antonyms, with its analysis of words in the linguistic context, and the use of metaphor, of which the people are such masters. Another section might provide the tools for a sociological analysis of the content of the texts.

These texts would not, of course, be used for mere mechanical reading, which leaves the readers without any understanding of what is real. Consistent with the nature of this pedagogy, they would become the object of analysis in reading seminars.

Add to all this the great stimulus it would be for those learning to read and write, as well as for students on more advanced levels, to know that they were reading and discussing the work of their own companions.

To undertake such a work, it is necessary to have faith in the people, solidarity with them. It is necessary to be utopian, in the sense in which we have used the word.

Notes

1. In languages like Portuguese or Spanish, words are composed syllabically. Thus, every non-monosyllabic word is, technically, *generative*, in the sense that other words can be constructed from its de-composed syllables. For a word to be authentically generative, however, certain conditions must be present, which will be discussed in a later section of this article. [At the phonetic level, the term *generative word* is properly applicable only with regard to a sound-syllabic reading methodology, while the thematic application is universal. See Sylvia Ashton-Warner's *Teacher* (1963; rpt. London: Virago, 1980) for a different treatment of the concept of generative words at the thematic level. — Editor]

2. Jean Paul Sartre, *Situations I* (Paris: Librairie Gallimard, 1974), p. 31.

3. The digestive concept of knowledge is suggested by "controlled readings" by classes that consist only of lectures; by the use of memorized dialogues in language learning; by bibliographical notes

that indicate not only which chapter, but which lines and words are to be read; by the methods of evaluating the students' progress in learning.

4. See Paulo Freire, "La alfabetización de adultos, crítica de su visión ingenua; comprensión de su visión crítica," in *Introducción a la Acción Cultural* (Santiago: ICIRA, 1969).

5. There are two noteworthy exceptions among these primers: 1) in Brazil, *Viver e Lutar*, developed by a team of specialists of the Basic Education Movement, sponsored by the National Conference of Bishops. (This reader became the object of controversy after it was banned as subversive by the then governor of Guanabara, Carlos Lacerda, in 1963.) 2) in Chile, the ESPIGA collection, despite some small defects. The collection was organized by Jefatura de Planes Extraordinarios de Educación de Adultos, of the Public Education Ministry.

6. Since at the time this article was written the writer did not have access to the primers, and was, therefore, vulnerable to recording phrases imprecisely or to confusing the author of one or another primer, it was thought best not to identify the authors or the titles of the books.

7. [The English here would be nonsensical, as is the Portuguese, the point being the emphasis on the consonant "d." — Editor]

8. The author may even have added here, "If, however, this should happen, apply a little mercurochrome."

9. [The Portuguese word here translated as *marginal man* is *marginado*. This has a passive sense: he who has been made marginal, or sent outside society, as well as the sense of a state of existence on the fringe of society. — Translator]

10. *La Situación Educativa en América Latina*, Cuadro No. 20 (Paris: UNESCO, 1960), p. 265.

11. [Here Freire stresses that learning to read and write is not just a mechanical acquisition of decoding skills, using the example of a decontextualized "family" of syllables. "Families" of syllables are often used in syllabic languages such as Portuguese and Spanish. — Editor]

12. Freire, "La alfabetización de adultos."

13. "There are two ways to fall into idealism: The one consists of dissolving the real in subjectivity; the other in denying all real subjectivity in the interests of objectivity." Jean Paul Sartre, *Search for a Method*, trans. Hazel E. Barnes (New York: Vintage Books, 1968), p. 33.

14. See Karel Kosik, *Dialéctica de lo Concreto* (Mexico: Grijalbo, 1967).

15. [Codification refers alternatively to the imaging, or the image itself, of some significant aspect of the learner's concrete reality (of a slum dwelling, for example). As such, it becomes both the object of the teacher-learner dialogue and the context for the introduction of the generative word. — Editor]

16. [Decodification refers to a process of description and interpretation, whether of printed words, pictures, or other "codifications." As such, decodification and decodifying are distinct from the process of decoding, or word-recognition. — Editor]

17. Re the oppressed consciousness, see: Frantz Fanon, *The Wretched of the Earth* (New York: Grove Press, 1968); Albert Memmi, *Colonizer and the Colonized* (New York: Orion Press, 1965); and Paulo Freire, *Pedagogy of the Oppressed*, (New York: Seabury Press, 1970).

18. See Fanon, *The Wretched of the Earth*; Freire, *Pedagogy of the Oppressed*.

19. See Louis Althussser, *Pour Marx* (Paris: Librairie François Maspero, 1965); and Paulo Freire, *Annual Report: Activities for 1968, Agrarian Reform, Training and Research Institute ICIRA, Chile*, trans. John Dewitt (Cambridge, MA: Center for the Study of Development and Social Change, 1969; mimeographed).

20. We observed in Brazil and Spanish America, especially Chile, that no more than seventeen words were necessary for teaching adults to read and write syllabic languages like Portuguese and Spanish.

21. See Paulo Freire, *Educação como Prática da Liberdade* (Rio de Janeiro: Paz e Terra, 1967); Chilean edition (Santiago: ICIRA, 1969).

22. Re the utopian dimension of denunciation and proclamation, see Lescek Kolakowski, *Toward a Marxist Humanism* (New York: Grove Press, 1969).

23. "The right, as a conservative force, needs no utopia; its essence is the affirmation of existing conditions — a fact and not a utopia — or else the desire to revert to a state which was once an accom-

plished fact. The Right strives to idealize actual conditions, not to change them. What it needs is fraud not utopia." Kolakowksi, *Toward a Marxist Humanism*, pp. 71–72.

24. "We have observed that the study of the creative aspect of language use develops the assumption that linguistic and mental process are virtually identical, language providing the primary means for free expansion of thought and feeling, as well as for the functioning of creative imagination." Noam Chomsky, *Cartesian Linguistics* (New York: Harper & Row, 1966), p. 31.

25. After the disappropriation of lands in the agrarian reform in Chile, the peasants who were salaried workers on the large latifundia become "settlers" *(asentados)*) during a three-year period in which they receive varied assistance from the government through the Agrarian Reform Corporation. This period of "settlement" *(asentamiento)* precedes that of assigning lands to the peasants. This policy is now changing. The phase of settlement of the lands is being abolished, in favor of an immediate distribution of lands to the peasants. The Agrarian Reform Corporation will continue, nevertheless, to aid the peasants.

26. Dario Salas, "Algumas experiencias vividas na Supervisão de Educação básica," in *A alfabetizção funcional no Chile.* Report to UNESCO, November 1968; Introduction by Paulo Freire.

27. Salas refers here to one of the best adult education programs organized by the Agrarian Reform Corporation in Chile, in strict collaboration with the Ministry of Education and ICIRA. Fifty peasants receive boarding and instruction scholarships for a month. The courses center on discussions of the local, regional, and national situations.

28. An analysis of the objectives and methodology of the investigation of generative themes lies outside the scope of this article, but is dealt with in the author's work, *Pedagogy of the Oppressed.*

The author gratefully acknowledges the contributions of Loretta Slover, who translated this article, and João da Veiga Coutinho and Robert Riordan, who assisted in the preparation of the manuscript.

Cultural Action and Conscientization

PAULO FREIRE

Existence *in* and *with* the World

It is appropriate at this point to make an explicit and systematic analysis of the concept of conscientization.[1]

The starting point for such an analysis must be a critical comprehension of man as a being who exists *in* and *with* the world. Since the basic condition for conscientization is that its agent must be a subject (that is, a conscious being), conscientization, like education, is specifically and exclusively a human process. It is as conscious beings that men are not only *in* the world, but *with* the world, together with other men. Only men, as "open" beings, are able to achieve the complex operation of simultaneously transforming the world by their action and grasping and expressing the world's reality in their creative language.

Men can fulfill the necessary condition of being *with* the world because they are able to gain objective distance from it. Without this objectification, whereby man also objectifies himself, man would be limited to being *in* the world, lacking both self-knowledge and knowledge of the world.

Unlike men, animals are simply *in* the world, incapable of objectifying either themselves or the world. They live a life without time, properly speaking, submerged in life with no possibility of emerging from it, adjusted and adhering to reality. Men, on the contrary, who can sever this adherence and transcend mere being in the world, add to the life that they have the existence that they make. To exist is thus a mode of life that is proper to the being who is capable of transforming, of producing, of deciding, of creating, and of communicating himself.

Whereas the being that merely lives is not capable of reflecting upon itself and knowing itself living *in* the world, the existent subject reflects upon his life within the very domain of existence, and questions his relationship to the world. His domain of existence is the domain of work, of history, of culture, of values — the domain in which men experience the dialectic between determinism and freedom.

If they did not sever their adherence to the world and emerge from it as consciousness constituted in the "admiration" of the world as its object, men would be merely determinate beings, and it would be impossible to think in terms of their liberation. Only beings who can reflect upon the fact that they are determined are capable of

Harvard Educational Review   Vol. 40   No. 3   August 1970, 452–477

freeing themselves. Their reflectiveness results not just in a vague and uncommitted awareness, but in the exercise of a profoundly transforming action upon the determining reality. *Consciousness of* and *action upon* reality are, therefore, inseparable constituents of the transforming act by which men become beings of relation.[2] By their characteristic reflection, intentionality, temporality, and transcendence,[3] men's consciousness and action are distinct from the mere *contacts* of animals with the world. The animals' contacts are a-critical; they do not go beyond the association of sensory images through experience. They are singular and not plural. Animals do not elaborate goals; they exist at the level of immersion and are thus a-temporal.

Engagement and objective distance, understanding reality as object, understanding the significance of men's action upon objective reality, creative communication about the object by means of language, plurality of responses to a single challenge — these varied dimensions testify to the existence of critical reflection in men's relationships with the world. Consciousness is constituted in the dialectic of man's objectification of and action upon the world. However, consciousness is never a mere reflection of, but a reflection upon, material reality.[4]

If it is true that consciousness is impossible without the world that constitutes it, it is equally true that this world is impossible if the world itself in constituting consciousness does not become an object of its critical reflection. Thus, mechanistic objectivism is incapable of explaining men and the world since it negates men, as is solipsistic idealism since it negates the world.

For mechanistic objectivism, consciousness is merely a "copy" of objective reality. For solipsism, the world is reduced to a capricious creation of consciousness. In the first case, consciousness would be unable to transcend its conditioning by reality; in the second, insofar as it "creates" reality, it is a priori to reality. In either case man is not engaged in transforming reality. That would be impossible in objectivistic terms, because for objectivism, consciousness, the replica or "copy" of reality, is the object of reality, and reality would then be transformed by itself.[5] The solipsistic view is equally incompatible with the concept of transforming reality, since the transformation of an imaginary reality is an absurdity. Thus in both conceptions of consciousness there can be no true praxis. Praxis is only possible where the objective-subjective dialectic is maintained.[6]

Behaviorism also fails to comprehend the dialectic of men-world relationships. Under the form called mechanistic behaviorism, men are negated because they are seen as machines. The second form, logical behaviorism, also negates men, since it affirms that men's consciousness is "merely an abstraction."[7] The process of conscientization cannot be founded upon any of these defective explanations of man-world relationships. Conscientization is viable only because men's consciousness, although conditioned, can recognize that it is conditioned. This "critical" dimension of consciousness accounts for the goals men assign to their transforming acts upon the world. Because they are able to have goals, men alone are capable of entertaining the result of their action even before initiating the proposed action. They are beings who project:

> We presuppose labor in a form that stamps it as exclusively human. A spider conducts operations that resemble those of a weaver, and a bee puts to shame many an

architect in the construction of her cells. But what distinguishes the worst architect from the best of the bees is this, that the architect raises his structure in imagination before he erects it in reality.[8]

Although bees, as expert "specialists," can identify the flower they need for making their honey, they do not vary their specialization. They cannot produce by-products. Their action upon the world is not accompanied by objectification; it lacks the critical reflection that characterizes men's tasks. Whereas animals adapt themselves to the world to survive, men modify the world in order *to be more*. In adapting themselves for the sake of survival, without ends to achieve and choices to make, animals cannot "animalize" the world. "Animalization" of the world would be intimately linked to the "animalization" of animals, and this would presuppose in animals an awareness that they are incomplete, which would engage them in a permanent quest. In fact, however, while they skillfully construct their hives and "manufacture" honey, bees remain bees in their contact with the world; they do not become more or less bees.[9]

For men, as beings of praxis, to transform the world is to humanize it, even if making the world human may not yet signify the humanization of men. It may simply mean impregnating the world with man's curious and inventive presence, imprinting it with the trace of his works. The process of transforming the world, which reveals this presence of man, can lead to his humanization as well as his dehumanization, to his growth or diminution. These alternatives reveal to man his problematic nature and pose a problem for him, requiring that he choose one path or the other. Often this very process of transformation ensnares man and his freedom to choose. Nevertheless, because they impregnate the world with their reflective presence, only men can humanize or dehumanize. Humanization is their utopia, which they announce in denouncing dehumanizing processes.

The reflectiveness and finality of men's relationships with the world would not be possible if these relationships did not occur in a historical as well as physical context. Without critical reflection there is no finality, nor does finality have meaning outside an uninterrupted temporal series of events. For men there is no *here* relative to a *there* that is not connected to a *now*, a *before*, and an *after*. Thus men's relationships with the world are per se historical, as are men themselves. Not only do men make the history that makes them, but they also can recount the history of this mutual making. In becoming "hominized"[10] in the process of evolution, men become capable of having a biography. Animals, on the contrary, are immersed in a time that belongs not to them, but to men.

There is a further fundamental distinction between man's relationships with the world and the animal's contacts with it: only men work. A horse, for example, lacks what is proper to man, what Marx refers to in his example of the bees: "At the end of every labor-process, we get a result that already existed in the imagination of the laborer at its commencement."[11] Action without this dimension is not work. In the fields as well as in the circus, the apparent work of horses reflects the work of men. Action is work not because of the greater or lesser physical effort expended in it by the acting organism, but because of the consciousness the subject has of his own effort, his possibility of programming action, for creating tools and using them to mediate between himself and the object of his action, of having purposes, of anticipating results. Still more, for action to work, it must result in significant products, which while distinct from the active agent, at the same time condition him and become the object of his reflection.[12] As men act upon the world effectively, transforming it by their work, their consciousness is in turn historically and culturally conditioned through the "inversion of praxis." According to the quality of this conditioning, men's consciousness attains various levels in the context of cultural-historical reality. We propose to analyze these levels of consciousness as a further step toward understanding the process of conscientization.

Historical Conditioning and Levels of Consciousness

To understand the levels of consciousness, we must understand cultural-historical reality as a superstructure in relation to an infrastructure. Therefore, we will try to discern, in relative rather than absolute terms, the fundamental characteristics of the historical-cultural configuration to which such levels correspond.

Our intention is not to attempt a study of the origins and historical evolution of consciousness, but to make a concrete introductory analysis of the levels of consciousness in Latin American reality. This does not invalidate such an analysis for other areas of the Third World, nor for those areas in the metropolises that identify themselves with the Third World as "areas of silence."

We will first study the historical-cultural configuration that we have called "the culture of silence." This mode of culture is a superstructural expression that conditions a special form of consciousness. The culture of silence "overdetermines" the infrastructure in which it originates.[13]

Understanding the culture of silence is possible only if it is taken as a totality that is itself part of a greater whole. In this greater whole we must also recognize the culture or cultures that determine the voice of the culture of silence. We do not mean that the culture of silence is an entity created by the metropolis in specialized laboratories and transported to the Third World. Nor is it true, however, that the culture of silence emerges by spontaneous generation. The fact is that the culture of silence is born in the relationship between the Third World and the metropolis. "It is not the dominator who constructs a culture and imposes it on the dominated. This culture is the result of the structural relations between the dominated and the dominators."[14] Thus, understanding the culture of silence presupposes an analysis of dependence as a relational phenomenon that gives rise to different forms of being, of thinking, of expression, those of the culture of silence and those of the culture that "has a voice."

We must avoid both of the positions previously criticized in this article: objectivism, which leads to mechanism; and idealism, which leads to solipsism. Further, we must guard against idealizing the superstructure, dichotomizing it from the infrastructure. If we underestimate either the superstructure of infrastructure it will be impossible to explain the social structure itself. Social structure is not an abstraction; it exists in the dialectic between super- and infrastructures. Failing to understand this dialectic, we will not understand the dialectic of change and permanence as the expression of the social structure.

It is true that the infrastructure, created in the relations by which the work of man transforms the world, gives rise to superstructure. But it is also true that the latter, mediated by men, who introject its myths, turns upon the infrastructure and "over-determines" it. If it were not for the dynamic of these precarious relationships in which men exist and work in the world, we could speak neither of social structure, nor of men, nor of a human world.

Let us return to the relationship between the metropolitan society and the dependent society as the source of their respective ways of being, thinking, and expression. Both the metropolitan society and the dependent society, totalities in themselves, are part of a greater whole, the economic, historical, cultural, and political context in which their mutual relationships evolve. Though the contest in which these societies relate to each other is the same, the quality of the relationship is obviously different in each case, being determined by the role that each plays in the total context of their interrelation. The action of the metropolitan society upon the dependent society has a directive character, whereas the object society's action, whether it be response or initiative, has a dependent character.

The relationships between the dominator and the dominated reflect the greater social context, even when formally personal. Such relationships imply the introjection by the dominated of the cultural myths of the dominator. Similarly, the dependent society introjects the values and lifestyle of the metropolitan society, since the structure of the latter shapes that of the former. This results in the duality of the dependent society, its ambiguity, its being and not being itself, and the ambivalence characteristic of its long experience of dependency, both attracted by and rejecting the metropolitan society.

The infrastructure of the dependent society is shaped by the director society's will. The resultant superstructure, therefore, reflects the inauthenticity of the infrastructure. Whereas the metropolis can absorb its ideological crises through mechanisms of economic power and a highly developed technology, the dependent structure is too weak to support the slightest popular manifestation. This accounts for the frequent rigidity of the dependent structure.

The dependent society is by definition a silent society. Its voice is not an authentic voice, but merely an echo of the voice of the metropolis — in every way, the metropolis speaks, the dependent society listens.[15]

The silence of the object society in relation to the director society is repeated in the relationships within the object society itself. Its power elites, silent in the face of the metropolis, silence their own people in turn. Only when the people of a dependent society break out of the culture of silence and win their right to speak — only, that is, when radical structural changes transform the dependent society — can such a society as a whole cease to be silent towards the director society.

On the other hand, if a group seizes power through a coup d'état, as in the recent case of Peru, and begins to take nationalist economic and cultural defense measures, its policy creates a new contradiction, with one of the following consequences. First, the new regime may exceed its own intentions and be obliged to break definitively with the culture of silence both internally and externally. Or, fearing the ascension of the people, it may retrogress, and re-impose silence on the people. Third, the government may sponsor a new type of populism. Stimulated by the first nationalist measures, the submerged masses would have the illusion that they were participating in the transformations of their society, when, in fact, they were being shrewdly manipulated. In Peru, as the military group that took power in 1968 pursues its political objectives, many of its actions will cause "cracks" to appear in the most closed areas of Peruvian society. Through these cracks, the masses will begin to emerge from their silence with increasingly demanding attitudes. Insofar as their demands are met, the masses will tend not only to increase their frequency, but also to alter their nature.

Thus, the populist approach will also end up creating serious contradictions for the power group. It will find itself obliged either to break open the culture of silence or to restore it. That is why it seems to us difficult in Latin America's present historical moment for any government to maintain even a relatively aggressive independent policy towards the metropolis while preserving the culture of silence internally.

In 1961, Janio Quadros came to power in Brazil in what was perhaps the greatest electoral victory in the nation's history. He attempted to carry out a paradoxical policy of independence towards the metropolis and control over the people. After seven months in office, he unexpectedly announced to the nation that he was obliged to renounce the presidency under pressure from the same hidden forces that had driven President Getulio Vargas to commit suicide. And so he made a melancholy exit and headed for London.

The Brazilian military group that overthrew the Goulart government in 1964, picturesquely designating their action a revolution, have followed a coherent course according to our preceding analysis: a consistent policy of servility towards the metropolis and the violent imposition of silence upon their own people. A policy of servility towards the metropolis and rupture of the internal culture of silence would not be viable. Neither would a policy of independence towards the metropolis while maintaining the culture of silence internally.

Latin American societies were established as closed societies from the time of their conquest by the Spanish and Portuguese, when the culture of silence took shape. With the exception of post-revolutionary Cuba, these societies are still closed societies today.[16] They are dependent societies for whom only the poles of decision of which they are the object have changed at different historical moments: Portugal, Spain, England, or the United States.

Latin American societies are closed societies characterized by a rigid hierarchical social structure; by the lack of internal markets, since their economy is controlled from the outside; by the exportation of raw materials and importation of manufactured goods, without a voice in either process; by a precarious and selective educational system whose schools are an instrument of maintaining the status quo; by high percentages of illiteracy and disease, including the naively named "tropical diseases" that are really diseases of underdevelopment and dependence; by alarming rates of infant mortality; by malnutrition, often with irreparable effects on mental faculties; by a low life expectancy; and by a high rate of crime.

There is a mode of consciousness that corresponds to the concrete reality of such dependent societies. It is a consciousness historically conditioned by the social structures. The principal characteristic of this consciousness, as dependent as the society to whose structure it conforms, is its "quasi-adherence" to objective reality, or "quasi-immersion" in reality.[17] The dominated consciousness does not have sufficient distance from reality to objectify it in order to know it in a critical way.[18] We call this mode of consciousness "semi-intransitive."[19]

Semi-intransitive consciousness is typical of closed structures. In its quasi-immersion in concrete reality, this consciousness fails to perceive many of reality's challenges, or perceives them in a distorted way. Its semi-intransitiveness is a kind of obliteration imposed by objective conditions. Because of this obliteration, the only data that the dominated consciousness grasps are the data that lie within the orbit of its lived experience. This mode of consciousness cannot objectify the facts and problematical situations of daily life. Men whose consciousness exists at this level of quasi-immersion lack what we call "structural perception," which shapes and reshapes itself from concrete reality in the apprehension of facts and problematical situations. Lacking structural perception, men attribute the sources of such facts and situations in their lives either to some super-reality or to something within themselves; in either case to something outside objective reality. It is not hard to trace here the origin of the fatalistic positions men assume in certain situations. If the explanation for those situations lies in a superior power, or in men's own "natural" incapacity, it is obvious that their action will not be orientated towards transforming reality, but towards those superior beings responsible for the problematical situation, or toward that presumed incapacity. Their action, therefore, has the character of defensive magic or therapeutic magic. Thus, before harvest time or sowing, Latin American peasants, and the peasants of the Third World in general, perform magical rites, often of a syncretistic religious nature. Even when those rites evolve into cultural traditions, they remain instrumental for a time; the transformation of a magical rite into an expression of tradition does not happen suddenly. It is a process involving, once again, the dialectic between objectivity and subjectivity.[20]

Under the impact of infrastructural changes that produced the first "cracks" in Latin American societies, they entered the present stage of historical and cultural transition — some more intensely than others. In the particular case of Brazil, this process began with the abolition of slavery at the end of the nineteenth century.[21] It accelerated during World War I and again after the depression of 1929, intensified during World War II, and continued with fits and starts to 1964, when the military coup violently returned the nation to silence.

What is important, nevertheless, is that once the cracks in the structure begin to appear, and once societies enter the period of transition, immediately the first movements of emergence of the hitherto submerged and silent masses begin to manifest themselves. This does not mean, however, that movements towards emergence automatically break open the culture of silence. In their relationship to the metropolis, transitional societies continue to be silent totalities. Within them, however, the phenomenon of the emerging masses forces the power elites to experiment with new forms of maintaining the masses in silence, since structural changes that provoke the emergence of the masses also qualitatively alter their quasi-immersed and semi-intransitive consciousness.

The objective datum of a closed society, one of its structural components, is the silence of the masses, a silence broken only by occasional, ineffective rebellions. When
this silence coincides with the masses' fatalistic perception of reality, the power elites
that impose silence on the masses are rarely questioned.[22] When the closed society begins to crack, however, the new datum becomes the demanding presence of the
masses. Silence is no longer seen as an inalterable given, but as the result of a reality
that can and must be transformed. This historical transition, lived by Latin American
societies to a greater or lesser degree, corresponds to a new phase of popular consciousness, that of "naive transitivity." Formerly the popular consciousness was semi-
intransitive, limited to meeting the challenges relative to biological needs. In the process of emerging from silence, the capacity of the popular consciousness expands so
that men begin to be able to visualize and distinguish what before was not clearly
outlined.

Although the qualitative difference between the semi-intransitive consciousness
and the naive transitive consciousness can be explained by the phenomenon of emergence due to structural transformations in society, there are no rigidly defined fron-
tiers between the historical moments that produce qualitative changes in men's
awareness. In many respects, the semi-intransitive consciousness remains present in
the naive transitive consciousness. In Latin America, for example, almost the entire
peasant population is still in the stage of quasi-immersion, a stage with a much longer
history than the present one of emergence. The semi-intransitive peasant consciousness introjected innumerable myths in the former stage that continue despite a
change in awareness towards transitivity. Therefore, the transitive consciousness
emerges as a naive consciousness, as dominated as the former. Nevertheless, it is now
indisputably more disposed to perceiving the source of its ambiguous existence in the
objective conditions of society.

The emergence of the popular consciousness implies, if not the overcoming of the
culture of silence, at least the presence of the masses in the historical process applying
pressure on the power elite. It can only be understood as one dimension of a more
complex phenomenon. That is to say, the emergence of the popular consciousness,
although yet naively intransitive, is also a moment in the developing consciousness of
the power elite. In a structure of domination, the silence of the popular masses would
not exist but for the power elites who silence them; nor would there be a power elite
without the masses. Just as there is a moment of surprise among the masses when
they begin to see what they did not see before, there is a corresponding surprise
among the elites in power when they find themselves unmasked by the masses. This
two-fold unveiling provokes anxieties in both the masses and the power elites. The
masses become anxious for freedom, anxious to overcome the silence in which they
have always existed. The elites are anxious to maintain the status quo by allowing
only superficial transformations designed to prevent any real change in their power of
prescription.

In the transitional process, the predominantly static character of the "closed society" gradually yields to a dynamism in all dimensions of social life. Contradictions
come to the surface, provoking conflicts in which the popular consciousness becomes
more and more demanding, causing greater and greater alarm on the part of the

elites. As the lines of this historical transition become more sharply etched, illuminating the contradictions inherent in a dependent society, groups of intellectuals and students, who themselves belong to the privileged elite, seek to become engaged in social reality, tending to reject imported schemes and pre-fabricated solutions. The arts gradually cease to be the mere expression of the easy life of the affluent bourgeoisie, and begin to find their inspiration in the hard life of the people. Poets begin to write about more than their lost loves, and even the theme of lost love becomes less maudlin, more objective and lyrical. They speak now of the field hand and laborer not as abstract and metaphysical concepts, but as concrete men with concrete lives.[23]

In the case of Brazil, such qualitative changes marked all levels of creative life. As the transitional phase intensified, these active groups focused more and more on their national reality in order to know it better and to create ways of overcoming their society's state of dependence.

The transitional phase also generates a new style of political life, since the old political models of the closed society are no longer adequate where the masses are an emerging historical presence. In the closed society, relations between the elite and the quasi-immersed people are mediated by political bosses, representing the various elitist factions. In Brazil, the invariably paternalistic political bosses are owners not only of their lands, but also of the silent and obedient popular masses under their control. As rural areas in Latin America at first were not touched by the emergence provoked by the cracks in society, they remained predominantly under the control of the political bosses.[24] In urban centers, by contrast, a new kind of leadership emerged to mediate between the power elites and the emerging masses: the populist leadership. There is one characteristic of populist leadership that deserves our particular attention: we refer to its manipulative character.

Although the emergence of the masses from silence does not allow the political style of the formerly closed society to continue, that does not mean that the masses are able to speak on their own behalf. They have merely passed from quasi-immersion to a naive transitive state of awareness. Populist leadership thus could be said to be an adequate response to the new presence of the masses in the historical process. But it is a manipulative leadership — manipulative of the masses, since it cannot manipulate the elite.

Populist manipulation of the masses must be seen from two different perspectives. On the one hand, it is undeniably a kind of political opiate that maintains not only the naiveté of the emerging consciousness, but also the people's habit of being directed. On the other hand, to the extent that it uses mass protest and demands, political manipulation paradoxically accelerates the process by which the people unveil reality. This paradox sums up the ambiguous character of populism: it is manipulative, yet at the same time a factor in democratic mobilization.[25]

Thus, the new style of political life found in transitional societies is not confined to the manipulative role of its leaders, mediating between the masses and the elites. Indeed, the populist style of political action ends up creating conditions for youth groups and intellectuals to exercise political participation together with the people. Although it is an instance of manipulative paternalism, populism offers the possibility of a critical analysis of the manipulation itself. Within the whole play of contradictions and ambiguities, the emergence of the popular masses in transitional societies prepares the way for the masses to become conscious of their dependent state.

As we have said, the passage of the masses from a semi-intransitive to a naive transitive state of consciousness is also the moment of an awakening consciousness on the part of the elites, a decisive moment for the critical consciousness of progressive groups. At first there appears a fragile awareness among small groups of intellectuals who are still marked by the cultural alienation of society as a whole, an alienation reinforced by their university "formation." As the contradictions typical of a society in transition emerge more clearly, these groups multiply and are able to distinguish more and more precisely what makes up their society. They tend more and more to join with the popular masses in a variety of ways: through literature, plastic arts, the theater, music, education, sports, and folk art. What is important is the communion with the people that some of these groups are able to achieve.

At this point the increasingly critical consciousness of these progressive groups, arising from the naive transitivity of the emerging masses, becomes a challenge to the consciousness of the power elites. Societies that find themselves in this historical phase, which cannot be clearly understood outside the critical comprehension of the totality of which they are a part, live in a climate of pre-revolution whose dialectical contradiction is the coup d'état.

In Latin America, the coup d'état has become the answer of the economic and military power elites to the crises of popular emergence. This response varies with the relative influence of the military. According to the degree of its violence and that of the subsequent repression of the people, the coup d'état "reactivates" old patterns of behavior in the people, patterns that belong to their former state of quasi-immersion. Only this "reactivation" of the culture of silence can explain the passivity of the people when faced with the violence and arbitrary rule of Latin American military coups (with the sole exception, up to now, of Peru).[26]

It must be emphasized that the coups d'état in Latin America are incomprehensible without a dialectical vision of reality; any attempt to understand them mechanistically will lead to a distorted picture. Intensely problematical, unmasking more and more their condition of dependency, Latin American societies in transition are confronted with two contradictory possibilities: revolution or coup d'état. The stronger the ideological foundations of a coup d'état, the more it is impossible for a society to return afterwards to the same political style that created the very conditions for the coup. A coup d'état qualitatively alters the process of a society's historical transition and marks the beginning of a new transition. In the original transitional stage, the coup was the antithetical alternative to revolution; in the new transitional stage, the coup is defined and confirmed as an arbitrary and anti-popular power, whose tendency before the continuing possibility of revolution is to become more and more rigid.

In Brazil, the transition marked by the coup d'état sets up recapitulation to an ideology of development based on the handing over of the national economy to foreign interests, an ideology in which "the idea of the great international enterprise replaces the idea of the state monopoly as the basis for development."[27] One of the basic requirements for such an ideology is necessarily the silencing of popular sectors and their consequent removal from the sphere of decisionmaking. Popular forces must, therefore, avoid the naive illusion that this transitional stage may afford "openings" that will enable them to reestablish the rhythm of the previous transitional stages, whose political model corresponded to a national populist ideology of development.

The "openings" that the new transitional phase offers have their own semantics. Such openings do not signify a return to what has been, but a give and take within the play of accommodations demanded by the reigning ideology. Whatever its ideology, the new transitional phase challenges the popular forces to find an entirely new way of proceeding, distinct from their action in the former period when they were contending with the forces that those coups brought to power.

One of the reasons for the change is obvious enough. Due to the repression imposed by the coup, the popular forces have to act in silence, and silent action requires a difficult apprenticeship. Further, the popular forces have to search for ways to counter the effects of the reactivation of the culture of silence, which historically engendered the dominated consciousness.

Under these conditions, what is the possibility of survival for the emerging consciousness that has reached the state of naive transitivity? The answer to this question must be found in a deeper analysis of the transitional phase inaugurated by the military coup. Since revolution is still a possibility in this phase, our analysis will focus on the dialectical confrontation between the revolutionary project (or, lamentably, projects) and the new regime.

Cultural Action and Cultural Revolution

It would be unnecessary to tell the revolutionary groups that they are the antagonistic contradiction of the Right. However, it would not be inexpedient to emphasize that this antagonism, which is born of their opposing purposes, must express itself in a behavior that is equally antagonistic. There ought to be a difference in the praxis of the Right and of revolutionary groups that defines them to the people, making the options of each group explicit. This difference between the two groups stems from the utopic nature of the revolutionary groups, and the impossibility of the Right to be utopic. This is not an arbitrary distinction, but one that is sufficient to distinguish radically the objectives and forms of action taken by the revolutionary and rightist groups.[28]

To the extent that real utopia implies the denunciation of an unjust reality and the proclamation of a pre-project, revolutionary leadership cannot:

a) denounce reality without knowing reality;
b) proclaim a new reality without having a draft project which, although it emerges in the denunciation, becomes a viable project only in praxis;
c) know reality without relying on the people as well as on objective facts for the source of its knowledge;
d) denounce and proclaim by itself;
e) make new myths out of the denunciation and annunciation — denunciation and annunciation must be anti-ideological insofar as they result from a scientific knowledge of reality;

f) renounce communion with the people, not only during the time between the dialectic of denunciation and annunciation and the concretization of a viable project, but also in the very act of giving that project concrete reality.

Thus, revolutionary leadership falls into internal contradictions that compromise its purpose, when, victim of a fatalist concept of history, it tries to domesticate the people mechanically to a future that the leadership knows a priori, but which it thinks the people are incapable of knowing. In this case, revolutionary leadership ceases to be utopian and ends up identified with the Right. The Right makes no denunciation or proclamation, except, as we have said, to denounce whoever denounces it and to proclaim its own myths.

A true revolutionary project, on the other hand, to which the utopian dimension is natural, is a process in which the people assume the role of subject in the precarious adventure of transforming and recreating the world. The Right is necessarily opposed to such a project, and attempts to immobilize it. Thus, to use Erich Fromm's terms, the revolutionary utopia is biophilic, whereas the Right in its rigidity is necrophilic, as is a revolutionary leadership that has become bureaucratic.[29]

Revolutionary utopia tends to be dynamic rather than static; tends to life rather than death; to the future as a challenge to man's creativity rather than as a repetition of the present; to love as liberation of subjects rather than as pathological possessiveness; to the emotion of life rather than cold abstractions; to living together in harmony rather than gregariousness; to dialogue rather than mutism; to praxis rather than "law and order"; to men who organize themselves reflectively for action rather than men who are organized for passivity; to creative and communicative language rather than prescriptive signals; to reflective challenges rather than domesticating slogans; and to values that are lived rather than myths that are imposed.

The Right in its rigidity prefers the dead to the living; the static to the dynamic; the future as a repetition of the past rather than as a creative venture; pathological forms of love rather than real love; frigid schematization rather than the emotion of living; gregariousness rather than authentic living together; organization men rather than creative and communicative language; and slogans rather than challenges.

It is indispensable for revolutionaries to witness more and more the radical difference that separates them from the rightist elite. It is not enough to condemn the violence of the Right, its aristocratic posture, its myths. Revolutionaries must prove their respect for the people, their belief and confidence in them, not as a mere strategy but as an implicit requirement to being a revolutionary. This commitment to the people is fundamental at any given moment, but especially in the transition period created by a coup d'état.

Victimizing the people by its violence, the coup reimposes, as we have said, the old climate of the culture of silence. The people, standing at the threshold of their experience as subjects and participants of society, need signs that will help them recognize who is with them and who is against them. These signs, or witnesses, are given through projects proposed by men in dialectic with the structure. Each project constitutes an interacting totality of objectives, methods, procedures, and techniques. The revolutionary project is distinguished from the rightist project not only by its objectives, but by its total reality. A project's method cannot be dichotomized from its content and objectives, as if methods were neutral and equally appropriate for liberation or domination. Such a concept reveals a naive idealism that is satisfied with the subjective intention of the person who acts.

The revolutionary project is engaged in a struggle against oppressive and dehumanizing structures. To the extent that it seeks the affirmation of concrete men as men freeing themselves, any thoughtless concession to the oppressor's methods is always a danger and a threat to the revolutionary project itself. Revolutionaries must demand of themselves an imperious coherence. As men, they may make mistakes, they are subject to equivocation, but they cannot act like reactionaries and call themselves revolutionaries. They must suit their action to historical conditions, taking advantage of the real and unique possibilities that exist. Their role is to seek the most efficient and viable means of helping the people to move from the levels of semi-intransitive or naive-transitive consciousness to the level of critical consciousness. This preoccupation, which is alone authentically liberating, is implicit in the revolutionary project itself. Originating in the praxis of both the leadership and the rank and file, every revolutionary project is basically "cultural action" in the process of becoming "cultural revolution."

Revolution is a critical process, unrealizable without science and reflection. In the midst of reflective action on the world to be transformed, the people come to recognize that the world is indeed being transformed. The world in transformation is the mediator of the dialogue between the people, at one pole of the act of knowing, and the revolutionary leadership, at the other. If objective conditions do not always permit this dialogue, its existence can be verified by the witness of the leadership.

Che Guevara is an example of the unceasing witness revolutionary leadership gives to dialogue with the people. The more we study his work, the more we perceive his conviction that anyone who wants to become a true revolutionary must be in "communion" with the people. Guevara did not hesitate to recognize the capacity to love as an indispensable condition for authentic revolutionaries. While he constantly noted the failure of the peasants to participate in the guerrilla movement, his references to them in his Bolivian diary did not express disaffection. He never lost hope of ultimately being able to count on their participation. In the same spirit of communion, Guevara's guerrilla encampment served as the "theoretical context" in which he and his companions together analyzed the concrete events they were living through and planned the strategy of their action.

Guevara did not create dichotomies between the methods, content, and objectives of his projects. In spite of the risks to his and his companions' lives, he justified guerrilla warfare as an introduction to freedom, as a call to life to those who are the living dead. Like Camilo Torres, he became a guerrilla not out of desperation, but because, as a lover of men, he dreamt of a new man being born in the experience of liberation. In this sense, Guevara incarnated the authentic revolutionary utopia as did few others. He was one of the great prophets of the silent ones of the Third World. Conversant with many of them, he spoke on behalf of all of them.

In citing Guevara and his witness as a guerrilla, we do not mean to say that revolutionaries elsewhere are obliged to repeat the same witness. What is essential is that they strive to achieve communion with the people as he did, patiently and unceasingly. Communion with the people — accessible only to those with a utopian vision, in the sense referred to in this article — is one of the fundamental characteristics of cultural action for freedom. Authentic communion implies communication between men, mediated by the world. Only praxis in the context of communion makes conscientization a viable project. Conscientization is a joint project in that it takes place in a man among other men, men united by their action and by their reflection upon that action and upon the world. Thus men together achieve the state of perceptive clarity that Goldman calls "the maximum of potential consciousness" beyond "real consciousness."[30]

Conscientization is more than a simple *prise de conscience*. While it implies overcoming "false consciousness," overcoming, that is, a semi-intransitive or naive transitive state of consciousness, it implies further the critical insertion of the conscienticized person into a demythologized reality. This is why conscientization is an unrealizable project for the Right. The Right is by its nature incapable of being utopian, and hence it cannot develop a form of cultural action that would bring about conscientization. There can be no conscientization of the people without a radical denunciation of dehumanizing structures, accompanied by the proclamation of a new reality to be created by men. The Right cannot unmask itself, nor can it sponsor the means for the people to unmask it more than it is willing to be unmasked. With the increased clarity of the popular consciousness, its own consciousness tends to grow, but this form of conscientization cannot convert itself into a praxis leading to the conscientization of the people. There can be no conscientization without denunciation of unjust structures, a thing that cannot be expected of the Right. Nor can there be popular conscientization for domination. The Right invents new forms of cultural action only for domination.

Thus, the two forms of cultural action are antagonistic to each other. Whereas cultural action for freedom is characterized by dialogue, and its preeminent purpose is to conscienticize the people, cultural action for domination is opposed to dialogue and serves to domesticate the people. The former problematizes, the latter sloganizes.[31] Since cultural action for freedom is committed to the scientific unveiling of reality, to the exposure, that is, of myths and ideologies, it must separate ideology from science. Althusser insists on the necessity of this separation.[32] Cultural action for freedom can be satisfied neither with "the mystifications of ideology," as he calls them, nor with "a simple moral denunciation of myths and errors," but must undertake a "rational and rigorous critique [of ideology]." The fundamental role of those committed to cultural action for conscientization is not properly speaking to fabricate the liberating idea, but to invite the people to grasp with their minds the truth of their reality.

Consistent with this spirit of knowing, scientific knowledge cannot be knowledge that is merely transmitted, for it would itself become ideological myth, even if it were transmitted with the intention of liberating men. The discrepancy between intention and practice would be resolved in favor of practice. The only authentic points of departure for the scientific knowledge of reality are the dialectical relationships between men and the world, and the critical comprehension of how these relationships are evolved and how they in turn condition men's perception of concrete reality.

Those who use cultural action as a strategy for maintaining their domination over the people have no choice but to indoctrinate the people in a mythified version of reality. In doing so, the Right subordinates science and technology to its own ideology, using them to disseminate information and prescriptions in its effort to adjust the people to the reality that the "communications" media define as proper. By contrast, for those who undertake cultural action for freedom, science is the indispensable instrument for denouncing the myths created by the Right, and philosophy is the matrix of the proclamation of a new reality. Science and philosophy together provide the principles of action for conscientization. Cultural action for conscientization is always a utopian enterprise. That is why it needs philosophy, without which, instead of denouncing reality and announcing the future, it would fall into the "mystifications of ideological knowledge."

The utopian nature of cultural action for freedom is what distinguishes it above all from cultural action for domination. Cultural action for domination, based on myths, cannot pose problems about reality to the people, nor orientate the people to the unveiling of reality, since both of these projects would imply denunciation and annunciation. On the contrary, in problematizing and conscienticizing cultural action for freedom, the annunciation of a new reality is the historical project proposed for men's achievement.

In the face of a semi-intransitive or naive state of consciousness among the people, conscientization envisages their attaining critical consciousness, or "the maximum of potential consciousness." This objective cannot terminate when the annunciation becomes concrete. On the contrary, when the annunciation becomes concrete reality, the need becomes even greater for critical consciousness among the people, both horizontally and vertically. Thus, cultural action for freedom, which characterized the movement that struggled for the realization of what was announced, must then transform itself into permanent cultural revolution.

Before going on to elaborate upon the distinct but essentially related moments of cultural action and cultural revolution, let us summarize our preceding points about levels of consciousness. An explicit relationship has been established between cultural action for freedom, conscientization as its chief enterprise, and the transcendence of semi-intransitive and naive-transitive states of consciousness by critical consciousness. Critical consciousness is brought about not through an intellectual effort alone, but through praxis — through the authentic union of action and reflection. Such reflective action cannot be denied to the people. If it were, the people would be no more than activist pawns in the hands of a leadership that reserved for itself the right of decisionmaking. The authentic left cannot fail to stimulate the overcoming of the people's false consciousness, on whatever level it exists, just as the Right is incapable of doing so. In order to maintain its power, the Right needs an elite who think for it, assisting it in accomplishing its projects. Revolutionary leadership needs the people in order to make the revolutionary project a reality, but the people in the process of becoming more and more critically conscious.

After the revolutionary reality is inaugurated, conscientization continues to be indispensable. It is the instrument for ejecting the cultural myths that remain in the people despite the new reality. Further, it is a force countering the bureaucracy, which threatens to deaden the revolutionary vision and dominate the people in the very name of their freedom.[33] Finally, conscientization is a defense against another threat, that of the potential mythification of the technology, which the new society requires to transform its backward infrastructures.[34]

There are two possible directions open to the transitive popular consciousness. The first is growth from a naive state of consciousness to the level of critical consciousness — Goldman's "maximum of potential consciousness." The second is the distortion of the transitive state of consciousness to its pathological form — that of the fanatic or "irrational" consciousness.[35] This form has a mythical character that replaces the magical character of the semi-intransitive and naive-transitive states of consciousness. "Massification" — the phenomenon of mass societies — originates at this level. Mass society is not to be associated with the emergence of the masses in the historical process, as an aristocratic eye may view the phenomenon. True, the emergence of the masses with their claims and demands makes them present in the historical process, however naive their consciousness — a phenomenon that accompanies the cracking up of closed societies under the impact of the first infrastructural changes. Mass society, however, occurs much later. It appears in highly technologized, complex societies. In order to function, these societies require specialties, which become specialisms, and rationality, which degenerates into myth-making irrationalism.

Distinct from specialties, to which we are not opposed, specialisms narrow the area of knowledge in such a way that the so-called "specialists" become generally incapable of thinking. Because they have lost the vision of the whole of which their "specialty" is only one dimension, they cannot even think correctly in the area of their specialization.

Similarly, the rationality basic to science and technology disappears under the extraordinary effects of technology itself, and its place is taken by myth-making irrationalism. The attempt to explain man as a superior type of robot originates in such irrationalism.[36]

In mass society, ways of thinking become as standardized as ways of dressing and tastes in food. Men begin thinking and acting according to the prescriptions they receive daily from the communications media rather than in response to their dialectical relationships with the world. In mass societies, where everything is prefabricated and behavior is almost automatized, men are lost because they don't have to "risk themselves." They do not have to think about even the smallest things; there is always some manual that says what to do in situation "a" or "b." Rarely do men have to pause at a street corner to think which direction to follow. There's always an arrow that deproblematizes the situation. Though street signs are not evil in themselves, and are necessary in cosmopolitan cities, they are among thousands of directional signals in a technological society that, introjected by men, hinder their capacity for critical thinking.

Technology thus ceases to be perceived by men as one of the greatest expressions of their creative power and becomes instead a species of new divinity to which they create a cult of worship. Efficiency ceases to be identified with the power men have to think, to imagine, to risk themselves in creation, and rather comes to mean carrying out orders from above precisely and punctually.[37]

Let it be clear, however, that technological development must be one of the concerns of the revolutionary project. It would be simplistic to attribute responsibility for these deviations to technology in itself. This would be another kind of irrationalism, that of conceiving of technology as a demonic entity, above and opposed to men. Critically viewed, technology is nothing more nor less than a natural phase of the creative process that engaged man from the moment he forged his first tool and began to transform the world for its humanization.

Considering that technology is not only necessary but part of man's natural development, the question facing revolutionaries is how to avoid technology's mythical deviations. The techniques of "human relations" are not the answer, for in the final analysis they are only another way of domesticating and alienating men even further in the service of greater productivity. For this and other reasons that we have expounded in the course of this article, we insist on cultural action for freedom. We do not, however, attribute to conscientization any magical power, which would only be to mythify it. Conscientization is not a magical charm for revolutionaries, but a basic dimension of their reflective action. If men were not "conscious bodies," capable of acting and perceiving, of knowing and re-creating, if they were not conscious of themselves and the world, the idea of conscientization would make no sense — but then, neither would the idea of revolution. Authentic revolutions are undertaken in order to liberate men, precisely because men can know themselves to be oppressed, and be conscious of the oppressive reality in which they exist.

But since, as we have seen, men's consciousness is conditioned by reality, conscientization is first of all the effort to enlighten men about the obstacles preventing them from a clear perception of reality. In this role, conscientization effects the ejection of cultural myths that confuse the people's awareness and make them ambiguous beings.

Because men are historical beings, incomplete and conscious of being incomplete, revolution is as natural and permanent a human dimension as is education. Only a mechanistic mentality holds that education can cease at a certain point, or that revolution can be halted when it attains power. To be authentic, revolution must be a continuous event. Otherwise it will cease to be revolution, and will become sclerotic bureaucracy.

Revolution is always cultural, whether it be in the phase of denouncing an oppressive society and proclaiming the advent of a just society, or in the phase of the new society inaugurated by the revolution. In the new society, the revolutionary process becomes cultural revolution.

Finally, let us clarify the reasons why we have been speaking of cultural action and cultural revolution as distinct moments in the revolutionary process. In the first place, cultural action for freedom is carried out in opposition to the dominating power elite, while cultural revolution takes place in harmony with the revolutionary regime — although this does not mean that it is subordinated to the revolutionary power. All cultural revolution proposes freedom as its goal. Cultural action, on the contrary, if sponsored by the oppressive regime, can be a strategy for domination, in which case it can never become cultural revolution.

The limits of cultural action are set by the oppressive reality itself and by the silence imposed by the power elite. The nature of the oppression, therefore, determines the tactics, which are necessarily different from those employed in cultural revolution. Whereas cultural action for freedom confronts silence both as external fact and introjected reality, cultural revolution confronts it only as introjected reality. Both cultural action for freedom and cultural revolution are an effort to negate the dominating culture culturally, even before the new culture resulting from that negation has become reality. The new cultural reality itself is continuously subject to negation in favor of the increasing affirmation of men. In cultural revolution, however, this negation occurs simultaneously with the birth of the new culture in the womb of the old.

Both cultural action and cultural revolution imply communion between the leaders and the people, as subjects who are transforming reality. In cultural revolution, however, communion is so firm that the leaders and the people become like one body, checked by a permanent process of self-scrutiny.[38] Both cultural action and cultural revolution are founded on scientific knowledge of reality, but in cultural revolution, science is no longer at the service of domination. On two points, however, there is no distinction between cultural action for freedom and cultural revolution. Both are committed to conscientization, and the necessity for each is explained by the "dialectic of overdetermination."

We have spoken of the challenge facing Latin America in this period of historical transition. We believe that other areas of the Third World are no exception to what we have described, though each will present its own particular nuances. If the paths they follow are to lead to liberation, they cannot bypass cultural action for conscientization. Only through such a process can the "maximum of potential consciousness" be attained by the emergent and uncritical masses, and the passage from submersion in semi-intransitiveness to full emergence be achieved. If we have faith in men, we cannot be content with saying that they are human persons while doing nothing concrete so that they may exist as such.

Notes

1. [Conscientization refers to the process in which men, not as recipients, but as knowing subjects, achieve a deepening awareness both of the sociocultural reality that shapes their lives and of their capacity to transform that reality. See p. 493. — Editor]
2. Re the distinction between men's relationships and the contacts of animals, see Paulo Freire, *Educação como Prática da Liberdade* (Rio de Janeiro: Paz e Terra, 1967).
3. Transcendence in this context signifies the capacity of human consciousness to surpass the limitations of the objective configuration. Without this "transcendental intentionality," consciousness of what exists beyond limitations would be impossible. For example, I am aware of how the table at which I write limits me only because I can transcend its limits, and focus my attention on them.
4. " 'Man, a reasoning animal,' said Aristotle.
    'Man, a reflective animal,' let us say more exactly today, putting the accent on the evolutionary characteristics of a quality which signifies the passage from a still diffuse consciousness to one sufficiently well centered to be capable of coinciding with itself. Man not only 'a being who knows' but 'a being who knows he knows.' Possessing *consciousness raised to the power of two*. . . . Do we sufficiently feel the radical nature of the difference?" Pierre Teilhard de Chardin, *The Appearance of Man*, trans. J. M. Cohen (New York: Harper & Row, 1965), p. 224.
5. Marx rejects the transformation of reality by itself in one of his "Theses on Feuerbach (III)," *Karl Marx, Selected Writings in Sociology and Social Philosophy*, trans. T. B. Bottomore (New York: McGraw-Hill, 1964), pp. 67–68.

6. In a discussion of men-world relationships during a *círculo de cultura,* a Chilean peasant affirmed, "I now see that there is no world without men." When the educator asked, "Suppose all men died, but there were still trees, animals, birds, rivers, and stars, wouldn't this be the world?" "No," replied the peasant, "there would be no one to say, this is the world."

7. We refer to behaviorism as studied in John Beloff's *The Existence of Mind* (New York: Citadel Press, 1964), Introduction.

8. Karl Marx, *Capital*, trans. Samuel Moore and Edward Aveling, ed. Frederick Engels (Chicago: Charles H. Kerr, 1932), p. 198.

9. "The Tiger does not 'de-tigerize' itself," said Ortega y Gasset in one of his works.

10. See Teilhard de Chardin, *The Appearance of Man.*

11. Karl Marx, *Capital.*

12. This is proper to men's social relations, which imply their relationship to their world. That is why the traditional aristocratic dichotomy between manual work and intellectual work is no more than a myth. All work engages the whole man as an indivisible unity. A factory hand's work can no more be divided into manual or intellectual than ours in writing this article. The only distinction that can be made between these forms of work is the predominance of the kind of effort demanded by the work: muscular-nervous effort or intellectual effort. Concerning this point, see Antonio Gramsci, *Cultura y Literatura* (Madrid: Ediciones Península, 1967), p. 31.

13. See Louis Althusser, *Pour Marx* (Paris: Librairie François Maspero, 1965).

14. José Luis Fiori, in a letter to the author. José Luis Fiori was an assistant to the author on his Chilean team to ICIRA, one of the best institutes of its type in the Third World.

15. It is interesting to note how this happens with the churches. The concept "mission lands" originates in the metropolis. For a mission land to exist, there must be another that defines it as such. There is a significant coincidence between mission-sending nations and metropolises as there is between mission lands and the Third World. It would seem to us that, on the contrary, all lands constitute mission territory to the Christian perspective.

16. Re "closed societies," see Henri Bergson, *The Two Sources of Morality and Religion*, trans. R. A. Audra and C. Brereton (Garden City, NY: Doubleday Anchor Books, 1954); and Karl Popper, *The Open Society and Its Enemies* (London: Routledge & Kegan Paul, 1949).

17. This mode of consciousness is still found to be predominant in Latin American rural areas where large property holdings *(latifundios)* are the rule. The rural areas constitute "closed societies" that maintain the "culture of silence" intact.

18. See Paulo Freire, *Pedagogy of the Oppressed* (New York: Seabury Press, 1970).

19. See Freire, *Educação como Prática da Liberdade.*

20. It is essential that modernization of backward structures ejects the sources of the magic rites that are an integral part of the structures. If not, while it may do away with the phenomenon of magic rites themselves, modernization will proceed to mythologize technology. The myth of technology will replace the magical entities that formerly explained problematical situations. Further, the myth of technology might be seen, not as the substitute for the old forces that, in this case, continue to exist, but as something superior even to them. Technology would thus be projected as all-powerful, beyond all structures, accessible only to a few privileged men.

21. The abolition of slavery in Brazil brought about the inversion of capital in incipient industries, and stimulated the first waves of German, Italian, and Japanese immigration to the south-central and southern Brazilian states.

22. Although we have not made a precise study of the emergence of black consciousness in the United States, we are tempted to state that, especially in southern areas, there are divergencies between the younger and older generations that cannot be explained by psychological criteria, but rather by a dialectical understanding of the process of the emerging consciousness. The younger generation, less influenced by fatalism than the older, must logically assume positions qualitatively different from the older generation, not only in regard to passive silence, but also in regard to the methods used by their protest movements.

23. See the excellent study on "The Role of Poetry in the Mozambican Revolution," *Africa Today, 16,* No. 2 (1969).

24. In Latin America, the Mexican, Bolivian, and Cuban revolutions broke open the closed structures of rural areas. Only Cuba, however, succeeded in making this change permanent. Mexico frustrated its revolution, and the Bolivian revolutionary movement was defeated. Nevertheless, the presence of the peasant in the social life of both Mexico and Bolivia is an indisputable fact as a result of that initial opening.

25. Francisco Weffort, in his introduction to Paulo Freire's *Educação como Prática da Liberdade*, points out that ambiguity is the principal characteristic of populism. A professor of sociology, Weffort is one of the best Brazilian analysts of populism today. The Center for the Study of Development and Social Change in Cambridge, Massachusetts, has recently issued a translation of this introduction, by Loretta Slover, for restricted circulation.

26. By the same phenomenon of the people's reversion to silence, Althusser explains how it was possible for the Russian people to put up with the crimes of Stalin's repression.

27. Fernando Henrique Cardoso, "Hegemonía Burguesa e Independencia Económica; Raízes Estruturias da Crise Política Brasileira," in *Revista Civilização Brasileira*, *17* (January 1968).

28. Re radicalization and its opposite, sectarianism, see Freire, *Pedagogy of the Oppressed.*

29. Re biophilia and necrophilia, see Erich Fromm, *The Heart of Man* (New York: Harper & Row, 1964).

30. Lucien Goldman, *The Human Science and Philosophy* (London: Jonathan Cape, 1969).

31. Freire, *Pedagogy of the Oppressed,* discusses both these forms of cultural action.

32. Louis Althusser and Etiene Balibar, *Para leer el capital* (Mexico: Siglo XXI, 1969).

33. One must reject the myth that any criticism of necrophilic bureaucracies that swallow up revolutionary proclamation strengthens the Right. The opposite is true. Silence, not criticism, in this case would renounce the proclamation and be a capitulation to the Right.

34. See Freire, *Pedagogy of the Oppressed.*

35. See Gabriel Marcel, *Man against Mass Society,* trans. G. S. Fraser (Chicago: A Gateway Edition, 1962).

36. In a recent conversation with the author, the psychoanalyst Michael Maccoby, Dr. Fromm's assistant, stated that his research suggests a relationship between mythologizing technology and necrophilic attitudes.

37. "Professionals who seek self-realization through creative and autonomous behavior without regard to the defined goals, needs, and channels of their respective departments have no more place in a large corporation or government agency than squeamish soldiers in the Army. . . . The social organization of the new Technology, by systematically denying to the general population experiences which are analogous to those of its higher management, contributes very heavily to the growth of social irrationality in our society." John MacDermott, "Technology: The Opiate of Intellectuals," *New York Review of Books,* No. 2 (July 31, 1969).

38. Even though these statements on cultural revolution can be applied to an analysis of the Chinese cultural revolution and beyond, that is not our intention. We restrict our study to a sketch of the relationship between cultural revolution and cultural action, which we propose.

No Longer Overlooked and Undervalued?
The Evolving Dynamics of
Endogenous Educational Research
in Sub-Saharan Africa

RICHARD MACLURE

Obstacles to the Development of
Endogenous African Educational Research

During the two decades following the success of independence movements across much of the African continent in the early 1960s, great hopes were invested in the rapid expansion of formal education systems. Yet since the end of the 1980s, education throughout sub-Saharan Africa has been persistently plagued by high rates of attrition, low achievement levels, shortfalls in infrastructure and learning materials, indications of poor teaching and low teacher morale, and disjunctions between school-based learning and subsequent job opportunities (United Nations Educational, Scientific and Cultural Organization [UNESCO], 2005). While the provision of universal access to basic education remains an as yet unattained imperative in most African countries, there is clearly also an urgent need to identify methods and strategies that will engender sweeping improvements in educational quality, relevance, and cost-effectiveness. It is now widely acknowledged that for this to occur, extensive ongoing programs of research are needed to shed light on the complexities of educational problems and to formulate appropriate policies of educational reform.

In many respects, existing knowledge of education systems and processes in sub-Saharan Africa is considerable. Yet most research published on education in sub-Saharan Africa has been produced by scholars and consultants who are employed in the universities, think tanks, and aid agencies of Northern countries.[1] Moreover, until quite recently, extensive public dissemination of endogenous educational research — studies that have been conducted by African researchers who live and work in their countries of origin — has been relatively scarce. This has been inevitable to some extent in light of the longstanding economic and sociopolitical travails that have afflicted African countries, and the vast technological and information disparities that exist between Northern countries and those of sub-Saharan Africa.

As elsewhere in the world, universities in Africa are ostensibly the main institutional foundations of autonomous national research. Yet despite the training and knowledge of their professorates, most university departments relegate independent scholarly research to a peripheral activity. The lack of financial and technical resources, the scarcity of journal subscriptions and recent books, and large student enrollments that necessitate heavy teaching loads have severely hampered the development and sustainability of endogenous research capacities within sub-Saharan African systems of higher education (Stren, 2001). With national universities generally overwhelmed by a combination of limited financial resources and steady growth in enrollment, scientific output from the whole of sub-Saharan Africa has been estimated at less than 1 percent of the world's output (International Development Research Centre/Association of Universities & Colleges of Canada [IDRC/AUCC], 2003). As a way to compensate, universities have customarily allowed for the creation of quasi-independent research centers that have attracted financial support from foreign backers and collaborative ties with Northern Africanist scholars. Institutes such as the Research Consultancy Bureau at Cape Coast University in Ghana and the Centre for Basic Research in Uganda have functioned essentially as consultancy firms, generating income for the universities that house them and complementing the relatively low university salaries of professors affiliated to these centers (Association for the Development of Education in Africa [ADEA], 1998). In fact, since adequate financial input for research is generally available through Northern-funded baseline studies and project evaluations, private research and evaluation consultancy groups have proliferated in sub-Saharan Africa. Yet as with all contracted research, the parameters of inquiry are defined by the contracting organizations, most of which are foreign to Africa. It is thus difficult for many otherwise well-trained researchers to establish their own independent research programs when they are understandably drawn to opportunity structures that offer attractive facilities and salaries (Association of African Universities & World Bank, 1997).

In light of the need to monitor and evaluate an array of processes and outcomes, specialized units have generally been established within African ministries of education to gather, analyze, and report on data pertaining to educational effectiveness and quality. Yet these ministries have rarely made effective use of the information they gather. As attested to in a recent comprehensive evaluation of aid to basic education, these ministries' failure to "link research to action is the most significant problem in the use of monitoring and evaluation in support of basic education" (Freeman & Faure, 2003, p. 51). A combination of factors, including staunch resistance to change and organizational cultures that impede the use of evaluative information, have rendered information gathering a frequently redundant and ineffective ministry exercise. Given these political, financial, and ideological hindrances to the development of independent research, concerns have often been expressed that African educational research has been dislocated from national contexts and has become largely the prerogative of researchers and institutions situated in North America and Europe.

Nevertheless, despite the weakness of African universities and the general disinterest in the practical merits of research and evaluation, endogenous African educational research has been resilient and voluminous in many respects. Until recently, however, much of it was conducted in relative obscurity and appeared only in unpublished manuscripts or reports that had limited readerships, and thus was usually quickly forgotten. This "subterranean" reality of African educational research became clear to me personally in the early 1990s while I was working on the synthesis of a series of national inventories of educational research sponsored by the Educational Research Network of West and Central Africa (ERNWACA). To the delight of those involved, many unpublished reports and manuscripts were unearthed by the inventory exercise. Yet the very fact that so much research had languished unused clearly signaled that endogenous African educational research was generally being overlooked and undervalued by educational policymakers and international scholars (Maclure, 1997; Namuddu & Tapsoba, 1993). This in turn generated questions about the degree to which autonomous national research capacities could be developed and maintained, and whether independent educational research conducted by African scholars could influence African educational policymaking and reform.

The relationship between endogenous research and national educational policymaking in fact emerged as a central theme of the inventory synthesis report, which concluded by outlining three main recommendations to enhance the quality and visibility of African educational research: (a) that substantial support be directed to strengthen educational research capacities, largely through training and the establishment of partnerships among African scholars; (b) that concerted efforts be made to disseminate nationally conducted research through as many channels as possible – publications, databases, newsletters, enhanced library resources; and (c) that links and regular forums for communication be established between African educational researchers and educational policymakers (Maclure, 1997). These were challenging objectives, particularly in view of the entrenched fiscal and administrative constraints that had weakened African governments and university systems. It was clear, therefore, that achieving these ends would require substantial external financial and technical assistance.

Now, a decade later, with African governments and international development agencies galvanized by the Millennium Development Goal[2] of ensuring that all children complete a full course of primary schooling by 2015 (United Nations, 2000), and with the empirical knowledge base of African education an undoubtedly significant factor in shaping national policies and programs, it is useful to reexamine the current state of endogenous African educational research and to assess whether or not it continues to be overlooked and undervalued. To some extent this is a vastly presumptuous task. Given the enormous political, linguistic, and demographic diversity of sub-Saharan Africa and the breadth of education as a multidisciplinary field that engages many institutions and scores of researchers, it is next to impossible to undertake an in-depth and comprehensive assessment of the status of African educational research. Furthermore, given the continued heavy dependence of African educational research on foreign funding, there may be questions about the degree to which African educational research can be fully independent and reflective of African sensibilities and concerns.

Nevertheless, in this essay, I will attempt to piece together an overview of the evolving state of endogenous African educational research by examining two modalities of educational research, one that is characterized by the direct control of international financial and technical assistance agencies (which I will refer to more simply as donor agencies), and another that is conducted largely under the auspices of formally established research networks that promote a praxis approach whereby research is oriented toward fostering policy-related reflection and dialogue. As I will show, despite diverse constraints and limitations, African researchers, by using both approaches, have been able to make considerable advances in contributing to the available knowledge base of African education and in participating more effectively in discourses of educational policymaking.

The Donor-Control Approach: Research as Product

Over the last two decades, following the corrosive effects of structural adjustment policies and the advent of the Education For All movement catalyzed by the 1990 Jomtien Conference,[3] a number of multilateral donor agencies — notably the World Bank and UNICEF — and bilateral donors — including the United States Agency for International Development (USAID), the Canadian International Development Agency (CIDA), and the United Kingdom's Department for International Development (DFID) — have sought to transform themselves from functioning solely as sources of financial and material aid into purveyors of policy advice and catalysts of educational reforms in sub-Saharan Africa (King & Buchert, 1999; McGinn, 2000; Samoff, 1999). Consequently, in order to ensure the credibility of their advisory functions, they have become keenly attuned to the value of evidence-based research and the content and dissemination of ideas that impinge directly on policies of African education. Given their inevitable concerns about the efficacy and outcomes of their own programs of assistance to education, these organizations have become major producers as well as consumers of research on African education, with much of their attention centered on issues closely related to their own program mandates (Buchert, 1998; Samoff & Stromquist, 2001). By and large, the objectives of donor-controlled inquiries are similar: to shed light on specific aspects or problems of education and to generate recommended courses of action for donor program staff and for host country counterparts (Reimers & McGinn, 1997).

To achieve these ends expeditiously, donors generally rely on a vast pool of education specialists, many of them African nationals, most of them hired on a contractual basis. While Africans are periodically designated as project leaders, they generally are appointed as coresearchers who work with or under the direction of Northern experts. Regardless of origin, however, education specialists who are involved in donor-controlled research and evaluation projects customarily share similar technical and disciplinary backgrounds. They usually hold graduate university degrees, often from Northern universities, and most have had previous and sometimes longstanding affiliation with donor agencies. Consequently, when collaborating on donor-controlled projects, they are generally bound together by mutual intellectual and professional perspectives that enable them to communicate easily and to work well together (Samoff, 1999).

With ample resources and expertise at their disposal, the World Bank and other major donors now wield substantial influence over the language and forms of inquiry and the overall orientation of applied educational research in most African countries. Although varying widely in terms of scope and quality, donor-controlled educational research has tended to generate or reinforce several common themes:

- Continued emphasis on the expansion of primary school placements and increased enrollment of girls, rural children, and other disadvantaged social groups (Tietjen, 1997; UNICEF, 2002; World Bank, 2000);
- Improved cost-effectiveness of education through more efficient fiscal and administrative capacities, and through the introduction of alternative "delivery" modalities, such as double-shift teaching and multigrade classrooms (Mattimore, Verspoor, & Watt, 2001; World Bank, 1999);
- Enhanced preservice and in-service teacher training as a way to foster improvements in the quality of classroom instruction and learning (Fiske, 1998; Gaynor, 1998; Perraton, Robinson, & Creed, 2001);
- Decentralized educational administration and strengthened local administrative systems and practices (Bray, 1996; Saunders, Riley, Craig, Poston, & Flynn, 2000; UNESCO, 2000; Watt, 2001);
- Combined support for and regulation of educational privatization and the establishment of autonomously managed community schools (Sosale, 2000; Watt, 2001; World Bank, 1999); and
- Enhanced donor coordination and emphasis on sectorwide strategies of educational assistance (Buchert, 1995; Freeman & Faure, 2003; Riddell, 2001).

While it is impossible to offer any comparative insights into the nature and content of donor-controlled research on these various issues, there is nonetheless a general tendency to focus on factors that are crucial to the continued expansion and improved efficiency of formal schooling. This is in line with a common donor agenda of specifying problems and prescribing solutions that generally include proposed system changes and external injections of financial and technical assistance. Yet this approach has attracted considerable criticism, particularly from Northern scholars (Reimers & McGinn, 1997; Samoff & Stromquist, 2001; Welch, 1998). As Samoff (1999) has argued, this approach to educational research is akin to a medical metaphor of inquiry in which education, particularly schooling, is regarded as a constellation of variables and outcomes that can be assessed through positivist methods determined in Northern institutional contexts. Because of this prescriptive approach, there rarely are indications of donor-controlled studies examining or questioning fundamental assumptions that relate to the purposes of education, to the cultural and linguistic dimensions of schooling, or to the social dynamics of classroom learning and interaction (Masemann, 1999; Welch, 1998).

At the heart of this medicalized approach to research is a power dynamic. Given the active involvement of donor agencies in the processes of knowledge accumulation and dissemination, and the corresponding dependence of African educational systems on foreign aid, agency-controlled research is essentially a top-down process (McNeely, 1995). Likewise, most of the principal authors of donor-controlled research that has focused on education in sub-Saharan Africa are non-Africans who are employed permanently in Northern institutions (Freeman & Faure, 2003). In line with the prescriptive research framework of the donor-control approach, the findings of donor agency studies are rarely subjected to extensive discussion outside of agency confines (Buchert, 1998). As such, African educational policymakers and other educational stakeholders — lower-level ministry bureaucrats, principals, teachers, and parents' associations — are generally regarded as recipients of validated knowledge that will facilitate the formulation and implementation of donor-proposed policy initiatives and reforms (Brock-Utne, 1995).

While donor agencies are frequently quite ready to embrace the language of stakeholder consultation and participation (Lavergne, 2004), and while there is clear indication of a growing African presence in donor-sponsored research and evaluation projects (even though there are still relatively few Africans functioning as principal researchers on these projects), ironically, in many instances the very *control* that donor agencies generally exercise over much of the process of knowledge production in Africa tends to hinder their effectiveness in influencing the perceptions and practices of those who work within education systems (Meier, 1999; Reimers & McGinn, 1997). Indeed, whether donor-agency studies have fostered major improvements in African education systems is a moot point (Freeman & Faure, 2003). For example, the goal of gender parity, particularly as it relates to the retention of girls in school and the quality of female learning, has proven elusive, as have questions about the long-term financial sustainability of expanding school systems and the faulty link between education and subsequent employment opportunities for the growing numbers of those leaving school. More recently, the HIV/AIDS pandemic, which has decimated the education profession in a number of southern African countries and left millions of children without parental support, has raised questions about alternative modalities of educational delivery that donor-directed studies have only recently begun to broach (World Bank, 2002).

Since the resolution of many abiding and looming problems depends substantially on coordinated actions by a range of educational stakeholders, there is growing acknowledgment of the need for a more symbiotic connection between researchers and policymakers, and for opportunities that enable stakeholders to share in the analysis of problems that they regularly confront (Reimers & McGinn, 1997). This has given rise to an alternative approach to endogenous African research, one that constitutes a combination of professional networking aiming to strengthen connections among African researchers and policymakers and the pursuit of research for purposes of collaborative reflection and policy-oriented dialogue. As I shall now discuss, it is this juxtaposition of networking and praxis-oriented research that appears to be augmenting the profile of endogenous African educational research as an increasingly significant factor in educational policy dialogue.

Networking and the Praxis Approach:
Research as Social Learning and Policy Development

Just as ideas of grassroots participation and capacity-building have been integrated into the mainstream rhetoric of international development over the last two decades (Chambers, 1983; Clark, 1995), so too has the notion of research as a basis of stakeholder learning and dialogue crept into development-policy discourse (Buchert, 1998; Maclure, 2000; World Bank, 2004). This has been a key theme underlying efforts to "Africanize" educational research and to strengthen links between endogenous research and educational policymaking through the development and expansion of professional networks. Although heavily dependent on external financial aid, a key aim of networking has been to stimulate greater autonomy and solidarity among African educational researchers and to augment their influence on the praxis of policy formulation and implementation (Stren, 2001). To this end, for well over a decade, two professional networks have devoted singular attention to enhancing the capacities, the productivity, and the profiles of African educational researchers and to fostering regional communities of researchers and decisionmakers. As a result, both networks have attained prominence among African governments and donor agencies alike. A brief overview of these networks — one regional, the other covering the entire subcontinent — provides insights into an approach to educational research in sub-Saharan Africa that differs markedly from the conventional donor-control model.

The Educational Research Network of West and Central Africa (ERNWACA)

In 1988, with support from the International Development Research Centre (IDRC), a group of West African education specialists formally launched the Educational Research Network of West and Central Africa (ERNWACA).[4] The impetus for doing so was largely the sense of isolation and lack of supportive professional environments that these researchers and their colleagues had long experienced in their own countries. Conceived as a bilingual network of researchers in Francophone and Anglophone countries, ERNWACA has steadily expanded and is now a well-established professional association with national chapters in thirteen countries in West and Central Africa and a membership of approximately 250 researchers.[5] With its headquarters located in Bamako, Mali, ERNWACA is administered by a permanent coordinator who communicates regularly with national members and other significant parties, including officials in national ministries of education and donor-agency representatives, and with educational scholars in Northern countries who have an abiding interest in African education. ERNWACA widely circulates a semiannual network newsletter that provides information on recent publications and colloquia, on forthcoming activities, and on the accomplishments of prominent West African educational researchers. Although initially relying heavily on the financial assistance of IDRC, ERNWACA has successfully broadened its base of support to include funding from USAID, UNICEF, UNESCO's Regional Bureau for Education in Africa, the German Foundation for International Development, the Swiss Development Corporation, and PLAN International.

In expanding its presence among educational researchers, ERNWACA has also helped to highlight their work and strengthen their connections with policymakers. Two types of ERWNACA activities have been especially notable in this process: (a) its inventories of existing educational research in member countries, and (b) its support for workshops, meetings, and projects that have enhanced the visibility of educational researchers and served as channels of communication between researchers and policymakers. What follows is a brief overview of these two sets of activities.

The First ERNWACA Inventory:
Two Decades of Post-Independence Educational Research

At the time of ERNWACA's formation, deliberations that immediately preceded and followed the 1990 Jomtien Conference on Basic Education for All frequently alluded to the imperative of strengthening the knowledge base for educational policymaking and reform (UNESCO, 1990; World Bank, 1988). Consequently, as a first tangible step in establishing a semblance of community among educational researchers across extensive national and linguistic boundaries, ERNWACA commissioned its newly created national chapters to undertake inventories of the published and unpublished products of educational research in each member country. Supported financially by IDRC and USAID, researchers in seven countries — Benin, Burkina Faso, Cameroun, Ghana, Mali, Sierra Leone, and Togo — embarked on a yearlong process of compiling and analyzing educational research manuscripts, reports, and publications.[6] By combing ministry archives and the libraries of universities and teacher-training colleges, the ERNWACA teams in each country uncovered a total of more than one thousand studies dating from the late 1960s to 1991. More than half of these included unpublished student theses and empirically grounded research papers. While the research uncovered encompassed an extensive range of topics, it was nonetheless possible to group the studies into thematic categories that revealed a broad pattern of an emerging educational crisis that has since become entrenched throughout much of the subcontinent. Very briefly, drawing from a selection of references cited in the national inventories, the findings in each category were as follows.

– Classroom Teaching and Learning: Shortcomings and Constraints

Over the years, teachers and their pupils have confronted a host of adversities: tenuous connections between the norms of family life and schooling (Essindi, 1977; Sow, 1985); severe deficiencies in infrastructures and materials that have undermined possibilities for effective teaching and fruitful learning (Wokwenmendam, 1981); pedagogical practices that have borne little relation to teacher training (Amegnonam, 1986; Mouthe, 1985); and curricular rigidities that have stifled innovation and reform (Diare, 1990; Koomson, 1990; Tetteh, 1989).

– Schooling and the Challenge of Community Engagement

Studies within this thematic cluster revealed two common findings related to community and schooling: persistent failures to establish sustainable income-generating cooperative and farm schools, and perennial difficulties in maintaining effective community management of local schools. Underlying these problems were the complex economic and socio-political dimensions of community life (Dougna, 1986; Rasera, 1986), and the contradictions between the professional and bureaucratic underpinnings of formal schooling and the decentralization of authority for purposes of community engagement in schools (Bediaku-Adu, 1987; Camara, 1987; Cisse, 1984; Gyilime, 1986).

– Education and Post-Educational Livelihoods

Another group of studies underscored the frequent disjuncture between formal schooling and the socio-cultural and economic contexts of local societies for reasons related to both educational supply and demand. On the supply side, there have been pronounced discontinuities between school curricula and labor market realities that have been shaped by weakened economies and the imposition of structural adjustment measures (Hode, 1987; Obanya, 1989). On the demand side, popular perceptions regarding the link between formal schooling and subsequent modern-sector employment remained largely constant, despite rising levels of unemployment among those leaving school (Megbemada, 1987).

– The Limits of Educational Innovation and Reform

The fourth broad category of research uncovered by the ERNWACA inventory project revealed the array of obstacles that has undermined efforts to fundamentally reform African school systems: weaknesses in planning (Gozo, 1977), lack of training and support for teachers and parent representatives (Konate, 1986), lack of consultation and local "ownership" of educational change (Sawadogo, 1984), and lack of recurrent resources for sustaining donor-sponsored innovations (Bockarie, 1979).

Implications of the First ERWNACA Inventory

Covering as it did only seven countries, the ERNWACA inventory was far from being an exhaustive survey of existing educational research in West Africa, let alone the rest of sub-Saharan Africa. Indeed, the lack of Nigerian involvement in the project was a significant caveat in what had been intended as a comprehensive review of educational research in the region. Most of the empirical research consisted of small-scale case studies that limited generalizability to broader political and economic problems affecting educational systems. It was also clear that diagnostic description far outweighed theoretical conceptualizations of educational issues, and that questions of validity and reliability were often ignored. This was not entirely surprising, however, since nearly two-thirds of the studies unearthed consisted of graduate student research essays and dissertations (the latter known as *mémoires* in Francophone countries). Other studies collated in the inventory included many unpublished seminar papers and a variety of technical reports, most of them earmarked for donor agencies and government ministries. Only 8 percent of the collated studies were published articles. The categories and breakdown of studies discussed in this first ERNWACA inventory are presented in Table 1.

For ERNWACA, this first inventory project underscored two key issues. First, despite the paucity of published research, this was an impressive volume of work that offered clear indication that African researchers had mapped out the terrain of many aspects of education in West and Central Africa. While there undoubtedly was room for capacity enhancement, this was ample evidence of a strong spirit of inquiry and evidence-based analysis that could provide fertile grist for the mill of African educational policymaking. Second, however, was the conundrum of a severe lack of dissemination. With the overwhelming proportion of endogenous educational research produced as unpublished theses and monographs that had languished in obscurity on archival shelves, it was clear that although many of these studies may have contributed to individual career advancement, they had added little to the publicly available knowledge base of African education and to educational policy deliberations.

Fortunately, however, the collation of these studies by national ERNWACA teams, and the subsequent publication of the inventory synthesis report (Maclure, 1997), had a substantial effect in boosting the visibility of endogenous African educational research. With the assistance of USAID and ADEA, the synthesis report was translated into French and was circulated widely among international donor agencies and ministries of education. Although it is impossible to assess the impact of this first inventory project, it clearly heightened awareness among senior ministry personnel and educational researchers themselves of the untapped potential of endogenous research as a source for policy reflection and deliberation.[7]

The Second ERNWACA Inventory: Focus on Quality

Partly as a consequence of the first inventory's success in highlighting previously unknown endogenous research in several member countries, in 2002 ERNWACA undertook a second compilation of studies that focused primarily on the issue of educational quality. Although not as wide-ranging as the earlier inventory, this second project was undertaken by researchers in eleven countries and resulted in the collation of more than five hundred research reports. In a summary report of this second inventory project, Obanya (2003) summarized the main findings of the principal topics covered by the inventory. Briefly, drawing from selected references, these main findings are summarized below.

– Preschooling

This category of research consisted of a number of descriptive studies, several of which highlighted the importance of teachers' remuneration and working conditions (Agusiobo, 1999; Nchungong, 1996; Onuchukwu & Ifeanacho, 2001).

– Teaching Effectiveness

A notable issue discerned in these largely qualitative studies was the significance of teachers' personality traits over and above their formal academic qualifications. The importance of teacher morale, as exemplified by the attributes of empathy, creativity, and cheerfulness, were deemed essential for effective teaching (Alota, 1999; Goerke, 1995; Sawadogo, 1999).

– Rural-Urban Dichotomies

Although a wave of decentralization policies throughout Western Africa has been oriented toward transferring resources and administrative control of schooling to rural regions, partly in an effort to enhance local ownership of schools and to increase the relevance of schooling to community life, continuing differences in examination results and in rates of attrition and repetition indicate ongoing fundamental gaps in the quality of urban and rural schools (Madumere-Obike & Oluwuo, 2001; Tchegho, 2003).

TABLE 1

ERNWACA First Inventory: Types of Research Data

Types of Research	Frequency
Mémoires (French)	557
Theses (English)	89
Government Reports	146
Joint Agency Reports	7
Donor Agency Reports	55
Published Manuscripts	85
Seminar Papers	37
Unpublished Papers	80
TOTAL	1,056

– Gender and Education

Studies on this topic have generally indicated that increased female enrollment in schools does not signify a reduction in discrimination against girls. Prevailing patriarchal values and norms manifested in curriculum materials and in classroom interactions appear to discourage girls from excelling in subjects such as math and science, and tends to hasten female dropouts (Amin & Fonkeng, 2000; Azie, 1998; Eta, 2000; Sedel, 1999).

– Language of Instruction

Despite policy rhetoric that is largely supportive of the use of national languages for regular classroom instruction, the lack of resources for curriculum development, textbook publishing, and teacher training, coupled with evidence of lukewarm interest among parents and concerns about the politicization of language selection in multilinguistic regions, have thwarted full-scale institutionalization of national language instruction in the primary school systems of Western and Central Africa (Afiesimama, 1995; Doumbia, 2000; Haidara, 2000; Ogbonna, 2002; Ohiri-Aniche, 2002).

Implications of the Second ERNWACA Inventory

Compared to the earlier ERNWACA-sponsored inventory of educational research that had been conducted before 1991, this second compilation of studies carried out within the more recent ten-year period revealed a much lower proportion of graduate student dissertations: 31 percent versus 61 percent. The percentage of published work also increased in this later review: 19 percent, compared to the relatively meager 8 percent in the first inventory. While a host of methodological factors prevents any definitive explanations for the differing levels of student work and published reports, particularly since Nigeria was included in the second review and not in the first,

Obanya (2003) nonetheless has surmised that these differences might be due in part to an ironic combination of deteriorating graduate studies programs in West Africa and increased opportunities and incentives for researchers to publish their work.

Like the first inventory, this second compilation of studies highlighted the extensive volume of largely independent endogenous educational research that continues to be conducted in ERNWACA member countries. Much of this work remains unpublished, however, and there was no indication that any of these studies had had an impact on policy deliberations. As Obanya (2003) observed,

> This exercise demonstrates that some serious research on the quality dimensions of basic education is going on in West and Central Africa, even though a good deal of this work is not known because of the poor state of research communication and archival culture. (p. 36)

Nevertheless, through the very process of conducting an inventory of existing research, and by posting the summative report of the inventory on its website, ERNWACA has contributed to growing awareness of endogenous research that has been focusing on an array of educational issues.

Research and Policy Dialogue

In addition to bringing to light many unpublished studies and providing regular updates of national researchers and their activities, within the past ten years ERNWACA has helped to sponsor a number of national and regional studies that have been conducted expressly for the purpose of informing policy dialogue and decisionmaking. While it is beyond the scope of this essay to determine the degree to which any of these studies have actually *shaped* the formulation and implementation of the policies that they were intended to influence, it is clear that endogenous research undertaken under the auspices of ERNWACA has attained a visibility and legitimacy in educational policy dialogue that was clearly not evident in the early 1990s. This is exemplified in Table 2, which outlines a selection of ERNWACA-coordinated national and regional studies that were aimed specifically at contributing to the educational policy deliberations of ministries and international donor agencies (ERNWACA, 2005a; ERNWACA, 2005b).

Since its inception, ERNWACA has been actively engaged in numerous meetings and conferences, most of which have brought together ERNWACA researchers with education ministry and donor agency personnel. Tables 3 and 4 present synopses of a series of national and regional meetings in 2004 – 2005, most of which were devoted to educational policy dialogue (ERNWACA, 2005a; ERNWACA, 2005b). As noted above, while it is not possible in this paper to demonstrate the degree to which researchers have affected the determination or modification of subsequent policies, suffice it to say that endogenous educational research has become increasingly an integral facet of educational policy dialogue in ERNWACA member countries.

As these studies and activities demonstrate, within the last ten years ERNWACA has established itself as a prominent association of African educational researchers that has a visible corporate presence in Western and Central Africa. Through a con-

TABLE 2

Recent Selected ERNWACA Studies: Topics and Countries

Complementarity between formal and nonformal education (Burkina Faso)

Study on the impact of armed conflict on the school system (Côte d'Ivoire)

Evaluation of the Ministry of Education's Scholarship Trust Fund for Girls (The Gambia)

Partnership dynamics in Koranic schools (Mali)

Study on conditions and quality of teachers (Niger)

Externally sponsored support for heightened girls' enrollment in primary schooling (Togo)

Factors affecting primary school pupil access and retention (Côte d'Ivoire and The Gambia)

Effects of community participation on access to and quality of basic education (Benin, Ghana, Guinea, and Mali)

Impact of conditionalities on educational reform policies (Benin, Ghana, Guinea, and Mali)

TABLE 3

National Colloquia Sponsored by ERNWACA, (2004–2005): Activity

Youth and HIV/AIDS conference (Cameroun)

Colloquium on teacher training (Cameroun)

Colloquium on policy-oriented participatory action research (Ghana)

Colloquium on HIV/AIDS in the education sector (Mali)

Colloquium on school management in the context of decentralization (Mali)

Colloquium on parental perceptions of education (Niger)

Colloquium on participatory action formative research (Nigeria)

Review of research and government policies on HIV/AIDS in the education sector (Senegal)

TABLE 4

Regional Activities Sponsored by ERNWACA or Involving ERNWACA Members from Two or More Countries (2004–2005): Activity

Colloquium on education, conflict, and perspectives for peace in Africa (Burkina Faso)

African Union Ministers of Education Conference (Algeria)

Governance, Equity, and Health Conference (Senegal)

UNESCO Regional Bureau for Education in Africa: 'Dakar + 5 Education for All' Forum (Senegal)

Colloquium on the UN Girls Education Initiative (Senegal)

Colloquium on research and education sector policy implementation (Niger)

Colloquium on gender, education, and skills development (Mali)

certed effort to highlight and disseminate endogenous educational research, to sponsor studies that have a direct bearing on policy issues, and to strengthen links among educational researchers and policymakers within and among its member countries, ERNWACA has enhanced the profile of endogenous research in discourses related to educational policymaking.

The Association for the Development of Education in Africa

Working on a larger scale than ERNWACA is the Association for the Development of Education in Africa. Originally established in 1988 as the Donors to African Education under the direction of the World Bank, in the early 1990s the organization's statute as an exclusive "donors' club" was abandoned in favor of its reformulation as an association of African ministries of education. In contrast to ERNWACA, whose core purposes have been to reinforce educational research environments through research dissemination and enhanced communication and collaboration among researchers and policymakers in Western and Central African countries, ADEA has a much broader mandate.

Headquartered in the offices of the International Institute of Educational Planning in Paris, ADEA's principal mission for more than a decade has been to promote partnerships among stakeholders and to contribute to capacity-building within ministries of education for better management of educational policies. As such, a key objective has been to strengthen the knowledge base of ministries of education through policy-oriented research and systematic communication between researchers and ministry officials. With an annual budget that has recently surpassed U.S. $5 million, ADEA is bankrolled almost entirely by donor agencies (Universalia, 2005). Reflecting the contribution of international donors, ADEA's steering committee, which is responsible for the oversight and governance of the organization, is comprised of twenty-one donor-agency representatives and ten ministers of education. Yet despite this two-to-one imbalance, selected topics of research and policy dialogue are largely a function of the priorities of African ministers (Universalia, 2005).

In pursuing its mandate of enhancing policy through research, ADEA has sponsored three ongoing sets of activities that adhere to the shared praxis of strengthening the interconnections of research, policy, and practice.

– Research Working Groups

The most prominent aspect of ADEA is its research working groups. Each group is coordinated by one or two educational specialists employed in African or donor-country institutions (Table 5). Together the working groups constitute a mix of Africans and non-Africans who are specialists in different aspects of education and who can participate in defining the topics and parameters of specific research projects. In keeping with the evolving nature of issues and problems, three ad hoc working groups have recently been created and two of the original thirteen have been disbanded. In addition, the erstwhile Working Group on Female Participation has become an independent pan-African nongovernmental organization (NGO), the Federation of African Women Educators.

Although diverse in composition and in their terms of reference, the working groups share the functions of undertaking research on specific areas of potential innovation and reform and disseminating the results of research to an audience that consists primarily of ministerial and donor-agency officials who have interests and responsibilities in the areas of inquiry. The purpose of research, therefore, is instrumental: to influence the perspectives and attitudes of key officials and thus affect the formulation of national education policies. As described by Marope and Sack (2005),

TABLE 5
ADEA Working Groups: Groups and Coordinating Institutions

Current Working Groups
Books and Learning Materials
      U.K.: Department for International Development
      South Africa: Read Educational Trust
Communication for Education and Development
      Benin: Comed Program-Wanad Center
Distance Education/Open Learning
      Mauritius: Tertiary Education Commission
Early Childhood Development
      Mozambique: Royal Netherlands Embassy
      Ghana: UNICEF House
Education Sector Analysis
      France: International Institute of Educational Planning
Education Statistics
      Netherlands: Ministry of Foreign Affairs
Finance and Education
      Senegal: Council for the Development of Social Science Research in Africa
      Canada: Canadian International Development Agency
Higher Education
      Ghana: Association of African Universities
Non-Formal Education
      Switzerland: Swiss Agency for Development and Cooperation
      U.K.: Commonwealth Secretariat
Teaching Profession
      U.K.: Commonwealth Secretariat
Female Participation
      Kenya: Federation of African Women Educators

Ad-Hoc Groups
HIV/AIDS and Education
      France: ADEA Secretariat
Quality of Education
      France: ADEA Secretariat
Postprimary Education
      France: ADEA Secretariat

Dissolved Working Groups
School Examinations
Education Research and Policy Analysis

the research activities of the working groups have contributed significantly to "the pedagogy of policy formulation" (p. 10). A recent evaluation of ADEA notes several examples of working group research influencing national policies (Universalia, 2005). In Niger, an agreement between the Ministry of Education and the Ministry of Finance regarding improvements in the disbursement of the country's annual education budget was facilitated by a study conducted by the Working Group on Finance and Education. In Chad, a policy ratifying community hiring of school principals followed recommendations outlined in a report by the Working Group on the Teaching Profession. Similarly, research and advocacy conducted by the Working Group on Female Participation and the Working Group on Early Childhood Development have contributed to policy developments in several countries that focus specifically on gender equity and preschooling (Universalia, 2005).

As articulated in ADEA's formal vision statement, the approach to research as conducted by the working groups is one that promotes "the development of synergies and in some cases the active participation of stakeholders" (ADEA, 2003, p. 1). By conducting research not with the aim of producing policy and program blueprints but as a way to generate a fluid and iterative relationship between policy-oriented inquiry, analysis, and dialogue, the working groups have helped advance the engagement of senior African education policymakers in ongoing research activities, something often absent from conventional Northern and donor-controlled research projects. This has invariably had the effect of enhancing the profile and the relevance of endogenous African research as a basis of policy deliberation and decisionmaking.

– Meetings and Conferences

In tangent with working group activities that aim to link researchers to policymakers around key policy issues, over the past decade ADEA has organized six biennial meetings that have enabled researchers, ministers of education, senior bureaucrats, and donor agency representatives to convene and discuss policy-related issues in an informal, collegial fashion. By incorporating working group reports as key background documentation, these "Biennials" (as they are referred to within ADEA) have focused on different themes.[8] For example, the unifying theme of the 2003 Mauritius Biennial was The Quest for Quality: Learning from the African Experience. In keeping with this central theme, the three-day meeting consisted of a series of working group reports that were followed by roundtable discussions and informal exchanges, all focused on experiences shared by various countries concerning the challenges of strengthening educational quality in both formal and nonformal educational settings. ADEA organizers work to ensure that Biennial discussions do not dwell solely on diagnoses of educational problems, but instead move on to examine evidence of promising policies and practices, as well as the institutional and contextual factors that underlie successful educational innovations (Marope & Sack, 2005). By incorporating working group reports as key background documentation, the Biennials have provided opportunities for policymakers to reflect on what has been achieved, how and why achievements have occurred, and what opportunities and challenges must be confronted to guarantee effective policy development and implementation (Universalia, 2005).

A similar agenda underlies ADEA's Intra-African Exchange Program which organizes cross-national research visits that allow senior officials to observe educational innovations and to discuss possibilities for replication as well as corresponding constraints. Launched in 1996, the program is intended to use existing regional capacities to capitalize on the diversity of experiences and expertise.

In terms of a broader international profile, a notable highlight for ADEA was the Tenth World Congress of Comparative Education that took place in Cape Town in 1998. The first major comparative education conference to be held in Africa, the congress provided an opportunity for African researchers to present their peer-reviewed studies — many of them undertaken under the auspices of ADEA — and to interact with policymakers from elsewhere in Africa and from other parts of the world.

– Publications and Databases

In line with its aim to promote research as a basis for policy-oriented dialogue, the ADEA secretariat has compiled a catalogue of some two hundred African educational research publications and documents. Many of these are now available online. Most of the working group research reports are also included on the ADEA website (http://www.adeanet.org). In addition, the secretariat produces a quarterly newsletter that publicizes the activities of the ADEA working groups and a monthly broadsheet that offers information on recently circulated reports and publications and on educational initiatives in different countries. Both the newsletter and the broadsheet are produced on-line and are also widely distributed to ministries of education, universities, donor agencies, and NGOs.

Another form of dissemination, however, has not been successful. In the mid-1990s, with technical and financial assistance from USAID, the ADEA Secretariat established two comprehensive online databases that were intended to provide continent-wide information on education in Africa for ministries of education and donor agencies. The Statistical Profile of Education in sub-Saharan Africa (SPESSA) was said to be user-friendly, offering an interactive and graphics framework for multiple searches and uses (Hartwell, 1999). The Program and Project Information System on Education was similarly designed to provide up-to-date information on externally funded educational projects and programs in sub-Saharan Africa. Unfortunately, although the SPESSA was updated in 1999, neither database has been maintained and they have thus lapsed into redundancy. This was due in part to the lack of data emanating from many countries, which effectively thwarted possibilities for maintaining the currency of the databases. There were also indications that the databases were of little use to stakeholders in African countries where access to the Internet has often been slow and sporadic (Universalia, 2005).

*The Merits and Limitations of Research Networking
and the Praxis Approach*

The studies, the reviews of research, and the range of dissemination activities carried out under the auspices of ERNWACA and ADEA by no means cover the extent of endogenous educational research conducted in sub-Saharan Africa. As mentioned at the outset of this essay, the breadth of education as a field of study does not allow for an in-depth, all-encompassing review of educational research in every African country. Nevertheless, the combination of networking and policy-oriented research that have been central to the mandates of these two professional associations have greatly enhanced endogenous African educational research in terms of its overall visibility and its relevance to educational policy deliberations throughout much of the subcontinent.

Three key factors have contributed to the success of these associations in augmenting the stature and influence of endogenous research. The first is the deliberate praxis orientation of the analytical work promoted and sponsored by these associations. To a large extent, this approach to research is rooted in a *raison d'être* that places less emphasis on standards of scientific rigor than it does on the social dynamics of research and the ensuing policy implications. By regarding research not as a meticulously collated and analyzed final "product" to be relayed to recipient decisionmakers, but rather as a catalyst of informed dialogue and negotiation among diverse educational policy stakeholders, these associations have attempted to situate research as an integral facet of educational policymaking and practice. From the perspective of this praxis approach to educational research, dialogue among key educational stakeholders that serves as the tangible link between knowledge creation and diffusion is as significant as the methodology of research and the content of knowledge acquired. Research, in other words, provides the springboard for collective learning and reflection that, once set in motion, may go beyond the parameters of the research itself.

This focus on collaborative stakeholder learning underscores a fundamental difference between the praxis orientation to research as exemplified by ERNWACA and ADEA and the more standardized procedures of donor-controlled research that generally focus on producing discrete research outcomes for purposes of formulating policy prescriptions and blueprints. The praxis approach is founded on the assumption that knowledge gathering and the utilization of knowledge are mutually reinforcing. Accordingly, there is a close symbiotic relation between inquiry, learning, and action, one not far from the precepts of participatory action research and the notion of indigenous knowledge as being "incarnated" in people's reflections and actions (World Bank, 2004). Indeed, as Marope (1999) has observed, this orientation is akin to a "self-study approach" that is meant to engage education officials in critically reviewing their own projects and programs. As such, "the development of a sustained culture of critical self-reflection . . . [takes] precedence over analytical sophistication" (p. 4).

A second critical factor, one that was not really foreseen when both ERNWACA and ADEA were first established, has been the advent of the Internet as a medium of dissemination. ADEA in particular has made effective use of this method of communication. Reports and publications, newsletters and news briefs, conference proceedings and *Who's Who* lists of African educational researchers are now regularly featured on ADEA's website and through ERNWACA's periodical electronic bulletins. The instantaneous nature of this form of communication and dissemination has greatly enhanced the visibility of African educational researchers and their work, not only among ministries of education and international donor agencies, but among Africanists and comparative education scholars in Northern countries. Indeed, given the universality and growing predominance of the Internet as a research tool in the North, there are indications that Northerners are becoming more knowledgeable about the scope and content of endogenous African educational research than are their African colleagues for whom access to the Internet is more expensive and cumbersome.[9] The advent of "networks of knowledge" (Stein, Stren, Fitzgibbon, & MacLean, 2001) that cross disciplinary, linguistic, organizational, and national lines, and that break free of formal, hierarchical structures in order to respond to broad social processes and policy issues, has proven to be enormously beneficial for African researchers. Through the combination of social capital and telecommunications afforded by research networks such as ERNWACA and ADEA, researchers in sub-Saharan Africa are attaining a greater and more independent voice in educational policy deliberations.

The third critical factor underlying the vibrancy of ERNWACA and ADEA has been a combination of dynamic leadership and sustained donor-agency support. Both of these associations have benefited from energetic and highly committed leaders. Since 1999, the regional coordinator of ERNWACA, Kathyrn Touré, has been indefatigable in developing links among educational researchers and decisionmakers, in encouraging the development of collaborative research projects, in disseminating research results, and in fundraising. Similarly, as the executive secretary of ADEA from 1996 to 2002, Richard Sack was instrumental in engaging ministries of education in the association's research activities and in promoting the dissemination of endogenous research as a vehicle for policy reform. His successor, ADEA's current Executive Secretary, Mamadou Ndoye, a former minister of education in Senegal, has likewise been described as having "considerable political and professional influence that helps him relate easily to donors and ministers alike . . . [and] being instrumental in facilitating dialogue and negotiating the numerous demands that are made on [ADEA]" (Universalia, 2005, p. 30). In large part because of such leadership, both ERNWACA and ADEA have been able to maintain a sustainable core of international financial and technical support.

Nevertheless, while networking and a praxis approach to research have undoubtedly raised the profile of endogenous educational research in sub-Saharan Africa, and while ministries of education appear more willing to heed the expertise of African educational researchers than they were before the early 1990s, evidence of the actual *impact* of endogenous African educational research on subsequent policy formulation and implementation remains sketchy and anecdotal.[10] To some extent this relates to the almost universal conundrum of the research/policy interface. Despite the proliferation of forums that have facilitated dialogue among African researchers and senior government officials, the formulation of African educational policies and the subsequent *implementation* of these policies are invariably constrained by extensive political, economic, technological, and sociocultural constraints. Lack of resources and weak systems of governance are major structural shortcomings that undermine the potential of praxis-oriented research from having an impact on educational policies and practices.

In addition, while ERNWACA and ADEA have benefited from the remarkable leadership of key individuals, particularly in terms of their organizational abilities and their collective energies in fostering communication and collaboration among researchers and decisionmakers, it is a truism that dynamic leadership is rarely sustainable. Likewise, sources of external financial support are finite, no matter how diversified they are. Without solid long-term institutional and financial foundations, the fortunes and accomplishments of professional networks in sub-Saharan Africa can quickly wane. This has been the fate of ERNWACA's counterpart — the Educational Research Network of East and Southern Africa (ERNESA) — which has lacked effective coordination in recent years, and therefore has lost most of its longstanding financial support.[11] This is clearly hazardous for African educational researchers who rely on network associations to provide them with significant opportunities to conduct and disseminate their research.

In addition, although research networks such as ERNWACA and ADEA can be highly effective in enhancing endogenous research capacity, they do not have the resources or the political influence to ensure long-term national institutional support for research within their member countries. In part this is because they are not bona fide *national* institutions. Despite the advantages of networking outlined above, ERNWACA and ADEA cannot singularly overcome problems associated with resource scarcity, political interference, and weak archival cultures that continue to render the conduct of independent research difficult in sub-Saharan Africa. While educational researchers and ministry officials have clearly benefited from their affiliations with these networks, there are others who have not been drawn into the orbits of these networks — particularly into inner circles of influence, such as membership in the ADEA working groups or participation in regional workshops and conferences (Universalia, 2005). For many outsiders, regionally and nationally conducted studies are still often either inaccessible or unknown. As Obanya (2003) has observed, the abiding lack of a culture of research communication continues to necessitate Herculean efforts to retrieve many endogenous research documents that are unpublished and excluded from databases.

In effect, professional networks are not fully grounded national institutions, and hence their ability to enhance research capacity and inculcate a culture of scholarly production and dissemination is constrained. Only through the strengthening of African universities, which are officially mandated to function as centers of teaching and research, coupled with reforms in systems of governance that are amenable to accommodating and supporting critical policy-oriented inquiry, will endogenous educational research be in a position to shift away from what has become an entrenched dependency on external financial and technical assistance. It is a dependency that is most obviously manifested through the direct involvement of African researchers in donor-controlled research and evaluation activities, but is also at issue under the auspices of research networks that must themselves rely on external assistance. Indeed, in the long run, if national universities have more resources to invest in strengthening their own institutional research capacities, regional and continental networking will likely become even more effective in facilitating the recognition and validation of endogenous African research.

Conclusion

The starting point of this essay centered on the following question: Is endogenous African educational research as overlooked and undervalued as it was over a decade ago when the first ERNWACA national inventories were conducted and ADEA was a fledgling offshoot of the Donors to African Education consortium? In broad terms the answer is mixed. Over the last ten years, a vast number of studies on education in Africa have been produced, many of them by African scholars working either individually or in partnership with Northern colleagues. Through various forms of networking, many of these studies have been widely disseminated and have attained substantial visibility. Yet the status of endogenous education research in much of sub-Saharan Africa remains ambiguous. Since most African universities are unable to function as major independent centers of social science research, African educational researchers have been highly dependent on funding from Northern sources. To a large extent, therefore, as outlined in this essay, the bulk of African educational research is currently being conducted in two distinctive ways: through studies that are commissioned and administered by international donor agencies in accordance with their own organizational mandates, and under the auspices of networks such as ERNWACA and ADEA that have promoted educational research as an essential process for enhancing the inevitable stakeholder discussions that underlie educational policies and practices. The differences in these two modalities of support entail fundamentally different purposes of research and consequently compel researchers to assume different roles and responsibilities. This then suggests that the status of endogenous African educational research must be qualified in terms of a postcolonial proviso: overlooked and undervalued — or recognized and appreciated — by *whom*?

Since the World Bank and other major donor agencies have assumed significant roles as knowledge producers and policy advisors to African governments, the donor-control approach to educational research is heavily funded and has thus become an attractive option for prominent African scholars. The studies these researchers undertake, sometimes as permanent agency staff members and at other times on a contractual basis, are obviously neither overlooked nor undervalued by the organizations for which they are undertaken. Nor are they overlooked by African governments that must negotiate the conditionalities of educational assistance programs with the agency sponsors of the studies in question. Indeed, in many respects there is little reason to critique the scope and quality of donor-controlled sector studies and program evaluations. The problem is not with the research *per se* — not the topics of inquiry, nor the methodologies that have been used, nor many of the findings that have resulted. Rather, as critics have frequently argued, it is the way agencies have so often attempted to *control* the entire progression of research from data collection and analysis to dissemination of results as a basis for policymaking and program implementation that is often flawed (Reimers & McGinn, 1997; Samoff & Stromquist, 2001). Within this modality of research support, where terms of reference are determined by the donor-agency sponsors, there is relatively little scope for autonomous intellectual expression. Although African researchers are now frequently involved in eliciting information and producing research findings for aid agencies, they do not *own* the research, nor do they control its dissemination and utilization. To a large degree, donor control of research has generated a profound degree of external dependency.

In contrast, the alternative strategy of networking and the adoption of a praxis orientation to research has helped not only to augment the status of endogenous educational research among African policymakers, but also has fostered processes of subjective dialogue and learning that are as significant as the completion and delivery of a final document to stakeholder recipients. In so doing, as exemplified most strikingly by ADEA's working groups, the combined strategy of networking and a praxis approach to research has tended to expand the role of policy stakeholders from being recipients of research products to becoming partners in research processes. Underlying this approach is the fact that research and policymaking are practices that are not mutually exclusive, but can be conducted as interrelated and mutually beneficial activities.

Whether it is conducted within the framework of the donor-control approach or as part of a more associational, praxis-oriented approach, the work of many African educational researchers is no longer overlooked and undervalued among those who are engaged in deliberating on educational policies in sub-Saharan Africa. Yet in circumstances where the emphasis is on the social and pedagogical aspects of the research process, there is less of a propensity to strive for a fully polished "product" capable of being disseminated beyond forums of face-to-face discussion or relatively easy website postings. As a result, research that is valued for its praxis orientation is rarely recognized in the realm of international scholarship for which the publication of books, scholarly articles, and other peer-reviewed forms of dissemination are critical for validation. For those who advocate the value of applied research, this may not be seen as a critical issue, for in African countries where there are so many pressing educational challenges, peer-reviewed scholarship may appear to be a needless distraction. Yet in a world where the standards of international scholarship are largely defined in Northern countries, this has an inevitable effect on North-South power imbalances. In the long run, if there is to be a more level playing field in terms of the influence of educational research in sub-Saharan Africa, then there is a case to be made for increased efforts to transform a greater volume of endogenous educational research into peer-reviewed endogenous educational *scholarship*. To achieve this, however, will require not just the continuation of professional networking, but a more substantive strengthening of national institutions of research. In effect, while networking and praxis approaches have contributed significantly to African educational research, they must invariably be regarded as measures that precede the revitalization of African college and university systems as centers of endogenous research.

Notes

1. This is a commonly accepted term for high-income, or developed, countries, many of which are geographically situated in the northern hemisphere
2. In September 2000, at the United Nations Millennium Summit, world leaders agreed to a set of eight time-bound Millenium Development Goals, which range from halving extreme poverty to halting the spread of HIV/AIDS and providing universal primary education, all by the target date of 2015.

3. In 1990 (March 5 – 9), delegates from 155 countries and representatives from over 150 organizations agreed at the World Conference on Education for All in Jomtien, Thailand, to universalize primary education and to greatly reduce illiteracy within a decade.

4. As Camerounian researchers were included in the network and because Cameroun is generally regarded as being situated in central Africa rather than in western Africa, the network included reference to the central region.

5. ERNWACA chapters exist in Benin, Burkina Faso, Cameroun, Côte d'Ivoire, The Gambia, Ghana, Guinea, Mali, Niger, Nigeria, Senegal, Sierra Leone, and Togo.

6. Three of the member countries — Nigeria, Niger, and Senegal — did not participate in this first network activity. The gap left by Nigeria was naturally significant, for it undoubtedly is a repository of a vast range of national research on education.

7. ADEA's former executive director, Richard Sack, once commented to me that on his trips to Africa he regularly distributed copies of the synthesis report to education ministers and senior ministry officials, and that this served as a useful reminder of the substantial "home-grown" talents of national researchers and the merits of them in policy dialogue.

8. The sequence of Biennials has been as follows:

> *Implementation of Educational Reforms* (France, 1993)
> *Formulating Education Policy: Lessons and experiences from Sub-Saharan Africa* (France, 1995)
> *Partnerships for Capacity Building and Quality Improvement* (Senegal, 1997)
> *What Works and What's New in African Education* (South Africa, 1999)
> *Reaching Out, Reaching All: Sustaining Effective Policy and Practice (Tanzania, 2001)*
> *Improving the Quality of Education* (Mauritius, 2003)

9. On several occasions within the past two or three years, through no prompting of my own, graduate students have referred to ERNWACA and ADEA studies that they have obtained from the Internet for inclusion in their term papers or seminar presentations.

10. An example of this localized connection between research and action is reflected in the experience of Tin Tua, a national NGO in Burkina Faso, which resuscitated a faltering state-supported literacy campaign in early 1990s and has since evolved into a federated system of community literacy centers and community-based primary schools. Underlying the dynamic of Tin Tua has been collaboration between a professor of linguistics, with an applied research background in adult education and Gulmancema, the *lingua franca* of the Gulma region of Burkina Faso, and local community leaders who were keen to revive and expand literacy training in their region (Faure, Maclure, Dao Sow, & Coulibaly, 2003).

11. Personal communication with IDRC personnel in Ottawa.

References

Association for the Development of Education in Africa [ADEA]. (1998). *Education research networks: Role and added value.* Retrieved January 26, 2005, from http://www.adeanet.org/newsletter/Vol10No3/en_10.html

ADEA (2003). *ADEA working groups: Taking stock, future prospects.* Retrieved January 26, 2005, from http://www.adeanet.org/newsletter/Vol15No1/V15N1_eng_coul.pdf

Afiesimama, A. (1995). Linguistic complexity in River's State: The position of language use in primary schools. In E. N. Emenanjo & O. M. Ndimele (Eds.), *Issues in African languages and linguistics: Essays in honour of Kay Williamson* (pp. 1–10). Aba, Nigeria: National Institute for Nigerian Languages.

Agusiobo, B. C. (1999). The early child-care curriculum development and implementation for functional education: Working towards the 21st century. *Nigerian Journal of Curriculum Studies, 6,* 3–9.

Alota, J. (1999). *Effects of teaching skills on pupils' performances.* Yaounde, Cameroun: École Normale Supérieure.

Amegnonam, K. (1986). *L'enseignement des sciences à l'école primaire: Formation et compétences des maîtres dans la recherche du materielle didactique au Togo.* Unpublished masters thesis, Division de la Formation des Personnels, Lomé, Togo.

Amin, M. E., & Fonkeng, G. E. (2000). Gender and the demand for primary education in Cameroun. *Advances in Gender Research, 4,* 5–17.

Association of African Universities and the World Bank. (1997). *Revitalizing universities in Africa: Strategy and guidelines.* Washington, DC: World Bank.

Azie, B. (1998). *Les déterminants des grossesses chez les jeunes filles des établissements sécondaires.* Abidjan, Côte d'Ivoire: École Normale Supérieure.

Bediaku-Adu, C. (1987). *The effects of parent-teacher coordination on the education of children in the Assin area.* Unpublished manuscript, University of Cape Coast, Cape Coast, Ghana.

Bockarie, S. L. (1979). *Curriculum diffusion project: Final report of the diffusion of core course projects in secondary schools.* Unpublished manuscript, International Development Research Centre, Ottawa.

Bray, M. (1996). *Decentralization of education: Community financing.* Washington, DC: World Bank.

Brock-Utne, B. (1995). Cultural conditionality and aid to education in East Africa. *International Review of Education, 41,* 177–197.

Buchert, L. (1995). From project to programme to sector-wide support: Some questions and concerns. *Prospects, 30,* 405–408.

Buchert, L. (1998). Education sector analysis in Africa: An evolving case in mutual North-South learning. *Prospects, 28,* 336– 48.

Camara, S. (1987). *Attitudes des parents face à l'école malienne (auto-financement).* Unpublished masters thesis, École Normale Supérieure, Bamako, Mali.

Chambers, R. (1983). *Rural development: Putting the first last.* London: Longman Group.

Cisse, B. S. (1984). *Les associations de parents d'élèves au Mali: Leurs perceptions sur l'école et sur leurs rôles et sur leur responsabilités dans le système scolaire malien.* Bamako, Mali: Rapport Institut International de Recherche et de Formation Éducation au Développement.

Clark, J. (1995). The state, popular participation, and the voluntary sector. *World Development, 23,* 593–601.

Diare, S. (1990). *Tentative d'analyse des causes de la déperdition scolaire: Cas des écoles de Hamdallaye Marche et mamadou Konate.* Unpublished masters thesis, École Normale Supérieure, Bamako, Mali.

Dougna, D. P. (1986). *Financement de l'éducation au Togo: Tendences et évolution.* Paris: Institut International de la Planification en Éducation.

Doumbia, A. T. (2000). L'enseignement du Bambara selon la pédagogie convergente au Mali : Théories et pratiques. *Nordic Journal of African Studies, 9,* 98–107.

Essindi, E. J. (1977). *Famille, école et éducation dans l'Afrique actuele.* Yaounde, Cameroun: École Normale Supérieure.

ERNWACA News # 8 (March, 2005). Retrieved March 1, 2005, from http://www.rocare.org/ERNWACA%20News_No.8.pdf

ERNWACA News # 9 (September, 2005). Retrieved September 20, 2005, from http://www.rocare.org/ERNWACA_News_No.9en.pdf

Eta, F. E. E. (2000). Dimensions of gender crisis in Nigerian education: A view from colleges of education. *The Nigerian Teacher Today, 8,* 13–19.

Faure, S., Maclure, R., Dao Sow, K.A., & Coulibaly, N. (2003). *Local solutions to global challenges: Toward effective partnership in basic education* (Country Study Report: Burkina Faso). The Hague: Netherlands Ministry of Foreign Affairs (Policy and Operations Department) for the Consultative Group of Evaluation Departments.

Fiske, E. B. (1998). *Education For All status and trends 1998: Wasted opportunities – When schools fail. Repetition and drop-out in primary schools.* Paris: UNESCO.

Freeman, T., & Faure, S. D. (2003). *Local solutions to global challenges: Toward effective partnership in basic education. Final Report.* The Hague: Netherlands Ministry of Foreign Affairs (Policy and Operations Department) for the Consultative Group of Evaluation Departments.

Gaynor, C. (1998). *Decentralization of education: Teacher management*. Washington, D.C.: World Bank.

Goerke, M. (1995). *Condition de l'enseignant: L'impact sur son rendement.* Lome, Togo: École Nationale Superieure.

Gozo, K. (1977). *L'inadequation du système d'enseignement togolais face au développement agricole.* Unpublished manuscript, Division de la Formation des Personnels, Lomé, Togo.

Gyilime, P. K. (1986). *The role of parent-teacher associations in the education of the Ghanaian child: A study of first cycle schools in the Kintampo education district.* Unpublished manuscript, University of Cape Coast, Cape Coast, Ghana.

Haidara, J. L. (2000). Introduction des langues nationales dans l'enseignement : Attitudes des maîtres de Bamako. *Nordic Journal of African Studies, 9*, 49–65.

Hartwell, A. (1999). SPESSA 1999: An easy way to access the most complete educational data for Africa. *ADEA Newsletter, 11*, 10.

Hode, M. N. (1987). *L'école nouvelle et la problematique de l'emploi en République populaire du Benin.* Unpublished masters thesis, École Nationale d'Administration, Cotonou, Benin.

International Development Research Centre & Association of Universities and Colleges of Canada (2003, May). *Research without (Southern) Borders.* Ottawa: Report of a roundtable, May 22–23.

Institut Pedagogique National. (1989). *Étude de la demande d'éducation en milieu rural au Mali.* Bamako, Mali: Rapport administratif.

King, K., & Buchert, L. (1999). *Changing international aid to education: Global patterns and national contexts.* Paris: UNESCO.

Konate, G. V. (1986). *L'instituteur face à la réforme du système éducatif voltaique: Réflexion à partir d'une enquête.* Unpublished masters thesis, Institut Pédagogique du Burkina, Ouagadougou, Burkina Faso.

Koomson, E. (1990). *A study of the factors that cause the incidence of dropout of pupils in juniour secondary schools.* Unpublished manuscript, University of Cape Coast, Cape Coast, Ghana.

Lavergne, R. (2004). *Strengthening aid effectiveness: Principles, operational implications, and approaches.* Hull, Quebec: Canadian International Development Agency.

Maclure, R. (Ed). (1997). *Overlooked and undervalued: A synthesis of ERNWACA reviews on the state of educational research in West and Central Africa*. Washington, DC: Academy of Educational Development.

Maclure, R. (2000). NGOs and education in sub-Saharan Africa: Instruments of hegemony or surreptitious resistance? *Education and Society, 18*, 25–45.

Madumere-Obike, C. U., & Oluwuo, S. O. (2001). Strategies for effective participation of rural communities in primary school administration in Nigeria. *Nigerian Journal of Profession Studies in Education, 8*, 8–14.

Marope, P. T. M. (1999). The prospective stocktaking review of education in Sub-Saharan Africa. *ADEA Newsletter, 11*, 3–5.

Marope, P. T. M., & Sacks, R. (2005). *The pedagogy of education policy formulation: Working from policy assets.* Paper presented at the Comparative International Education Society Conference, Stanford University.

Masemann, V. L. (1999). Culture and education. In R. F. Arnove, & Torres, C. A. Torres. (Eds.), *Comparative education: The dialectic of the global and the local* (pp. 115–133). Lanham, MD: Rowman & Littlefield.

Mattimore, A., Verspoor, A., & Watt, P. (2001). *A chance to learn: Knowledge and finance for education in Sub-Saharan Africa.* Washington, DC: World Bank.

McGinn, N. F. (2000). An assessment of new modalities in development assistance. *Prospects, 30*, 437–450.

McNeely, C. L. (1995). Prescribing national education policies: The role of international organizations. *Comparative Education Review, 39*, 483–507.

Megbemada, Y. (1987). "*Jeunesse et emploi [Youth and employment].*" Paper presented at the National Seminar on Rural Youth Productivity and Assistance, Cotonou, Benin: l'Institut de Formation Sociale Economique et Civique.

Meier, W. (1999). *In search of indigenous participation in education sector studies in sub-Saharan Africa*. Unpublished manuscript, University of Ottawa, Ottawa.

Mouthe, J. (1985). *Analyses des resources utilisées dans le système éducatif Camerounais,* Unpublished manuscript, Centre National d'Éducation, Yaoundé, Cameroon.

Namuddu, K., & Tapsoba, J. M. S. (1993). *The status of educational research and policy analysis in sub-Saharan Africa: A report of the DAE working group on capacity-building in educational research and policy analysis*. Ottawa: International Development Research Centre.

Nchungong, C. (1996). *Improving the quality of teaching in Cameroun nursery schools*. Yaoundé, Cameroun: École Normale Supérieure.

Obanya, P. (2003). *Emerging trends in research on the quality of education: A synthesis of education research reviews from 1992 – 2002 in eleven countries of West and Central Africa*. Bamako, Mali: ERNWACA.

Obanya, P. (1989). Going beyond the educational reform document. *Prospects, 29,* 333–347.

Ogbonna, S. O. (2002). Parental preferences for medium instruction in primary schools: Implications for teaching Nigerian languages. *Universal Basic Education Forum, 1,* 22–35.

Ohiri-Aniche, C. (2002). The place of Nigerian languages in the new Universal Basic Education (UBE) scheme in Nigeria. *African Journal of Curriculum and Instruction, 1,* 4–16.

Onuchukwu, O., & Ifeanacho, M. J. (2001). Education versus indoctrination: A critical appraisal of nursery education in Port Harcourt. *Nigerian Journal of Professional Studies in Education, 5,* 4–13.

Perraton, H., Robinson, B., & Creed, C. (2001). *Teacher education through distance learning: Technology, curriculum, cost, evaluation: Summary of case studies*. Paris: UNESCO.

Rasera, J.–B. (1986). *Coût et financement de l'éducation au Benin*. Cotonou, Benin: Rapport de consultation.

Reimers, F., & McGinn, N. (1997). *Informed dialogue: Using research to shape education policy around the world*. Westport, CT: Praeger.

Riddell, A. (2001). *Sector wide approaches in education: Implications for donor agencies and issues arising from case studies of Zambia and Mozambique*. Stockholm: Swedish International Development Cooperation Agency.

Samoff, J. (1999). Education sector analysis in Africa: Limited national control and even less national ownership, *International Journal of Educational Development, 19,* 249–272.

Samoff, J., & Stromquist, N.P. (2001). Managing knowledge and storing wisdom: New forms of foreign aid? *Development and Change, 32,* 631–656.

Saunders, L., Riley, K., Craig, H., Poston, M., & Flynn, A. (2000). *Effective schooling in rural Africa (Report 2): Key issues concerning school effectiveness and improvement*. Washington, DC: World Bank.

Sawadogo, A. (1999). *Les innovations pédagogiques et leurs effets sur l'enseignement primaire burkinabe: Cas des classes multigrades et des classes à double flux*. Ouagadougou, Burkina Faso: École nationale d'administration et de magistrature.

Sawadogo, P. (1984). *La cooperative scolaire à l'école primaire*. Unpublished manuscript, Centre Pédagogique National, Ouagadougou, Burkina Faso.

Sedel, C. (1999). *Les rélations de genre et la scolarisation primaire en milieu rural Senoufo (nord de la Côte d'Ivoire)*. Abidjan, Côte d'Ivoire: École 2000.

Sosale, S. (2000). *Trends in private sector development in World Bank education projects*. Washington, D.C.: The World Bank.

Sow, O. (1985). *Échec scolaire au Mali: Aspects socio-économiques*. Unpublished manuscript, École normale supérieure, Bamako, Mali.

Stein, J. G., Stren, R., Fitzgibbon, J., & MacLean, M. (Eds.) (2001). *Networks of knowledge: Collaborative innovation in international learning*. Toronto: University of Toronto Press.

Stren, R. (2001). Knowledge networks and new approaches to "development." In J.G. Stein et al. (Eds). *Networks of knowledge: Collaborative innovation in international learning* (pp. 133–150). Toronto: University of Toronto Press.

Tchegho, J.-M. (2003). *La décentralisation, l'éducation, l'unité nationale*. Yaoundé, Cameroun: Éditions Demos.

Tetteh, N. J. (1989). *A study of the causes of dropping out in first cycles schools in the Ningo traditional area*. Unpublished manuscript, University of Cape Coast, Cape Coast, Ghana.

Tietjen, K. (1997). *Educating girls in sub-Saharan Africa: USAID's approach and lessons for donors* (Technical Paper No. 54). Washington, DC: USAID, Health and Human Resources Analysis for Africa Project.

United Nations (2000). United Nations millennium declaration: Resolution adopted by the General Assembly. New York: Author.

United Nations Children's Fund. (2002). *Quality education for all: From a girl's point of view*. New York: Author.

United Nations Educational, Scientific and Cultural Organization [UNESCO]. (1990). *World declaration on education for all and framework for action to meet basic learning needs*. Paris: Author.

UNESCO. (2000). *Education For All assessment 2000: Sub-Saharan Africa. Regional synthesis report*. Paris: Author.

UNESCO. (2005). *EFA global monitoring report: The quality imperative*. Paris: Author.

Universalia. (2005). *Evaluation of the Association for the Development of Education in Africa (ADEA)*. Ottawa: Author.

Watt, P. (2001). *Community support for basic education in sub-Saharan Africa*. Washington, DC: World Bank.

Welch, A. R. (1998). The cult of efficiency in education: Comparative reflections on the reality and the rhetoric. *Comparative Education, 34*, 157–175.

Wokwenmendam, Z. (1981). *Disponibilité des materiels didactiques et leur utilization dans l'enseignement du calcul et des sciences d'observation*. Unpublished manuscript, École normale superieure, Yaounde, Cameroun.

World Bank (1988). *Education in Sub-Saharan Africa: Policies for adjustment, revitalization, and expansion*. Washington, DC: Author.

World Bank. (1988). *Education sector strategy*. Washington, DC: Author.

World Bank (1999). *Education sector strategy paper*. Washington, D. C.: Author.

World Bank. (2000). *Effective schooling in rural Africa (Report 3): Case study brief on rural schooling*. Washington, DC: Author.

World Bank. (2002). *Education and HIV/AIDS: A window of hope*. Washington, DC: Author.

World Bank. (2004). *Indigenous knowledge: Local pathways to global development*. Washington, DC: Author.

I am most grateful to the editors of *HER* for their careful reading of earlier drafts of this paper and for their suggested revisions. In addition, I have very much appreciated Benjamin Piper's encouragement and helpful comments on earlier drafts.

PART TWO

Transitions and Reform in
International Education

PART TWO

Introduction

Education systems change. These changes are a result of demographic shifts within communities; the effect of diseases, natural disasters, or conflicts; debates about curriculum, pedagogy, and the importance of teachers; relative wealth and the availability of public funding; and broader international debates about economic policy. Given the inevitability of such shifts, education systems must be able to react with both effective policy and flexibility toward local classroom realities. In preparing for these changes and transitions, it is important to explore and understand the motivations for, responses to, and consequences of education reform. This section of the book investigates a variety of facets of education reform. These five chapters include settings that range from the supranational to the local, and they address issues as diverse as how education reforms are designed, what the effects of reform are at the local level, how women fit into the broader spectrum of reforms, and how national reforms affect local institutions and individuals.

In the opening chapter, "Education in Tanzania," former Tanzanian President Julius K. Nyerere shares his assessment of education in his country twenty-three years after gaining independence from Britain. Nyerere's essay is a remarkably honest assessment of the progress, or lack thereof, that Tanzania's citizenry and government achieved in education following independence. He sets the context of education in his country and describes the role education played in social and economic development. The Tanganyika Africa National Union political party that Nyerere led before independence demanded more access and equity in education than the British colonial regime was willing to give, since the British were concerned about the political, social, and economic power that increased access to education would provide. From the very beginning of Nyerere's political career, education was a critical factor in his thinking about how to improve education in Tanzania. Nyerere's vision of education for self-reliance suggested a unique approach to education that was largely dependent on and related to the broader scope of African socialism that he proposed for the continent and implemented in Tanzania. Education for self-reliance called for the highly educated elite to use their education to support the rest of the community, and required that part of this elite's education be similar to the manual agricultural life that the rest of the nation experienced. In this article, Nyerere critically examines the ability of his concept of education for self-reliance to take hold in schools and in classroom practice. He analyzes Tanzania's success in the spheres of primary, secondary, and higher education, technical training, and education for children with disabilities, arguing that while the realization of his ideas proved elusive, significant progress had been made. He concludes by outlining the areas Tanzania would need to focus on in the future. In many ways, Tanzania followed his advice, thus adding to his legacy even after he served his public duty. Nyerere retired from the presidency in 1985, the year this essay was published, so this essay can be seen as his postscript to Tanzania's attempts to implement his wide-ranging vision for educational development.

While Nyerere examined the ability of students in Tanzania's education system to deal with shifts at the national level, Frances Vavrus investigates the effects of significant shifts in international policy on local practice and individual communities. In "Adjusting Inequality: Education and Structural Adjustment Policies in Tanzania," Vavrus employs ethnography of policy methods to examine the effects of structural adjustment programs and economic reforms initiated by the World Bank and the International Monetary Fund (IMF) on the experiences and choices available to secondary school students in rural Kilimanjaro, Tanzania. She makes a convincing case for the importance of understanding a local setting in the development of international and national policy, and for investigating the impact policy change in non-educational sectors has on educational realities. Vavrus's research also provides a glimpse into the multiple local consequences of the policy of user fees, or tuition, for school access that were implemented over the last fifteen years in Tanzania and elsewhere in sub-Saharan Africa. These user fees became ubiquitous in public education after policy shifts within the World Bank and IMF in the "austerity era" of the 1980s. Vavrus's data suggest a reexamination of the assumed benefits of globalization and show that international trends affect local realities. Her essay is rich with student voices and local context, and she argues persuasively that policy research need not always be done at the macro level. In fact, her policy ethnography is evidence that one of the more critical investigations of the effectiveness of any policy is to examine how that policy affects local communities.

In "Women and Education in Eritrea: A Historical and Contemporary Analysis," Asgedet Stefanos investigates the relationship between gender and education across eras of conflict in Eritrea. Using interviews with Eritrean women, Stefanos describes the history of women and education in Eritrea during the Italian occupation, the resistance movements of the 1970s and 1980s, and the period since Eritrean independence in 1993. Stefanos argues that the Italian colonialists almost entirely ignored the schooling of women, and that the major Eritrean resistance movements improved the status of women. As the Eritrean Patriotic Liberation Front (EPLF) began its resistance, first against the Italians and then against the Ethiopians, women were given increasing roles in the political cadre and the armed forces, and, slowly, more recognition in the education system. The greater role women had in the EPLF party was mitigated, however, by their lack of real decisionmaking power. Moreover, Stefanos identifies continuing cultural barriers against expanded access to education for women as a major impediment to real gender equity in education in Eritrea. Interviews with a sample of Eritrean women of various positions, ages, and education levels suggest that the role of women in the newly independent Eritrean state is still far from equitable. Some of the women interviewed hearken back to the age of the resistance as the best time for women's rights, as women's issues have increasingly taken a back seat to other concerns since Eritrea became independent. Stefanos calls on the Eritrean government to actively address the gender disparities apparent in the formal education system and governmental leadership.

"Black Dean: Race, Reconciliation, and the Emotions of Deanship" is Jonathan Jansen's autobiographical account of his experience as dean of the College of Education at the University of Pretoria. Jansen provides evidence supporting Vavrus's point that national and international policy shifts affect local practice and individual realities. Jansen describes his experiences as the first Black dean of the formerly all-White University of Pretoria in South Africa. He provides rich descriptions of ironic situations where the predominately White faculty is forced to adjust to a Black dean and supervisor. Jansen describes a faculty of education facing other transitions — more emphasis on publishing, an increased number of Black and Colored faculty, and a controversial shift in the relative place of the Afrikaans language in the institution. Jansen's chapter contributes to the literature in the areas of higher education, language of instruction, school leadership, education in postconflict societies, the deanship, and ethnic relations in South Africa. He offers insights into how school leaders and higher education administrators can personally deal with the difficult transitions associated with the increased access to higher education that comes with the eradication or erosion of racial and gender impediments.

In his important contribution to the literature on the quality of education, the importance of instructional quality, and the relational dimension of teaching, Fernando Reimers contributes a new essay to this book, "Teaching Quality Matters: Pedagogy and Literacy Instruction of Poor Students in Mexico." Reimers draws on data collected from a nationally representative sample of sixth-grade students in Mexico. This dataset allows Reimers to investigate whether teaching quality matters, as measured by student perceptions. His multiple regression models suggest that it does matter, and that the magnitude of its effect on student achievement is as significant as the effect of students' background, including socioeconomic status. Reimers' argument is that the recent international push toward increased access and equity has often ignored the quality of education, and teacher quality more specifically. He suggests that the next frontier of international education policy is to develop education reforms and programs that purposefully increase education quality, particularly teacher quality.

Being aware of broad national and international shifts in politics and policies, understanding how and why education systems change as a result, and attending to the implications of these changes for local education realities are critical parts of the continual improvement of education in Southern countries. These authors reveal a broad range of transitions that affect education systems across the globe. As will be evident throughout this section, these authors' work has implications for both macro-level policy reform and individual-level best practices in the context of education reform.

Education in Tanzania

JULIUS K. NYERERE

Tanzania's educational policy is based on three philosophical assumptions: first, that every human being is fundamentally of equal worth and has equal rights; second, that the individual becomes meaningful to him or herself and to others only as a member of society; and third, that basic literacy and numeracy liberate the human personality, and are thus valuable in their own right quite apart from the contribution that literacy and numeracy make to the nation's economy and to the individual's economic situation. If one does not share these assumptions, Tanzania's whole development strategy — as well as its education policies — will seem to have involved a huge waste of resources and will not be judged as having been successful. If these assumptions are shared, the strategy makes sense, and can be judged a qualified success. The word "qualified" refers to the implementation of our policies, to the effects of ambition clashing with the limits of resources, and to impatience clashing with the need to get the people's full understanding and involvement before introducing change.

Education is not something which is done just in schools. The process of education begins to shape the children before they ever enter a classroom. Education starts in the home at the time of a child's birth and continues as the child grows up in the local community. Education is affected by the social mores, the physical and social environment, the press, radio, and so on. It is an administrative necessity which causes governments to establish a "Ministry of National Education." However revolutionary its intentions and effects, education is strongly influenced by the past and serves to influence but not to control the future. Formal education in any country is bound to be — and from society's point of view is intended to be — an element in maintaining or developing the social, political, and economic culture of that society. For Tanzania, therefore, formal education is intended to develop the potential of individuals, making them better able to contribute to their own well-being and to the development of the society in which they live.

The more common approach to educational development in older societies is one in which its structure has developed gradually in response to ongoing needs rather than having been planned as a comprehensive strategy. In a country like ours, where the mainland came into independent existence in December 1961, the importance of

Harvard Educational Review   Vol. 55   No. 1   February 1985, 45–52

education to the society's development, as distinct from the development of the individual, brings as a consequence a structure of educational activity which naturally influences national consciousness and which leads to deliberate policy planning. However, an understanding of the function of education and its requirements in the circumstances of a new state is not automatic. This understanding develops usually from an attempt to apply, in the context of local conditions and aspirations, the structure and the experience of countries with which the new nation has had recent historical contact. That is certainly what happened in our case.

Since 1967, Tanzania's national policies have been based on the philosophy of "Socialism and Self-Reliance," as outlined in the Arusha Declaration. This means that our aim is, first, to produce an educated people who are able to understand their own needs and the actions which these needs imply; and second, to provide access to further knowledge as individuals come to need it. Further we intend to have an educational system that encourages the development of the human instincts of cooperation and a sense of service. In other words, we are concerned with attitudes. We also hope to equip our people with the ability, as well as the willingness, to develop themselves and their community, and this involves imparting the skills required by modern society.

The framework outlined above applies to the entire United Republic of Tanzania, which includes the island of Zanzibar. Our philosophy is implemented on the island differently than on the mainland. Under our Constitution, primary-and secondary-level education in Zanzibar is controlled by the government of Zanzibar and is distinct from the Union government. The island's primary and secondary educational system is somewhat different, and is in some ways more advanced than on the mainland, although the problems and constraints are common throughout the United Republic. Most of what follows relates to the education policies of the mainland government.

Having defined its educational purpose as providing all of its citizens with the basic skills of literacy and numeracy, as well as basic principles of agriculture, health care, and an understanding of history and the constitution, that pertain to their ability to be active and, we hope, productive members of our developing society, Tanzania places a special emphasis on mass education. The provision of more advanced educational opportunities is planned in light of the nation's need to equip some of its people with the ability to provide special service in particular fields. These opportunities are regarded as a privilege, not a right, and carry with them obligations to the community. A program of mass education presupposes the existence of an established and competent national administrative system, and the existence of a large number of people qualified to teach. Yet, when mainland Tanzania became independent, we had hardly any civil servants working in the administrative, or even in the executive, grades of the small civil service who had received a full secondary school education. At the time of independence, our few trained teachers were already employed in their fields. The shortage of educated people was so great that many of the experienced teachers in both secondary and primary schools had to be transferred from education to do other types of needed work in the new government.

During the first decade of independence, educational policy placed emphasis on the expansion of secondary and tertiary educational opportunities. As a result, between 1961 and 1971, the number of pupils enrolled in government secondary schools increased from just under 12,000 to almost 33,000. There was also a great expansion in the provision of places in Form V, from 236 in 1961 to 1,608 in 1971; in our system, it is only after graduating from Form VI that a pupil can become qualified to enter the university or be trained as a secondary school teacher. It was only in the late 1950s that Africans in Tanganyika (the name of our nation when it was a British colony) began to take the advanced-level examination at the end of Form VI, and even in 1961 only 176 had done so. The racially separate school systems of the colonial period had allowed some Asian and European children to take this examination, and a few were, or became, Tanzanian citizens. Yet even with these additions, the total number of people with university qualifications was ludicrously small for a new nation whose population was then 10.5 million.

The Dar es Salaam University College was established in October 1961, during the preindependence period of internal self-government. Fourteen students were enrolled in that year. In addition, 194 Tanzanians were attending the other University Colleges of East Africa, and 1,312 were studying overseas, either at the university or pre-university level. By 1971 the University College of Dar es Salaam had become a full university, with faculties of law, arts, social science, science, medicine, and agriculture. Thus in 1971, there were 2,028 Tanzanian students at this and other East African universities. Further expansion has taken place at Dar es Salaam since then, with many new departments and an engineering faculty being added. In 1984, the faculty of agriculture, forestry, and veterinary science split off to form the basis of the new Sokoine University of Agriculture at Morongoro. There are now 3,409 undergraduates and 584 postgraduate students at the two universities in Tanzania, as well as a small number of students taking specialist university or other professional courses outside the country. No fees are charged to Tanzanians for university-level education, but students who have post-secondary education of any type are obliged to serve in specified public service fields for five years or a little less, depending on the length of the course in which they matriculated.

This necessary emphasis on secondary and post-secondary education during the first decade of independence meant that the expansion of primary education did little more than maintain the proportion of school-age children attending school. Nonetheless, in my Ten Year Report issued in 1971 to the party, I was able to say that the number of primary schools had increased from 3,100 to 4,705, and the number of primary school pupils had gone up from 486,000 to 848,000. Further, those figures conceal other important advances. In particular, by 1971 all primary school pupils were able to go straight through a seven-year course; in 1961, the majority had been eliminated by a competitive examination at the end of the fourth year of school. Also, radical revisions had been made in the curricula and syllabi (with most textbooks being revised accordingly), and the schools were being reorganized in accordance with the policy of "Education for Self-Reliance."

In 1974 we decided that we could no longer delay the introduction of universal primary education, and that it must be achieved within three years. This decision was consistent with our philosophy and was the result of insistent public demand. By the end of 1977 we had 2,194,000 primary school pupils and continued to expand, first to include the few children who lived too far from schools, and second to keep up with the rapidly increasing population. As a result, there were 3,552,000 pupils enrolled in about 10,000 primary schools by the end of 1983.

This tremendous increase in enrollment was only made possible by supplementing the normal teacher training program with a system of "Distance Teacher Training." Primary school graduates between the ages of seventeen and twenty-eight were carefully selected by education officials in cooperation with village committees who were familiar with the applicants. These graduates were prepared to teach primary school through a combination of specially designed correspondence courses and radio programs; they attended training sessions with teachers specifically prepared to help them and participated in in-service training given by the more qualified teachers. At the end of their three years of distance training, the teacher trainees attended residential courses of a few weeks' duration at national teachers colleges. The process culminated in a final examination. Out of the 45,534 young people selected for this training, 35,028 finished and qualified as primary school teachers, Grade C. Grade C teachers are those with primary education plus two years residential teacher's training. These new teachers overcame many difficulties, including having to survive on a trainees' honorarium of 150 Tanzanian shillings-a-month (at that time equivalent to about 20 U.S. dollars and now equivalent to about 9 U.S. dollars) during the three years. Like other teachers at that grade, they then became eligible for further in-service training so as to attain higher grades.

At the same time, the full-time teachers' training colleges were expanded, so that by the end of 1983 there were over 2,000 students taking a Grade C course, 6,100 taking a Grade A course, and 1,482 taking a diploma in Education. This makes a total of over 9,600 teachers in residential training in addition to the university students taking education courses as part of their degree. In preparation for the planned expansion of day secondary schools, student entry for the two-or-three year teachers' diploma course increased to over 1,000 students in July 1984. Further, many of the diploma-trainee teachers, as well as a few primary school teacher trainees, are being prepared in specialist subjects — including courses in agriculture, music, commerce, science, teaching of the handicapped, and so on. Yet more has to be done. There is currently a shortage of 28,000 Grade A primary school teachers and 888 more qualified teachers are needed to bring the existing secondary schools up to full strength.

Despite the urgent need and desire to educate all Tanzanian children, we realized very early that rapid Tanzanian development depended upon the men and women who had already passed school age — it was they who would have to begin the transformation of our economy and lay the foundations of our social and political progress. Yet, at independence, an estimated 75 percent of the adults on the Tanzanian mainland were considered illiterate; up until 1970 adult literacy work was being done largely by voluntary effort. Quite clearly, this situation could only be rectified by a serious and deliberate effort, and by incorporating adult education into the national plans. Also in 1970, the first challenge to eliminate illiteracy in six districts was made to the government and party, and at about the same time a UNESCO-assisted pilot project for functional literacy got underway. Everyone was encouraged by the results, so, in 1971 the first national campaign to eradicate illiteracy was begun. The work has continued through the Ministry of National Education, assisted by experts from UNESCO, and funded by Sweden and a few other countries.

The campaign is based on the principle of combining literacy with the spread of vocational skills needed by the people in the villages and towns. Eleven different series of books, linking literacy teaching with knowledge of such things as better crop husbandry, animal husbandry, and child welfare. Post-literacy programs have also been designed and introduced through specially written books on topics such as agriculture, mathematics, political education, rural construction, health, and English.

In order to motivate learners and encourage adult teachers, as well as government and party leaders, four national literacy and post-literacy tests have been given to date (1975, 1977, 1981, and 1983). After each test, certificates are awarded at village ceremonies — often by visiting district, regional, or even national leaders — and every effort is made to stress the importance of the achievement. As a result of this continuing effort, and the allocation of over 6 percent of the government's education expenditures to adult education, it is now estimated that, based on exam results from the Ministry of Education, only 15 percent of Tanzania's 20 million population is illiterate, and almost 1.5 million adults have so far been involved in the post-literacy programs.

One remaining problem is that of making reading material available, especially to those people in the rural areas. Our national library service has branches in some of the major towns, and we have tried to establish village library linkages to the central service or to the adult education system. This work is handicapped, however, by the same financial and foreign exchange problems which adversely affect the school programs. Nonetheless, seven rural newspapers are published, with 50,000 copies distributed monthly, and efforts are being made to publish Swahili books of interest to the peasants and workers. We have our own national publishing firm, and one or two international publishers also publish books in our national language. In addition, radio provides a vital and effective supplementary educational tool.

The emphasis given since 1974 to primary school education and to adult education does not mean that the provisions for secondary school settings have been ignored. As our main efforts shifted to mass education, the rate of secondary school expansion has inevitably declined, but it has never stopped. Consequently, whereas in 1971 there were 7,780 children who entered Form I through competitive examination, in 1983 the comparable figure was 9,899 children. The total enrollment in government secondary schools in 1983 was 39,737 (27,040 boys and 12,697 girls). Most of these schools have a special bias towards a particular type of instructional activity. Five out of the eighty-five government secondary schools have a technical bias, forty-one an agricultural bias, thirty-three a commercial bias. The result is, for example, that at the end of Form IV those who enter a school that has a technical bias leave as qualified craftsmen in the areas of mechanical, electrical, or civil engineering.

In addition to government secondary schools, nonprofit, private, fee-paying secondary schools are permitted, provided they are registered and accept government inspection on the same basis as government schools. By 1983, 31,500 children were attending such private schools. The Ministry tries to ensure that the pupils accepted for private secondary schools have attained a reasonably high standard in the primary schools and, while the private school teachers in general are not as highly qualified as those in our government schools, the Ministry is able to insist on their competence.

Whether in government or private schools, all secondary school students attend school for four years. At the end of that period they are examined, and those who are academically qualified are then selected to continue in Forms V and VI, offered primarily in government secondary schools. In 1961, there were Form V places for only 176 students; by 1983, the figure was 2,114 (out of 15,834 who were eligible to take the Form IV examination). Many other students who complete the four-year secondary course are selected for training as teachers, technicians, agricultural extension officers, health workers, and so on. Those who continue to the end of Form VI are eligible for entry to the university, for education diploma courses, or for further training in agriculture, medical and technical work, and other fields.

Until now, boarding schools have been the most common form of secondary education. This policy was adopted because we have so few schools in relation to our need and also because we wanted to be sure that young people who have been selected from the rural areas have, as much as possible, an equal opportunity to attend such schools. Indeed, most of the existing day secondary schools are those inherited from the old Asian school system, although racial segregation in education was ended almost immediately after independence. Although our current economic crisis has forced us this year to charge a small fee to cover food costs at secondary schools (we are making provisions for those students whose parents honestly cannot pay), boarding schools are very expensive to run. We have therefore decided that the planned expansion in secondary schools will take the form of day schools, with the boarding secondary schools reserved for students whose family or personal circumstances make school residence essential.

Quite apart from academic education, however, the Tanzanian government has in recent years become increasingly concerned with expanding technical training of all kinds and at all levels. The general lack of even the most basic mechanical and technical understanding is a major factor contributing to the backwardness of our agricultural system and the short lifespan of our imported machines. Agriculture, elementary science, and in a few cases construction or workshop skills, are taught in primary schools, but only at a very rudimentary level. We intend, eventually, to establish post-primary technical centers throughout the country. So far, only 316 have been put in place, and many of these are lacking even the most essential basic equipment. A number of voluntary agencies run small vocational training centers, as do various government ministries and departments, and we have also begun to establish an apprenticeship system. National trade tests are conducted by the government for craftsmen. Presently there are two technical colleges for post-Form IV students, with another one under construction. In spite of this activity we still have numerous obstacles in this area. We are hampered by an acute shortage of technical teachers. Financial problems, especially foreign exchange, inhibit expansion even at the planned rate.

Another area in which there is an urgent need for much greater progress is the education of our physically and mentally handicapped children and young people. Our policy is to integrate such children into the normal schools as far as possible; for example, a number of the primary schools in towns, and four of the secondary boarding schools, have teachers who are specially trained to help blind pupils. Special schools for children who are seriously physically handicapped or mentally deficient require great dedication, highly trained teachers, and sometimes considerable capital expenditure. Until now, most of these services have been established and are run by voluntary agencies, especially Christian missions, and they receive a capitation grant and other forms of help from the government. But the vast majority of handicapped children still have no opportunity for an education; for example, there are now only two very small new schools for the mentally afflicted.

Tanzania's efforts in the educational field have not been conducted without difficulties. Our country is, according to the World Bank's classification, one of the world's twenty-five poorest nations — our highest ever per capita annual income in 1980 was about 280 U.S dollars. This means that in 1983, although 22.1 percent of the total government recurrent expenditure was devoted to education (with the regional and local authorities also making a very sizeable contribution), it amounted to little more than 1.25 billion Tanzania shillings — which at the current rate of exchange is approximately 73.5 million U.S. dollars. An additional 23 million U.S. dollars (much of it gifts from abroad) were allocated to educational development expenditures.

These financial constraints hamper every aspect of formal education despite herculean efforts by our villagers and our teachers. It is made worse by the even greater shortage of foreign exchange with which to buy books, stationery, and equipment. Thus, for example, the teacher in an average primary school class will have fifty children who have to share about seventeen textbooks in each subject. Sometimes there is also a shortage of pencils and exercise books. Our secondary schools and universities also suffer very greatly from a lack of books; we have to import all our paper as well as almost all the tertiary-level books. The teaching of science and technical subjects is particularly badly hit by the foreign exchange shortage, for almost all of the needed equipment has to be brought in from outside the country.

Summing up, and looking back over twenty-two years of independence, Tanzania can legitimately be very proud of its achievements in education. We have not done everything we would have liked or aimed to do. We have done more than most people outside Tanzania believed to be possible. We had help from friends. At the beginning, some of our education administrators, most of our secondary school teachers, and almost all of our university academic staff were expatriates, often paid for by various aid arrangements. Even now we have many non-Tanzanians teaching in the science and professional departments of our universities and a few volunteers from overseas teaching English, science, or math in our secondary schools. But the vast bulk of the work, and the financial burden of our education policy have fallen upon the people of Tanzania.

So what have we put in place since independence at the end of 1961? We now have an educational policy designed by us to suit our needs, which we are endeavoring to implement despite the difficulties of making the fundamental changes they require. Curricula and syllabi have been redesigned in all subjects in the twenty-two years since independence so as to lead us toward our educational objectives. All primary school texts, some secondary school textbooks, as well as those for adult education, have been written or rewritten. Two universities have been established, with entry de-pendent upon academic merit. We now have three and a half times as many students in government secondary schools, and more than seven times as many children in primary school. All our children can get a seven-year education ensuring the elimina-tion of illiteracy among the younger generation. Our adult population is now 85 per-cent literate, and millions of people are attending adult education classes, which we hope will increase the percentage of literate adults even more. Also, we have begun a widespread plan for technical education at all grade levels.

These advances have been achieved by a poor and underdeveloped country which started independence with only one hundred African university graduates, and which has simultaneously been working to bring basic health care to all of its people, build-ing an infrastructure of communications and public utilities, expanding its agricul-tural production, and creating the foundations of its industrial sector.

Nonetheless, the brutal fact is that Tanzania's educational advance has been virtu-ally halted, and our people are having to struggle even to defend the positions we have already won. The national economy has been battered by events over which we have no control. Our national per capita income is now 26 percent lower than it was in 1980 as a result of the continually worsening terms of trade, the years of drought, the war we were forced to fight when Idi Amin's Ugandan troops invaded Tanzania, the international economic recession, plus a reduction in our own productive capac-ity following the import strangulation of our modern sector.[1] Meaningful educa-tional expansion is thus precluded by ever-increasing financial constraints. Indeed, despite all our efforts, there has been a decrease rather than the needed increase in real expenditures on education during the last four years. As a result, even existing school equipment and modern buildings are deteriorating through want of spare parts and maintenance.

In light of the desperate national scarcity of foreign exchange, the little money available has to be allocated to directly productive activities. Also, reduced govern-ment expenditures have to be concentrated on essential and immediate day-to-day expenses such as teachers' wages and the minimal purchase of books. Therefore, we are now forced to concern ourselves with questions such as: how to maintain univer-sal primary education as our population increases and at the same time improve the quality of teaching; how to provide adult and post-primary education at its present levels; and how to meet the minimum training needs of young people leaving school if they are to become productive and active members of our society.

We are determined to do these things. In socialism, as we understand it, education is the right of all citizens and not something which should only be provided for a plu-tocratic elite or as a form of charity for the poor. Our national economic and social policies are determined in that context. We will continue to adjust our economy to meet the dire circumstances in which we have to operate, but we will not change the direction of our efforts despite what the impact of the world economic recession, the unjust international economic order, international financial institutions, or climatic disaster can do to us. We are convinced that if we can hold on to our educational ob-jectives despite the enormous economic sacrifices now being imposed upon us, our educational achievements will eventually benefit us economically. They have already begun to show their worth both socially and politically. Not once in all our parliamentary or party economic debates has anyone suggested that we should stop any of our public educational activities in order to reduce the strain of high taxation burdens at a time of declining personal incomes. Tanzania now has an aware people, consciously involved in the present economic struggle and increasingly exerting their social and political power for their own ends. On that basis we shall refuse to go backward now, and we shall make further advances in the future.

Note

1. "Import strangulation of the modern sector" refers to the fact that the modern sector of the economy, which consists primarily of imported machinery, equipment, and so on, seizes up when there is a foreign exchange shortage because the spare parts, replacements and imported inputs cannot be obtained.

Adjusting Inequality: Education and Structural Adjustment Policies in Tanzania

FRANCES VAVRUS

One of the most important developments in the field of education has been the growing interest in qualitative approaches to policy studies. With an emphasis on cultural analysis, most qualitative studies demonstrate that the intended outcomes of policy are only one part of a much larger picture of how policy is interpreted through local practice. To study this phenomenon, researchers have developed a particular type of qualitative approach to policy research, namely, the ethnography of policy (Levinson & Sutton, 2001; Shore & Wright, 1997). Stephen Ball, whose scholarship has helped strengthen this strand of qualitative policy research, writes: "Ethnography provides access to 'situated' discourse and 'specific tactics' and 'precise and tenuous' power relations operating in local settings" (1994, p. 2). What most ethnographic studies of policy share, then, is an emphasis on relations of power, on cultural practices that affect policy interpretations, and on sustained engagement with residents in a local setting (Walford, 2001, 2002).

This article explores ethnographically the effects of one type of policy — structural adjustment — in a community on Mount Kilimanjaro in northern Tanzania, where I have worked intermittently as a teacher and researcher for the past decade. The community, Old Moshi, is located in the Moshi Rural District of the Kilimanjaro Region. It has a population of approximately 20,000 people in two administrative wards, and each ward is further divided into four villages with their own primary schools, churches, and political leaders (Moshi, 1994). Old Moshi is a relatively prosperous community in rural Kilimanjaro, due to the rainfall and volcanic soil that enhance agricultural production and the proximity of several public and private secondary schools.

Structural adjustment policies, or SAPs, are macroeconomic policies designed to enable countries with large outstanding debts, like Tanzania, to repay their loans and balance their budgets. These policies, developed by the World Bank and the International Monetary Fund (IMF), vary somewhat from one country to another, but

Harvard Educational Review   Vol. 75   No. 2   Summer 2005, 174–201

they generally include the privatization of national industries and assets, the promotion of agricultural crops for export, the devaluation of the national currency, and the reduction of government spending on social programs, such as food subsidies, health care, and education. Although the ultimate decision to "adjust" rests with the national government, debtor nations are unlikely to receive further loans from the World Bank or the IMF unless these general macroeconomic reforms are implemented.

The impact of structural adjustment on the education sector in heavily indebted countries has been studied by researchers interested in policy implementation in Africa and Latin America (Moulton, Mundy, Walmond, & Williams, 2002; Reimers, 1994), and in the influence of international financial institutions on national education policies in these world regions (Mundy, 1998; Samoff, 1994a, 1999). However, there has been little research addressing the relationship between the macro-level changes brought about by SAPs and the local lives and livelihoods that are reshaped when a comprehensive set of policy reforms is implemented. This study takes a close look at how policies that are developed by international financial institutions and implemented at the national level affect local opportunities for 1) education, 2) employment, and 3) health, the social sectors most affected by structural adjustment. This ethnographic study of these three sectors reveals perceptions of both increased opportunity and growing inequality as a result of SAPs.

My ethnographic analysis culminates in a theoretical framework of relative deprivation that helps explain the social categories and cultural premises associated with structural adjustment on Mount Kilimanjaro. The concept of relative deprivation has been developed by social psychologists and sociologists to explain the conditions under which the actual or perceived differential treatment of a group (or of an individual) leads to political action or violence (Crosby, 1982; Klandermans, Roefs, & Olivier, 2001). It provides a useful framework for explaining the conditions under which social cleavages based on race, class, or ethnicity become the impetus for collective mobilization against those that an aggrieved group holds responsible for an unjust situation. In this article, I develop a theory of relative deprivation to explain the perception among many people on Mount Kilimanjaro that social inequalities are increasing even though macroeconomic conditions are improving.

In the sections that follow, I engage in a cultural analysis of relative deprivation that focuses on the "'situated' discourse and 'specific tactics'" of secondary school-age youth and adults in Kilimanjaro whose lives have been "adjusted" by changes in policy (Ball, 1994, p. 2). The first two sections present the methodology of the study and an overview of structural adjustment. The remaining sections provide an ethnographic account of adjustment organized around the three domains that emerged from my analysis of the qualitative and quantitative data: 1) access to secondary school; 2) opportunities for formal employment; and 3) risk of HIV infection among young women of secondary school age. These domains represent the three issues informants most often cited to explain recent social and economic changes in their community. The final section of the article considers the implications of this analysis for future educational research on structural adjustment and on the ethnography of policy.

Methodology

The negotiation of the shifting boundary between cultural outsider and insider during the course of field research is one of the central methodological challenges facing ethnographers. This study, which spans seven years, from 1996 to 2003, reflects my changing status vis-à-vis the residents of Old Moshi, where this research was conducted. Prior to beginning my doctoral fieldwork in 1996, I taught English at Njema Secondary School in Old Moshi during the 1993 school year.[1] Since I was newly married, my neighbors marked this important aspect of my identity by calling me "Mrs. Timothy," the wife of Timothy, a fellow teacher at the school. Eventually I was able to carve out my own role, separate from that of my spouse, by becoming the school librarian and supervising a group of students who worked with me to rehabilitate the aging facility.

Three years later, in 1996, Timothy and I returned with our infant son, August, to conduct a year-long ethnographic study of schooling at Njema. Following local custom, "Mrs. Timothy" became "Mama Augustino." This change in appellation not only signaled a different stage in my life course, according to the residents of Old Moshi; it also reflected an important shift in my local identity as I moved from being seen primarily as a neophyte wife and teacher interested in children's education and health to a mother and researcher who needed to understand these issues for the sake of her son and her scholarship. Similar to other ethnographers whose children accompanied them during fieldwork, August's presence helped to minimize, although never eliminate, the gulf between cultural outsider and insider (Cassell, 1987). His presence also helped me negotiate my own status as a researcher, teacher, and parent, rather than giving priority to one over the others during this extended period of fieldwork.

When I returned to Old Moshi in 2000 to begin a longitudinal research project for a postdoctoral fellowship, my former neighbors warmly greeted me as "Mama Augustino." However, my research assistant corrected them, explaining that I was now "Doctor Frances" because I had received my PhD. At first I was concerned that this more impersonal moniker would distance me from the parents I wanted to interview, but my three subsequent trips to the community have demonstrated that my status as a professor has not diminished the insider status granted to me several years earlier. Moreover, this elevated status has given me access to officials who were previously reluctant to meet with a graduate student but who are now most willing to discuss educational matters with a visiting scholar.

One reason why local residents and officials have generally embraced my ongoing research is because of the historical support for education in the Kilimanjaro Region. The Chagga are the dominant ethnic group in the region and 95 percent of the population in Old Moshi (Vavrus, 2003). Although the Chagga constitute only 5 percent of Tanzania's total population, their strong identification with schooling, Christianity, and commercial coffee farming for nearly a century has resulted in a disproportionate number of the country's schools being built in Kilimanjaro by parent organizations, churches, and the state. Moreover, Chagga accomplishments in the areas of education and economic development from the colonial era to the present have earned them a reputation as one of the most "modern" of Tanzania's many ethnic groups (Setel, 1995). For these reasons, Kilimanjaro continues to be an intriguing region in which to explore questions of cultural, economic, and educational change.

To examine such questions in Old Moshi, I utilized multiple research methods, including document analysis, interviews, focus group discussions, surveys, and participant observation (see Table 1). Throughout this study, I have been engaged in an analysis of documents about the educational, employment, and financial sectors in Tanzania published by the World Bank, the IMF, and various ministries in the country to understand how changes in "inter/national" policy affect local cultural practice. This analysis led me to use the term "inter/national" to signal the blurred distinction between policies formulated by international financial institutions, such as the World Bank and the IMF, and the national policies of heavily indebted poor countries like Tanzania.

The individual interviews and focus group discussions involved secondary school students at Njema Secondary School, the focal school in the study, and their parents. The interviews with students took place in 1996 and focused on their school achievement and their future educational and employment plans. The interviews with students' parents during the same year also touched on these topics, but added questions about the conditions of life today and in the past. The focus group discussions involved some of these students from 1996, who reconvened in 2001. A second set of discussions was held with parents and teachers at four primary schools in Old Moshi, where I am engaged in a separate longitudinal study of education and reproductive health. I met with these adults in 2001 and 2002 to discuss the results of the first phase of the longitudinal study that began in 2000.

The survey data come from two sources: 1) a follow-up study in 2000 of the young women and men who had been students at Njema in 1996; and 2) the longitudinal study of primary school students that started in 2000. Out of the 225 former students to whom the survey was mailed, 112 completed and returned it. They were asked to complete a questionnaire and write an essay about their views on the Tanzanian economy, their employment prospects, their educational aspirations, and their reproductive health awareness. The second survey, part of the longitudinal project, asked students in their final two years of primary school to answer questions about their educational and employment plans, and their knowledge of basic health and HIV/AIDS prevention. It also contained questions designed to ascertain their level of literacy and numeracy. For each of the 277 primary school students in the study, one of their adult guardians — a parent, grandparent, or another relative — was interviewed about the family's educational history, birth history, socioeconomic status, and expectations for the child in the study.

The final method employed in this ethnography is observation. In 1996, I was engaged in participant observation as a teacher at Njema Secondary School and as a parent of a young child living in Old Moshi. To capture my observations, I recorded day-to-day conversations and events in my field notes. Field notes are the principal way of collecting and analyzing observational data; indeed, as Dewalt and Dewalt argue, "*observations are not data* unless they are recorded in some fashion for further analysis" (1998, p. 271; emphasis in original). In this case, the observations were focused on classroom interactions among teachers, students, and the school administration, as well as events in the Old Moshi community, such as weddings, funerals, and holiday celebrations. I have included field note excerpts alongside verbatim quotes from interviews and focus group discussions to illustrate how a theory of relative deprivation emerged through the process of triangulation, the primary means of enhancing internal validity in an ethnographic study by obtaining multiple sources of data about the issue being explored (Handwerker & Borgatti, 1998).

The qualitative data generated through observations and interviews were studied systematically through domain analysis. Domains, "the first and most important unit of analysis in ethnographic research," are culturally relevant categories that consist of "cover terms" — or labels — and the more specific "included terms" that together express cultural knowledge about a concept (Spradley, 1979, p. 100). Domains are also the building blocks for theory generation; in this study, three domains emerged from my analysis of the terms and phrases used repeatedly by participants. Each domain — 1) access to schooling; 2) opportunities for formal employment; and 3) risk of HIV infection among young women — was comprised of several emic cover terms for the more numerous included terms that share a semantic relationship with one another.[2] For example, the included terms "good time," "buy things," and "gifts" were grouped under the cover term "temptations" (*vishawishi*). This cover term formed the core of the domain "risk of HIV infection among young women" because it was these sexual and material temptations that informants believed put young women at risk. Figure 1 uses this example to illustrate the process of analysis for the other two cover terms as well, namely, "difficult life" (*maisha magumu*) and "there is no employment" (*hakuna ajira*). Each cover term forms the core of a domain, such as maisha magumu for access to schooling and hakuna ajira in the case of opportunities for formal employment. Combined with the analysis of the documents and surveys, this procedure allowed me to address the question of how inter/national structural adjustment policies affect material conditions and cultural discourses of education, employment, and HIV/AIDS at the local level.

Structural Adjustment: An Overview and an Analysis in Tanzania

Before examining the local effects of structural adjustment policies, it is important to understand the historical context in which they emerged. The policies that have been implemented in Africa, Asia, the Caribbean, and Latin America were developed during the debt crisis of the late 1970s and early 1980s. Many countries, most notably Mexico and Brazil, were poised to default on their loans to foreign banks. Commercial banks were worried that loans to debtor nations would not be repaid, and the governments of donor nations were concerned that rapidly growing debt in the Third World could destabilize their own economies as well. Beginning in Mexico, the IMF granted the government a loan on the condition that it engage in a series of macroeconomic reforms, such as reducing social spending and subsidies for certain consumer goods (Peet, 2003). The World Bank also began structural adjustment lending to a number of other countries at this time in exchange for implementing policies to restructure their economies (Woodhall, 1994). In addition to reducing government expenditures, eliminating trade barriers, and devaluing the currency, SAPs encour-

TABLE 1
Methodological Approaches, 1996–2003

Dates	Methods	Description of Participants
1996	Interviewing and focus group discussions	Njema Secondary School students (13–35 years old)*
	Interviewing	Parents in Old Moshi
	Participant observation	Students at Njema and four other secondary schools in northern Tanzania
2000	Survey	Elementary school students at four schools in Old Moshi (11–16 years old) and their guardians
	Mail-in survey	Former Njema students
2001	Survey (follow-up)	Guardians of elementary school students in the 2000 study
	Focus group discussion	Guardians of elementary school students, teachers, and community leaders
	Focus group discussion	Former Njema students
2002	Presentation/discussion of results of 2000 and 2001 surveys	Guardians of elementary school students, teachers, and community leaders
2003	Observation	Njema Secondary School and four elementary schools
1996–2003	Document analysis	—

*The wide age range at Njema Secondary School reflects the presence of several older male students who returned to school after military training or training as lay ministers. The median age of students at the school was 16.5 years.

aged the establishment of cost-sharing programs, whereby fees are charged to users of educational and health services. By the middle of the 1980s, with economic stagnation growing in Latin America and Africa, three-quarters of Latin American countries and two-thirds of those in Africa were implementing some combination of these structural adjustment policies (Peet, 2003).

In Tanzania, the macroeconomic situation grew considerably worse in the late 1970s and early 1980s because of its war with neighboring Uganda, declining prices on the world market for its leading export crops, the increasing cost of importing oil, and shortcomings in its own domestic policies (Kerner & Cook, 1991; Ponte, 2002; Rugumisa, 1989; Wagao, 1990). However, the socialist government of then president Julius Nyerere was reluctant to negotiate with the IMF (Harrison, 2001). Six years after Tanzania's independence from Britain in 1961, Nyerere enacted his vision of self-reliant rural development through a set of policies known as *ujamaa*, or African socialism (Nyerere, 1962, 1967b). By 1967, it was evident that the regional and class disparities inherited from the colonial era were still largely intact, and Nyerere was concerned that gradual changes in policy were inadequate to address these fundamental inequalities (Coulson, 1982). Therefore, Nyerere put forth a "blueprint for socialist development" that was intended to build a self-reliant nation that met the needs of the rural, agricultural majority (Hyden, 1980, p. 96). In contrast to the free-market orientation of the IMF, the Nyerere government sought to improve conditions in the country by increasing state involvement in the economy, from nationalizing many commercial institutions to regulating crop prices through state agricultural marketing boards. The state also played a major role in job creation: by the mid-1970s, almost two-thirds of the wage-earning positions in Tanzania were controlled by the government (Tripp, 1997).

Nyerere was also strongly committed to active state involvement in education. As early as 1963, secondary school fees at government-supported schools were eliminated, and fees for primary schooling were abolished ten years later (Samoff, 1994b). These policy changes contributed to the dramatic rise in primary school enrollment rates from approximately 903,000 children in 1971 to 3,500,000 by 1981 (World Bank, 1999). Secondary school enrollment increased steadily as well because of the expansion of schools for African students in the decades following independence (Bureau of Statistics, 1995).

Yet the economic crisis that began in the late 1970s did not dissipate, and this led the Nyerere government to create its own economic reform policies (Lugalla, 1997). To the government's dismay, its early national restructuring policies did not lead to the anticipated improvements in the economy, nor did they go as far as the IMF required before Tanzania would qualify for a loan (Harrison, 2001). By the mid-1980s the economic situation had reached its nadir, and the new president, Ali Hassan Mwinyi, "had little choice but to conclude an agreement with the IMF" (Tripp, 1997, p. 80).

Since 1986, with the support of the IMF and the World Bank, Tanzania has instituted a number of structural adjustment policies designed to improve its macroeconomic performance. These specific restructuring activities include devaluing the Tanzanian shilling, creating greater opportunity for foreign investment, eliminating consumer and agricultural subsidies, and reducing civil service employment (Ponte, 1998; Wagao, 1990). In the education and health sectors, user fees were reintroduced after years of free service, and private schools and clinics began to proliferate in a reversal of the ujamaa-era policy of government provision of social services (Samoff, 1994b; Turshen, 1999). Requirements for family contributions to schooling grew considerably, even though the value of parental income was declining (Bureau of Statistics, 1995; Kuleana, 1999; Maarifa ni Ufunguo, 2001); therefore, many low-income families had to choose between education for their children and other basic needs. As a result of these policy changes, gross primary school enrollment rates declined from around 90 percent in the early 1980s to somewhere between 66 percent and 75 percent a decade later (Global Challenge Initiative, 2000; World Bank, 1999).[3]

What have been the macroeconomic outcomes of these structural adjustment policies in Tanzania? After nearly two decades of SAPs, the results suggest that these changes have had their intended effect on the national economy. For example, from

FIGURE 1
Data Analysis and Theory Construction

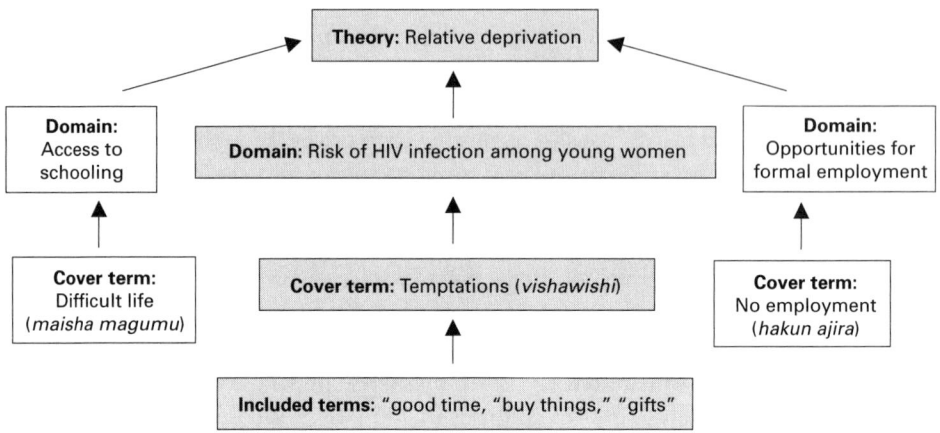

1986 to 1993, Tanzania's growth rate averaged 4 percent, compared to 2 percent between 1976 and 1985, and the economy grew annually from 2.7 percent to 5.6 percent during the period from 1996 to 2001 (International Monetary Fund [IMF] & International Development Association [IDA], 1999; Mramba, 2002).[4] In general, IMF, World Bank, and Tanzanian government figures show that, since the mid 1990s, growth has increased, import duties have been reduced on many consumer goods, and inflation has declined from double digits to below 5 percent (Mramba, 2002). In addition, since 1993–1994, there has been a steady decline in the value of the Tanzanian shilling against the dollar, thereby improving the climate for foreign investment. For example, the exchange rate was 405 Tanzanian shillings to the dollar in 1993, but declined to 1,050 shillings to the dollar by 2003 (Financial Management Service, 2003). Opportunities for foreign investment improved further when the government privatized state-owned assets: More than 50 percent of the public sector institutions scheduled for privatization in 1993 have been sold, and the government is now working on the privatization of its major utilities (IMF & IDA, 1999; Mramba, 2002).

Economic growth and the reduction of inflation are goals that few policymakers or citizens question, but there has been considerable controversy over the reduction in civil service employment as a result of privatization. The number of public sector jobs plummeted during the second half of the 1980s because structural adjustment policies encouraged the government to sharply reduce the size of its labor force (Wagao, 1990). Between 1990–1991 and 2000–2001, there was a 15 percent decline in public sector employment and a concomitant rise in the number of households involved in the informal sector — the nonstate sector that includes licit and illicit activities — of the economy from 25 percent to 33 percent of households (National Bureau of Statistics, 2003).

Another contentious aspect of structural adjustment is that it has not alleviated Tanzania's crippling foreign debt. The IMF determined in 1999 that the country had an "unsustainable debt burden" even though it had been carrying out SAPs for more than a decade, and recommended that debt relief be provided under the terms of the Heavily Indebted Poor Country — or HIPC — Initiative (IMF & IDA, 1999, p. 37). The HIPC Initiative is a program developed by the IMF and the World Bank in 1996 to link poverty reduction, debt reduction, and macroeconomic reform. Eligible countries prepare a Poverty Reduction Strategy Paper that describes the policies a government will implement to redirect money that would have gone to debt servicing to cover some of the costs of basic social services, such as education and health (World Bank, 2001). In 2001, the IMF and the World Bank deemed Tanzania's Poverty Reduction Strategy Paper satisfactory, and they announced that three billion dollars, or roughly 54 percent of the country's external debt, would be eliminated (Mramba, 2002; World Bank, 2001). However, the country is still paying back the remainder of its outstanding debt and continuing to take on new loans.

By conventional measures, the macroeconomic situation in the country has improved during the era of structural adjustment. The economy is growing, inflation is down, and a significant portion of the country's massive debt has been eliminated. One must then ask whether the positive changes in the economy have had an equally constructive impact on the education, employment, and health sectors.

Most observers, the World Bank included, concur that inequality of educational opportunities has increased from the mid-1980s to the present, with a growing gap between those who can afford user fees and other school-related expenses and those who cannot (Lassibille et al., 2000; Maarifa ni Ufunguo, 2001; World Bank, 1999). The major Tanzanian educational policies of the 1990s, the Education and Training Policy and the Basic Education Master Plan, included user fee provisions; not unexpectedly, primary school gross enrollment rates declined. Two years ago, in a reversal of policy, school fees at the primary level were eliminated once again.[5] Since 2002 there has been a resurgence in primary school attendance with the elimination of school fees, but also growing discontent with the low quality of education in Tanzania's already overcrowded schools (Maarifa ni Ufunguo, 2002).

A more striking and sustained effect of structural adjustment policies on the education sector is the growing inequality of opportunity at the secondary level because of the steady increase in fees and related expenses at private and public (government-sponsored) facilities during the past decade. For instance, the proportion of secondary school students whose parents are peasant farmers has declined as the burden of cost-sharing on families has increased (Lassibille et al., 2000). Inequalities are also evident in the sharp difference between secondary school enrollment rates for students whose families are in the lowest quintile for household expenditures (2% enrollment) and for those whose families are in the highest quintile (15% enrollment) (World Bank, 1999).

The major impact of structural adjustment on the employment sector has already been noted, namely, the decline in the number of civil service jobs and the rise of the informal sector. Of particular interest to this study are the changes in opportunities for youth employment in general and for female employment in particular. The most comprehensive study of the labor market during the years of adjustment, the Tanzania Integrated Labour Market Survey, shows that age- and gender-based inequalities have increased during the past decade (National Bureau of Statistics, 2003). For example, there was an overall rise in youth unemployment throughout the 1990s such that young people between the ages of fifteen and twenty-four now make up 44 percent of the unemployed population in the country, compared to 33 percent a decade ago. In addition, the sector with the highest paying jobs — the parastatal, or public, sector linked to the government — is shrinking as a result of structural adjustment (President's Office, 2004); however, those who do hold jobs in this sector are 81 percent male and 19 percent female. As for gender disparities in income, the labor survey concludes, "For employees with paid income, females earn less than males. This is true in every sector of employment." Women, far more often than men, report that they are "economically inactive" because they do not have formal employment (National Bureau of Statistics, 2003).

The impact of structural adjustment policies on the health sector, and especially on women's health, has been mixed. Tanzania, along with many other African countries, has been engaged in a process of privatizing health services since the mid-1980s (Turshen, 1999). In Kilimanjaro, this change in policy has led to the founding of private hospitals, well-stocked pharmacies, and clinics that provide high-quality care to those who can afford it. It has also meant, however, that the quality of service at public hospitals and clinics has deteriorated, as doctors opt for the more profitable private sector. Today, even the poorest families must pay something to be treated at "public" facilities. For some people this means foregoing treatment altogether.

The relationship between structural adjustment policies and the escalation of the HIV/AIDS crisis in Tanzania is more difficult to ascertain because their co-occurrence does not necessarily mean causality. The first AIDS cases were identified in Tanzania in the early 1980s, the same period when SAPs began, and the disease has spread rapidly ever since. Today, approximately one and a half million out of the country's 35 million residents, or 8 percent of the adult population, are living with HIV/AIDS (UNAIDS, 2001). The epidemic has had an especially serious impact on Tanzanian youth: Young women and men between the ages of fifteen and twenty-four account for 60 percent of the new HIV infections in Tanzania, and young women in this age group are six times as likely to be infected as their male counterparts (UNICEF, 2000).

For youth in Kilimanjaro, the necessity of migrating from a rural community to an urban center to find employment has undoubtedly contributed to the spread of HIV. As Setel (1999) notes in his research on AIDS in Kilimanjaro, these simultaneous changes — SAPS and AIDS — have created a feeling among many young women and men in the region that they have been hit by two crises at the same time: "For young people, this alignment of structural forces proved to be a fatal and paradoxical bit of serendipity. At the moment environmental conditions for youth had reached their worst, and many became involved in the black market (*magendo*) and informal sector activities, HIV arrived" (p. 147). The pages to follow examine these multiple factors that contribute to the sense that life is growing more difficult, and more dangerous, at a time when the national macroeconomic indicators suggest growing opportunities and a higher standard of living.

Adjusting Inequality in Old Moshi

Structural adjustment policies have had numerous demonstrable effects — both positive and negative — on the economy, education, and health in Tanzania. Yet an analysis of policy outcomes tells only one side of the story; an ethnography of policy goes beyond this to explore "the frameworks of cultural meaning people use to interpret their experience and generate social behavior" (Levinson & Sutton, 2001, p. 3). In this section, I provide background information about Old Moshi to establish the cultural framework through which to explore the meaning of maisha magumu (difficult life), hakuna ajira (there is no employment), and vishawishi (temptations), the cover terms central to the three domains of access to secondary schooling, opportunities for formal employment, and risk of HIV infection among young women, respectively. These emic terms inscribe local beliefs about the lives people should desire, the preferred routes toward establishing those lives, and the forces that often impede youth and adults along the way. In this case, what many people perceive as having gone awry are government policies they believed would make life less difficult, create more jobs, and improve access to education.

Old Moshi is an ideal site to explore ethnographically the effects of structural adjustment policies at the local level because of its combination of a high level of commitment to children's schooling and a high degree of integration in the global economy through trade in coffee. This community, where people overwhelmingly identify as Chagga and as Lutherans, consists of eight villages organized vertically along the verdant slopes of Mount Kilimanjaro.[6] Most adults in Old Moshi are farmers whose families grow the staple food, bananas, and the major cash crop, coffee. In addition to farming, adults and youth are often engaged in other forms of labor, including teaching, carpentry, and clerical work in the town of Moshi, the capital of the Kilimanjaro region. Formal education is highly valued in this community, which boasts eleven primary schools and three secondary schools. Relative to the rest of rural Tanzania, the residents of the Kilimanjaro Region, and of Old Moshi in particular, have greater access to schooling, health services, and the commodities associated with prosperity because of their proximity to important intra- and international trading networks.

For these reasons, there is a widespread view of the Chagga as "educated persons," a historically and culturally produced identity that bestows privilege upon those who have the positive attributes associated with schooling in a particular community (Levinson & Holland, 1996).[7] The concept of the educated person is central to my analysis because it enables one to understand how deprivation is experienced in a relatively prosperous community like Old Moshi. As I discuss below, it is the perception of deprivation relative to others — in one's immediate or imagined community — that makes SAPs especially difficult for those who associate being educated with being able to afford the plethora of consumer products and services now available in Tanzania. However, if the material effects of structural adjustment were uniformly negative, then this would be a far less complex story. Instead, the sense of deprivation today is produced by the very fact that more commodities are available, more schools do exist, and macroeconomic conditions are better than they have been in many years; nonetheless, these changes have not produced a sense of prosperity for the majority. It is by examining local meanings of terms like maisha magumu, hakuna ajira, and vishawishi that one begins to understand both the tangible hardships faced by many people in this community and the social cleavages that are exacerbated when opportunities are not available to all who identify themselves as educated persons.

Inequality of Opportunities for Secondary Education

The aspect of structural adjustment that has received the most criticism from teachers, parents, and students during the seven years of this study has been the growing inequalities in secondary schooling due to ever-increasing school fees. Parents felt the effects of this aspect of cost-sharing policies most directly while also bearing the brunt of other macroeconomic reforms. For example, the devaluation of the Tanzanian shilling was noted as a serious problem by many parents. With the value of their currency declining, costs increasing, and more goods available for the educated parent to purchase, adults in Old Moshi generally believed that life was more difficult today than in the past. The comments of one Njema student's father are typical of remarks made by others:

> In the past, you could give a child 200 shillings when going to school, and he would be satisfied with that for a term.[8] Today, even if you give him 10,000 shillings [approximately $20 in 1996], he'll frown at you and think that this is very little money. . . . Our currency has been devalued a lot, and getting money is extremely difficult now. Getting money is difficult, but once it is earned, it is easily spent. (Interview)

Parents frequently linked structural adjustment and its effects on educational inequality to the increase in the price of commodities relative to their income. Goods such as cement and iron sheets to build houses are now the standard for "educated" people, who do not want to live in homes made of earthen blocks that were the norm in the past. However, it is costly to buy such items out of a family budget that must also cover school costs, health care, and other domestic expenses. As noted earlier, the value of the Tanzanian shilling has declined steadily during the years of structural adjustment. This diminution in the value of one's income has created a sense of frustration among parents who once had government jobs that paid them a monthly wage adequate to cover their needs and wants. One father of a student at Njema fits this description, and he had a great deal to say about how rising costs, declining incomes, and increasing desires for a certain standard of living make life difficult today:

> Difficult life [maisha magumu] is perpetuated by our government not examining carefully how people with low incomes live. . . . A kilogram of meat, for example, now costs 1,200 shillings [approximately 60 U.S. cents in 1996], but a person has no means of getting that amount of money although she needs to eat meat to stay healthy. . . . Besides this, the prices of other commodities have also tripled. It is true that if one has not yet built a permanent house, it is impossible to do so now. A corrugated iron sheet costs between 4,000–5,000 shillings [approximately $2.25], but one has no means to get that money. Even a bag of cement costs 4,000 shillings now. How can one build? Tell me, don't you think those are problems? (Interview)

Eating meat on a daily basis and living in a house with a corrugated iron roof are two of the many examples parents provided of the standards to which educated parents hold themselves that are increasingly difficult to reach because of changes in government policy. A common complaint among Old Moshi residents was the government decision to eliminate agricultural subsidies and price supports for farmers, especially for coffee farmers like themselves. During the ujamaa period, the Nyerere government provided subsidized agricultural inputs, such as fertilizers, pesticides, and seeds, for smallholder farmers throughout the country (World Bank, 1994). Additionally, the government regulated the market for many food crops, including coffee, and it also subsidized the price of basic foodstuffs — maize flour, for example — as a sign of its commitment to covering the basic needs of the population (Ponte, 1998).

Since the beginning of structural adjustment in the mid-1980s, Tanzanian agricultural policy has changed considerably. The government, on the advice of the World Bank, "has advocated a gradual shift towards private sector ownership of commercial enterprises, and the use of market determined prices and incentives in the agricultural sector" (World Bank, 1994, p. xxiii). Specifically, these changes include the elimination of subsidies for fertilizers (Cooksey, 2003) and the reduction of agricultural import restrictions so that Tanzanian farmers must now compete with products from other parts of the world, such as the North Atlantic, where farming is still heavily subsided by the state (Kristof, 2002; World Bank, 1994). This competition has led to a precipitous drop in the price that farmers receive for their coffee: Farmers in Kilimanjaro received approximately 1,000 shillings [approximately 50 cents] for a kilogram of coffee in 1998 (Maarifa ni Ufunguo, 2001), but by 2003 the price had fallen to a mere 200 shillings per kilo, or around 20 U.S. cents (Cooksey, 2003).

As I learned more about the geographical differences in coffee farming in Old Moshi (with those living at the base of the mountain and nearer to the town of Moshi being less likely to grow coffee), I wondered whether dependence on farm income affected educational opportunity at the secondary level. The survey administered to children in four primary schools was designed to ascertain the factors associated with starting secondary school upon completion of the primary level. The four primary schools in the study are located in geographically disparate parts of Old Moshi. Sokoni, the school nearest to town, is the largest school, with some 1,200 students (as of 2002) in Standards — or grades — 1–7. Mbali Primary School (257 students), in contrast, is the smallest school and lies farthest from town and at the highest altitude of the four schools on Mount Kilimanjaro. Bonde and Miti primary schools lie between these two schools, and the size of their student populations are also somewhere between the other two — 412 students at Bonde and 535 at Miti. Both schools also enroll students whose parents grow coffee, but the families tend to have more diversified sources of income than families living near Mbali Primary School.

The 2000 survey for children and adults found that the families whose children attended Mbali had the fewest household resources. For example, only 2 percent of the Mbali students' homes had electricity, compared to 10 percent at Bonde, 46 percent at Miti, and 77 percent at Sokoni. Similarly, nearly one-third of the families at Mbali reported that they often had inadequate food to eat, while only 12 percent of the

Bonde families and virtually none of the Miti and Sokoni families reported this problem. Given the high cost of secondary schooling in Tanzania today, it is not surprising that the differences in resources paralleled the differences in matriculation rates: 83 percent of the children at Sokoni started secondary school in 2001, compared to 60 percent at Miti, 49 percent at Bonde, and 30 percent at Mbali Primary School. In contrast, the educational levels of the students' parents were quite similar: With the exception of Mbali, where no fathers had gone to secondary school, 43 percent to 56 percent of students' fathers at the three other schools had had some postprimary education. The educational opportunities for students' mothers were even more similar, with around 10 percent of those at Sokoni, Bonde, and Mbali, and 20 percent at Miti having completed some postprimary schooling (Vavrus, 2003).

Further analysis of the survey data provided additional evidence about the growing economic and educational polarization in Old Moshi. In brief, it showed that families who are most dependent on the sale of coffee for their income but are unable to hire workers to help pick the beans are less likely to have children who start secondary school. This describes the typical family whose children attend Mbali Primary School, and it lends support to the sentiments expressed during focus group discussions that dependence on coffee for family income has a negative impact on children's opportunity for secondary schooling (Vavrus, 2003).

Dependence on agricultural income in general becomes an educational problem when subsidies and price guarantees for farmers are removed *and* secondary school fees increase beyond the average yearly income of smallholder farm families. Parents, especially at Mbali Primary School, frequently lamented the current hardships for poor farm families. This was evident in a focus group discussion at Mbali, where a father presented his analysis of the local situation in relation to the more prosperous conditions at Sokoni. His comments had particular resonance on the damp day when we held the discussion and sat shivering in a classroom that had no windowpanes to keep out the cold air or flooring to keep our feet dry:

> This entire building was built by the energies of the parents, the parents who began in 1978. [They made] contributions — money, money, money! And at that time we had coffee! . . . Now, it has reached the point where people are unable [to give] due to the downfall of the economy, especially due to this coffee crop, and the school is the way it is now. Here on the ground, there is no flooring; there are no windows; there are no doors. When a pupil is in a classroom like this one, she is filled with doubts. She is not hopeful. If it rains, it rains inside. There at Sokoni, the buildings are well built, and the walls are painted. When a pupil looks at the wall, she becomes hopeful. When she treads on the floor, she is hopeful. The pupils here are eaten by chiggers from this ground. Now such conditions do not allow the child to learn anything. Even when the teacher tells her to do some work, she scratches herself. Now it is not possible for the education level to rise. It will continue to fall, fall, fall because the building itself is not promising . . . and the parents themselves lack energy due to the poor economy.

The sentiments of this father and others like him suggest that inequality of opportunity for secondary schooling stems from the complex conditions that constitute *maisha magumu,* which include a sense of deprivation relative to one's more prosperous neighbors. Maisha magumu, as the phrase is used locally, conveys a sense of deprivation among residents of rural communities with the most limited incomes but whose parental aspirations are as great as those of more prosperous residents, whose lives they observe and use as a gauge against which to measure their own success and their children's opportunities. Life is difficult in part because changes in agricultural and educational policies have affected the poorest farming families most significantly. However, it is also difficult because poor families are judged, and judge themselves, as "educated" against the same standards that apply to more prosperous families in neighborhoods like Sokoni. These standards throughout Old Moshi now include providing an adequate supply of certain kinds of food for one's family, living in sturdy homes with an iron roof, and sending one's children to a school with windows on the walls and flooring below.

Limited Opportunities for Formal Employment

The changes brought about by structural adjustment policies have affected youth employment in Old Moshi in multiple ways. In this section, I consider three changes in relation to the cover term hakuna ajira ("there is no employment"). The first two — the growing disdain for agricultural labor among secondary school graduates and the belief that the government ought to provide jobs for its citizens — reflect important shifts since the ujamaa period, when agriculture was privileged in national development policy and state planning in the employment sector was the norm. The third change in employment opportunities stems from the privatization of Tanzanian industries, especially as factories are sold to the highest bidder, who may or may not be Tanzanian.

Agricultural and vocational education were touted by President Nyerere in his 1967 Education for Self-Reliance policy, arguing that schools should have farms that teach children to appreciate the collective farming and the practical skills that he believed characterized — or had once characterized — life in rural Tanzania (Nyerere, 1967a). Agriculture continues to be the backbone of the Tanzanian economy, and this sector currently employs more than 80 percent of young people in the country (National Bureau of Statistics, 2003). The problem with this employment picture for secondary school graduates in Old Moshi is that one of the local features defining educated persons is their ability to hire others to do the manual labor on their farms. As noted in the section above, it is generally the poorest families who cannot hire farm laborers and the wealthier families who can.

Secondary school youths' aversion to agricultural labor was something I noted many times in my field notes, where I recorded observations and comments made by students about this form of work. The following excerpt, written two months into my fieldwork in 1996, describes the typical conditions under which students engaged in agricultural labor and their sentiments regarding it:

> There were a lot of absences today, especially of the girls. I thought at first it was due to the rain, but then it seemed that the girls who were absent were those who had been punished last Friday. On my way home at 9:30 a.m., I saw several girls in their regular, non-school clothes hoeing the ground along the road up to school. . . .

[They] told me that this was their punishment — to farm all week instead of going to class. . . . Right after tea, as I was going past the Form III room, I heard several boys spreading the word that they would be going to the shamba [farm] instead of to class. These boys didn't sound pleased by this news.

It wasn't until later in the year that the pattern of agricultural labor as punishment became apparent to me as I began to analyze my field notes and to incorporate questions about my observations in interviews with parents and students. Although agriculture is one of the vocational tracks in some Tanzanian secondary schools (Stambach, 2000), Njema did not offer it. Instead it offered science and commerce tracks, which were more in line with local sentiments about the careers for which schools ought to prepare students. A few male students did report during interviews that they wanted to become farmers upon graduation, but the far more typical response was that farming was a last resort. For example, Robert, an older student at Njema, explained that if his plan to find a "good" job after graduation failed, only then he would consider agriculture or informal employment:

> Actually, I haven't yet decided what to do considering the fact that the [economic] situation of our country is still bad. There is no employment [hakuna ajira]. So, I'll simply see. Whatever comes, that's what I'll do. In the event that I miss everything [all job prospects], I will have to operate my own business, whether agricultural or petty trading. (Interview)

Observational, interview, and survey data about agricultural labor formed a critical part of my understanding the term hakuna ajira in this community. Almost every family in Old Moshi engages in farming to some extent, and there are opportunities to sell the produce one grows at nearby markets. However, as the field note data suggested, agricultural labor is often used as punishment in secondary schools, and students are generally loath to assume a career in farming because it is not what "educated persons" do these days. Hakuna ajira, I began to realize, does not literally mean there is no work of any sort in Tanzania, but that there is little employment that secondary school graduates find suitable.

A second aspect of hakuna ajira that was revealed in interviews with parents is its use to contrast current policies with past manpower planning programs of the Nyerere government. Through its firm grip on the economy in the 1960s and 1970s, the government became the principal employer in the country, and secondary school and college graduates felt assured of finding employment. During interviews with parents in 1996, many of whom benefited from this aspect of socialist planning, they complained that the government no longer felt responsible to find employment for educated youth. Many of them were nostalgic for the more state-centered development of the past, even though most Chagga in Kilimanjaro were never strong supporters of Nyerere's socialist policies (Howard & Millard, 1997). The interviews with two fathers conveyed common sentiments:

> *Mr. Mauki:* Ahaa, as far as I know, the parents who were lucky to educate their children to the secondary level at that time didn't have a problem because the child could secure a job. The government would allocate him a job. That is one important thing I noted: The government would find him a job.

Mr. Ringo: Another problem, I think, is that although we are giving them [children] an education, they don't have a future. That means, ehh, it's okay if we set targets for them to complete their education. But once the student completes school, given the existing situation, where does she go to next? This is because the nation has laid out no plan for placing these youth after they graduate. The government doesn't have such a program that shows what should follow when they finish their education in private or public secondary schools. . . . So, what we are saying is that we educate them, but we don't have any future for them.

These quotes illustrate the use of several "included terms" encapsulated by the broader cover term hakuna ajira (Spradley, 1979, p. 100). For example, "secure a job" came up repeatedly in reference to past employment opportunities for secondary school graduates, while "no plan" and "no future" were frequently used to describe the current state of affairs. Moreover, for many youth in the study, opportunities for formal employment today exist only for those with "connections" because, as one young man put it, finding a job in Tanzania relies on a system of "who knows whom, not who knows what." Thus, even if these youth, as educated persons, have a good deal of knowledge, they believe their lack of connections deprives them of job opportunities and that their government is not going to find employment for them.

The notion that there are fewer employment opportunities today for secondary school graduates is related to a third aspect of hakuna ajira that came up often in focus group discussions with my former students: the privatization of Tanzanian industries. When I returned to Old Moshi in 2000, I began hearing a verb that I had not encountered when I lived there in 1993 and 1996, *kubinafsisha* — meaning "to privatize." By this time, the government's proposals to privatize the parastatal industries had fully materialized, and people who worked in Moshi and other towns and cities in the country were feeling the effects. Discussions with my former students in 2001 were filled with tales of people losing their jobs when companies were sold and of workers' rights being violated, especially when the new owner was South African. During the apartheid era, Tanzania provided a safe haven and training facilities for African National Congress members, and the Nyerere government was consistently a vocal opponent of the White regime. Today, however, South Africa is viewed with a combination of envy and resentment as its citizens are seen as buying up land, hotels, and, most troubling to some of the Kilimanjaro elite, the national airline, which now sports a hybrid Tanzanian/South African flag and has many White South African pilots. If government policies were working as they should, according to the local cultural framework, then it would have been Tanzanians buying the breweries, exporting flowers from their farms to Europe, and flying the Air Tanzania planes. Although this has happened in some cases, the general feeling in 2001 was that privatization policies have had a negative impact on job prospects for educated Tanzanian youth and have created opportunities for foreigners to work in their place.

This sense of privatization policies gone awry was quite apparent in the focus groups with secondary school graduates. In one group, a question was asked about why employment was more of a problem today than in the 1980s. A young woman began by stating, "The number of people and the privatization of factories. They've been bought by private individuals, and they won't belong to the government again."

She was then interrupted by her male colleague, who began describing a particular case of privatization that many people mentioned to me in 2001: the sale of a nearby brewery to a South African owner. He complained:

> The people who bought the breweries were rich people, and they brought their own people to work there. . . . Then they started bringing the wheat, the wheat needed for the beer, from South Africa, but there wasn't enough wheat for all the beer they wanted to produce so they even bought the farms to grow the wheat here. If the farms had not been privatized — the government land was also privatized — they would have been buying the wheat [from Tanzanians], but now they bought the farms, too. So the wheat then comes from their land because they bought the land, and they have bought the breweries. And the labor, the laborers also come from South Africa!

From the perspective of these secondary school graduates, privatization is forcing Tanzanian youth to compete on a much broader playing field that extends beyond the borders of the country to the southernmost part of the African continent. Their sense of deprivation is derived not only from comparisons to their parents' generation, when job security through the government was almost a given for an educated person, or from comparisons with colleagues whom they perceive as having better social contacts. It also comes from assessing their situation relative to those from other countries who are now working in positions they would like for themselves.

Increased Risk of HIV Infection among Young Women

The changing nature of the labor and commodity markets as a result of structural adjustment policies has affected the lives and longings of Tanzanian secondary school–age youth, especially among young women. According to local cultural frameworks in Old Moshi, these changes have had a particularly negative impact on the reproductive health of young women from low-income families because they are prone to giving into temptations (vishawishi) that may result in unwanted pregnancies or in HIV infection. According to this cultural logic, the limited opportunities for young women to find employment outside the agricultural and informal sectors, coupled with the high cost of schooling and the consumer goods now available in the country, create the ideal conditions for men with wealth or influence to become "sugar daddies" for those who can afford neither school fees nor the accessories and clothing sported by their better-off female peers (Bledsoe, 1990; Komba-Malekela & Liljestrom, 1994). Thus, when young women feel deprived of the opportunities or the commodities that others enjoy, they are confronted with vishawishi, most often in the form of sexual relationships with men who can provide these things for them.

The problem of limited employment opportunities for secondary school graduates — male and female — was evident in both the questionnaire and the essays completed by my former students in 2000. However, it was the female respondents who linked this problem further to temptations. Similar to the results of the Integrated Labour Force Survey discussed above, there were clear gender differences in employment patterns for these students after graduation (National Bureau of Statistics, 2003). For example, approximately 50 percent of the former male students were still in school at the upper secondary or tertiary levels; 40 percent were employed; and 10 percent reported being idle at their parents' homes without any formal employment. In contrast, around 30 percent of the young women were still enrolled in school; 30 percent were employed; and 40 percent described themselves as "idle." Although these young women and men had received financial support from their families to attend lower secondary school (O-level studies), the results of the questionnaire suggest that parents often support their sons' education and employment aspirations to a greater extent than their daughters'.

This lack of support was linked in the young women's essays to employment, idleness, and sexual risk. For example, Martha wrote:

> Honestly, Dr. Frances, I ask you to look for a way to help me to achieve at least a higher level of education. I think you know how tempting it is for youth to stay idle. I have tried to join various groups to run away from such temptations. For example, I have joined the choir group and also learned sewing.

Although the essays made a number of connections between idleness and temptations, it was during the focus group discussions with some of these students in 2001 that this link was expanded to include explicit references to sexual risk for young women. Vishawishi, my former students argued, may refer to sexual temptations when a man and a woman are strongly attracted to each other, but it is the temptation to have sex with men, especially with men who can provide school fees, desirable commodities, or simply a "good time," that places young women from poorer families at risk of contracting HIV/AIDS. These views were conveyed during the following exchange about the reasons why young women have higher rates of HIV infection than young men:

> *Erick:* They like to have fun. They are deceived by men who give them all kinds of things, provide all kinds of fun. However, that man who her gives her a good time is also the one who infects her with the virus.

> *Rita:* Her friends have the ability to buy things, but she can't. So when she's given these things, she's content. But every now and then they [young women] get the virus.

> *Question:* OK, but *why* do young women have a higher rates of AIDS and . . .

> *Erick:* Young women like to look good. A man can have one girlfriend, but if a young woman is not satisfied by the things she gets from him, she goes to another man. If she gets someone who can buy her more [things] than this one, she leaves him and goes to the next. (Focus Group Discussion)

The belief that young women are particularly motivated to exchange sexual favors for material gain was a common perspective among the female and male participants in the focus group discussions, but this gendered sense of responsibility for HIV infection was tempered by the accusations against older men who "tempt" female students from low-income families (see Mbilinyi & Kaihula, 2000). The young men in the focus groups, in particular, suggested that the older generation poses a far greater temptation for secondary school–age women than do male students, whose pocket money barely covers their own expenses. While young women can get pregnant and infected with HIV from having sexual intercourse with their male peers, it does appear that their health risks are greater with older men: According to the Tanzania Demographic and Health Survey, men above thirty years of age are less likely to use condoms with their partners than are men between the ages of fifteen and twenty-nine (Bureau of Statistics Tanzania & Macro International, 1997). The same survey shows that more than 95 percent of women who have completed primary school know about condoms and about AIDS. However, as one former Njema student put it, "it's like talking to people who are deaf" when one tries to convince young women to forego the immediate, tangible benefits of high-risk sex for the assurance of long-term health by insisting that their partners use condoms. Another participant spoke at length about this dilemma in response to a question about why schoolgirls become pregnant if they know about contraceptives:

> *Ibrahim:* This is a very good question, because those men from outside the school give them gifts. When they are at school, as we said before about life being difficult [maisha magumu], if someone comes from a poor family she's only given bus fare [by her parents]. She gets to the school canteen and others are drinking sodas. . . . If she gets somebody, maybe she just has bus fare, she finds somebody who can give her 10,000 or 20,000 shillings [approximately $8–$18 by 2001] or other gifts. It's easy to be captured in this way and to be lifted from this state of poverty. That's how they find themselves pregnant by people from outside the school, because [male] students are not given a lot so they don't have enough money to give the girls. But the person from outside is not a student and has time to work and get money to give to the girls. And many men from outside the school think that school girls are not affected by HIV because they assume young girls in general are not infected.

Ibrahim's views were typical of others in that he linked temptations to the lack of commodities that others have, including inexpensive ones like sodas and costly items like school fees. Most young people agreed that the material dimensions of maisha magumu, the sense of deprivation relative to others, and the presence of vishawishi in the form of men with money and influence together create the conditions of sexual risk confronting young women from low-income families.

If this is the case, what role can education play in combating the spread of AIDS in communities like Old Moshi? One view holds that the more years a woman spends in school, regardless of social class or family income, the lower her likelihood of HIV infection. The so-called "education vaccine" is thought to operate through cognitive and interpersonal channels: Women who have completed more years of school usually have greater knowledge of methods to prevent AIDS and may feel more empowered to discuss safe sexual practices with their partners (Vandemoortele, 2000). From this perspective, the best way to combat the disease is to send more girls to school and to develop prevention programs based on individual behavioral change (Green, 2003).

The young people in this study, however, questioned the role of education because, as noted above, they see it as "talking to the deaf" unless one addresses concomitantly the cultural and economic reasons why young women are at risk of HIV infection in the first place. Some anthropologists, most notably Paul Farmer (1996, 1999), similarly contend that poverty reduction efforts that target women are the active ingredient in any social vaccine against the disease. Farmer's argument, like that of many participants in this study, is based on the belief that sexual risk cannot be understood without examining inter/national policies, such as SAPs, that affect young people's lives (Simmons, Farmer, & Schoepf, 1996). While education and behavior-change programs can certainly play a role in promoting safer sex, these interventions cannot be the primary prophylaxis against AIDS when conditions of poverty create enormous inducements for low-income women to engage in high-risk behavior. The development of policies that run counter to SAPs, such as reducing user fees at the secondary school level and increasing state involvement in the employment sector, would appear to be the most effective inoculation against AIDS for youth in this community.

Implications for Inter/national Education

This article has attempted to illustrate how an ethnography of policy can deepen one's understanding of the cultural practices and economic conditions that affect policy interpretation at the local level. Inter/national structural adjustment policies rarely attend to local settings unless it is to hail them as sites for cost-sharing or decentralization programs. In contrast, I have examined SAPs by looking at the meanings of terms that convey sentiments about economic restructuring in one rural community in Tanzania. The meaning of hakuna ajira ("no employment"), for example, must be understood within a specific historical, social, and economic context in Old Moshi that links concerns about the privatization of industries and the shrinking civil service to a rejection of agricultural and informal labor by educated youth. Maisha magumu and vishawishi express a similar sense of relative deprivation that structural adjustment policies have fostered on Mount Kilimanjaro, as more goods and services have become accessible for some but not for the majority. In a community that has long been privileged relative to the rest of the country, it is widely believed that government policies are supposed to make life better, not worse, and yet the devaluation of the Tanzanian shilling, the devolution of financial responsibility for education from the state to the local level, and the privatization of government farms and factories have done just that for many families. Although SAPs have created greater economic and educational opportunities for some people, they have generated a sense of frustration among others, especially among those who see more things they cannot afford at a time when educated parents and their offspring feel entitled to them.

What, then, are the implications of this ethnography for the field of education? One of the most important is the need to consider a broad range of issues beyond schools themselves that influence the inequality of educational opportunity. In this study, school fees at the secondary level have an obvious impact on class stratification through education; however, there are also factors that may seem unrelated to schooling that are in fact linked to it in crucial ways — particularly for the poor and the near poor. For people living on or near the margins, anything that makes life more difficult, such as the elimination of agricultural subsidies or the reduction of the price of coffee beans, can push schooling further out of reach. If we want to more fully understand the dynamics of educational inequality, then we must examine more comprehensively the relevance of factors outside the domain of education that bear on schooling opportunities in the United States and abroad.

A second implication of this study concerns the financing of education when government expenditures do not keep up with the growing demand for schooling. The solution to this problem in both the United States and in heavily indebted countries like Tanzania has been to place greater financial responsibility on parents and students themselves. In many countries, this responsibility has been formalized through cost-sharing policies that require students to pay fees to continue in primary or secondary school. In the United States, education at these levels remains largely a public responsibility, but the increasing stratification in the quality of public schooling reflects a de facto cost-sharing policy: Parents' financial contributions through "voluntary" donations and various fundraising activities offset cuts in government funding at schools serving middle- and high-income students. However, schools serving low-income students usually cannot generate the same amount of supplemental revenue, and the quality of children's education suffers. This study of structural adjustment in Tanzania serves as a harbinger of what may lie ahead if cost-sharing becomes the de jure education policy in other countries as well.

Finally, this article highlights the growing importance of ethnographic studies of policy for students and scholars of education the world over. An international perspective on education promotes a deeper understanding of the policies and practices that appear to be national in origin but may, in fact, have been formulated in another country or in an international institution. The distinction between international and domestic education has grown increasingly tenuous in an age when ideas about best practices and sound policy travel across borders at astonishing speed. Ethnography allows one to maintain a focus on the specificity of local and national contexts while simultaneously exploring how international policies affect the "frameworks of cultural meaning" (Levinson & Sutton, 2001, p. 3) of the participants in our research. In this way, one can begin to understand how educational inequalities are adjusted, and ideally alleviated, both locally and globally.

Notes

1. The names of the schools and the individuals in this article are pseudonyms.
2. The term "emic" refers to the point of view of the actors involved in a situation and to their understanding of the events in their lives (Schwandt, 1998).
3. The gross enrollment rate expresses the relationship between the number of children enrolled in primary school relative to the number of children of primary school–age in a population.
4. One ought to view with some skepticism the interpretations of economic "success" based solely on national aggregated data because regional differences often tell a different story (Ponte, 2002). Moreover, data are often inconsistent from one source to the next, as Samoff has demonstrated in his analysis of the education sector in Tanzania (1994a).
5. A likely reason for this abrupt change in policy in Tanzania (and in other African countries) is that the U.S. Congress voted to oppose IMF and World Bank loans that have cost-sharing provisions (Global Challenge Initiative, 2000). Now, by law, the U.S. executive directors at the IMF and World Bank are supposed to vote against loans that require user fees for primary education and health services.

6. For details on the demography and topography of Old Moshi, see Vavrus (2003, Introduction and ch. 5).

7. In the pages that follow, I draw upon the concept of the "educated person" developed by Levinson and Holland (1996) when I discuss local notions of "educated parents" and "educated youth." Levinson and Holland use the concept to explore how historically and culturally specific notions of education become embodied in those who have experienced particular kinds of schooling. In this study, the educated parent refers to a type of educated person with certain dispositions and attitudes regarding their children's education.

8. The third-person singular pronoun in Swahili (*yeye*) does not distinguish between male and female referents. Therefore, in some cases it is difficult to determine whether a person is speaking of a boy or a girl. Throughout this article, I have alternated "he" and "she" as the translation for *yeye*, but it should be noted that gender was not specified in the interviews and focus group discussions.

References

Ball, S. J. (1994). *Education reform.* Buckingham, England: Open University Press.

Bledsoe, C. (1990). School fees and the marriage process for Mende girls in Sierra Leone. In P. R. Sanday & R. G. Goodenough (Eds.), *Beyond the second sex: New directions in the anthropology of gender* (pp. 284–309). Philadelphia: University of Pennsylvania Press.

Bureau of Statistics. (1995). *Selected statistics series: 1951–1992.* Dar es Salaam, Tanzania: President's Office, Planning Commission.

Bureau of Statistics Tanzania, & Macro International. (1997). *Tanzania demographic and health survey 1996.* Calverton, MD: Author.

Cassell, J. (Ed.). (1987). *Children in the field: Anthropological experiences.* Philadelphia: Temple University Press.

Cooksey, B. (2003). Marketing reform? The rise and fall of agricultural liberalisation in Tanzania. *Development Policy Review, 21*(1), 67–91.

Coulson, A. (1982). *Tanzania: A political economy.* New York: Oxford University Press.

Crosby, F. (1982). *Relative deprivation and the working woman.* New York: Oxford University Press.

Dewalt, K., & Dewalt, B. (1998). Participant observation. In H. R. Bernard (Ed.), *Handbook of methods in cultural anthropology* (pp. 259–299). Walnut Creek, CA: AltaMira Press.

Farmer, P. (1996). Women, poverty, and AIDS. In P. Farmer, M. Connors, & J. Simmons (Eds.), *Women, poverty, and AIDS* (pp. 3–38). Monroe, ME: Common Courage.

Farmer, P. (1999). *Infections and inequalities: The modern plague.* Berkeley: University of California Press.

Financial Management Service. (2003). *Treasury reporting rates of exchange as of December 31, 2003* [Online]. Available at http://www.fms.treas.gov/intn.html

Global Challenge Initiative, & Integrated Social Development Centre. (2000). *Year 2000 country profile: The status of Tanzania with the IMF and the World Bank.* Unpublished report.

Green, E. C. (2003). New challenges to the AIDS prevention paradigm. *Anthropology News, 44*(6), 5–6.

Handwerker, W. P., & Borgatti, S. P. (1998). Reasoning with numbers. In H. R. Bernard (Ed.), *Handbook of methods in cultural anthropology* (pp. 549–593). Walnut Creek, CA: AltaMira Press.

Harrison, G. (2001). Post-conditionality politics and administrative reform: Reflections on the cases of Uganda and Tanzania. *Development and Change, 32,* 657–679.

Howard, M., & Millard, A. V. (1997). *Hunger and shame: Child malnutrition and poverty on Mount Kilimanjaro.* New York: Routledge.

Hyden, G. (1980). *Beyond ujamaa in Tanzania: Underdevelopment and an uncaptured peasantry.* Berkeley: University of California Press.

International Monetary Fund, & International Development Association. (1999). *Tanzania: Preliminary document on the Initiative for the Heavily Indebted Poor Countries* [Online]. Available at http://www.imf.org/external/np/hipc/pdf/tza.pdf

Kerner, D. O., & Cook, K. (1991). Gender, hunger, and crisis in Tanzania. In R. E. Downs (Ed.), *The political economy of African famine* (pp. 257–272). Philadelphia: Gordon and Breach.

Klandermans, B., Roefs, M., & Olivier, J. (2001). Grievance formation in a country in transition: South Africa, 1994–1998. *Social Psychology, 64*(1), 41–54.

Komba-Malekela, B., & Liljestrom, R. (1994). Looking for men. In Z. Tumbo-Masabo & R. Liljestrom (Eds.), *Chelewa, chelewa: The dilemma of teenage girls* (pp. 133–149). Uppsala, Sweden: Scandinavian Institute of African Studies.

Kristof, N. (2002, July 5). Farm subsidies that kill. *New York Times*, p. A19.

Kuleana. (1999). *The state of education in Tanzania: Crisis and opportunity*. Mwanza, Tanzania: Kuleana Center for Children's Rights.

Lassibille, G., Tan, J. P., & Sumra, S. (2000). Expansion of private secondary education: Lessons from recent experience in Tanzania. *Comparative Education Review, 44*(1), 1–28.

Levinson, B., & Holland, D. (1996). The cultural production of the educated person: An introduction. In B. A. Levinson, D. E. Foley, & D. C. Holland (Eds.), *The cultural production of the educated person: Critical ethnographies of schooling and local practice* (pp. 1–54). Albany: State University of New York Press.

Levinson, B., & Sutton, M. (2001). Introduction: Policy as/in practice—A sociocultural approach to the study of educational policy. In M. Sutton & B. Levinson (Eds.), *Policy as practice: Toward a comparative sociocultural analysis of educational policy* (pp. 1–22). Westport, CT: Ablex.

Lugalla, J. L. P. (1997). Development, change, and poverty in the informal sector during the era of structural adjustments in Tanzania. *Canadian Journal of African Studies, 31*, 424–451.

Maarifa ni Ufunguo. (2001). *Cost sharing: A case study of education in Kilimanjaro*. Unpublished manuscript.

Maarifa ni Ufunguo. (2002). *A follow up to the 2000 study: Cost sharing: A case study of education in Kilimanjaro* [Online]. Available at http://www.ufunguo.org/csfr/

Mbilinyi, M., & Kaihula, N. (2000). Sinners and outsiders: The drama of AIDS in Rungwe. In C. Baylies & J. Bujra (Eds.), *AIDS, sexuality and gender in Africa: Collective strategies and struggles in Tanzania and Zambia* (pp. 76–95). London: Routledge.

Moshi, C. A. (1994). *A comprehensive report on a local government elections study done in Old Moshi East Ward-Moshi Rural District in September/October 1994*. Unpublished report.

Moulton, J., Mundy, K., Walmond, M., & Williams, J. (2002). *Education reforms in Sub-Saharan Africa: Paradigm lost?* Westport, CT: Greenwood Press.

Mramba, B. P. (2002). *Speech by the Minister of Finance Honorable Basil P. Mramba (MP) introducing to the National Assembly the estimates of government revenue and expenditure for the financial year 2002/2003 on 13 June 2002* [Online]. Available at http://www.tanzania. go. tz/humanf.html

Mundy, K. (1998). Educational multilateralism and world (dis)order. *Comparative Education Review, 42*, 448–478.

National Bureau of Statistics. (2003). *Integrated labour force survey, 2000/01, analytical report* [Online]. Available at http://www.tanzania.go.tz/humanf.html

Nyerere, J. K. (1962). Ujamaa: The basis of African socialism. In J. K. Nyerere (Ed.), *Ujamaa: Essays on socialism* (pp. 1–12). Dar es Salaam, Tanzania: Oxford University Press.

Nyerere, J. K. (1967a). Education for self-reliance. In J. K. Nyerere (Ed.), *Ujamaa: Essays on socialism* (pp. 44–75). Dar es Salaam, Tanzania: Oxford University Press.

Nyerere, J. K. (1967b). Socialism and rural development. In J. K. Nyerere (Ed.), *Ujamaa: Essays on socialism* (pp. 106–144). Dar es Salaam, Tanzania: Oxford University Press.

Peet, R. (2003). *Unholy trinity: The IMF, World Bank, and WTO*. London: Zed Books.

Ponte, S. (1998). Fast crops, fast cash: Market liberalization and rural livelihoods in Songea and Morogoro Districts, Tanzania. *Canadian Journal of African Studies, 32*, 316–348.

Ponte, S. (2002). *Farmers and markets in Tanzania: How policy reforms affect rural livelihoods in Africa*. Oxford, England: James Currey.

President's Office. (2004). Macroeconomic policy framework for the plan/budget 2004/05-2006/07. [Online]. Available at http://www.tanzania.go.tz/pdf/MACROPOLICY_ FRAME_2004_Prx. pdf

Reimers, F. (1994). Education and structural adjustment in Latin America and Sub-Saharan Africa. *International Journal of Educational Development, 14*, 119–129.

Rugumisa, S. (1989). *A review of the Tanzanian economic recovery programme*. Dar es Salaam, Tanzania: TADREG.

Samoff, J. (1994a). Responses to crisis: (Re)setting the education and training policy agenda. In J. Samoff (Ed.), *Coping with crisis: Austerity, adjustment and human resources* (pp. 219–266). London: Cassell.

Samoff, J. (with S. Sumra). (1994b). From planning to marketing: Making education and training policy in Tanzania. In J. Samoff (Ed.), *Coping with crisis: Austerity, adjustment and human resources* (pp. 134–172). London: Cassell.

Samoff, J. (1999). Education sector analysis in Africa: Limited national control and even less national ownership. *International Journal of Educational Development, 19,* 249–272.

Schwandt, T. A. (1998). Constructivist, interpretivist approaches to human inquiry. In N. K. Denzin & Y. S. Lincoln (Eds.), *The landscape of qualitative research* (pp. 221–259). Thousand Oaks, CA: Sage.

Setel, P. (1995). *Bo'n town life: Youth, AIDS, and the changing character of adulthood in Kilimanjaro, Tanzania*. Unpublished doctoral dissertation, Boston University.

Setel, P. (1999). *A plague of paradoxes: AIDS, culture, and demography in northern Tanzania*. Chicago: University of Chicago Press.

Shore, C., & Wright, S. (Eds.), (1997). *Anthropology of policy: Critical perspectives on governance and power.* London: Routledge.

Simmons, J., Farmer, P., & Schoepf, B. G. (1996). A global perspective. In P. Farmer, M. Connors, & J. Simmons (Eds.), *Women, poverty, and AIDS* (pp. 39–90). Monroe, ME: Common Courage.

Spradley, J. P. (1979). *The ethnographic interview.* Fort Worth, TX: Holt, Rinehart, and Winston.

Stambach, A. (2000). *Lessons from Mount Kilimanjaro: Schooling, community, and gender in East Africa.* New York: Routledge.

Tripp, A. M. (1997). *Changing the rules: The politics of liberalization and the urban informal economy in Tanzania.* Berkeley: University of California Press.

Turshen, M. (1999). *Privatizing health services in Africa.* New Brunswick, NJ: Rutgers University Press.

UNAIDS. (2001). *AIDS epidemic update: December 2001* [Online]. Available at http://www.unaids.org/epidemic_update/report_dec01

UNICEF. (2000). *Tanzania 2000 annual report.* Unpublished document.

Vandemoortele, J. (2000). *Absorbing social shocks, protecting children and reducing poverty: The role of basic human services* (Staff Working Paper EPP-00-001). New York: UNICEF.

Vavrus, F. (2003). *Desire and decline: Schooling amid crisis in Tanzania.* New York: Peter Lang.

Vavrus, F. (2004). The referential web: Externalization beyond education in Tanzania. In G. Steiner-Khamsi (Ed.), *Lessons from elsewhere: The politics of educational borrowing* (pp. 141–153). New York: Teachers College Press.

Wagao, J. H. (1990). *Adjustment policies in Tanzania, 1981–1989: The impact on growth, structure and human welfare.* Florence, Italy: UNICEF.

Walford, G. (Ed.) (2001). *Ethnography and education policy.* Oxford, England: Elsevier Science.

Walford, G. (2002). When policy moves fast, how long can ethnography take? In B. A. U. Levinson, S. L. Cade, A. Padawer, & A. P. Elvir (Eds.), *Ethnography and education policy across the Americas* (pp. 23–38). Westport, CT: Praeger.

Woodhall, M. (1994). The context of economic austerity and structural adjustment. In J. Samoff (Ed.), *Coping with crisis: Austerity, adjustment and human resources* (pp. 28–39). London: Cassell.

World Bank. (1994). *Tanzania: Agriculture.* Washington, DC: Author.

World Bank. (1999). *Tanzania: Social sector review.* Washington, DC: Author.

World Bank. (2001). *Tanzania debt relief* [Online]. Available at http://web.worldbank.org/WBSITE/EXTERNAL/NEWS/0,,contentMDK:20035067~menuPK:34460~pagePK:64003015~piPK:64003012~theSitePK:4607,00.html

I would like to thank Lesley Bartlett and Priya G. Nalkur for their insightful comments on earlier versions of the manuscript and for their support during the review process.

Women and Education in Eritrea:
A Historical and Contemporary Analysis

ASGEDET STEFANOS

In 1961, the Eritrean people launched a national liberation struggle in response to Haile Selassie's unilateral incorporation of Eritrea as part of Ethiopia. In 1970, a group of Eritrean activists formed the Eritrean Peoples Liberation Front (EPLF), which became the predominant organization to shape and forge the war of liberation. This struggle was enormously successful in mobilizing and uniting the Eritrean people. In 1993, against great odds and without the sponsorship of a major world power, Eritrea gained its national independence. Early on, the EPLF asserted that the liberation struggle must take the form of a national democratic revolution and took steps to establish forms of democratic organization in the liberated areas.[1] In addition, the EPLF claimed that there was an interrelated need for both national independence and an egalitarian social revolution and that the former could not be attained without pursuing the latter. In 1974, the EPLF made a major decision to admit women into its ranks and to mount a comprehensive series of policies to foster women's emancipation[2] in the society as a whole.

During the contemporary period (1961–1997), Eritrea and Eritrean women have been undergoing massive social changes. This article explores whether and to what extent Eritrean women have been achieving emancipation, and, if so, what role education has played in that process. It assesses the changes that have occurred for women in the realm of education, during the armed struggle and after national liberation, by examining systems of schooling and learning opportunities — both formal and nonformal — available to women, curricula and pedagogical methods, and supports to promote the EPLF's stated goal of gender equity in education.[3] This assessment of women and education in contemporary Eritrea draws from the policies, programs, and commentary of Eritrea's political leadership and, in addition, from the perceptions and experiences of a diverse sample of Eritrean women, who were interviewed in 1983 and 1997. In a Third World society, particularly one undergoing major social change, the impact of education on women can be grasped only in the context of evaluating conditions in other realms of their lives, including family life, the economy, and politics.[4] Consequently, this article analyzes these other spheres, par-

Harvard Educational Review Vol. 67 No. 4 Winter 1997, 658–688

ticularly when developments within them have affected how women have responded to educational reforms.[5] In addition, it discusses whether the dynamics of the revolutionary process itself have facilitated or burdened the political leadership's campaign for gender equity in education and women's capacity to pursue opportunities for schooling and learning.

The analysis of women and education in Eritrea during the contemporary period needs to be situated in a broader historical context. Accordingly, this article provides an overview of the general social condition of Eritrean women and the forms of learning and degree of educational access available to them in both the period of pre-colonial traditional society and the eras of Italian (1889–1941) and British (1941–1952) colonialism.

Women and Education in Eritrea in Traditional Society and Under Colonial Regimes

Before and during colonialism, Eritrean women's status was severely subordinate in educational and sociopolitical spheres. However, Eritrean women's dependent position was not static. Depending on the particular contradictions posed by changing socioeconomic and political conditions, women created spaces for themselves within the existing structures to gain some degree of cultural and social autonomy and self-determination.

The history of women's education in Eritrea demonstrates that broad social factors and specific developments in education that were relatively emancipatory for men — liberating them from natural, social, or ideological restraints — often have had quite different, and even opposite, effects upon women. These disparities between women's and men's experience were rooted in the social forces that systematically created obstacles for women's educational equity.[6] For example, under the Italian colonial regime of the 1940s, Eritrean women, in contrast to men, did not significantly partake in the educational and economic expansion of the period.[7] Those women who found access to learning and urban employment got locked into the informal sector of the economy, turning domestic duties into economic activities. A major reason for the separation of the sexes in education was the colonialists' disregard for women and for their productive capacity. This stance reinforced the prevailing indigenous system of gender inequality in education.[8]

Eritrean Women and Education in Traditional Society

In traditional Eritrea,[9] women's status was established within two distinct semi-feudal socioeconomic systems — agricultural and pastoral — and two conservative religious value systems — Coptic and Muslim.[10] For both sedentary highlanders and pastoral semi-nomadic lowlanders, the family was a crucial unit of learning and cultural activities.[11] The family was hierarchical, patrilineal, and authoritarian, with strict sexual and generational divisions of labor.[12]

Traditional formal education was established for religious purposes. Secular education can be generally characterized as informal and nonformal education. Traditional learning patterns reflected the agricultural and pastoral life of Eritrea, and were suited to the needs of the people; education fitted the young for their roles in communal life. Skills and crafts were handed down, along with traditions, customs, and knowledge of the complex system of rights and duties that ordered the society. Education was usually rounded-off by initiation ceremonies or "regimental" training, marking the young person's entry into full adult status. Thus, traditional Eritrean education was functional and utilitarian with respect to the social and economic roles women and men were called upon to fill.[13]

Religious education, controlled by the Coptic Church for the Christian highlanders and by the Mosque for the Muslim lowlanders, tended to buttress the political and social preeminence of men. The aim of this education was to prepare males for religious vocations and, in a few cases, for secular occupations that required literacy. Clerical authority was supportive of the upper-rung social groups and conservative in its view of women's place in society. Theological schooling for girls was not deemed worthwhile because women were always excluded from the ecclesiastical hierarchy and from temporal duties of governance in their communities. The majority of Eritrean women remained nonliterate.

Girls received much of their education from their mothers, who focused on the "sacramental" duties associated with being a wife and mother. Women's exclusion from public roles and the strict sexual division of labor determined that girls needed to learn skills directly connected to household management, child care, and health care. The early training of either Christian highland or Muslim lowland girls also focused on a limited range of religious activities and the social codes of "proper" family relationships. They learned to be courteous and subordinate, and to defer to males, even those younger than themselves. They came to expect that, once they became matriarchs, they in turn would accrue power and status over younger female household members.[14]

Within the family, women were given chief responsibility for household management. At the young age of five or six, daughters began to assume an array of tasks, such as caring for siblings, gathering firewood, carrying water, milking sheep and goats, pounding dried grains for brewing, and churning milk into butter. Women also learned various crafts, including spinning cotton, weaving baskets, and decorating household items and their homes.[15]

Early marriage meant that most girls would leave their homes before becoming of significant labor value to their families. The future bride was selected by the groom's parents with an eye to the continuity of the family's lineage (bearing male heirs) and proper household management. Girls often married well before puberty, as early as ten to twelve years of age. Once married, the young bride acquired further training under the tutelage of her mother-in-law.

In the predominantly agrarian society, women participated actively in the economic sphere. Eritrean Highland women were essential to the economy, farming the land along with men. They cleared acreage, weeded, harvested, winnowed, tended livestock, and ground grain into flour. Despite their active economic role in agricultural production, Highland women's status was subordinate to men's within the rural economy. Men were the sole owners of agricultural produce, and the fruits of their wives' and daughters' labor was their undisputed property. Men made unilateral deci-

sions in the distribution of surplus produce and had total control over formal barter-
ing transactions.

By contrast, female labor was not necessary among the nomads, who raised only cattle, and women were under significant subjugation. The constant movement of the
family in search of pastures meant an isolated and rough existence for women. They
were totally secluded and covered up while traveling on camel back, and then restricted
in a small tent at a temporary campsite where they prepared the family meal, pushing it
under the tent for the men of the family to eat. These nomadic women's activities consisted of building the frame of the hut and staying out of sight in it except to care for
small children, while men moved around freely with their cattle and sat in the open air
socializing with other men. The complex interaction of ecological necessity and Islamic
religious laws resulted in a stark asymmetry between the sexes.[16]

Eritrean Women and Education during Colonialism

Eritrean educational institutions under Italian colonialism had a pattern of deliberate
exclusion of females and sex-differentiated schooling. Beginning in 1889, the Italians
introduced a capitalist economy, heavy taxation, and expropriation of land, which increased pressure on men and women alike. When men migrated to cities, women
were left behind in the rural areas.[17] Usually only males were employed in the cash
crop plantations and in mines and urban factories. Thus, women were excluded from
the cash economy and were dependent on men.

Under both Italian (1889–1941) and British (1941–1952) colonialism, there was
no effort to educate or develop the skills of women, since it was considered unnecessary to secure political domination and economic exploitation. In addition, Western
patriarchal conceptions of acceptable sex roles contributed to different educational
opportunities for boys and girls.[18]

Italian colonialism brought limited modern education to Eritrea — male Eritreans
received education up to a fourth-grade level.[19] A handful of state vocational schools
were established to train boys as noncommissioned officers, artisans, clerks, male
nurses, and plantation workers. There were also Catholic and Protestant missionary
schools, which largely excluded females, that were designed primarily to garner
Eritrean converts, and only secondarily to train subalterns for the colonial administration.[20] Post-primary education was minimal, since the Italians were concerned
that higher education might inculcate in Eritreans an anti-colonial outlook.[21] After
almost sixty years of Italian colonization in Eritrea, only a small, predominantly male
segment of the population could claim rudimentary schooling,[22] and only a minority
with "assimilated status"[23] were given the opportunity to pursue their education.

Generally, the British were less stringent than the Italians in restricting educational opportunity. They oversaw a notable expansion of schools in villages and
towns. The rewards of schooling were visible, and Eritreans' desire for education increased rapidly. They began to enter white-collar professions as teachers, lawyers, entrepreneurs, and newspaper reporters, fervently taking advantage of the new educational programs. Nevertheless, these limited educational opportunities were largely
reserved for males.

Both the secular and missionary educational systems constructed by the Italians and British shared characteristic features of colonial education. They negated Eritrea's history and culture and claimed that history began with the civilizing presence of colonialists.[24] Placing no value on Eritrean customs and institutions, they introduced European standards of behavior and general outlook into the educational system. This pedagogical bias was the "de-Africanization of nationals."[25]

In the shift from traditional to colonial education, two factors remained constant: females were generally denied access to formal schooling, and educators sponsored deliberate patterns of sex-differentiated roles. Education, even literacy, was not considered useful for women as they performed their daily tasks.

The few schools established for girls were run by missionaries. Curricula focused on general literacy education and on subjects that upheld the stereotypical role of women, with home economics as the principal subject. The schools' curricula included domestic duties such as sewing, embroidery, and cooking. Learning these skills constituted a girl's vocational education and socialized her to become an industrious and obedient woman.

A major component of missionary schools for girls was the promotion of converts and implanting religious principles in Eritrean families by turning girls into Christian wives and mothers. While most Eritrean women had little or no chance for wage-earning, schooling for girls was valued by all because it could provide a better opportunity for securing husbands who had good educational and economic standing. An unmarried educated and/or Christian woman's choices were limited to joining a convent and working within a missionary structure as a single woman. Some women married fellow male converts or evangelists.

In large part, Italian and British rule exacerbated Eritrean women's economic subjugation and reinforced their exclusion from education. Increased economic activity in the urban areas and Italian land confiscation brought a migration of Highland men out of the rural areas. This shift of men from working on farms to work on cash crop plantations and in mines and urban factories placed additional pressure on women in the rural areas.

Women, who never were property owners, were also excluded from the cash transactions and technical innovations of the modern sector, since only Eritrean males engaged in business activities. This exclusion also increased women's economic marginality. Colonialists' cultural prejudice and patriarchal biases led them to ignore Eritrean women. Not having access to wage employment, women could not learn the new skills that paid jobs offered. Thus, conservative Western conceptions of gender roles and capitalism's sexual division of labor were grafted onto existing traditional features of Eritrean women's subordination. The result often combined the worst elements of these diverse forms of gender inequality.

When women moved to the urban areas that arose with colonialism, job opportunities for Eritreans in the modern sector were far broader for males than for females, and jobs were stratified by gender. In the colonial hierarchy, the Eritrean women held the lowest position — the few girls who had access to training and skills were only prepared for household labor and for the humbler occupations in the modern sector.

In the early Italian colonial period, most families lived apart — men in the cities and towns close to work, their wives and children in the villages. The wives lived on their husbands' remittances, together with whatever subsistence farming they could muster. Normally husbands visited their homes once or twice a year, usually around planting and harvesting season to work on the family plot. Many male workers found this a double burden and ceased returning to their villages, yet continued to send money to their spouses. Many men lived with other women in the city and thus became even more estranged from their wives in the countryside.[26] Some married women in the villages led a miserable and lonely existence under the control of their in-laws. They were mostly viewed as misfits and treated as lowly workers. They were expected to raise their children and to wait indefinitely for husbands who often never returned.

Unlike other European colonialists, the Italians left the traditional family code untouched. Accordingly, abandoned women had no legal recourse. However, the contradictions between the traditional and colonial economic systems inadvertently created possibilities for women. In response to their men's departure to plantations and the city, some women left their villages and went to cities looking for jobs. Also lured to the city were those few women who did not conform to the social norms of the traditional village and were viewed as outcasts — widowed women, women without dowries, and divorced women. The city offered these women wider horizons and a certain freedom to start a new life. Some entered the informal market of brewing, handicraft, selling foodstuffs, and laundry work, while others gradually worked their way into agricultural industries.

By the 1940s, some women began to enter light industrial sectors such as textiles, matches, and coffee factories, where they were paid lower rates than men and endured long hours and harsh treatment. Despite discriminatory wages and unhealthy working conditions, urban employment gave women an alternative to marriage and a chance to earn their own money. Some created opportunities for themselves by turning domestic labor into an economic activity, serving in Italian households as maids, cooks, and nannies. They boarded with Italian families and supported their parents, siblings, and extended families with their wages. Many of them decided to forego marriage in order to lift their family members from poverty, expecting that in old age they would be supported by one of the many relatives they had helped.[27]

Existence in the city enabled some Eritrean women to exercise greater control over their social lives and their choice of male partners. Among these were a group of females who owned and ran bars. While a number of them offered sexual favors to Eritrean and Italian male customers, most were respectable small business women who garnered extraordinary independence and were notable figures in the urban social milieu. They resisted the sexual advances of colonialists, and later on, many actively contributed to the national liberation movement. Generally, the urban areas provided anonymity and a certain measure of autonomy for women who were escaping the control of extended families and the village. It provided women with a rare opportunity to reinvent themselves. Sharing similar experiences, women residing in cities created networks and solidarity amongst themselves. The majority of these women were nonliterate.

Women and Education in Eritrea during
the National Liberation Struggle and after Independence:
Policies and Programs

An examination of both the traditional period and the eras of Italian and British colonialism indicate that education was undervalued and constricted and that Eritrean women in particular were greatly impeded in pursuing schooling and all forms of learning. The contemporary period (1961–1997), which commences with the launching of the war for national liberation, represents a radical departure in that educational resources have been greatly expanded, and there has been a significant break with the longstanding prohibition against women pursuing educational opportunities.

Education was viewed by political leaders as integral to the national liberation struggle, and is currently valued by policymakers as a core element of nation-building. In the view of both the EPLF and the government, the broad educational arena relates to both formal and nonformal learning; to efforts at consciousness-raising, including those that occur outside of schools; and to all opportunities for building skills. The design of and strategy for education is linked to a larger social vision that is egalitarian, responsive to the interests of peasants and workers, independent, oriented to self-reliance, and able to mobilize effectively all human and material resources.

Educational goals and objectives that were pursued during the liberation struggle have been adopted and expanded by the post-independence government. The broad educational strategy has a range of core components. First, there has been an effort to highlight Eritrea's history and heritage, and thereby eliminate the colonized mentality. Second, education has been designed to expose elements of the traditional culture that retard social and economic transformation, such as disdain for certain vocations, religious zealotry, and superstition.[28] There is an emphasis on training people in the scientific method in the study of both nature and society. There is a commitment to ensure that education engages and is accessible to the vast majority of people, rather than to a small, highly specialized elite. Accordingly, nonformal schooling has been given equal status to formal learning; both are seen as critical to developing the resources of the independent nation. In addition, the curriculum is anti-elitist; all subject areas highlight the everyday experiences encountered by students and are rooted in the concrete challenges of local life. The cleavage between mental and manual labor is seen as a false dichotomy that promotes an undesirable divide between exalted thinkers and denigrated laborers. Accordingly, the educational system combines learning with productive work. The pedagogical approach promotes active learning and collective cooperation. Teachers are encouraged to play a role in designing educational materials and to act as co-learners with, rather than transmitting agents to, their students. A great deal of emphasis is placed on peer learning, and students are involved in shaping educational experiences.[29]

In the mid-1970s, the EPLF recognized the need to engage the full and active participation of Eritrean women in the liberation struggle. With this recognition came a commitment that has continued beyond independence to establish educational equity between the genders. Education was recognized as crucial in transforming women and enabling them to redefine their private and public roles. It has been a critical avenue for developing the consciousness of a newly emancipated woman, for disarming the objections of men and mothers, and for providing skills that permit females to operate on an equal footing with males in the reconstruction of Eritrean society.

The strategy for integrating the masses of women into a new educational system included combating the material and attitudinal barriers to access.[30] A fundamental obstacle was the parental view that a girl's only goal was to prepare for and succeed in getting married and that female education was an unnecessary frill or, worse yet, a costly distraction. Aside from notions about male superiority, there was an economic basis to parents' opposition to education for girls: the need for children to help with the persistent demands of domestic and agricultural labor. While some parents anxiously ceded time for schooling to sons, they stiffened when it came to daughters. The EPLF recognized the need for an intensive political education campaign in the liberated areas to confront parental resistance to female education. In mass gatherings and individual meetings, the EPLF's political activists explained to elders and parents the value of making education available to all young people. They noted that gender discrimination in schooling undermined the liberation effort and sometimes sternly criticized those who withheld education from their daughters. The cadres organized communal assistance for those families who relied on their daughter's extra hands, and the school calendar was often planned to minimize interference with periods of peak agricultural activity.

However, once access to education was established in the countryside, girls often lagged behind in their school work, and their dropout rate was high. Parents would often turn up to retrieve their daughters for work "because something unexpected had come up."[31] During the national liberation struggle, the EPLF was not able to block fully such parental interference, but it did work to accelerate its ability to help village girls to move to base areas to pursue their education.

The EPLF's Revolution School, established in the base area in 1980, became a site for advancing approaches to education that promoted female emancipation and reduced male chauvinism. It attempted to combat sexual stereotyping in its structure, methods, and curriculum. At the Revolution School, girls and boys were equal partners in all aspects of school life. Both boys and girls engaged equally in academics, gymnastics, maintenance, cooking, fetching water from the well, and building construction.[32] The integration of both genders into all school activities was considered essential to ensure that girls were able to experience fully an emancipatory environment and to participate in new learning and training opportunities.

In contemporary educational settings, curriculum materials include new images of women, such as handling tools or military equipment.[33] School texts discuss women's relationship with family, their work outside the home, domestic chores, and parenting, eliciting discussion on the value of women's work and their place in society. They note women's achievements in the revolution, including their new roles as combatants, teachers, mechanics, and engineers.

There is little systematic statistical data to measure the impact of the EPLF's campaign to give girls access to school. A 1987 EPLF report indicated that 40 percent of Revolution School students were female — an extraordinary increase from girls' almost total exclusion from schooling.[34] However, there is little doubt that the Revolution School benefited from the singular energy and control applied to it by the Front, and that its achievements on behalf of girls were not representative of schooling throughout the liberated territories or the country as a whole.

With independence, the new government took on the massive responsibility of education throughout the nation and of developing an expanded educational system that continued to promote female emancipation. The preeminence of education as the means to advance national reconstruction and development was upheld. The Ministry of Education's policy guidelines committed the government to compulsory basic education, including instruction in local languages, and eventually ensuring universal access to schooling.[35]

Other Realms: Alternative Venues for Learning by Women

The EPLF and the post-independence government have launched a multi-prong attack on impediments to women's emancipation. This campaign goes beyond reshaping the educational system to engage and be accessible to females. Substantial interventions have occurred in economics and politics, and, to a lesser degree, in the domain of family life. In each of these arenas, interventions from above have opened up a range of opportunities for women to develop consciousness, acquire new knowledge, and pursue skills once unavailable to them. The contemporary leaders of Eritrea view education and learning not as a discrete, segregated activity, but as an integral component of individual and collective socioeconomic initiatives and efforts. Accordingly, one must include women's advances in politics, economics, and domestic life as additional avenues for breakthroughs in female education and learning.

Adopting a classical Marxist perspective, Eritrean leaders have viewed the economy as the decisive realm in which to secure the liberation of the Eritrean masses as a whole, and of Eritrean women in particular. Economic transformation is perceived as key to overcoming the oppressive class relations and impoverishment that have victimized the vast majority of both men and women. It is believed that the mobilization and integration of women into the labor force is essential for successful economic development of the nation. In the leadership's view, women's full participation in economic life as wage laborers helps to dissipate their traditionally inferior social status and subjugation. Accordingly, during the liberation struggle and since independence, a range of interventions to overcome obstacles and prohibitions to women's economic activity have been launched. The national Constitution[36] asserts that women have a right to work in all economic sectors and that the principle of "equal pay for equal work" must be gender-free. A decisive intervention establishes women's rights to own and work the land in the countryside, and for nomadic women to own herds.[37] As a modern economic sector has been revived and expanded during the liberation struggle and since independence, women have gained entry into a range of wage labor fields that under colonialism had been the preserve of men. Females work in rural poultry and vegetable cooperatives and state farms, in quarries and mines, in factories, and as part of maintenance and repair units. They have assumed front-line and administrative positions in the human service agencies proliferated first by the Front, and then later by the government. They have converted unpaid household activities into retail operations by selling foodstuffs, baskets, pottery, and processed hides. Women entrepreneurs, a recent phenomenon, have developed small-scale businesses, primarily in the service and retail sectors, owning and running restaurants, bars, groceries, and clothing stores.[38]

The Eritrean leadership also asserts that substantial interventions to open up the arena of politics to women are necessary if gender oppression is to be addressed and if women are to be mobilized for nation-building. While leaders regard economic rights as the fundamental lever for changing women's status, they have viewed political empowerment for women as key to energizing and guaranteeing the emancipatory process.

Beginning in 1974, women's political mobilization and integration became a major priority of the EPLF. It strove to eliminate the substantial obstacles to women's participation in political activity. During a succession of nationalist efforts prior to the EPLF, women had been relegated to highly circumscribed, marginal activity. The EPLF broke with this legacy. The Front, which prior to this point had been exclusively male, formally welcomed and recruited women to join its ranks as cadre, a step which concretely legitimized women's capabilities to play political roles.[39] In addition, the EPLF proclaimed women's right to vote and to run for office. Local organizers actively criticized men's resistance to this process. Under the EPLF's tutelage, women became a presence and had an active voice in the newly organized village and urban assemblies that were established in liberated regions.[40] One indicator of the political empowerment of women is that, at the point of independence in 1993, they represented 30 percent of the Front's membership.[41] However, despite its sustained push for inclusion of women in the political arena, the current government (and the EPLF) have never acknowledged a need for females to assume positions within the core national or regional leadership. There were no women in the EPLF's Central Committee and currently only a few women are in high government positions. None are viewed as key players in major policy decisionmaking.[42]

Women's political activism has, nonetheless, given them a major opportunity to exercise new skills. Previously confined to family life, women developed their capabilities as they increasingly spoke in public and participated in shaping group opinions and decisions in the transformed political arena. With their views about public matters now making a difference, women had new incentives to learn about and analyze regional and national issues. These activities were instrumental in breaking women's internalized view of themselves, upheld by men, that they were "naturally" weak, shy, indecisive, and deferential. The taboo on women being forceful and taking initiatives in public was weakened, and men began to face criticism for chastening and disciplining such women as "hard-headed" and "unruly."

A major EPLF initiative was to welcome women into the liberation Army as active combatants.[43] Thus, women gained entry into the independence struggle's highest status and most revered role, which once again broke decisively with male prerogatives, stereotypes, and self-stigmatization. Women had won access to the decisive fulcrum of the national liberation effort.[44]

In the mid-1970s, the EPLF established a women's organization, the National Union of Eritrean Women (NUEW).[45] The Front chose women cadre to head

NUEW and to frame its mission, which was to engage Eritrean women activists at the grassroots levels; to form consciousness-raising groups so that women could break with internalized stigma and become active supporters of the Front's strategy to open up educational, political, and economic arenas to women; and to confront male domination legitimized by traditional and religious attitudes. The NUEW has continued since independence, and its branches have become ardent supporters of government initiatives that specifically abolished male privilege and of policy initiatives that support areas seen as central to the support and development of women, such as education, health care, and child care. Overcoming the initial resistance to unorthodox, militant female cadres, NUEW members entered the cloistered sanctums of women's *wushati* (or women's room)[46] and became highly adept at incrementally organizing cautiously conservative women. The NUEW has vigorously recruited women supporters for the Front and post-independence government that Eritrean male leadership could not have recruited. Nevertheless, while the NUEW has had an independent sphere of activity and significant Front and government support, those in its top ranks have always been selected by the national (male) leadership, which has also defined its overall mission and mode of operation.

During the liberation struggle and since independence, Eritrean leaders have crafted policies and programs that affect the realm of family life. These interventions into the family represent an additional route by which consciousness has been shaped and obstacles reduced that bear directly upon female's ability to gain access to education and opportunities for new learning and skills. Legislation has been enacted that abolishes customary common laws that enshrined male control over women in the domestic realm. Laws were passed that gave women rights equal to men's to choose a marriage partner, pursue divorce, and own family property. At the same time, they have encoded the preeminence of secular law over practices emanating from Coptic Christian and/or Muslim religious tenets that had legitimized women's submissiveness and absolute male authority in family matters.[47] These laws have had an enormous impact on Eritrean women's self-esteem and stature as full participants in family matters, and have also strengthened their sense of themselves as social beings and members of the larger society who are motivated to pursue schooling and educational goals, as well as economic and political interests.

The government has recognized that women are, by custom, singularly and disproportionately responsible for domestic labor and child care, and that these burdens impede their ability to pursue education, learn job-market skills, or fully enter into wage labor. Efforts have been made to lessen women's household work by establishing childcare centers, communal laundries, and flour mills. Attempts have been made to educate men so that they accept rather than block women from pursuing these alternatives to tending to children's needs or domestic chores. At the same time, the Eritrean leaders have claimed that a large-scale development of institutional infrastructure to lessen women's burdens in family life is contingent upon significant economic modernization. This is an example of a classical Marxist orientation that views economic advancement of the masses as the key catalyst for overcoming women's oppression and male dominance. Accordingly, the Eritrean leadership has abstained from pursuing initiatives to directly intervene in male privilege and sexism within the family. There are no educational campaigns to pressure, enlighten, or teach skills to men so that they can perform more household tasks, care effectively for children, or gain new appreciation for daughters. No programs have been created to challenge a culture that frees men to pursue public leisure activities and entertainment with each other, while women tend to their homes separately. Further, the government has been highly cautious in the area of sexual practices that oppress women. It has only tentatively and sporadically questioned customs, such as female seclusion, polygamy, and female circumcision. It seems probable that relatively unchallenged male sexism within family life emboldens fathers and husbands to undercut government-sanctioned drives to expand female access to educational opportunity.

Women's Perceptions and Experiences

Eritrean political leaders' goals and policies for advancing female opportunities in education need to be measured against the concrete aspirations and experiences of Eritrean women. This article seeks to establish a sense of grassroots perceptions and perspectives. A group of Eritrean women were interviewed about their encounters with education during the national liberation struggle and after independence.[48]

These women were drawn from a diverse range of ages, places of birth, ethnic groups, primary languages, religious affiliations, and educational levels (if any).[49] These women saw themselves as participating in the liberation struggle, and were aware of the post-independence government's goal of national reconstruction and development. They shared this perspective with the vast majority of contemporary Eritrean women and men. They represent both cadre and mass participants, the level and status of their activity varies, and there are significant differences in the degree to which they feel connected to (or distanced from) Eritrean leaders and nationally organized political efforts.

These women express the view that the decisive mid-1970s leadership decision to integrate women fully into national liberation and development was essential to insure the success of these efforts. They do not believe that the leadership's commitment to women's emancipation was inevitable, and they give male national leaders credit for this decisive break with the legacy of male supremacy. Genet, a single fifty-year-old civil servant with the Public Works Department in Asmara, says:

> Women's oppression is deep-seated and multifarious. . . . [Eritrean leaders] have embraced "the women's question". . . [which] has given women the opportunity to participate and to fight against their specific oppression. This is an important concession. . . . The [leaders] did not have to do that . . . it is a daring act.[50]

These women define education broadly. When they discuss education, they include both nonformal and formal learning, focus on both knowledge acquisition and skill building, place great emphasis on consciousness-raising activities, and highlight the positive psychological and developmental effects of education as much as its practical benefits. They often depict the revolutionary process itself as a nonformal setting that promoted the intellectual growth of its female participants. These women view education as a core arena in which reforms have had a significant impact on

Eritrean women's gains toward emancipation. They generally regard the effects of opportunities for women in education as more substantial and fundamental than changes in the economy — the public realm viewed as the decisive lever for gender equality by Eritrean leaders. Keddes, a college-educated woman from a middle-class family, characterizes education as "pivotal" in enabling women to pursue new rights and access to female participation in politics and economic life:

> For women, education is a critical measure to deepen their awareness about and to develop the means of change in their personal lives. Also, through the acquisition of training and skills women can successfully move into public life that was previously inaccessible to them. I would also say that education is pivotal in transforming the entire society into an egalitarian social system and a productive economic entity.

Many women perceive education as necessary in order for women to recognize and understand the nature of their oppression and to overcome self-stigmatization and, thereby, to embrace and participate in emancipatory efforts. As Asma, a thirty-four-year-old Muslim woman from a peasant family, describes:

> Education [is] the major element in the creation of a new Eritrean woman. Education helps [women] to understand the need for that change, thus empowering us to become major protagonists in our own name.

Yelsu, a thirty-year-old Coptic Christian woman from one of the Highland regions, couples the depiction of education as the key to women's social liberation with the guarantee it provides that children — the future of the nation — will pursue educational advancement:

> Education of women is the sure way to promote the social position of women . . . but it [also] equips them to impart their knowledge and training to the children they bear and raise within the household. So the next generation would grow up with new attitudes and values.

Time and again, these women reflect on how their participation and achievements in education were unimaginable until the reforms advanced by the Eritrean leadership. They note the scarcity of learning opportunities available to girls, the economic pressures that prevented their participation in schools, and the traditional beliefs and attitudes against women's intellectual development. Leila, an ex-combatant from a nomadic peasant family, notes that in her village "it was unthinkable for a girl to be sent to school" or attain rudimentary literacy. Women from towns and cities indicate that there, too, girls who pursued schooling were extremely rare.

Women place great value on the institutionalization of a curriculum open to both genders in all its dimensions. They depict the constraints that had been previously placed on female students. Senayit, a thirty-eight-year-old front-line medic, states:

> Before, there was a differential between females' and males' educational goals. Girls who remained in school were urged to take home economics and homemaking courses. . . . I had wanted to study the sciences. I dreamed of being a doctor. . . . There was no way I could do this in the [traditional] school system.

A reformed pedagogical approach that focused on lessons drawn from everyday life and concrete experience, rather than on rote textbook learning, greatly benefited female students, who had been steeped in the detailed narratives and ruminations of an oral culture. Some women indicate that schools' inclusion of collective manual labor as part of the educational experience and equal regard for both intellectual and physical activities also benefited females, who even more so than males had been traditionally restricted to and associated with manual tasks.

Many women characterize education (and revolutionary activity in general) as a "great awakener" that has catalyzed enormous growth in both understandings of self and of a larger social landscape. Twenty-six-year-old Mamet, a former member of the Eritrean Liberation Army, says:

> There is no yardstick to measure the revolution's influence over my life. Now I have better understanding about myself and others. . . . Before I came here, my interest in life was geared exclusively towards family affairs. I did not know anything about my country and the world beyond.[51]

Zewdi, a thirty-six-year-old Catholic single woman from a working-class background, says:

> I have undergone immense changes since I joined EPLF [and] because of . . . my academic achievement. . . . Today I can understand about my surroundings and about the world. My horizon has broadened.[52]

Emancipatory reforms for females in education are linked with interventions to achieve gender equality in the economy and politics. Senayit observes that the introduction of a gender-equal curriculum could not benefit females if the job market had remained rigidly segregated by gender: "[Gender-based curricula] reflected the sex-segregated labor force where women received lowly jobs and were easily dispensed with. Girls were [routed] into vocations such as secretaries and seamstresses." Sarah, a forty-five-year-old college graduate who holds a professional position at the Ministry of Culture, notes: "Because of the limitation of women's role [in the economy], women did not have the incentive to continue their education."

The Eritrean government regards economic modernization as the key factor in enabling females to fully access education. National leaders believe that once the nation has the financial capability to develop and distribute education resources and families have greater economic well-being, girls will be able to take fuller advantage of new educational rights and opportunities. In contrast to this official view, the women interviewed generally regard male dominance and sexist attitudes within the family as the major impediments to females' accessing and utilizing the reformed educational arena. Time and again, they delineate how traditional family beliefs and practices block female participation in schools and learning. Although they recognize this as a manifestation of patriarchy — the rule of the father — they note that mothers have helped reinforce the tenet that education is unnecessary and undesirable for girls.[53] Leila, a forty-year-old married Muslim woman, relates:[54]

> My father had some education but my mother did not go school. My parents felt that a girl should learn from her mother how to be a good housekeeper, mother and

wife, and the man will take care of the activities outside the home. In fact I was told the Prophet Mohammed has said that women should concern themselves only with family activities. So, it was unthinkable for a girl to be sent to school.

Twenty-two-year-old Rishan states:[55]

> When I was a little girl, villagers had a tremendous curiosity and enthusiasm for education. The elders used to accept contributions from farmers and request that the Italian administration establish schools, but it was to send boys not girls . . . [by saying] contemptuously that "a female will always remain a female so why waste time educating her." Women have never been seen as having the ability to cultivate their minds.

Mamet agrees: she says that even in the urban areas, parents always feel conflicted about sending their daughters to school. Interviewees stress that families' opposition to female education is rooted in their view that the priority for daughters is to help mothers with domestic chores and to be trained and socialized to become obedient and dutiful wives. Families have viewed education as a source by which girls can become defiant and morally corrupt. Yelsu explains:

> With better education girls may refuse to marry the men who already have paid the dowry; scholastic ambitions might tempt girls not to give their full attention to their "proper role" as wives and mothers; higher education may instigate giving up one's culture and the traditional status accorded childbearing; and, moral danger arising from imported values and new ways of life. . . . [My parents felt] they were being very liberal by allowing their daughters to go to school in the first place. However, as the girl gets older, they worry she may be interested in boys and before it is too late they consent to the first eligible suitor who appears. In my own case, they insisted that my education had improved my chances for a superior husband and that they could not understand why I rejected him. They kept saying, "but he is from a good family, educated and well-off." They felt that I could not get a better suitor than him.

Given the weight that respondents place on the patriarchal family's traditional resistance to females' access to education, they are extremely heartened by the reforms in education that include pedagogical approaches that challenge male students' sexist sense of superiority, and that allow boys opportunities to work and study alongside girls.

Women's Perspectives on Other Realms for Learning

When the women interviewed discuss national policies to achieve gender equality in realms other than education — the economy, politics, and family life — they note and value the increased power and material benefits that females won through these reforms. At the same time, they stress that the emancipating policies in these realms also provided women with additional educational opportunities to develop knowledge, consciousness, and skills. Keddes readily links women's new economic rights to own property, till the soil, sell products, and be wage laborers to changing relations with their husbands: "She can be an independent person rather than an appendage to a man." She couples female economic emancipation with the broader endeavor of women gaining a "foothold [into and] . . . learn[ing] the skills of public life." She then asserts that to achieve all this, "a women needs to have . . . education. Schooling would enable a woman to know what is possible and to acquire training and skills." Many respondents often note the intellectual growth that occurs as women encounter new work opportunities. As Yelsu states: "Access to employment enabled women to gain not only personal earnings and economic security, but it also broadened their horizons towards new experiences and ideas that were previously inaccessible to them when they were isolated in their homes." These women stress that intensive education and consciousness-raising have been key in making men more accepting of female economic equality and in motivating women to pursue new economic opportunities. As Sarah says:

> Some conservative rural villages have accepted the notion of women's right to own land. But this happened after conducting a long and arduous political education and discussion with the entire village community and not the least with women themselves.

Leila describes vividly how things have changed for women:

> [When I was young,] it was forbidden for women to plough the land and engage in all kinds of activities like selling grains or vegetables . . . [our] society does not find it acceptable for women to do these things. [It] is considered an insult to her husband. . . . Even if she is an able-bodied women and her husband is sick or she becomes widowed, she has to hire a field hand to do this specific job. This rule is something that no woman would dare break for she will be an outcast. . . . Now [women] are doing all these new things. We [women] are opening our eyes to a new way of life. Even our husbands are open to these new ideas. I only hope it remains like this when the war is over. . . . I like it better this way.

To these interviewees, women's full and equal participation in politics is a critical milestone in the movement toward gender equality. They often speak of their newly gained political understandings and activity as eventually producing a consciousness about their own oppression as women and the need to overcome it. Zewdi notes that, when joining the Front and commencing political activism,

> all I wanted is [to] stand on equal grounds with the enemy and avenge the misery and devastation it has brought to our people. I learned that there were other dimensions to struggling for national liberation, that we need to eradicate other types of oppression in our midst. There is prejudice, poverty, and illiteracy and there is also gender oppression. [Eventually] I ma[de] the connection between my political and my personal oppression. . . . Now, I consider it a bonus to exercise my rights, not only as an Eritrean but also as a woman.

Women embrace their admittance to the army because it not only allows them to exercise their patriotic fervor and desire for national liberation, but also because it is a decisive "testing ground" to demonstrate that their skills and tenacity are equal to men's. As Sarah explains, "in the course of the liberation struggle, no women fighters have deserted . . . whereas there were many men who deserted."

These women often see political activism as yielding more than political gains. To them, it also empowers women and creates a consciousness that females are able to forge their own destinies. Yelsu says that "the emancipation of women is not something that will be handed to us. We should earn it, through our own struggle." These women recognize that women's political participation results in enhanced power, but they also value political work because it also gives females opportunities to learn and to acquire new skills. Genet explains:

> [As a top political organizer assigned to a rural village,] I find my work challenging and gratifying because I relate with different types of people and their issues. . . . [I] have a chance to upgrade [my] skills. . . . There are new issues and challenges that one runs into all the time. I am always learning.

The NUEW is perceived as guarantor of women's political space and its organizers are viewed as uniquely capable of opening other women's eyes to the nature and need to overcome female oppression. As Mamet relates:

> We can go to inner sanctum of women's *wushati* and talk to them. It's even better to have a meeting . . . there, because they become very animated and direct. . . . And joining an all-female organization does not violate their sense of propriety. . . . Through the local [NUEW] chapter, women can participate [fully] in public life.

The interviewees place great value on interventions to foster gender equality within family. As Genet notes, "women's oppression has thrived . . . in the privacy and quiet corners of people's homes."[56] Respondents credit the new egalitarian laws about marriage, family property ownership, and divorce with giving women privileges and autonomy that were once the exclusive preserve of their men folk. At the same time, they stress that new, more emancipated family dynamics help women to speak up for themselves and to expand their abilities. Women now share with men decisions about family budgets. They have greater voice in planning children's (male, as well as female) futures. They speak of a whole range of familial discussions and decisionmaking that their spouses now engage in with them "where there is respect for each other's views." Women who are widowed and divorced describe how egalitarian family laws enabled them to exercise new capabilities and rights to raise their children effectively.

Increased Criticism from Below and Indications of Demoralization: Shifts during the Early Post-Independence Years

Fourteen years after the initial interviews, which were conducted during the liberation struggle in 1983 and four years into independence, the commentary of women respondents indicated much continuity in their attitudes and perspectives. All spoke with energy about the successfully waged liberation war, the welcome end of combat traumas and losses, and the myriad tasks and changes occurring since independence. Many have positions integral to national reconstruction, and some are associated with the government or with nonprofit organizations that receive state funding. All speak with pride about their individual participation in Eritrea's struggle for and achievements under independence. Most remark, without regret, that they have participated in experiences and activities that could not have been anticipated, given their gender and, for many, economic background. Many possess an intimate knowledge of regions of the country, ethnic groups, and second (and third) languages that were not connected to their own birthplaces, identities, and upbringings — a form of cosmopolitanism that was rare amongst most Eritreans twenty-five years ago and unimaginable for its constricted and cloistered females.

Nevertheless, the interviewees are generally far more critical of and pessimistic in 1997 about the Eritrean leadership's efforts toward gender equality and women's emancipation than they were in 1983 in the midst of the liberation struggle. There are more indications of bitterness, charges of bad faith, and evidence of alienation and demoralization. Ironically, many look back on the liberation war as "a better time" for women's rights and empowerment — "when we were living most heartily." Even so, these harsher appraisals do not just focus on the years since independence, but also on the decades of the liberation struggle itself. The respondents' critical commentary focuses on general aspects of Eritrean women's condition and does not concentrate in particular on female access to and pursuit of education. However, their insights are suggestive of how and why the drive to create gender equality in the educational realm may be losing momentum.

A large number of respondents characterize women as experiencing a range of difficulties and encountering frustrations and disappointments. They believe there is a resurgence of male reactions against women's gains during the liberation struggle and that Eritrean leaders either minimize this phenomenon or do not regard challenging it as a major priority. Eritrean women believe that the government's predominant focus is on economic modernization and that it has displayed a tendency to regard women's emancipation as a side issue or distraction. Many of these critics believe that leaders point too readily to disappointments in current international financial aid or the low levels of national resources as a rationale for why there is waning momentum for women's advancement. They assert that their leaders have long overvalued large-scale economic development as a contingency for gains in gender equality. These women have a revisionist view (often amending their own earlier appraisals) that during the liberation struggle there were gaps in the Front's pursuit of women's emancipation and that, with independence, for a variety of reasons, these deficiencies have intensified.

A large number of women are critical about what they regard as the government's relative abandonment of women activists — particularly those who were combatants in the liberation army. In the view of those women interviewed, the condition of the vast majority of female cadre is not an "insiders" issue. They regard the status of former women fighters and society's regard for them as a reasonable indicator of how the masses of Eritrean women — and the struggle for gender equality — are faring in post-independence Eritrea. Female members of the liberation army were largely rural peasants and working class (in contrast to the small number of female cadre who served in administrative noncombat positions, who were more educated and came from families with better economic circumstances).[57] While these respondents feel that all Front activists — both men and women — have not received as much care as they deserve, they feel this tendency has been harshest on females in general, and military personnel in particular.

They note that women fighters often had little or no education prior to joining the struggle, and that while many attained literacy during the liberation years, their further education was stymied by the imperatives of war. Many developed new skills during the struggle, but they were inadequately developed and are not well matched to the peacetime economy. Further, unlike upper-level female noncombatant administrators, the women fighters have few networks among men, which are critical to advancing in post-independent Eritrean society. To its credit, Eritrea has undertaken a massive demobilization of its army, recognizing that modernization is the work of civilians and that a permanent mobilization can undercut economic and political development. However, a significantly greater percentage of women than men have been demobilized[58] and this has accelerated the difficulties of former female members of the liberation army. As Sarah relates:

> The [demobilized] women have few marketable skills . . . they live a miserable and impoverished life. They come and tell me that "you were right, we should have looked out for ourselves and acquired some education and useful skill. All we thought about was contributing to the revolutionary effort. Perhaps we were duped." Now, you see them in terrible shape, poorly clothed, unhappy, with *madia*[59] on their faces, walking the streets of Asmara.

Some respondents believe that women cadre faced covert and unsanctioned disaffirmation during the liberation years. They do not view this as having been imposed by male Eritrean leaders, but as a manifestation of chauvinist attitudes among Front members that were not effectively challenged either by the leadership or by women themselves. Noting that no women combatants ever achieved the three highest officer ranks in the army, Keddes said that the effect was to keep women locked in the ranks or lower leadership roles that, ironically, required more physically demanding activity:

> It meant women combatants had years of carrying heavy weapons and supplies, climbing difficult terrain. They sustained multiple injuries and eventually their performance stagnated or declined because age catches up on you. Even though there have been many skilled female combatants, they never rose beyond the rank of *hailee*[60] — we hit a "glass ceiling." We were told that the promotion required a higher level of training and educational background. Of course many of the females were peasants, who became literate after they joined and did not get beyond sixth-grade level of education. Due to their upbringing, they were viewed as having tremendous ability to withstand the physical hardship of guerrilla fighting. So the men said women were put where their labor is needed most. However, this was an excuse, since these factors do not limit peasant or working-class men from acquiring high status.

During the liberation struggle, many women activists had much exposure to a collective life, which despite its gaps in gender equality allowed women to work and live side by side with men, to perform tasks formerly reserved for males, and, in many instances, to have their effectiveness judged without bias. As they often say, "the revolution was a great equalizer." In this context, they abandoned the subservient and diffident stance that women had traditionally assumed. In today's civil society and economy, these women are often penalized for their "emancipated ways." Discussing demobilized women, Rishan notes that they often

> cannot get a job, because they are discriminated against. Even when they seek jobs like waitressing or store clerk position, employers say "we want women who have pleasant smiles and look appealing." [More traditional] women break their gaze and smile, and can put up with occasionally verbal abuse from male bosses and co-workers. Whereas these women know their rights and expect fair treatment. So they are shunned.

Many parents of women activists have begun to castigate them for going on a wayward path and abandoning cherished traditions during the years of struggle. A number have one or two children or are childless, which is condemned as a symptom of failure. Many women note that there is currently a notable "conservative backlash" in civil society against "liberated females." For example, in towns and cities, there has been a resurgence of elaborate weddings, and women are returning to traditionally feminine dress and finery. Symbols of women's delicacy and submissiveness have regained renewed acceptability as well.

Women respondents also characterize a current resurgence of men's supremacist attitudes. They assert that Eritrean leaders have reduced their commitment to organized mass education and consciousness-raising around gender issues and that this emboldens men to behave chauvinistically. They believe that this trend is marked among many men who were active during the liberation struggle. For example, they note that the divorce rate among Front members is over 35 percent.[61] While some of these divorces can be viewed as an indicator of modernity, respondents believe that they are predominantly initiated by men, who pursue younger women as partners and largely abandon responsibility for the children from their first marriages. These women believe that one aspect of the "women's liberation" is that men have embraced open forms of irresponsibility that used to be condemnable. As Keddes explains, "now that men have no monopoly over family property, they believe it is alright to leave a woman outright and then, only through the goodness of their hearts, would they assist former wives in raising their children."

Analysis and Conclusion

The twenty-three year collective effort in Eritrea to address longstanding female oppression in general, and to eliminate women's exclusion from education in particular, has had substantial successes. Statistical data demonstrates that women have achieved significant access into the contemporary educational system that has developed during the past two decades. For example, in 1992–1993, 45 percent of primary school students and 28.5 percent of high school graduates were female. In addition, there were 3,085 women teachers representing 37 percent of elementary, 17 percent of middle, and 10 percent of high school faculties.[62] The magnitude of this achievement is appreciated when it is contrasted with Eritrea's traditional and colonial epochs, when women's involvement in education was viewed as largely unnecessary and undesirable. Nevertheless, while women now participate as students, teachers, and, to a lesser extent, policymakers, they are still in the minority. Further, after initial breakthroughs and successes, there is evidence of a leveling off of effort and success, as indicated, for example, by persistently high dropout rates for females and the government's inattention to the factors that promote that trend.[63]

National leaders have adopted comprehensive and creative policies to promote gender equity in education, which suggests the authenticity of their effort. During and after the liberation struggle, government officials have defined broadly the components of education, focusing not only on formal schooling and youth, but also on nonformal educational efforts, adult education, and on-the-job training as core elements of the new educational system. This has been advantageous for women, who have needed many and flexible opportunities for learning to overcome the diverse obstacles that had marginalized them historically. Nonformal educational programs have insured that, as women gain entry to education, it is not just a small, privileged minority who have become involved and that major deficits, such as pervasive female nonliteracy, are addressed. Adult education programs are available to the many middle-aged and elderly females who shouldered much responsibility for liberating the nation and stabilizing its independence. Adult education has also helped win parents' acceptance of the merits of schooling and their daughters' rights to become students. The official emphasis on consciousness-raising as a core component of education has been vital in motivating females to pursue educational opportunities and in lessening male opposition to gender equality in this realm. Educational policymakers' attention to skill development, and not simply to the acquisition of knowledge, has helped women grasp the relevance of education in enriched, concrete terms, in contrast to previous generations, who were led to view women's schooling as, at most, a transitory stepping stone to a more desirable husband.

The interviewees in this study testify to the efficacy and accomplishments of the contemporary effort to emancipate Eritrean women from the constraints that kept them from getting an education. They describe the radical departure of current educational policies from the legacy of female exclusion from schooling, delineate the manner in which institutional supports have facilitated their pursuit of formal and nonformal learning, and marvel at their significant individual advances in knowledge and skill. These women place great value on educational reforms undertaken in the context of a broad, far-reaching national campaign to overcome their oppression. They believe that their participation in new educational programs has often been catalyzed and strengthened by their involvement in the realms of politics, the economy, and domestic life. They are a living testimony to contemporary gains in educating women. From adolescents to grandmothers, from peasants residing in remote regions to inhabitants of the capital city, from those who have recently attained basic literacy to those who have attended college — Eritrean women collectively demonstrate an impressive level of intellectual curiosity, analytic adeptness, and confidence in the value of their own perceptions and opinions. They address a range of issues — national economic policies, power dynamics in local political organizations, the intricacies of male chauvinistic practices, the transmission of internalized stigma from mother to daughter, the effects of sexual mores — that were literally unimaginable as topics for women two decades ago.

I found evidence in my analysis of government documents, national newspapers, meetings with public officials, and 1997 interviews with Eritrean women that there is currently a loss of momentum and, perhaps, a reversal in the movement to fully integrate women into public life, including education. The majority of women are concerned and somewhat skeptical about the government's ability to sustain a commitment to advance women's rights and status. They note that leaders are increasingly preoccupied with economic development. They see evidence that high-level officials believe that to pursue vigorously "the women's question" distracts from the collective unity and sacrifice required for modernization. Women suspect that leaders are ceding a need for them to return to more traditional roles in order to stabilize a massive reconstruction effort. For example, respondents believe the government is complacent in not implementing the kind of infrastructural supports — such as daycare centers and laundry and cooking establishments — that are particularly vital to facilitate women's participation in educational, political, and economic activity. Women activists consistently place far greater emphasis than do government leaders on the need to aggressively confront male sexism and privilege within the family and the cultural beliefs that legitimize female subordination. The current official focus on economic development is viewed as intensifying the government's relative disengagement from the cultural struggle around women's emancipation. In addition, the rapid decline in mass consciousness-raising activities is viewed by women as a major setback in efforts to enhance women's self-esteem and to reverse male chauvinism. The interviewees believe that the government's posture has the effect — even if not intended — of lending support to a conservative backlash within society against gender equality and "the new emancipated woman." The social organization and culture forged within the Front during the liberation struggle allowed female and male members to live and work together in a way that was far more egalitarian than gender relations in the larger society. Respondents poignantly characterize women cadre as increasingly ostracized in public and private life, and view the government's inattentive support of former Front members, particularly females, as contributing to their isolation and demoralization.

Official speeches and policy documents demonstrate the government's narrowing focus on economic modernization and a dearth of new ideas and programs to push forward on women's liberation. A female official, selected by the government, who monitors programs directed to women, conveys current official complacency when she asserts that governmental structural interventions to ensure gender equality have been "largely achieved and now it is women's turn and responsibility to move forward on their own."[64]

In my own view, there are significant indications that government policymakers are turning away from an active campaign to eliminate women's oppression. I believe that longstanding weaknesses and fault lines in the Eritrean leadership's pursuit of gender equality have contributed to this shift. First, despite significant advances in the public arena, women were never able to break into the highest rankings of national political leadership, and this was never established as an emancipatory goal. Further, the NUEW has never been a fully autonomous organization. Those in senior positions of NUEW have always been selected by the top male leaders of the government (and formerly the Front), who also have defined its overall mission and sphere of operation. NUEW has never departed from or critiqued the agenda and priorities of the national leadership. The assertion that NUEW funding comes solely from nongovernmental organizations (NGOs) seems more a government strategy to inspire NGO support than evidence that the women's organization has a truly independent financial base. Despite an impressive record of substantial creativity in mobilizing women at the grassroots level, the NUEW has never established itself as an independent player that can pressure policymakers to attend to women's interests. The EPLF's initial embrace of women's emancipation was tied to a strategy to fully enlist marginalized groups into the liberation war. Eritrean leaders' commitment to gender equality has never been fully extricated from this pragmatic instrumentalism, and has thereby been vulnerable, especially once a major component of that commitment — the war effort — was no longer a factor.[65] While Eritrean activists have lessened their theoretical reliance on classical Marxism,[66] this orientation is still influential in the nation's political dialogue, and it systematically demotes women's oppression by making it a condition dependent on more basic social inequities.[67]

Many of the women interviewed discuss how they embraced the national revolutionary leadership, admired its success in forging independence, and were exhilarated by its sponsorship of women's emancipation. They speak of their devotion, their willingness "to hold nothing back and make every sacrifice" to the revolutionary cause. They often note that — given the legacy of women's subordination — females have "a duty" to be extraordinary in their performance and "to pass every test," as Zewdi put it. These themes, which are persistent, suggest that, in some sense, women switched their dutiful allegiance from the father — the domestic patriarch — to the liberating nation and its male leaders. It is understandable that strands of subservience remain in how women have positioned themselves in relation to the contemporary struggle to create a modern Eritrea. In my own view, women's vigorous criticism of the national leadership and its policies signals a major step forward in female assertiveness and independence. While the critical attitudes of these women activists are generated by setbacks to the struggle for gender equality, they represent a maturation of their capabilities and confidence in shaping public life.

Finally, Eritrea's current context and situation — nationally and internationally — promotes obstacles and challenges to a vigorous pursuit of women's rights and equality. The people of the nation have undergone a harrowing and traumatic struggle to achieve peace and independence. There is an understandable yearning for calm, amicability, and freedom from conflict. In this atmosphere, many — including former female activists — are zealously seeking the normalization of everyday life. This can result in a decline in the collective will and interest to pursue arduous battles against forms of female subjugation that have been entrenched for centuries. Even when they suffered from massive exploitation themselves, Eritrean men vigilantly guarded and preserved their dominance over women. Imperial powers chose not to tamper with or challenge these male prerogatives. It has been indeed "a daring act" and enormously courageous that contemporary Eritrean male leaders and women activists made women's rights and equality a major component of their vision and program for liberation and social revolution. In these early years of independence, Eritrea faces the monumental task of national reconstruction within an international political arena and world economy that largely marginalizes Africa and exempts itself from financial support to Third World societies.[68] This creates more pressures to blunt a sustained mobilization against women's oppression within Eritrea — a social struggle that will inevitably generate domestically pronounced tensions and opposition. It will take many more "daring acts" by both national leaders and Eritrean women to push forward the struggle for gender equality.

Notes

1. *"Eritrea: New Society Is Being Born," Eritrea Information, 4,* No. 9 (1982), 12.

2. I have opted to use the term "emancipation," which is defined as a release from oppressive constraints. It is also the opposite of oppression, which is the imposition of unjust restraint on the freedom of individuals and groups. From these definitions it follows that there are conceptual connections between oppression and emancipation. The diverse Western feminist literature on women's liberation does not explicitly define the term, focusing instead on the question of *why* and *how* women are oppressed. However, feminists implicitly outline the concept of women's emancipation by suggesting different strategies to achieve women's liberation. For the purpose of this article, I conceived the term "emancipation" as a process of setting women free from restraint. Emancipation is not viewed as some finally achievable state or situation, but rather as the process of eliminating forms of oppression as they continue to arise. Thus, the domain of women and human liberation is constantly redefined and extended. Eritrean women's emancipation is therefore viewed from a perspective that presupposes a dynamic rather than a static view of society. Because of this, education is viewed as a critical element in changing Eritrean women's self-concept, autonomy, and options to participate in a democratic society. For further discussion, see Asgedet Stefanos, "African Women and Revolutionary Change: A Freirian and Feminist Perspective," in *Mentoring the Mentor: A Critical Dialogue with Paulo Freire,* ed. Paulo Freire, James Fraser, Donaldo Macedo, Tanya McKinnon, and William Stokes (New York: Peter Lang, 1997); Andrew Parker, Mary Russo, Doris Sommer, and Patricia Yaeger, eds., *Nationalisms and Sexualities* (London: Routledge, 1992); Seth Kreisberg, *Transforming Power: Domination, Empowerment, and Education* (Albany: State University of New York Press, 1992); Carmen Luke and Jennifer Gore, eds., *Feminisms and Critical Pedagogy* (London: Routledge, 1992); Albert Memmi, *The Colonizer and the Colonized* (Boston: Beacon Press, 1967).

3. See Rosemarie Buikema and Anneke Smelik, *Women's Studies and Culture* (London: Zed Books, 1993); Ann Diller, Barbara Houston, Kathryn Morgan and Maryama Ayim, *The Gender Question in Education: Theory, Pedagogy and Politics* (Boulder, CO: Westview Press, 1996).

4. For a discussion on the EPLF's and the Eritrean government's education goals, see Ministry of Labor and Human Welfare Report, *Initial Report on the Implementation of the Convention on the Rights of The Child,* (Asmara, Eritrea: Government of the State of Eritrea, 1997), pp. 60–62. In addition, as works in critical pedagogy have pointed out, education can be an important site of ongoing contestation and control. Likewise, resistance theorists indicate colonial struggles are also a rejection of domination and an assertion of self-determination. So, both revolution and education are interdependent in asserting the possibility of human agency, or the belief in the individual's ability to make a difference, to bring about an egalitarian society. See Paulo Freire, *Pedagogy of the*

Oppressed (New York: Continuum, 1970); Michael W. Apple, *Ideology and Curriculum* (New York: Routledge, 1990); Henry A. Giroux, *Theory and Resistance in Education* (South Hadley, MA: Bergin & Garvey, 1983); Paulo Freire and Donaldo Macedo, *Literacy: Reading the Word and the World* (Westport, CT: Bergin & Garvey, 1987); Paul Willis, *Learning to Labour* (New York: Columbia University Press, 1977).

5. The strategy of Eritrean education is to attack the structural constraints to women's access to education. See Asgedet Stefanos, *An Encounter with Revolutionary Change: A Portrait of Eritrean Women,* Diss., Harvard Graduate School of Education, 1988, p. 295; Sheila Parvyn Wamahiu, ed., *Girls' Education in Eritrea,* (Asmara, Eritrea: Ministry of Education and UNICEF, 1996), p. 6.

6. See Jane Gaskell and John Willinsky, eds., *Gender In/forms Curriculum: From Enrichment to Transformation* (New York: Teachers College Press, 1995); Miriam David, *The State, The Family and Education* (London: Routledge & Kegan Paul, 1980).

7. For detailed discussion on women's access to formal education during Italian and British colonial rule, see Stefanos, *An Encounter with Revolutionary Change,* pp. 203–206.

8. Stefanos, *An Encounter with Revolutionary Change,* p. 205.

9. Here, the term "traditional" is used to differentiate between socioeconomic structures that predated colonization and those that took shape during colonialism. Economic development theorists use the term traditional to suggest "backward" in contrast to "modern." They characterize traditionalists as "rural, unproductive, consumptive, uneducated, irrational, uncompetitive, unmotivated, acquisitive . . ." Modern is defined as "urban, productive, autonomous, motivated, literate, rational, punctual, efficient . . ." See David McClelland, *The Achieving Society* (New York: Irvington, 1976, rpt.); Alex Inkeles and David H. Smith, *On Being Modern* (Cambridge, MA: Harvard University, 1974); Daniel Lerner, *The Passing of Traditional Society: Modernizing the Middle East* (New York: Free Press, 1958).

10. There was also a minority of Protestant and Catholic highlanders in traditional Eritrea. Stefanos, *An Encounter With Revolutionary Change,* p. 204.

11. There are nine distinct national/linguistic groups within Eritrea — Tigre, Kebessa (Tigrinya), Belen, Denkel, Sahho, Barya and Beza (Kunama), Ben Amir, and Beja. For a detailed account of the history of Eritrea and its sociocultural groups, see Stefanos, *An Encounter with Revolutionary Change,* pp. 70–186.

12. A people and socioeconomic system that do not fit into these broad categories are the Kunamas. They were both agriculturalists and pastoralists. They did not adhere to a monotheistic religion. Their society followed a matrilineal descent line. Social relations were relatively nonhierarchical.

13. Stefanos, *An Encounter with Revolutionary Change,* pp. 188–197.

14. These expectations were gleaned from my interviews with Eritrean women in 1983. See "Women's Perception and Experiences of Their Personal Status Within the Family," Stefanos, *An Encounter with Revolutionary Change,* pp. 348–353.

15. Women carry singular responsibility for household management. Asma, an interviewee from a peasant background, stated: "I rarely saw my mother sitting down doing nothing. She always worked. The work within the home is solely hers. She prepared the daily family meal, raised her children, and took care of the sick and the old in the family. My father did not perform any duties within the home even when it is not farming season, because tradition did not permit him to do so. [However,] my mother was also expected to 'lend a hand' during planting and harvesting season," Stefanos, *An Encounter with Revolutionary Change,* p. 346.

16. Studies of pastoral societies are comparatively sparse and a focus on women even more rare. In order to have a fuller picture of Eritrean women, the differing structures and experiences of semi-nomadic women should be studied in their own right. Stefanos, *An Encounter with Revolutionary Change,* p. 193.

17. By the 1940s, one-fifth of the Eritrean population was urbanized. See Jordan Gebre-Medhin, *Peasant and Nationalism in Eritrea* (Trenton, NJ: Red Sea Press, 1989), p. 61.

18. Italy, like all other European colonial regimes in Africa, had Victorian sensibilities about women's position within its own society and so was less interested in women in the colonies. For an analysis of colonialists' view of African women, see Fanon's classic analysis of Algerian women's position during French colonial period: Frantz Fanon, *A Dying Colonialism* (New York: Grove Press, 1965).

19. Italians had a separatist and functional view of education for Eritreans, which led them to a policy that government education can only go as far as the fourth-grade level. Kennedy Nicholas Trevaskis, *Eritrea: A Colony in Transition* (London: Oxford University Press, 1952), p. 33.

20. The various Catholic and Protestant missionaries were fiercely competitive among each other, which was aggravated by the fact that in the Highlands, where their activities were based, Eritreans were conservative Coptic Christians who viewed conversion as ludicrous. Promises of schooling and health services were used as major inducements to enter the mission orbit and become a convert. Stefanos, *An Encounter with Revolutionary Change*, p. 203.

21. Trevaskis, *Eritrea: A Colony in Transition*, p. 33.

22. In contrast to a rigid policy of noncontinuation of schooling beyond fourth-grade level, mission schools allowed some Eritreans to pursue their education further. Trevaskis, *Eritrea: A Colony in Transition*, p. 34.

23. Children who were fathered by Italians were conferred Italian citizenship and were permitted to enjoy the full benefit of Italian education in segregated parochial schools. Stefanos, *An Encounter with Revolutionary Change*, p. 204.

24. Trevaskis quotes from an official confidential memo to Italian headmasters by Signor Festa, Director of Education in Eritrea, in 1938: "By the end of fourth year, the Eritrean student should be able to speak our language moderately well; he should know the four arithmetical operations within normal limits; he should be a convinced propagandist of the principles of hygiene; and of history he should know only the names of those who have made Italy great." Trevaskis, *Eritrea: A Colony in Transition*, p. 33.

25. See Asgedet Stefanos, *Women and Education in Guinea-Bissau: An Analysis of Theory and Practice*, Qualifying Paper, Harvard Graduate School of Education, 1981, p. 19. Also, see Amilcar Cabral, *A Return to the Source* (New York: African Information Service and PAIGC, 1973); Donna Landry and Gerald Maclean, *The Spivak Reader* (New York: Routledge, 1996); Homi K. Bhabha, *Nation and Narration* (London: Routledge, 1990); Stephanie Urdang, *Fighting Two Colonialisms: Women in Guinea-Bissau* (New York: Monthly Review Press, 1979).

26. Family life worsened during British and subsequently under Ethiopian regimes: "The colonialists' neglect of the rural areas has caused the disintegration of Eritrean families. Starting from the Italian period, male members migrated to cities in search of work. Years went by before their families saw them and many did not return. Sometimes men decided to move on rather than come back penniless. As the situation worsened, both men and women increasingly began to go further and further away from their homes, to the other African countries, the Gulf states, Europe and the United States." Stefanos, *An Encounter with Revolutionary Change*, p. 371.

27. It was not desirable for Eritrean women to become maids in Italian homes.

28. Traditionally, some occupations were viewed as not "proper." For example, there was a deep-seated prejudice against musicians, singers, leather-workers, jewelry-makers, and blacksmiths. These groups were shunned and intermarried among themselves. Stefanos, *An Encounter with Revolutionary Change*, p. 198.

29. As has been discussed, the barriers for girls to access education had been sturdy and long-standing. Prior to the liberation struggle, nonliteracy among Eritrean women was over 90 percent. Seyoum A. Haregot, *The First Year: Fourth Quarter Report, May–July, 1996* (United Nations Office for Project Services, Second-Phase—Support for Public Sector Management Programme, Project ERI/94/006), p. 33.

30. "Relationship Between Society and School," *Eritrea Information, 5*, No. 3, (1983), 7.

31. "The Revolution School Achievement and Problems," *Eritrea Information*, p. 11.

32. Stefanos, *An Encounter with Revolutionary Change*, p. 298.

33. For example, there were themes of "mother's brigade," "mother's day," or "working-mothers" and the portrayal of women in official iconography "with a gun in one hand and a baby in the other" that were promoted as manifestations of interest in women's issues. However, there was no similar representation of men hailed as images of "fathers work-brigade" or "fathers with a child in one hand and a gun in the other." For a detailed discussion on this, see Stefanos, *An Encounter with Revolutionary Change*, p. 427.

34. "The Revolution School Achievement and Problems," *Eritrea Information,* p. 10.

35. Even though "basic education" (seven years of schooling) has been promoted as a requirement regardless of gender, the government has ceded that it has not created the educational capacity to make compulsory schooling a viable alternative. See Ministry of Labor and Human Welfare Report, *Initial Report on the Implementation of the Convention on the Rights of the Child,* pp. 64–73; Wamahiu, *Girls' Education in Eritrea,* p. 6; Department of Research, *Eritrea: Basic Education Statistics and Essential Indicators 1995/96* (Asmara, Eritrea: Ministry of Education, 1996).

36. See *Draft Constitution of Eritrea* (Asmara, Eritrea: Constitutional Commission of Eritrea, July 1996), p. 19.

37. Traditionally, property and livestock ownership had been an unassailable male prerogative. As the EPLF applied the principle of "land to the tiller" in liberated areas, it distributed land directly to refugees and landless peasants, a vast majority of whom were women. In post-independent Eritrea, the Land Reform Proclamation has provided equal access to female land ownership. See "National Democratic Program" in Stefanos, *An Encounter with Revolutionary Change,* pp. 446–447; *Draft Constitution of Eritrea,* p. 20.

38. The majority of women who are self-employed are found in the service and retail sectors, 38 percent and 39 percent, respectively, while only 18 percent are in manufacturing and less than 1 percent are in commercial farming. Haregot, *The First Year: Fourth Quarter Report,* p. 37.

39. The push for this shift came concurrently from below. Increasingly, in the cities and towns, females — particularly high school and college students — were becoming visible in organized nationalist clandestine activities. For a detailed discussion on women's political participation, see Stefanos, *An Encounter with Revolutionary Change,* pp. 279–285.

40. The Front's campaign for breaking with male political domination was clearly connected to its own needs for active supporters to wage the battle for national liberation under its leadership. The EPLF saw women, along with marginalized ethnic groups, landless peasants, and youth, as naturally more sympathetic to its egalitarian agenda and drive against traditional beliefs that upheld the status quo, than the men who had a grip on local and family privilege and power. For more information about the EPLF's view of gender equality, see Stefanos, *An Encounter with Revolutionary Change,* pp. 274–279.

41. The Minister of Education, His Excellency Osman Saleh, in his Opening Address to the Workshop on Girls' Education, in September 1996, Wamahiu, *Girls' Education in Eritrea,* p. 6.

42. In the executive branch, there are two women out of fourteen ministers — one is a Minister of Tourism and the other is a Minister of Justice; there are four women directors — of Postal and Communication, Central Personnel Administration, Social Affairs, and National Union of Eritrean Women. There are no women as provincial governors. While women comprise 31.3 percent of all government employees, they outnumber men in clerical and custodial services. Haregot, *The First Year: Fourth Quarter Report,* p. 37.

43. Women represented 20 percent of active combatants in 1983 and 30 percent in 1993. The inclusion of well-trained women into the army helped lessen the impact of the vastly larger number of troops under Ethiopian command. International journalists regularly highlighted the numbers and performance of female EPLF fighters as a unique feature in Eritrea's independence struggle. They observed that the Front's iconic imagery of a woman with a gun in hand was not solely a symbol of new female assertiveness and freedoms, but rather a familiar happenstance in areas under Front control. Stefanos, *An Encounter with Revolutionary Change,* pp. 274–279.

44. In interviews, women combatants said that they fought to the death, partly because of what they knew about the atrocities that Ethiopian soldiers inflicted on female POWs. They felt that the sexism of the enemy soldiers made them more determined as fighters.

45. All rural and urban residents were organized into one of "five mass organizations according to social class or groups — women, youth, peasants, workers, and professionals." Stefanos, *An Encounter with Revolutionary Change,* p. 271.

46. Among settled agriculturalists, *wushati* is a small room within the hut that is reserved for women only. Male members older than five are by tradition prohibited from entering this room.

47. See Stefanos, *An Encounter with Revolutionary Change,* pp. 292–293.

48. In 1983, I interviewed twenty-four women in eleven towns and villages in the northeastern and northwestern regions of Eritrea. I returned to Eritrea in January 1997 to do follow-up interviews, and was able to locate eighteen women from my original study and to broaden my sample to eight additional women, some of whom held key positions in the new post-independence government.

49. The interview sample represented an age range of sixteen to sixty-five; single, married, divorced and widowed; Tigre, Kebessa, Denkel, Sahho, Kunama, and Belen nationalities; Coptics, Muslims, Catholics, Protestants, and various African religious orientations; nonliterate to college-level education; political activists and non-activists; peasants, factory workers, medical doctors, and students.

50. During the national liberation struggle, Genet worked as a coordinator of refugee women in the village of Arrarib. She received her elementary education at a Catholic missionary school and had an arranged marriage at the age of fifteen. She subsequently resumed her schooling and got a certificate in business administration.

51. After military demobilization, Mamet invested the $4,000 [in U.S. dollars] compensation from the government in a cotton plantation project. Since the project was not well conceived, she along with many others lost her lifelong investment. She is presently unemployed. Her marriage failed, and she and her two small children are presently living with ex-combatant friends.

52. Zewdi works as a store clerk, after completing her high school level education.

53. As some respondents indicated, occasionally there were mothers and often brothers who were ardent supporters of their schooling.

54. Leila is of Sahho nationality. She and her husband own a gift store in Massawa.

55. Rishan, an ex-combatant, is presently working as a parking lot attendant in the capital city. Her parents are farmers and Coptic Christians from Kebessa. She was in fifth grade when she joined the liberation front.

56. Many respondents described vividly the low status of females within their families when they were children. Asma states, "In the family, a women is not considered an equal human being to a man. She is there to serve him. A father chooses her husband. . . . She is prohibited from leaving the house." Keddes adds, "In our home, our oldest brother assumed the second command to our father. . . . My mother deferred to him. Even my younger brothers had better rights than me. . . . Men do not want women to be independent. Even when they are oppressed themselves, men feel that women are their domain . . ." Sarah, who is from a middle-class urban family, says, "My mother kept careful watch over me. When parents find a girl playing with her brothers, she will be told to go inside the house and sit there or do something useful. If a girl protests, the explanation given by all mothers to their daughters is, 'boys can play and be rambunctious, but a girl must be quiet and stay in the house, and keep busy. Besides, a girl should not expect to be treated equally with boys.'"

57. In post-independence Eritrea, this same group of women currently occupy the mid-level administrative and moderately prestigious white-collar jobs. See Stefanos, "Appendix E: Biographical Charts," in *An Encounter with Revolutionary Change*, pp. *466–467.*

58. Women representation in the military has been reduced from 30 percent to 10 percent. "Of those who were demobilized, only 14 percent had skills that can be translated into employment or income-generating activities." Haregot, *The First Year: Fourth Quarter Report*, p. 39.

59. Facial skin discoloration caused by stress.

60. The military hierarchy starts with being in charge of a *gujelle*, a unit of ten people; then *ganta* (composed of three *gujelles*); *hailee* (three *gantas*); *bottolini* (three *hailees*); *brigade* (three *bottolonis*), and finally *Kefle-Serawit* (three *brigades*). Sarah states "that up to the *hailee* level, the work is physically demanding — one has to be physically fit for a guerrilla warfare, carrying heavy weapons and supplies, walking and climbing difficult terrain. In addition, one has to endure multiple injuries. But, once you become a *bottolini* leader, what is demanded is leadership ability based on your experience and training for strategic plans and supervising ancillary divisions such as medical, economic, and other units."

61. Interview with the director of *BANA* — Eritrean Women War Veteran Association.

62. Haregot, *The First Year: Fourth Quarter Report*, pp. 4–50.

63. In 1997, Mamet provided two relevant examples of government disinterest — the decline in mass consciousness-raising programs to deal with parental attitudes toward female education and the dearth of interventions to lighten domestic labor, which gets relegated to females and promotes removing girls from schools.

64. This same remark was offered by the three women officials who held top positions within the post-revolutionary government.

65. Asgedet Stefanos, *An Encounter with Revolutionary Change*, William Monroe Trotter Institute Research Report No. 33 (Boston: University of Massachusetts, 1996), pp. 72–74.

66. Like most Third World revolutions, Eritrea's approach to women's issues was influenced by an instrumental reading of two well-known texts: Frederick Engels, *The Origin of the Family, Private Property and the State,* ed. Eleanor Burke Leacock (New York: International Publishers, 1972), and V. I. Lenin, *The Emancipation of Women* (New York: International Publishers, 1966). In this approach, moving women into the public sector was viewed as key to solving women's problems. The privileging of the role of production over women's familial relations has been functional to the struggle for national liberation during armed conflict and the drive for economic development after liberation. The appeal for women to fulfill the general needs of the society legitimizes the reproduction of sexual divisions of labor both in the work force and in the home.

67. According to Senayit, recent official theoretical acceptance of a mixed economy "with heavy emphasis on privatization is not advantageous to women, who will have difficulty gaining a foothold in the free-for-all of individual entrepreneurship — where men's longstanding dominance in business will have unchecked reign."

68. Although the Eritrean government does not have any debt to service, its ability to raise funds has been severely hindered by its devastated economy and the overall poverty of its people. Eritrea is one of the poorest countries in the world, with a GDP per capita below U.S. $120-$150, less than half the U.S. $300 average for sub-Saharan African countries. Ministry of Labor and Human Welfare Report, *Initial Report on the Implementation of the Convention on the Rights of the Child,* p. 5.

Black Dean: Race, Reconciliation, and the Emotions of Deanship

JONATHAN DAVID JANSEN

As I drove through the gates of the University of Pretoria, I was already tense. Years of living under apartheid had involuntarily stressed the muscles and sharpened the mind to attack even the slightest hint of racial aggression when entering unfamiliar, White territory. It did not help that the entrance was guarded, as if by design, by one of the tallest buildings on the South African campus — a cold, white, rectangular edifice that dwarfed any soul entering the gates. The two security guards at the "boomgate" approached the car. I felt some relief, as both were Black: "Brothers," I thought. I announced that I was the new dean of education and that I would therefore appreciate entrance through the gates. One of the guards laughed uncontrollably: "Nice one, comrade, I've heard that one before." I burst out laughing, imagining myself in his shoes. I would certainly share the same incredulity if a Black man, coming through the gates of this former bastion of apartheid, suddenly declared himself dean. I went through the motions of filling out the visitor's form, having learned a long time ago that you do not argue with the person at the tail end of an authoritarian system — whether it be a university or a shop or a church. As I moved through the gates, I said to myself, "If I struggle with you, comrade, how on earth am I going to make it with my White colleagues?"

First Impressions: Symbols, Images, Uncertainty

I introduced myself to the vice principal of the university.[1] A wonderful person, I thought, who spoke English (rather than Afrikaans) and appeared quite genuine in his manner. This relaxed me. Together we walked over to the faculty of education, where I would take up the position of dean — the first Black dean in more than 100 years in this faculty.

The walk through the main entrance of the faculty building was riveting, and my tension returned. On the walls hung the imposing frames of four serious-looking White men, all Afrikaners, all former deans. I tried to stare back, wondering how any student, Black or White, could possibly feel welcome and at home under the glare of

Harvard Educational Review   Vol. 75   No. 3   Fall 2005, 306–326

these serious patriarchs. I had to take down these portraits, I thought. All along the corridor — a long bureaucratic hall with little doors, one alongside the next — ran a string of old black-and-white photographs dating back to the early part of the century, including one of the first graduating education classes of the University of Pretoria. In every photograph there were somber-looking individuals, grey and uniformed. Each photograph told a story. One was of the De Lange Commission: A few Black faces betrayed the identities of those regarded in much of the Black community as "sell-outs" and "collaborators" with the apartheid government of the 1980s as it sought, under pressure, to bring minimalist reforms to a crumbling, racist education system. Coming to this White university, was I simply another collaborator?

I had been invited to serve as dean at the University of Pretoria by its new and charismatic vice chancellor, who was determined to transform this former White Afrikaans university into an African institution that was, as he put it, locally relevant and internationally competitive. His vision and commitment created the space and the opportunity for bold leadership in the deanship. In order to make my decision to accept, I had consulted many friends, most of them radicals, then and now. Many of them felt that this was a chance to assist in creating a genuinely South African university rather than let this formidable institution continue as a White remnant of apartheid. Others reminded me, correctly, that I had always insisted I would never work in a White South African university. But surely things had changed, I rationalized. This was a South African university that needed to be transformed to serve all South Africans.

The Role of Emotions

I write about the deanship in terms of the emotional experiences of leadership by a Black person within what was once (and to some still is) regarded as one of the bastions of White Afrikaner power. To me "emotions" signal not a discussion about weakness or pathology, but a vital if neglected component of leadership in organizations. In the literature on leadership, organizational change, and educational reforms, the neglect and significance of emotion are being recorded simultaneously (Beatty, 2000; Fineman, 2000; Hargreaves, 1998; Hochschild, 1983; Maddock & Fulton, 1998). None of this literature, however, deals with emotions and leadership in the context of higher education or, specifically, matters of race and leadership in divided societies. The business and organizational literature still tends to focus on the management of other people's emotions, normally employees (Green & Butkus, 1999). The education literature focuses almost exclusively on the emotional labor of teachers (Hargreaves, 1998). What about deans? What about deans of faculties of education? What about Black deans? What about Black deans in White universities? I begin this writing, therefore, with both a positive impression of the small but growing literature on emotions and a recognition of its limitations.

In describing the process of educational change and the emotions of deanship, I focus on problems of race and gender and their interaction with institutional leadership. I show how correlates of institutional culture — such as authority, *beleefdheid* (politeness), silencing, and the construction of insiders and outsiders — constrain and instruct leadership action. I demonstrate how language functions as a powerful political instrument for restraining change. I conclude by arguing that leadership in such contexts requires constant emotional balancing, even as the task of change is relentlessly pursued.

The methodology employed in this study rests on recordings of critical incidents in my life as dean over a three-year period (July 2000 through March 2003) as dean of the faculty of education at the University of Pretoria, South Africa's largest residential university, with about 40,000 residential students and an additional 10,000 students in distance education programs. This record of events has been composed from direct observation of daily events, participation in meetings, interviews with faculty members, and the reading of university policies in relation to institutional practices.

Creating Initial Zones of Comfort and Authority

With the vice principal, I walked into a meeting of department heads chaired by the acting dean. All White, all men, all Afrikaners. They jumped to their feet to greet me. I encouraged the meeting to continue and left after a few minutes to survey my new office. The meeting with my secretary was most uncomfortable. She was in a state of panic, jumping around as the vice principal introduced me. For a senior Afrikaner woman who had served several White, conservative deans, this must have been most traumatic. Now I was alone, and I knew I had to break the tension. I called her in and encouraged her to tell me how she would like the office organized, and asked how I could best support her in her role as the dean's secretary. Gradually, we both relaxed. In those moments, I realized that I would have to initiate grounds for any *toenadering* (coming together, meeting to reconcile) with my colleagues by creating a non-threatening, nonracial space in which they would feel free to talk, work, and live with their new dean. But my historical commitment to "servant leadership," while workable within the Black university I had just served as dean and vice principal, created emotional and political dilemmas in this White university. Seared into my consciousness as a young boy, I remember watching my father wash the floors in homes of rich White people in Cape Town, working as, in the language of those days, a servant. If I remained true to my commitments and values as a dean, servant leadership would mean sacrificing my time, energy, and emotions for the sake of my colleagues. On the other hand, this was risky and could be interpreted as the Black dean "knowing his place" and being willing to continue servitude in this White institution. I decided to take the risk, but with a high degree of alertness to any possible misinterpretation of my service commitments. Thus, in my interviews with each staff member, I made the point I had made more comfortably in other places: *I am here to serve you.*

During those individual interviews, and in the typical slog of meetings facing an administrator, I realized that to a large extent my fears about the acceptance of my authority as dean were unwarranted. At this university, unlike any other I had worked in, the dean was regarded as a great and formidable authority figure. I found that I was not expected to discuss things; I was expected to pronounce on things. The unbridled power of this university's administration and the efficiency of this cultural system was light-years away from the University of Durban, Westville, where I had worked as academic leader for six years.

A typical example of the cultural differences between the two university environments occurred when I was called on to chair a selection committee for a new faculty member. The selection panel included the union representatives of the academic staff and senior faculty. I listened to the discussions and tried to summarize individual positions around the table in order to formulate a proposal that reflected the consensus of the panel. After a majority of the panel agreed on a candidate, I asked one more time if this person's name could be forwarded to "admin" for appointment. The panel agreed. Then a senior professor caught me completely off guard. "Despite all this," he said, "at the end of the day it is your decision as dean as to whom you would appoint." I was stunned. The question ran through my mind: Why have a committee? I stayed with the majority decision.

My conversations with individual colleagues constituted the richest form of "data" on the institution, on the deanship, and on the possibilities for change. One of my standard practices as dean has been to meet with faculty members to inquire about their current rank as academics, their career goals, and the support they required from my office to attain their personal goals. The interviews were difficult, as colleagues struggled to open up with this stranger in their midst, a Black dean asking probing personal questions about their careers. At the same time, most of my colleagues really appreciated what they said was "the first time ever" that they were asked about their intellectual goals and what they required from the dean to make these goals happen in their lives.

Gradually, my colleagues opened up. Women academics were remarkably consistent as they recollected stories of abuse at the hands of former deans and department heads. A typical story was the following:

> I disagreed with the dean in a meeting. He called me aside and told me that that was the last time I would ever disagree with him again. He also told me that my career was over, and that while he was dean I would never get [a] promotion. Final. I was destroyed, and I learned that you never, ever disagree with your dean.

If this confidence represented one voice among many, I would have considered the possibility that the colleague in question was a difficult person or that the dean in question had had a bad day. But I heard stories like these over and over again, in various forms, during those interviews. I tried to contain my anger at this devastating abuse of women academics (all of them White Afrikaner women). I realized that this was a systematic attack on women, which helped explain why there had never been a woman as dean or department head in this faculty of education's century of existence. It explained the relentless Dutch-Calvinist logic of the Afrikaners, in which the man was responsible to God and the woman to the man, "in subjection." It explained why women simply did not speak in any of the initial faculty meetings until I insisted on such participation. It explained the phenomenon of Afrikaner patriarchy.

Race, Gender, Distance, and Emotion

But there was another revelation that came through during these interviews with women faculty — the difficulty of dealing with a Black dean in private conversations about careers. The White women, with notable exceptions, were very uncomfortable in this private space. They did not appear relaxed, and they sat far away from me at the table. I noticed the distance and discomfort. I searched for explanations even as I conducted the interviews, trying as hard as possible to create a comfortable and relaxed atmosphere. It struck me that this was probably the first time in their entire lives, shaped and molded by apartheid, that my female colleagues had ever occupied space alone in a room with a Black male adult figure, who also happened to be their senior authority in the faculty. All those racist myths, I thought, about pure White women being ravaged by a Black man must have left indelible marks on the consciousness of these colleagues. I realized, in those moments, that the struggle would have to be fought on both sides of the table. My own anger at what I perceived to be a racial and gendered distancing had to be managed, and their fears about racial and gendered stereotypes had to be overcome.

Trust was to become the essential ingredient in relationship-building. I had entered a microcosm of the real-life cauldron of racial reconciliation after apartheid, something that was difficult, messy, emotional, and unpredictable. It certainly lacked the glamour and elegance of Nelson Mandela's celebrated autobiography, *Long Walk to Freedom,* or the triumphant mood of the myriad of publications on the South African "miracle." In my first nine months at the University of Pretoria, it was women academics who gradually began to open up, to share, and to commit to a vision of transformation in which I made it clear that women and Black academics would be readily affirmed in my tenure as dean.

My relationship with Afrikaner men was very different. Some of them simply did not show up for the interviews, despite repeated attempts by my secretary to schedule these meetings. After about a month, this got to me, and I suspected that there might be real racial dilemmas faced by these White men (no more than five) in discussing what inevitably were personal and revealing topics. I decided to call them myself and insist that they show up immediately for the planned interviews. I did not want to use that tone as a dean, but I believed that this situation, bolstered by my intuitive sense that race was the problem, justified my insistence.

The men, with few exceptions, did not open up during those interviews. They were "fine." The fact that they were not publishing was not because they did not know how to do research, but simply because there was no time. My job, I was told, was simply to provide the space and the resources, and they would "get on with the job." It was as simple as that. These interviews were probably the most difficult for me. It was here that I realized that huge emotional and political chasms had to be crossed. The men across the table had all done military service, under compulsion, for the apartheid state. Some, I noticed from their curricula vitae, were captains in the apartheid military. Others were members of a secret society of White men, the Afrikaner *Broederbond.*[2] I had hated these institutions — the visible and the secretive — as my political awareness developed while I was an undergraduate student on the politically charged campus of the University of the Western Cape. Later, as a young teacher in the volatile townships of the rural and urban Western Cape, I witnessed the viciousness of the apartheid machinery in the daily lives of Black people. Now I suddenly felt these emotions awakened as I tried to cross racial chasms in the face of, at best, the quiet hostility of the faculty members. Within months and with my encouragement, some of these reluctant men left the faculty of education, either on early retirement or resignation. They were not going to change, and I was not going to allow them to stagnate; a simple and decent way of dealing with this was for them to leave. Gradually, but after a much longer time than with the women, several of the Afrikaner men also opened up and became centrally involved in the administration of the faculty of education.

From Beleefdheid to Openness

With both Afrikaner men and women, there was another serious impediment to faculty transformation, something called beleefdheid. It is a strange Afrikaans word that probably means politeness, but carries with it a sense of hypocrisy — polite to the extent of being dishonest. The institutional culture, I observed, was averse to public conflict.

How did this problem express itself during my efforts to democratize the faculty of education? After undertaking a strategic review of the strengths and limitations of the faculty, I presented a detailed report to a full meeting of all academic and administrative staff, together with an action plan. The report contained some dramatic, wide-ranging proposals for action, including a one-year forced sabbatical for eighteen young academics to give them exposure to the best universities in the world, and a series of steps to build a more diverse faculty that affirmed Black and women colleagues.

There was, after an hour of presentation, not a single word of critical feedback from this packed meeting. In fact, the few who spoke said simply that "this was fine." I realized there was a problem. I would never know how well or badly I was doing as dean because beleefdheid insists that you do not confront anyone, tradition requires that the dean must be right, and past experience suggested that disagreement with authority could terminate a career. The only opposition I received to my action plan was my suggestion that the portraits of those four patriarchs should come down. But it came in the form of an anonymous letter slipped under my door. This puzzled and infuriated me. I encouraged and looked forward to challenge and criticism, but not the cowardice of anonymous correspondence. I sent the word out on the online bulletin board that such notices were unacceptable in a democracy. At the next heads of department meeting, I bemoaned the fact that the only criticism, though couched in a very *beleefd* manner, was delivered under my door. Halfway through my lecture, the former acting dean raised his hand and confessed, "It was I."

I now was even more determined to change the culture of the faculty by encouraging greater openness. I used the faculty online bulletin, called *Opforum*, to list some provocative ideas for change in the hope that it would stimulate discussion. Nothing happened. I noted this silence on *Opforum*. Very apologetic comments started to come from younger academics, but at least there were grounds for dialogue. I did not evaluate those comments or counter proposals, but simply allowed much of the dialogue to flow. Several comments from the older academics were intensely angry and awkward, representing the opposite of direct, intelligent engagement. It was as if after decades of being shut up, their words were not coming through in the constrained yet challenging manner typical of rigorous academic exchange. I accepted that it would take time to modify these angry outbursts into the kind of critical, informed dialogue that remained riveting in style and content. As new faculty joined from the outside, *Opforum* became a regular site for expressing ideals, for engaging new policies, for challenging the dean.

Faculty Leadership within the Broader Institution

It is one thing trying to change a faculty within a university; it is another matter when the entire institution is steeped in a top-down, authoritarian culture that reinforces and replicates this negative behavior across the campus. The most troubling event in which I participated as a dean at the University of Pretoria was my first senate meeting, the senate being a universitywide decisionmaking body. About 165 persons attended — mainly White, male Afrikaners. A thick agenda appeared; in less than an hour, the meeting was rushing to a close. The chairperson, a fine scholar and a graduate of *Tukkies*, had done what his predecessors had done before: simply list an item and make a decision.[3] There was no discussion, and even when discussion was called for, the audience knew not to engage. One of the issues on the agenda concerned the restructuring of the faculty of veterinary sciences. Although drastic cost-cutting measures and possible staff losses were on the horizon, there was still no serious discussion. I raised my hand and asked, "What is the educational rationale for such a decision in the vet school?" I explained that while the financial rationale was clear, the senate, being the highest academic decisionmaking body in a university, had an obligation to ask questions about the academic basis for faculty decisions. I was clearly out of order, and I sensed that immediately from the silence that followed. There was an awkward fumbling as the chair and the dean of the veterinary school scrambled for explanations outside of the financial calculus that had come to determine so much of what universities in South Africa (and the rest of the planet) do under conditions of managerialism, markets, and globalization. I was tolerated with polite answers. Then something else completely unexpected happened.

A young Afrikaner actuarial scientist, apparently buoyed by this unexpected questioning in the hallowed halls of the senate, started to raise his own series of questions about the restructuring. To put it mildly, he was eaten alive. He suffered a series of aggressive counter-punches from the leadership of the institution. To his credit, he refused to back down. I got the distinct impression that the reason this young professor was so aggressively treated was that he was supposed to know better; he was one of the *volk* and should have known his place in an authority-driven culture where knowledge, wisdom, and the final word rested with his superiors. I could be tolerated as the ignorant outsider — the Black dean who, if challenged, would raise inevitable racial questions about White aggression in this cathedral of Afrikanerdom. This experience, more than any other, made me realize how faculty-based transformation can be impeded and constrained by institutional inertia with respect to critical issues of dissent, democracy, and affirmation.

Black Dean, Public Intellectual

Curiously, as the number of Black academics increased in the first nine months of my deanship, race was seldom mentioned as a problem within the faculty. In fact, it appeared as if the senior staff who stayed were quite eager to appoint Black academics in some of the departments. But the problem of race did surface once in an unforgettable experience. I had always regarded myself as a public commentator on education policy issues and a public critic of racism in any society. So it appeared perfectly natural that when I was asked by a left-wing Dutch journal to write and comment on race and racism six years after apartheid, I would write about my personal observations and experiences. I wrote about the persistent attacks on Black people by White farmers, about the (Black) CNN reporter and her husband who had just been attacked by White policemen, about racial slurs I tolerated every day in the suburbs of Pretoria, about Black children segregated within classrooms of allegedly desegregated schools, and so forth. When the article appeared, in Dutch, I placed the journal on the reading room table where guests waited to see the dean. Shortly thereafter, two of my senior colleagues, both Afrikaner men, came to see me. They had read the article. They were offended by what I had said about Afrikaners. The picture, one colleague insisted, was "one sided" and did not talk about the wonderful things happening among races in the country. Afrikaners were portrayed in a negative way. I was told, politely, that the article needed to be "balanced."

I was left surprised and slightly off balance. I explained that public writing was a matter of personal perspective, that every case cited in the magazine was authentic, that my goal was not to add to the literature on "the South African miracle," and that I write what I like. It was the first and the last time that race ever surfaced in a discussion during my deanship. That article was circulated to all the principals of Afrikaans high schools in the area: Everybody now had a view of the Black dean. I realized then that race and racism, neatly packaged and stored away by reconciliation politics and institutional *beleefdheid*, must be put on the table for frank and honest discussion. As in so many parts of South Africa, we had not worked through the emotions and experiences of racism in ordinary life, in established institutions, in schools or universities or bars or churches. This unfinished business could come back to haunt us.

The Language of Leadership: When Is It Race?
When Is It Language?

If race was not the obvious and explicit dividing line in the faculty, the problem of language certainly had potential to derail transformation. I had not understood, until I came to Tukkies, how deep, sensitive, and entrenched the issue of the Afrikaans language was to the university community, its alumni, and to language activists on the outside. The *laager* was drawn on the language issue by language politics on the outside and changing language demographics on the inside.[4] The minister of education made it clear that, historically, Afrikaner universities were using language (that is, the Afrikaans language) to limit access to non-Afrikaans language speakers (that is, mainly Black students). On the other hand, the changing language demographics within some Afrikaans universities had raised alarms in Afrikaner cultural circles and among prominent academics.

At the University of Pretoria, for example, the most dramatic shift in student demographics was not in terms of race, but in terms of language. By 2001, the sharp increase of English-speaking students (a large proportion of whom were White) on the campus had approached 50 percent, with the university now forced to offer more and more classes in English, in addition to those traditionally offered in Afrikaans. In the faculty of education, this problem was whispered about in the corridors and tearoom but, as usual, seldom directly with the dean. Only once did a senior colleague raise the complaint — as if it were not his own — "*dat die plek verengels*" (that the place is being Anglicized). What he meant was that the increasing number of Black and non-Afrikaans-speaking staff (I had also recruited White English speakers as part of my broad-based strategy for diversity) had changed the language of communication in the faculty. I decided early on not to address the language issue directly, but to allow the changing staff composition to create the new language policy. At some point, of course, the language problem was bound to erupt. And it did so in a most gentle manner.

I was chairing a faculty meeting in which a number of policy issues were being decided on — though not language. The participants in the meeting made various comments and offered feedback almost entirely in Afrikaans; occasionally there were comments in English. I used both languages, though mainly English, at this meeting. An additional problem was that the documentation for the meeting had been written only in Afrikaans. Toward the end of that meeting, in a calm but deliberate way, a Black South African academic, recruited from her graduating doctoral class at Michigan State University, stopped the meeting with these comments, "I am a new member of staff. I am really trying to participate in this meeting and to make a contribution to the faculty of education. But I am finding this very difficult because all the documents and communication are in Afrikaans. I appeal to you to consider those of us who do not understand Afrikaans." A sympathetic silence fell on the meeting, largely because of the kind and gentle manner in which the point was made. I decided not to lead the response from the chair, and to see what happened. Senior colleagues in the room insisted that, as a practical matter, documentation should be produced in both languages and one even insisted that (also as a practical matter) our meetings should be conducted in English only when non-Afrikaans speakers are present. The proposal on dual-language documentation received enthusiastic body-language responses; the English-only meetings, perhaps less so. But this interruption was perhaps the single most important change in the cultural and language direction then taken in the life of the faculty of education.

The language problem will not go away as easily, as this episode might suggest. Since then, I have participated in several national and media-inspired debates on the future of Afrikaans. I still hear quiet grumbling, especially among older staff, about the loss of status of Afrikaans in the life of the faculty. I still wonder why the debate on Afrikaans in the twenty-first century remains so deeply mired in the history of Afrikaner-English struggles, ongoing since at least the 1890s. And I have realized that, despite being a Black dean, my growing competence in Afrikaans creates access to people and politics that I would not have enjoyed without this simple but powerful device.

My most important challenge as dean, though, came in my relationship with the principals of Afrikaans schools. Soon after I arrived, I reorganized the annual School Principals' Symposium, an annual meeting of school leaders from the traditionally White schools around the university. The invitation list was broadened so that the symposium would include a more diverse grouping of principals, including those from the Black schools around Pretoria. In addition, a Black jazz ensemble consisting of former street children was hired to perform the music. The two speakers at the symposium were both English-speaking, from Australia and the United States. I did not realize that this reorganization would cause dissension in the ranks of the Afrikaans principals. As was the custom at the university, none of these complaints reached my office directly — the discontent was shared with my senior colleagues and with the marketing division of the University of Pretoria. Another source of discontent was the concern expressed among some of the school principals that the place was being Anglicized. Indeed, the marketing brochures and the new website appeared only in English. To make matters worse, a member of my staff had sent one of the principals an invitation — in English! The discontent that followed was, again, not raised with me directly but with my colleagues. But not with the Black dean. How was this issue to be approached? These tensions had potentially serious repercussions for the faculty of education.

The school principals sent messages, again indirectly, that they would advise their students against registering at the University of Pretoria since it no longer represented the language and cultural interests of Afrikaans speakers. They would rather redirect their students to the Potchefstroom University for Christian National Higher Education, or to the Rand Afrikaans University, or even to Stellenbosch University in the Cape. This would be disastrous for undergraduate education, since Afrikaans families were the only ones in South Africa that still sent their children to study to become teachers (and ministers). Students from Black families simply had not found teaching attractive as a profession, a perception fueled by violence in schools, retrenchments of teachers, negative images of teaching reinforced by politicians, and the popular television series *Yizo Yizo*, which portrays constant incidents of rape, murder, and dysfunction in township schools. In a very real sense, therefore, the future of the faculty depended on the steady recruitment and enrollment of White, Afrikaans-speaking students. But I did not act on the basis of either veiled threats from the Afrikaans schools (as taxing as this was emotionally) or because of a narrow financial interest in the sustainability of the faculty of education (as attractive as this was strategically). I decided to act on the basis of a simple principle, namely, that all universities belong to all South African students — and that included Afrikaans speakers. My role as dean, therefore, was to ensure that Afrikaans speakers felt as comfortable at the University of Pretoria as any other language group, and I would do my best to ensure this. I started visiting each principal of the Afrikaans high schools, to introduce myself, to present the faculty's commitment to that school, and to inquire as to how our service could be better rendered to the Afrikaans-speaking community of schools. It would be part of a broader set of visits to Black and English-speaking schools.

The anxiety about Afrikaans will continue in my relationship with schools, for it is only generated in part by what the faculty of education does. These concerns are nested within the broader actions of the university itself, as well as the political machinations of government officials who often use the language issue for symbolic "point scoring" in the face of a declining number of Black students passing high school and entering university. But the relationship between a faculty of education and its "feeder schools" demonstrates the emotional dilemmas of a Black dean in powerful ways. On the one hand, I had to recognize the privileged and protected role afforded Afrikaans in the past century, often at the expense of indigenous African languages; on the other hand, I had to promote a public position that encouraged a broader language inclusiveness — even for White Afrikaans speakers. It was often difficult to constrain my own emotions and feelings about language injustice in South Africa (after all, I speak Afrikaans because I was forced to under apartheid). As a dean, these constraints on my emotions have been very difficult to manage, especially when I have felt that language was being used as a proxy for race. In particular, I became concerned that some insiders and outsiders described language as the primary problem of institutional transformation when it was actually the changing racial demographic that really unsettled them.

Black Outsider, White Insiders: Negotiating Authority

If the rules of the game in institutional life were based simply on open and fair participation by all persons, regardless of color, then my life as a dean would be relatively easy. I realized that after I left a room of all-White administrators, I could not always be assured that what was agreed among us would stand after consultation with fellow *broeders* (brothers). It struck me time and again that I was, and for the foreseeable future would be, an outsider.

My outsider status became especially clear when the minister of education decreed that the college of education (Pretoria Teachers College) be incorporated into the university as part of the newly restructured higher education system. The decision by the government to close or incorporate more than 100 colleges was motivated by reports that the quality of teacher preparation at most of these institutions was very poor; that these colleges, as artifacts of apartheid, were irrationally distributed across regions of the country to serve previous racial and ethnic communities; and that the colleges were over-producing teachers at a time when teacher rationing was being pursued to reduce the salary bill to the national government.

Until 2001, colleges were part of the provincial education departments and were therefore regarded, in legal terms, as "a provincial competence." Incorporation would mean that colleges would lose their status (and existence) by becoming part of a university (or technikon) and, therefore, would be classified as "national competence" under direct authority of the minister of education. Before my arrival in July 2000, the University Council and the College Council had already agreed on incorporation for reasons that made rational sense: The two institutions, both White and Afrikaner, had long relationships of working together, they were within a 10-minute drive from each other, and the cultural fit, of course, was perfect.

It was evident to me that the agreements reached before my arrival had several flaws. For example, in letter and spirit, the agreement anticipated the wholesale transfer of staff from the college into the university and, for most of them, into the faculty of education. This created three problems. First, there was a competency problem, since most of these staff were not trained to do university-level teaching and research. Second, there was an equity problem in that the majority of college staff were White and simply bringing them into the university would further hinder the goal of building racial diversity in the faculty of education. Third, there was a financial problem in that the traditionally small lecturer-to-student ratios in a college meant that if the college was reconfigured into a university, the faculty of education would be seriously overstaffed, given the university tradition of one lecturer teaching large undergraduate classes. This meant that as a consequence of the incorporation process, of the ninety-odd staff, only about fifteen to twenty would make the selection process.

Time after time, when I met the university administrators, they not only appeared to understand the problem as I sketched it but they vigorously supported my proposal for taking less staff. I initially was buoyed by the fact that my senior colleagues supported me on this matter. But as soon as I left their offices, the senior college administrators would march in and change the substance of our agreement. Initially I thought I should relent a little, since these processes are always political and involve serious horse-trading among stakeholders. But later it really frustrated me that I could not understand why my seniors would agree with me so vociferously, and then change the agreement. It was only much later that I understood my disadvantage. These were colleagues who had worked together for many years, as broeders, and had forged cultural, linguistic, social, and political ties that were firm and loyal. They attended the same church, served on the administration of the same rugby and sports clubs, and shared *braais* (barbeques) and fishing trips. In addition, their children knew and married each other. My proposals disturbed those racial and cultural ties of the fraternity. Once I realized what was going on, I tightened my proposals for staffing, refused to back down, and sent some strongly worded correspondence to my administration. I am told by several sources that as the position of the Black dean became clear, there were some nasty scenes in which traditional loyalties, racial loyalties, and cultural loyalties were questioned. I understood then, in graphic terms, how the institutional rules were culturally written in ways that exclude some and include others. I also realized that leadership required assertion that challenged those rules, or else the transformation of White universities would remain an illusion of the political class and, more importantly, an impediment to greater inclusiveness.

Black Dean: Affirmative Action Appointment?

Dealing with the university administration and staff was one kind of experience; dealing with students was a different emotional challenge in the deanship. The challenge in the undergraduate class was that more than 95 percent of the students were White, and of this group, almost all were Afrikaans speakers. The reverse was true of the postgraduate class. I have always enjoyed working with students, which explains why I have always taught a class, regardless of whether I was dean or vice principal.

One day, a young staff member asked me whether I would do a guest lecture for her class in comparative education. She mumbled something about my need to meet students and her awareness of the fact that I appeared to be shielded from them. What happened next, seconds before I took the podium, rendered me speechless.

The senior faculty member for comparative education had also decided to attend the class, along with other (I suppose) curious members of the academic staff — since I could not believe they had an interest in the role of symbolic politics in comparative education. The senior colleague introduced me to the students, displacing (by custom and invitation) the person who invited me. She said:

> This is our new dean. Now normally when one meets someone like this, we think of affirmative action and that such a person came in because they are Black. Well, I wish to assure you that this is not the case with this man; he studied at Stanford and is a prolific researcher, and widely respected. You may even have seen him on television. So I introduce to you Professor Jansen.

Until that point, I had decidedly not thought of myself in relation to affirmative action. Now that my colleague had raised the question, I suddenly felt aware of the argument that those bright, White eyes in front of me might very well see me as a special treatment candidate. Even if they did not, the seeds for such thought had been planted among students in this, my maiden lecture. For the first time in my life, I started a lecture not knowing quite what to say. As is so often the case, I had to submerge these emotions for later reflection and get on with the job. I would like to think that the students in that lecture were soon made to forget that this was the dean, or that he was Black, or that he came in through the back door. However, I could not be sure.

Asserting Personal and Professional Authority

Another incident I wish to draw on in my emotional journey as dean in a historically Afrikaner university concerns my relationship with the academic community outside of the faculty of education. I experienced two strains in this relationship with the broader campus. One strain was a strong expression of support for changing the faculty of education. Many of the "education" initiatives on campus, I found, had proceeded as if there was no faculty of education. I pondered whether the law school would allow a major discussion on legal issues to be chaired and led by the medical school or the education faculty. This isolation of the faculty of education, I was told repeatedly, was a result of our own doing. People on the campus felt that education was aloof, outdated, inward looking, and, quite simply, a nonentity in the educational life of the campus. The historical attachment to "fundamental pedagogics," an Afrikaner variant of Dutch phenomenology with a particularly conservative bent, was referred to in derisory terms on the campus. To this group of people, the new dean could rescue education and create new synergies with other faculties and departments. The second strain was a strong expression of hostility toward my leadership within the campus. I noted that there were several senior colleagues on parts of the campus who were decidedly unfriendly, even challenging, of the new dean. Two episodes come to mind.

The first episode occurred when a senior colleague from administration came to instruct me on how to submit annual faculty reports. There was no discussion, simply a statement of "this is what I want you to do." I have always reserved judgment, in initial contacts of this sort, as to whether this was a racist attitude or simply the kind of authoritarian style that this group of people used in communication. However, I perceived this as an aggressive approach by a colleague. In this case, I assumed that both could be true and asked him to leave my office. It was the first time that I "snapped" and let down my emotional guard with fellow colleagues from another part of the campus.

Sometimes my emotions are provoked by a very different kind of encounter that on the surface appears friendly but may carry with it a particularly venomous racism. One of the deans insisted on greeting me with the phrase "my friend." In another time and place, this might be regarded as a genuine, sincere effort to make a new person feel welcome. But this was South Africa, and I had witnessed countless times how in a group where the Black person was a minority, a typical White male greeting would acknowledge everybody else by their first names or titles, and then turn to the Black person with the line, "my friend." It was a distinctly patronizing, offensive practice among White males in South Africa. I have never in my life inside South Africa heard a White man introduce himself to another White man in such terms. The first time my fellow dean used the term I let it slide, not ready so early on to really challenge this provocative racialized practice. The next time, however, I stopped, and in a large audience made it very clear that he would never again address me as his "friend" — in part since I hardly knew him, and in part because I had a name. He never did this again.

Taking the Message More Broadly

My most vivid recollection of the University of Pretoria was in a public lecture. The university holds a regular series of lectures on "innovation," and this typically involves some high-tech motivational speech on the growing significance of science and technology on campus and in the world. I was asked to present and entitled my talk, "Why Tukkies Cannot Develop Intellectuals." I knew this was putting the ideological cat among the long-rested Tukkies pigeons. I also knew that this was a platform to address a broader set of concerns about institutional transformation, such as racism, sexism, authoritarian practices, and their suffocating effect on the development of intellectuals. I seriously thought I would be disinvited, given the title alone. I prepared a written paper, something I seldom do for campus talks or school presentations, because of the time that this takes when you have three or four such invitations every week. But I wanted to think through my experiences and record them, since I hoped the talk could really chip away at the core of authoritarian practices and beliefs that continued to keep the University of Pretoria from becoming a genuinely humane environment for Afrikaner women, Black people, and any person who dared to hold themselves as different from the dominant, White, patriarchal, "Christian" culture. I expected few people to show up for this lecture. The senate hall was packed beyond my expectations.

I argued that intellectuals develop under one of two conditions: severe repression or genuine democratic conditions — neither of which existed at the University of Pretoria. I inquired whether Tukkies had ever publicly acknowledged how its laboratories were used as research sites for the apartheid scientific and military establishments. I suggested that "the only thing worse than being Black at Tukkies was being a woman." For while there was historically a symbolic point at which Black South Africans could claim to have been free, such a moment had never materialized for Afrikaner women. I reported on incidents of student abuse in our authoritarian system and the hypocrisy of religious cover for what we do. I demonstrated that our institutional commitment to change was narrow and instrumentalist, and at odds with building a culture of innovation in which ethics, politics, and values would become the steering mechanisms for moving toward an open, diverse, and democratic learning culture. There was sustained and intense applause. Speaker after speaker acknowledged most of what had been shared as accurate; there were accolades and encouragement. Several noted that this was the first time in their twenty or thirty years that an event like this had ever happened on campus. I did not expect this. My goal was to rattle conceptual and ideological cages, not to be praised.

This was a turning point in my own emotional disposition toward Tukkies. In those moments, I realized that in this large university there was a critical mass of scholars with an acute understanding of the cultural and ideological problems weighing down on the institution — problems that stood in the way of a broader transformation of the University of Pretoria. I also understood, toward the close of the event, that being a Black dean held distinct advantages. I could see and respond to institutional problems from a position that few other colleagues shared. It was an emotional high point, for I sensed the possibility not only of change, but of transformation.

Reflections on Race, Method, Emotions, and Deanship

My initial objective was simply to record my life and experiences as a Black dean at the University of Pretoria. I did not intend to publish this material, in part because I was uncertain of its external and internal reception. As I started to discuss the material with friends inside and outside the faculty, there appeared to be a genuine interest in reading and engaging the experiences represented in this article. With the passage of time, it also became easier for me to talk about these often sensitive human emotions and institutional experiences. What started as a personal and private set of reflections gradually became a public and professional matter. The last objective of this article, therefore, is to describe the complex and difficult process of institutional transformation from records of personal observation and through the lens of human emotions.

In my conceptual frame I place my life, as it were, on the line. I open up to the emotional challenges and struggles of being a Black dean in a White university. I try to show that actions in the deanship are not simply rational and technical decisions, but deeply emotional and political decisions. I demonstrate that these emotions emerge from and are shaped by the very real and recent context of apartheid, with its dual horrors of racial oppression and economic exploitation. I try to shake off innocence by showing that as dean I am not immune to intense personal struggles with change and commitment in the context of a historically White university, or to organizational culture as it shapes and sustains racial and gendered attitudes among staff and students. I have tried not to present either myself or the people I work with as "emotionally anorexic" (Fineman, 1993, p. 9) but as people living through and expressing the real dilemmas, uncertainties, contradictions, failures, and successes of a changing institution and a changing country seven years after the legal termination of apartheid. In declaring my methodological point of departure, I present moments of emotional withdrawal or "backing up," perhaps even silence, but also moments of emotional assertion, perhaps even aggression.

On the one hand, therefore, I am implicated in Hochschild's (1983) disturbing observation that "this [emotional] labor requires one to induce or suppress feelings in order to sustain the outward countenance that produces the proper state of mind in others" (p. 7). On the other hand, I also express moments that Sergiovanni (1992) labels as

> leadership by outrage . . . the practice of kindling outrage in others [that] challenge[s] the conventional wisdom that leadership should be pokerfaced, play their cards close to their chest, avoid emotion, and otherwise hide what they believe and feel (p. 130).

This kind of writing also raises, of course, the issue of ethics. Is it right, in the first place, to write other people's stories? I think this is fairly common and, in the case of people living, it is good methodological and ethical practice to consult them. But this is relatively easy in cases where the stories told are positive ones about personal achievements, such as Reddy's (2000) life histories of Black South African scientists, or heroic struggles such as Lather and Smithies's (1997) account of North American women living with HIV/AIDS. But what if, as in this case, the stories are less celebratory of individuals or even an institution, as captured in this narrative built around critical incidents? I believe that in both cases, but especially the latter, it is important to share the draft writings with the individuals or incidents written about, not only to inform them about the narrative but also to secure their advice and comment in improving or sharpening the story of changes and continuities in a faculty of education. In addition, I have tried not to mention names of specific individuals or list the dates of specific events. At the same time, I believe it is critical to bring into open dialogue the kind of writing and reflection that challenges the status quo, whether in political or methodological terms, as part of an ongoing process of transforming not only how we practice education, but also how we think about and experience it.

The research context for reflection on race, emotion, and the deanship is a very turbulent one. The University of Pretoria, as should by now be clear, is a historically White university with roots in Afrikaner history, politics, and language. It is not only South Africa's largest residential university, but also its wealthiest. It has benefited from leadership by a particularly entrepreneurial vice chancellor with a strong personality and a keen insight that has helped the University of Pretoria enjoy a credible reputation after apartheid. In his terms, the university had to become "internation-ally competitive and locally relevant." Yet, in a memorable phrase, he recalls that "while I might have turned the ship around, it still drifts in the same direction."[5] He has made firm if not sufficient commitments to challenging the racial privileges of the University of Pretoria. He hired three Black deans and one (Afrikaner) female dean. He invested considerable resources in attracting Black doctoral and master's students. And, he has made "employment equity" one of the focal points for change during his tenure. Despite all these actions, he has not been able to transform qualita-tively and substantively the cultural capital with which power is sustained at lower levels in the university. By this I mean curriculum changes, changes in staffing at departmental levels, and changes in the overall institutional culture and practice.

South African universities are beginning to realize that simply changing the struc-tures of an institution is one thing; changing the cultural essence of a university is a completely different challenge. This reflective essay shifts the emphasis from the structural and organizational to the personal and individual; from policies declared to practices experienced; from official intentions to everyday life; from behavior to emo-tions. At the same time, the narrative in this essay shows the interplay between the in-dividual and institutional levels of university life.

Studies on the interaction between race and gender in institutional contexts are vir-tually unknown in South African educational and social research. This narrative not only describes the different roles between White men and White women in relation to the Black dean, but also the changing roles of these three groups as the project of fac-ulty restructuring proceeded. Afrikaner women had a stronger sense of new "space" for their academic advancement through various policy messages from the dean's office. Afrikaner men, for whom ascendancy to departmental headship, and the deanship, was almost a rite of passage, clearly felt a sense of loss in the new deal. What requires further research and reflection in this context is the role of institutional culture in Afrikaans universities as yet another variable in determining gender-race interactions with the Black dean over time (Jansen, 2005). Such a narrative would have to take into account the various traditions served by Black universities, White English universities, and the White Afrikaner universities as outlined in the historic address of Professor Jakes Gerwel in 1987 on the occasion of his inauguration as vice chancellor of the University of the Western Cape in Cape Town, South Africa.

There is still very little written on the complex ways in which race, gender, culture, and history come together to define the possibilities and the limits of change. In this respect, I am very conscious of the fact that while race has been privileged in the ac-count of life inside Tukkies, I am also clear in the narrative that gender is a critical factor in institutional life. The people most threatened by the changes in South Af-rica, and at the University of Pretoria, are White Afrikaner men. Time after time I was told as dean that the changes undertaken in the faculty in fact disadvantaged men. And this was true. For over 100 years women never became department heads in the faculty of education, and now male ascendancy was no longer inevitable. I had announced, several times, that the next dean would be a woman and that 2000 was the last year that there would be no woman as department head. Young and middle-aged men, in particular, were especially distraught that they now had to compete on an even slate with women. Whereas men previously were almost guaranteed top positions, this was now dependent on a fair and equal process that was also committed to affirming women. In this regard, the writings of Cameron McCarthy and others (McCarthy & Crichlow, 1993) offer powerful starting points for understanding the relational terms between Black and White women academics in universities.

In looking back on this written account of my experiences as Black dean, I hope to have made several marks on the growing literature on leadership in education. First, I hope to have shown that in leadership research, context matters. It is the broader context of apartheid, and how it was resolved, that enabled this kind of leader to emerge (I would never have held such a position under apartheid) and that required this kind of leadership to build and then bring together an increasingly diverse faculty. It is not, however, enough to assert that context matters; I hope this narrative shows how context shapes and constrains decisionmaking within the deanship.

Second, I hope to have broken through the decidedly ethnocentric character of research on leadership that holds Western norms and trends as the standard against which to judge particular kinds of leaders and leadership styles. For example, I am not at all sure that Western disillusionment with heroic leaders is applicable in a context that enabled Nelson Mandela to emerge and in which there is little cynicism with, in fact even expectation of, strong and visible leaders. Third, I hope to have shifted the focus from a voluminous literature on school leadership to the relatively sparse research terrain on academic deans as leaders.

Fourth, I hope to have created windows for viewing leadership not as a simple technical, rational, and logical frame approached through a toolbox of finite techniques, but as a complex political and emotional process in which the outcomes are not always predictable and measurable. Finally, I hope I was able to lay the groundwork for further studies on leadership under conditions of social transition. In the context of South Africa's negotiated political settlement, this essay shows that transformative leadership inevitably involves living with and balancing a set of tensions: the tension between affirmation and inclusion, between retention and restitution, between caring and correction, between accommodation and assertion, and between racial reconciliation and social justice.

Notes

1. The vice principal in South Africa is equivalent by rank to a vice president in a North American university.
2. There were often two ways to know that one was a part of this secret society. First, colleagues would volunteer this information and even list this association on their curriculum vitae. Second, it was generally known that no senior position in the academic, corporate, or political world could be attained without Broederbond membership.
3. The University of Pretoria started as the *Transvaalse Universiteits Kollege* (Transvaal Education College), with the acronym TUKS and the affectionate reference, Tukkies.
4. The laager refers to the ways the Afrikaners, during the great movement (or great *trek*) from the Cape colony into the interior during the nineteenth century, would draw their ox wagons into a circle to defend against an attacking enemy. The word has come to take on symbolic meaning to refer to any defensive or inward-looking behaviors of those calling themselves Afrikaners.
5. Johan van Zyl, former vice chancellor, in private conversation with the author.

References

Beatty, B. R. (2000, December). *Emotion matters in educational leadership.* Paper presented at the Australian Association for Research in Education Annual Conference, Sydney, Australia.

Fineman, S. (1993). *Emotions in organizations.* Thousand Oaks, CA: Sage.

Fineman, S. (2000). *Emotions in organizations* (2nd ed.). Thousand Oaks, CA: Sage.

Green, T. B., & Butkus, R. K. (1999). *Motivation, beliefs and organizational transformation.* Westport, CT: Quorum.

Hargreaves, A. (1998). The emotions of teaching and educational change. In A. Hargreaves, A. Lieberman, M. Fullan, & D. Hopkins (Eds.), *International handbook of education change, part one* (pp. 558–575). Dordrecht, Netherlands: Kluwer Academic.

Hochschild, A. R. (1983). *The managed heart: Commercialization of human feeling.* Berkeley: University of California Press.

Jansen, J. D. (2005). The color of leadership. *Educational Forum, 69,* 203–211.

Lather, P., & Smithies, C. (1997). *Troubling the angels: Women living with HIV/AIDS.* Boulder, CO: Westview/Harper Collins.

Maddock, R. C., & Fulton, R. L. (1998). *Motivation, emotions and leadership: The silent side of management.* Westport, CT: Greenwood.

Mandela, N. (1995). *Long walk to freedom: The autobiography of Nelson Mandela.* Randburg, South Africa: Macdonald Purnell.

McCarthy, C., & Crichlow, W. (Eds.). (1993). *Race, identity and representation.* New York: Routledge.

Reddy, J. (2000). *Life histories of Black South African scientists.* Unpublished dissertation, University of Durban Westville, South Africa.

Sergiovanni, T. (1992). *Moral leadership: Getting to the heart of school leadership.* San Francisco: Jossey-Bass.

Teaching Quality Matters:
Pedagogy and Literacy Instruction of
Poor Students in Mexico

FERNANDO REIMERS

In this chapter, I examine a topic inadequately addressed in current discussions about education in developing countries: teaching quality. I argue that teaching quality is important if schools are to help students develop capabilities of consequence to improve their life chances, especially if students cannot develop those capabilities in other institutions. I further argue that we need to think about teaching quality as a complex process, one that incorporates both normative and positive elements and that integrates what teachers do with how students make meaning and understand what their teachers do. The focus of this paper is on the relationship between teaching quality and the literacy skills of marginalized children. In supporting these arguments with empirical analysis of a nationally representative sample of sixth graders in Mexico, I address two research questions: How do variations in the literacy skills of various groups of sixth graders relate to the different circumstances they experience at home? How do their literacy skills relate to the teaching they experience in schools? I conclude that teaching quality, as reported by students, is as related to learning outcomes as parental education and other home advantages. This finding is important: While the intergenerational transmission of educational advantages within families is widely accepted as a sociological and psychological fact, the importance of instructional quality and the conceptualization of teaching quality are not as widely established or accepted.

Much contemporary rhetoric about education in developing countries focuses on the factors that influence student attendance and the attainment of more years of schooling. The Millennium Development Goals, for example, a compact to reduce poverty incidence in the developing world by the year 2015, include two goals explicitly related to education: achieving universal primary education, and promoting gender equality in primary and secondary education (United Nations, 2000).[1] These goals refer only to the targets of access to school and quantitative educational attainment as measured in years of schooling completed. Similarly, the Education For All goals established at the Jomtien and Dakar conferences identify six education goals:[2] expansion of early childhood care, universal access to free and compulsory primary education, access to appropriate learning and life-skills programs, improvement in adult literacy rates, elimination of gender disparities, and improvement in education quality. While quality is acknowledged as a goal in the Education For All framework, it receives significantly less conceptual development than the quantitative targets of educational expansion.

The concern with educational opportunity in developing countries should go much further than the current emphasis on access and completion of a basic education. It should focus instead on how teachers can help students develop capabilities that help expand their options in life. These options refer to pathways to achieve personal goals, thus enhancing personal freedom. They include pathways to maintain health, to secure shelter, to obtain resources and use them effectively, to care for dependents, and to devote one's energies to activities consistent with personal goals and values. These capabilities increase the chances of employment, or of well-remunerated employment, and expand options in life because work and remuneration contribute to obtaining food, shelter, health, and care for others. Enhanced capabilities also provide more choice regarding what kind of work to pursue, thus increasing the odds of making choices consistent with personal goals and values. Similarly, capabilities that enhance political efficacy have similar consequences in expanding personal options. More options translate into more freedom to make choices according to personal goals and values.[3]

Attention to quality of education requires a focus on the intended purposes of instruction, as well as on the processes that help teachers achieve those purposes. I define teaching quality as this dual concern with purposes and pedagogies. Quality teaching is thus the teacher-mediated process that helps students gain the knowledge, skills, and capabilities that are of value in expanding their freedoms and increasing the opportunity to maximize health and well-being.[4] Note that I include the definition of curriculum — that is, the actual instructional goals or standards — as a component of quality, as teachers who are efficient in teaching a low-level, irrelevant, or outdated curriculum cannot be deemed to teach with quality. In this chapter I focus on a single instructional purpose: developing the literacy skills of students. Literacy is a fundamental skill, which provides the foundation for further learning and enables students to access the printed texts essential for further education, for participation in most jobs, and for informed political participation.

To examine the relationship between teaching quality and literacy skills, I analyze student achievement in a curriculum-based language test for a nationally representative sample of sixth graders in Mexico. I look at the relationships among literacy outcomes, parental literacy, and teaching quality, for both students whose parents are literate and those who are the first in their families to read. This choice of focus is intentional. The institutional dynamics of schools are best examined when they set out to do that which only they can do. For example, schools are uniquely positioned to develop literacy in societies where large segments of the population are not literate. More so than the culture of families, the culture of the school is a written culture, one in which children are exposed, many for the first time, to printed words, and are given the opportunity to learn to decode print and understand texts. The ambition to make all people literate is a relatively recent social objective. As a result, in a developing society such as Mexico, it is possible to find many children who are the first in their family to be schooled.

Mexico is unique among Organisation for Economic Co-operation and Development (OECD) countries because it has a much greater percentage of children who have parents with low levels of education, thus providing a good opportunity to study how teaching quality matters to this group. On average in all the OECD countries, 2 percent of 15-year-olds who attend school have mothers and fathers who did not go to school, and an additional 8 percent have mothers and 7 percent have fathers who completed only elementary school. In Mexico, 15 percent of students have mothers who did not go to school and 11 percent have fathers who did not. Thirty-eight percent have mothers who only completed elementary school, and 32 percent have fathers who completed only that level.[5] For comparison, in the U.S. student population, 1 percent of students have parents who did not go to school, and 2 percent have parents who only completed elementary school.

Educational Opportunity: From Access to Quality

In the aftermath of World War II, the governments that signed the Universal Declaration of Human Rights accepted that education was a basic human right in the hope that this would help create the conditions to promote global peace and security. The creation of the United Nations, and specifically of the United Nations Educational Scientific, and Cultural Organization (UNESCO), mobilized significant expansion in access to schools, especially in the developing world. In Mexico, expansion in educational enrollments was twenty fold between 1920 and 1998, and with it educational attainment expanded significantly. Those age fifty-one today have completed an average of three grades of primary school, compared with nine years of schooling completed by those age twenty-five (Reimers, 2000).

As a result of this massive educational expansion, many children throughout the world were the first in their families to gain access to school. It was believed that such access would expand their capabilities, thus expanding their life opportunities as compared with their parents and contributing to improved living conditions of the most socially marginalized. A similar faith in the power of schools to teach children living in poverty and thus to reduce poverty has been at the root of the expansion of educational access and the improvement of quality in a number of countries since the 1950s.

Governments in many parts of the world have supported education in the expectation that it would increase the chances of marginalized children. As part of the Johnson administration's U. S. War on Poverty in the 1960s, the federal government supported significant funding of initiatives to improve the educational conditions of schools serving the poorest children through Title I of the Elementary and Secondary Education Act. On another continent, the Netherlands contemplated transferring resources to schools serving working-class children through the Social Priority Policy in 1974 and the Educational Priority Policy in the 1980s (Driessen & Mulder, 1999). In the early 1980s, the French government, under François Mitterrand, supported the creation of Priority Action Zones (*zones d'éducation prioritaire*), which allowed coordination at the local level of teachers, social workers, health officials, and police officers in delivering integrated services to poor children. The Disadvantaged Schools Program in Australia, launched in 1975, promoted better links between schools and neighboring communities, and focused on the development of basic literacy and numeracy skills. Belgium's Educational Priority Policy, launched in 1991, provided extra resources and support to targeted ethnic minority groups in elementary and middle school. In Britain, Prime Minister Tony Blair supported similar initiatives—the Educational Priority Areas — beginning in 1998. In 1993, the Mexican government initiated a bold education reform that included, among other goals, supporting the learning chances of poor children.

Education Quality Matters

In spite of government claims that education initiatives can expand the chances of the poor, there is ongoing controversy on the tradeoffs between quality and access. Hanushek (1995), for instance, has suggested that education quality is central in expanding the life chances of individuals and that efforts to expand access, therefore, should be attentive to the quality of the education provided. He explains how differences in earnings associated with different levels of educational attainment cannot be simply attributed to the gap in years of educational attainment, as the students who have attained the higher levels of education are also those who performed at the higher academic levels at the lower levels — those performing at very low levels are not able to advance to higher levels (Hanushek, 1995). In a response to Hanushek, Kremer (1995) rebuts, "We have insufficient evidence to conclude that quality should be a higher priority than ensuring that schools are available for more children" (p. 247). The debate is, indeed, ongoing. More recent efforts by development organizations to include quality as a priority are deficient in that the conceptualization of quality is poor, often equated with teacher credentials or student performance on achievement tests.

When studies have tried to examine the impact of quality directly, the results have been mixed. This is no doubt in part because of the inherent difficulties of defining and measuring quality, which lead researchers to take varied approaches and make synthesis challenging. Among the few studies looking directly at teacher practices, some have found very modest relationships between teacher practices and student achievement (Good & Brophy, 1987; Mayer, 1998). Other studies have found that even as teachers' use of higher order instruction improves student achievement, it also increases the gap between more and less advantaged students (Von Secker, 2002).

In contrast to these findings documenting the limited impact of teaching, recent research provides evidence that classroom conditions and teaching do matter. The Tennessee STAR project assessed what happened when children were assigned to different class sizes under experimental conditions. One of this study's findings is that poor and minority children benefited most from studying consistently in small classes in the first three grades (15 vs. 22 students per teacher). Smaller classes allowed teachers to use differentiated instruction (Grissmer, 1999; Nye, Hedges, & Konstantopoulos, 2002). The same study emphasized that a series of educational experiences with good teachers — that is, teachers whose students achieved at higher levels — has important effects on student achievement and that poor teachers can set students back several years. Another large national longitudinal study of complete school restructuring programs found that poor children, when they receive high-quality instruction, can achieve at levels comparable to the national average. This study highlighted the importance of implementation in determining the success of these programs (Stringfield & Datnow, 1998). A recent review of fourteen studies of improvement programs found that better prepared teachers, smaller classes, more integrated schools, and more demanding curricular materials led to improvements in achievement for the lowest performing students (Orfield & DeBray, 1999). Experimental studies of the impact of specific higher-order instruction and peer collaboration find a significant influence on math achievement and engagement among the lowest-achieving students (Ginsburg-Block & Fantuzzo, 1998). Others have found that teacher practices are related to student achievement in curriculum-based mathematics tests in California, and that professional development influenced the development of these teacher practices (Cohen & Hill, 2000). Similar results on the relationship between teacher practices and student achievement have been found in science (Burkam, Lee, & Smerdon, 1997). Emerging research suggests further that instruction emphasizing higher-order thinking skills positively influences student achievement (National Center for Education Statistics, 1996; Stein & Lane, 1996). A study of the relationship between classroom instruction, teacher professional development, and the mathematics achievement of eighth-grade students finds that classroom practices have a greater effect than teacher characteristics, professional development, and student socioeconomic status (SES). The total impact of teacher quality variables is greater than that of student SES (Wenglinsky, 2002). However, most of these studies have been conducted in the United States and there is limited evidence on this topic for developing countries.

Controversial findings about the effects of teaching have initiated ongoing controversies over the power of schools to teach disadvantaged children at high levels. It is not surprising, then, that support for education reform worldwide is focused away from pedagogy and teaching quality. As a result, more than fifty years after the Universal Declaration of Human Rights was drafted, many education systems provide patently unequal opportunities for children of marginalized social backgrounds, as compared with their more advantaged peers.

Literacy Acquisition: The Role of Families and Teachers

Schools share their role in shaping the capabilities of students with families. When children first come to school, they have spent a large part of their most critical developmental years with their families. Once they are in school, families play a fundamental role in shaping their school experience. What families expect of schools, how they understand the role schools can play in helping children develop, what they believe about the institutional objectives of the school are all important factors that mediate the effects of schooling on children. For example, families decide whether to send their children to school at all, at what age to do it, how regularly to allow children to attend school, how much time to devote to school endeavors at home, and how to support the demands schools place on children at home. In sum, families make decisions about how or whether to use their resources, their time, their social relationships, and their money for the purpose of schooling children. These decisions are to a great extent influenced by the resources that families have and by their own school experiences.

When parents or guardians or an older sibling has been schooled, families are in a better position to understand the school culture and thus to make decisions about the use of family resources to support the children's school experiences. Some of these decisions are made long before children begin school. For example, it is known that in order to develop language and literacy skills, it is helpful to engage children in conversation early on and to read to them (Snow, Burns, & Griffins, 1998). Children who grow up in such an environment have a richer vocabulary and are more likely to develop prereading skills, which makes it easier for them to acquire early literacy skills in school (Hart & Risley, 1995; Scarborough, Dorich, & Hager, 2001). Some children in fact arrive in school already reading. But not all families understand the importance of providing children with these experiences, and some lack the skills and resources to provide them; children thus arrive at school with very different levels of preparedness (Dickinson & Tabors, 2001). They continue their schooling careers with different levels of support at home. To sum up, differences at home resulting from the different ways families support the development of preliteracy and literacy skills place children at different levels of preparedness to learn to read.

Mexico offers a rich context in which to examine the role of families in supporting literacy because there is much heterogeneity in the resources and school experiences of parents. Due to the recent expansion in access to education in Mexico, many of the children who begin and complete primary education today are the first to do so in their family. One in five children has at least one parent who cannot read.[6] How does parental literacy matter? What difference does it make to the opportunities of children to become literate, especially when compared to the quality of their teachers?

Research Design

In this paper, I analyze the results of a survey administered by the Mexican Ministry of Education to a nationally representative sample of students in the sixth grade in the year 2000 (Evaluación De La Educación Primaria, 2000). The survey included a curriculum-based test and a series of questions, including aspects of the support they received at home and their perceptions of the teaching they experienced. This survey was administered to a nationally representative stratified random sample of 44,195 students. Students were first given questionnaires about family characteristics and about experiences in school, and then were administered a curriculum-based language test that was designed to cover competency in the language arts curriculum of sixth grade, the last year of the primary school cycle. The test had twenty-five items focusing on reading comprehension.

In the survey on teacher quality, students were asked to rate to what extent they understood their teacher, found the classroom rules to be clear, found the teacher helpful when they did not understand, felt they learned a lot in class, thought their teachers expected them to learn much, and to what the extent the teacher answered their questions when they did not understand. Students could rate their teachers in these dimensions as always/consistently or occasionally/never. Note that 2.6 percent of the students did not answer the question of whether their fathers could read and 3.8 did not answer the question of whether their mothers could read. That is, only 13 percent said explicitly that their mothers could not read and 8 percent said explicitly that their fathers could not read. Those children who did not answer any of these questions will be excluded from the analysis comparing first-generation students to those with literate parents. That is, I will only compare students who explicitly answered the question, and in this analysis each student was given a score equal to the number of questions answered correctly on the test, each question receiving an equal weight in the final score.

Results

The large percentage of students with at least one illiterate parent is a result of recent educational expansion, as children are now afforded opportunities to attain levels of schooling their parents did not have. Based on the school survey administered to sixth graders in 2000 on which this study is based, 85 percent of students said their mothers could read and 88 percent said their fathers could, and 79 percent said both of their parents could read. I will call those who said that at least one of their parents could not read first-generation students, because they express this intergenerational change in accessing school; that is, they are the first in their families to read. For the most part, I will not differentiate between those who have only one literate parent vs. two, or whether the parent who can read is the mother or the father.

Children in Mexico whose parents are literate are more likely to do well on the curriculum-based language test (see Table 1). Student academic performance on the curriculum-based language test increases with each additional parent who is literate, and the advantages of having two literate parents are significantly greater than those of having only one literate parent. The advantage of having one literate parent is 40 percent greater when the parent who can read is the mother. The joint effects of dual-parent literacy are even greater. Students with two illiterate parents correctly answer, on average, 9.68 questions of the 25-item language test, compared to students with one literate parent, who answer ten questions correctly, and to students with two literate parents who answer twelve questions correctly. On this test, the language advantage of students with two literate parents equals about half a standard deviation of the score distribution, which parallels the order of magnitude of differences — between one-half and three- quarters of a standard deviation — in achievement associated with socioeconomic status found elsewhere (White, 1982). The magnitude of the advantages associated with parental literacy should remain the baseline against which to assess the advantages associated with teaching quality.

A well-established finding of the research on early literacy is that exposure to print and being read to are important contributors to the development of literacy (Snow, Burns, & Griffin, 1998). Predictably, more educated parents are more likely to report that they read to their children when they were small. The number of books in the home is also clearly related to the parents' level of education. Among those who have not completed elementary education, 35 percent said they did not have books at home; among those who completed elementary schooling, this percentage declined to 27 percent; and for those with some high school, only 3 percent reported that they do not have books at home. Conversely, among the parents without primary education, the percentage who said they had more than fifty books at home was 5 percent; among those with some high school this figure was 9 percent; for high school graduates it was 16 percent; for parents with some college it was 29 percent; and for college graduates it was 45 percent. Similar support for early literacy is found in the structured environments of preschool. The likelihood of attending preschool is higher for those students whose parents are more educated. Fifty-eight percent of the children whose parents had no schooling attended preschool, compared to 71 percent of those whose parents had completed elementary school and 78 percent of those whose parents had some college.

In the analyses that follow, I examine how these differences relate to the reading skills of students. Some of these observed differences might be the paths through which parental literacy influences student literacy (e.g., reading to children early in life), others might be confounds, or competing explanations, where the true causes are associated with parental literacy (e.g., the greater propensity of children of illiterate parents to work for pay). Given that this study's principal purpose is to examine the contribution of good teaching relative to home advantages, distinguishing paths from confounds in the home advantages is not critical. Home advantages can be taken as an integral set of factors that will be left — to some extent — unpacked.

The different literacy environments first-generation students are exposed to early in life suggest that they begin school at a significant disadvantage for literacy compared to their more privileged peers. Perhaps the most promising approaches to support them have little to do with the language instruction offered by their teachers and more to do with addressing these early disadvantages. Early experiences at home and in preschool are undoubtedly critical, and their importance has been well established by other research (see Snow et al., 1998, for a review). Relatively less is known about how pedagogy matters to children's ability to achieve the language curriculum objectives.

Since reading acquisition is a staged process toward more advanced levels of literacy (Chall, 1996), I hypothesize that this progression is not solely determined by early literacy experiences. Many first-generation children do reach the sixth grade and perform on the language test at levels comparable to children of literate parents and proceed to middle school, even if they are proportionately fewer than students with literate parents. The question this paper addresses, therefore, is how much teachers in the sixth grade matter, relative to home circumstances and to social background.[7]

What differences do the literacy resources at home, time, and parental support make to the reading literacy of students completing their elementary education? To

TABLE 1

Student Achievement in Literacy Test by Parental Literacy

		Mean	(SD)	N
Number of Parents Who Read				
None		9.7	(3.9)	1,524
One		10.0	(3.8)	5,884
Two		12.1	(4.3)	34,936
Total		11.7	(4.3)	42,344
Mother	*Father*			
Illiterate	Illiterate	9.7	(3.9)	1,524
	Literate	10.0	(3.8)	3,915
	All fathers	9.9	(3.9)	5,439
Literate	Illiterate	10.0	(3.8)	1,969
	Literate	12.1	(4.3)	34,936
	All fathers	12.0	(4.3)	36,905
All	Illiterate	9.9	(3.8)	3,493
	Literate	11.9	(4.3)	38,851
TOTAL		11.7	(4.3)	42,344

Source: Evaluación De La Educación Primaria 2000, Secretaria de Educación Publica, Mexico.

examine this question, I fitted a multiple regression model predicting student performance on the language test based on the literacy of parents. I then compared it with a second model that include a predictor for the most influential home differences, such as whether there are many books at home; whether students read books, comics, magazines, or newspapers; whether their motivation for higher grades was to please parents or teachers; whether they planned to continue in school; and whether they worked regularly or occasionally (Table 2). Children who have two literate parents scored on average 1.75 points higher on the 25-point test than those whose parents are illiterate. Parental literacy explains 4 percent of the variation in student learning outcomes. Taking into account the other previously mentioned observed differences between first-generation students and their peers at home explains 10 percent of variation in student learning outcomes (Model 2 in Table 2). When examined jointly, each of these conditions proved to be significantly associated with student achievement on the test. They diminished the differences associated with parental literacy by 26 percent. However, substantial advantages remained for children of literate parents, even after taking into account the differences associated with these factors. The factor associated with the larger differences was student work, which was 30 percent greater than the advantages associated with parental literacy. Arguably, some of the examined factors could be part of the process through which literate parents support

TABLE 2

*Ordinary Least Square Regression Results Predicting Student Reading Literacy
by Literacy of Parents and Other Individual Differences between Students*

β		Unstand-ardized	Standard-ized	t
Model 1: Contribution of Parental Literacy to Language Competency (n=42,343)				
(Constant)		9.68		90.1 ***
Mother reads		0.35	0.03	2.4 *
Father reads		0.30	0.02	2.4 *
Both read		1.75	0.16	11.0 ***
Adjusted R-square	0.04			
F	537 ***			
Model 2: Contribution of Parental Literacy plus Home Advantages (n=41,418)				
(Constant)		9.20		61.2 ***
Mother reads		0.06	0.00	0.5
Father reads		0.04	0.00	0.3
Both read		1.30	0.12	8.2 ***
There are many books at home		0.50	0.06	11.8 ***
Read books		0.44	0.05	−7.3 ***
Read comics		0.34	0.02	−4.1 ***
Read magazines		0.49	0.04	6.5 ***
Read news		0.30	0.02	−3.1 ***
Please parents		0.86	0.10	12.0 ***
Please teachers		0.96	0.10	12.6 ***
Plan to continue in school		1.22	0.07	14.7 ***
Works always		−2.08	−0.16	−33.0 ***
Works sometimes		−1.42	−0.15	−31.1 ***
Adjusted R-square	0.10			
F	345 ***			

Source: Evaluación De La Educación Primaria 2000, Secretaria de Educación Publica, Mexico.

***p<.001, *p<.05

their children, while others could be correlates of parental literacy and potential confounds.

From Differences at Home to Differences in School

The differences between first-generation students and their peers with literate parents do not end with the differences in the support they find at home, but extend into how they experience school and how they describe the teaching quality they experience.

First-generation students are more likely to report that what they most enjoy about coming to school is the classes, rather than practicing sports or spending time with friends. Among first-generation students, 64 percent said what they most liked was classes, 18 percent said sports, and 17 percent said being with friends. Among students with two literate parents, by contrast, 47 percent say what they most like is classes, 23 percent sports, and 30 percent to be with friends. First-generation students are as likely as other students to believe their school is in a safe locality, to feel safe in school, and to find their classrooms comfortable. They are less likely to say that their classmates bother them and just as likely to fight with other children in school. They are also as likely to say that they have good friends among classmates.

First-generation students are as likely to enjoy going to school as any other child. The percentage of children who said they enjoyed going to school was 90 percent for students with no literate parent, 91 percent for those with one literate parent, and 93 percent for those with two literate parents. Those students who enjoy attending school experience more academic success, they have higher language competency as measured by higher test scores, they are less likely to have repeated a grade, and they are more likely to understand their teachers. Among first-generation students, for instance, 92 percent of those who understand most of what their teachers explain enjoy coming to school, compared to 78 percent of those who say they hardly understand what their teachers explain.

In spite of the fact that first-generation students value their teachers more as a reason for wanting to succeed academically and to enjoy coming to school and attending their classes, they are less likely to experience effective teaching. They are less likely to understand the teacher presentations; less likely to understand the norms established by the teacher; less likely to find that their teachers help them when they don't understand; less likely to say they learn a lot in class; less likely to believe their teacher wants them to learn a lot; and less likely to find their teachers respond to their questions.

Teaching Quality and the Success of First-Generation Students

Teaching can be characterized in a number of ways. The indicators I use in this study are based on basic teaching qualities: the ability to teach in ways that students understand, to be responsive to inquisitive students, to communicate clear norms for academic work, to be helpful to one's students, to convey that one expects them to work hard, and to convey the expectation to achieve at high levels. The six domains I have identified as characterizing good teaching are the final result of all these unobserved qualities of teacher-student communication. I have chosen them because they reflect my normative understanding of what is an appropriate learning environment for children. These basic characteristics of good teaching are consistent with teaching practices found to be associated with student learning. Jere Brophy (1999), in synthesizing decades of process-product research on teaching, identifies twelve conditions of effective teaching: a supportive classroom climate, opportunity to learn, curricular alignment, establishing learning orientations, coherent content, thoughtful discourse, practice and application, scaffolding student task engagement, strategy teaching, cooperative learning, goal oriented assessment, and high achievement expectations. The six dimensions named in this study partially reflect those conditions.

These six aspects of teaching are deceivingly simple. The range and depth of skills necessary to be understood by one's students arguably include expert or at least adequate knowledge of subject matter and how to teach it, and knowledge of one's students and their prior knowledge. Given the approach I have followed in this study, I cannot disaggregate these different pedagogical components in terms of their individual relative contributions or interactions. My level of analysis is above that level of specificity in the study of pedagogy because student reports are inferences above the direct observable data that would allow proper categorization of teacher behaviors into these pedagogical components. I am focusing on the final product of these various components — how teaching is experienced and reported by students. Students do not necessarily experience teaching in ways that allow them to distinguish these different pedagogical components, but rather as an integral experience in which all of these components are subsumed. In this sense, their reports and judgments of teaching probably integrate information from multiple interactions with their teachers and in different domains, combining aspects that reflect teacher mastery of the domain, of pedagogy, and of the nature of the teacher-student relationship. Thus, when we ask them whether they can understand their teachers or whether their teachers are helpful, we are asking for a judgment that reflects a level of inference no different than the judgments college and graduate students make when they rate their professors, or the judgments people make when evaluating the professional competency of a colleague, a subordinate, or a supervisor. We have grounds to make these inferences, but we aggregate so much information into these perceptions that it may be hard to identify all the direct data that led us to this summative judgment, or to recall these data adequately to categorize them according to pedagogical content knowledge, subject-matter competency, or pedagogical competency, which are not common in our ordinary meaning-making processes.

By relying on students' reports, I am acknowledging that good teaching has an inherently subjective element — that it is in the mind of students, personally experienced. I assume that unpacking all the elements that go into the mix of producing teaching probably involves exchanging many different sorts of information: facts and ideas, as well as feelings and emotions, verbal and nonverbal interactions, and utterances as well as silences. When a student says she understands her teacher or that she believes her teacher expects her to work hard and achieve at high levels, this is probably the result of multiple direct and subtle clues that characterize the history of interactions between this student and her teacher. It is also possible that the student's history influences how she makes sense of these interactions and the ensuing inferences she draws about whether she can understand her teacher and whether the teacher expects her to work hard. It would be extremely challenging, perhaps impossible, to design forms of direct measurement of these many interactions that combine to lead the student to conclude she can or cannot understand her teacher, or that her teacher wants her to achieve at high levels.[8]

As mentioned earlier, students were asked to rate to what extent they understood their teacher, found the classroom rules to be clear, found the teacher helpful when they did not understand, felt they learned a lot in class, thought their teachers expected them to learn a lot, and to what the extent the teacher answered their questions when they did not understand. Students could rate their teachers in these dimensions as always/consistently or occasionally/never.

Most of these questions ask the students to evaluate the effectiveness of the teacher's direct instruction. Characterizing direct instruction is part of an established process-product tradition in studying teaching, which examines the extent to which variations in teacher practices explain variations in student achievement (Brophy & Good, 1986). Because student achievement is mediated by students' understanding, this type of questioning is the most direct way to assess teacher effectiveness as perceived by students. The use of student perceptions to characterize classroom environments is an established approach that provides robust measures of classroom environments: they pool student's experience over many lessons because they reflect student views, which mediate instruction and student achievement (Baek & Choi, 2002; Fraser, 1986).

The question of whether students believe their teachers expect them to learn addresses the process through which teacher expectations influence student achievement. Research establishes that teacher expectations have an influence on student achievement because they are communicated to students and thus influence students' self-concept, need to achieve, aspirations, and interactions with teachers (Brophy, 1983).

Teaching Quality and Literacy Skills

Differences in how students report their teachers' instruction relate to differences in their performance on the reading literacy test (Table 3). As explained earlier, "good" or quality teaching is defined as that which leads to student understanding of teacher explanations; the provision of clear classroom rules; an environment where students state their teachers help when they don't understand; where students believe they learn a lot in class; where students believe their teachers want them to learn a lot; and where students state that teachers answer their questions. The Pearson correlation coefficients between individuals' performance on the test are significantly related to individual reports of teaching practices on the six dimensions explored here.[9] On average, students who report that their teachers are good in each of these practices obtain higher test scores than those who report that their teachers are not effective. These differences are statistically significant and represent 1/5 to 2/5 of a standard deviation of the language scores. These differences associated with good teaching compare to an advantage of a half a standard deviation in the language scores associated with parental literacy.

TABLE 3

Average Differences in Student Language Ability for Students Who Describe Their Teachers Teaching Differently (Good Teaching vs. Poor Teaching).

	Language Score Mean	(SD)	N	F	Gap in means	(%)
I understand the teacher when she explains something						
No	10.9	(4.0)	20,245	1095 ***	1.3	(12)
Yes	12.3	(4.4)	23,950			
Total	11.6	(4.3)	44,195			
Classroom rules are clear						
No	11.2	(4.2)	22,947	513 ***	0.9	(8)
Yes	12.1	(4.4)	21,248			
Total	11.6	(4.3)	44,195			
My teacher helps when I don't understand						
No	11.0	(4.2)	15,758	640 ***	1.1	(10)
Yes	12.0	(4.3)	28,437			
Total	11.6	(4.3)	44,195			
I learn a lot in class						
No	11.1	(4.2)	14,840	418 ***	0.9	(8)
Yes	11.9	(4.3)	29,355			
Total	11.6	(4.3)	44,195			
My teacher wants me to learn a lot						
No	10.2	(4.2)	5,954	764 ***	1.6	(16)
Yes	11.9	(4.3)	38,241			
Total	11.6	(4.3)	44,195			
My teacher answers my questions						
No	11.1	(4.2)	19,077	565 ***	1.0	(9)
Yes	12.1	(4.3)	25,118			
Total	11.6	(4.3)	44,195			
Mother reads						
No	9.9	(3.9)	5,559	1174 ***	2.1	(21)
Yes	12.0	(4.3)	37,474			
Total	11.7	(4.3)	43,033			
Father reads						
No	9.9	(3.8)	3,510	708 ***	2.0	(17)
Yes	11.9	(4.3)	38,994			
Total	11.7	(4.3)	42,504			
Both parents read						
No	9.9	(3.8)	7,545	1668 ***	2.2	(22)
Yes	12.1	(4.3)	34,936			
Total	11.7	(4.3)	42,481			
Number of parents who read						
None	9.7	(3.9)	1,524	806 ***	2.4	(25)
One	10.0	(3.8)	5,884			
Two	12.1	(4.3)	34,936			
Total	11.7	(4.3)	42,344			

Source: Evaluación De La Educación Primaria 2000, Secretaria de Educación Publica, Mexico.

***$p < .001$

Quality Teaching, Home Advantages, and Reading Skills

The joint effect of these six student descriptions of their teachers on their language test performance is greater than the joint effect of all the individual differences examined earlier, as shown in Table 4.[10] In other words, a child whose teacher is reported to be of high quality — defined by a student report indicating these six domains — can have better reading skills than a child whose teacher is not reported as being of high quality and a child who has all the home advantages described earlier. These differences remain when examined separately for first-generation students and for students with two literate parents. This analysis confirms that there are clear advantages to student literacy associated with how students describe their teachers' effectiveness.

To contrast the relative contributions of good teaching and parental literacy, I compare the reading literacy of first-generation students with those with two literate parents, based on whether they characterize their teachers as good or bad in the same series of quality indicators: students say they understand their teachers; the teacher rules are clear; their teachers help when they don't understand; their teachers want them to learn a lot; and their teacher answers their questions. I characterized students exposed to "good teaching" as those who gave positive characterizations of their teachers in the six indicators and "bad teaching" as those who gave negative characterization of their teachers in the six indicators. Notice that these are somewhat extreme cases, as most students respond to these six questions with some combinations of positive and negative answers. The results (Table 5) show that there is an advantage equal to two thirds of a standard deviation associated with good teaching for first-generation students, and an advantage of a third of a standard deviation associated with good teaching for students with literate parents. Furthermore, first-generation students who experience good teaching have a small advantage over those students with literate parents who experience poor teaching. The likelihood that this event will happen, however, is very rare, as first-generation students are three times more likely to experience good teaching than poor teaching, while students with literate parents are ten times more likely. That is, the odds that students will experience good teaching are more than three times greater for students with literate parents than for first-generation students. Exposure to poor teaching for first-generation students worsens inequalities in reading literacy significantly, as students with literate parents and good teachers have language scores a full standard deviation higher than first-generation students with poor teachers. Good teaching slightly reduces the gap associated with parental literacy, by 1/5 of a standard deviation.

There are admittedly difficulties with using student characterizations of teaching as indicators of teaching quality. To some extent, some student responses may be influenced by students' literacy skills, and are thus not an independent assessment of the pedagogy they experience. The relationship between pedagogy and literacy may also be one of simultaneous causation and successive feedback loops, rather than unidirectional. That is, teachers may be more responsive to the students when students do well, do homework, and have parents who are responsive. As teachers are more responsive, students continue to do better, which further causes the teachers to be more responsive. Alternatively, when students are doing poorly they may perceive that the

TABLE 4

Ordinary Least Square Regression Results Predicting Reading Literacy
by Student Characteristics and Good Teaching (n= 41,143)

β	Unstan-dardized	Standardized	t	
Model 1: Contribution of Parental Literacy, Home Advantages and Good Teaching				
Constant	8.98		60.62	***
Mother reads	0.06	0.00	0.44	
Father reads	0.04	0.00	0.30	
Both parents read	1.12	0.10	7.20	***
There are many books at home	0.41	0.05	9.74	***
Read books	0.44	0.08	11.71	***
Read comics	0.34	0.04	6.51	***
Read news	0.44	0.02	4.63	***
Read magazines	0.31	0.03	4.13	***
Please parents	0.11	0.01	2.47	*
Please teachers	0.91	0.06	12.09	***
Plan to continue in school	0.96	0.06	11.65	***
Works always	−1.96	−0.15	−31.43	***
Works sometimes	−1.28	−0.14	−28.29	***
I understand the teacher	0.86	0.10	20.73	***
The teachers rules are clear	0.37	0.04	9.09	***
My teacher helps when I don't understand	0.36	0.04	8.11	***
I learn a lot in class	0.25	0.03	5.65	***
My teacher wants me to learn a lot	0.56	0.04	8.50	***
My teacher answers my questions	0.34	0.04	8.03	***
Adjusted R-square	0.12			
F	306 ***			

Source: Evaluación De La Educación Primaria 2000, Secretaria de Educación Publica, Mexico.

***p<.001, *p<.05

teacher expects them to do poorly, a perceived expectation manifested in low grades. In other words, student performance influences teacher grading, which influences a student's perception of how their teacher sees them, which further influences student performance. Student characterizations of the teaching they experience do not allow us to model the chain of events linking those characterizations to what teachers do. Perhaps it is impossible to model these relationships with a series of linear, one-way paths. However, whether they are the results of linear systems of causation or of dynamic systems with feedback loops changing over time, these characterizations reflect

TABLE 5

Average Differences of Student Achievement for Students Experiencing
Good and Bad Teaching by Parental Literacy

	N	Mini-mum	Maxi-mum	Mean	(SD)
First-generation students					
With good teaching	788	0	26	11	(4.0)
With bad teaching	265	0	25	9	(3.5)
Students with literate parents					
With good teaching	5,851	0	26	13	(4.4)
With bad teaching	572	0	24	11	(4.0)

	Difference (%)	Odds
Good teaching advantage		
For first-generation students	29.54	2.97
For students with literate parents	24.25	10.23
First-generation with good teaching vs. Student with literate parents with bad teaching	3.2	
First-generation with bad teaching vs. Student with Literate parents with good teaching	−35.88	
Parental literacy advantage		
With good teaching	20.4	
With bad teaching	25.52	

Source: Evaluación De La Educación Primaria 2000, Secretaria de Educación Publica, Mexico.

nonetheless how students experience teaching and account for perceived teaching quality. As such, this information is valuable in its own right from a perspective that values students' thoughts, feelings, and perceptions as important aspects of the teaching-learning process.

Conclusion

In this article I have shown that first-generation students in Mexico are capable of equally high levels of literacy performance as their peers whose parents are literate. However, many first-generation students attain lower levels of achievement on a language test. How students describe their teachers is a greater predictor of literacy competency than the home advantages represented by parental literacy.

Student-described teacher practices have a significant and consistent relationship with student literacy competencies. Students, including first-generation students, describe a number of teachers as effective. When teachers are not characterized as consistently effective, it is systematically first-generation students who describe their teachers as least effective. The advantages associated with simple good teaching practices, such as replying to student questions, holding high expectations for students' work, establishing clear classroom rules, and providing explanations that students can understand, are larger than the advantages associated with parental literacy. Given that first-generation students are already more inclined to see their teachers as their motive to want to succeed academically, this compounds the powerful associations between good teaching and student success.

This paper has focused primarily on examining differences in how sixth-grade Mexican students characterize their teachers' teaching. The differences that students experience are important in and of themselves, irrespective of how they relate to conditions observed by others. Students make their own meaning from their experiences with teachers — about how responsive teachers are to them and about what expectations they have for their own academic success. By definition, they are more likely to be on their own when constructing these meanings than their peers who are not the first in their families to go to school. First-generation students have to translate school culture for their parents, whereas those whose parents have been to school can count on others to provide a perspective on the significance of daily school experiences.

The test of good teaching is partially in the minds of students — in whether students judge it to be good — even if their subjective rules or preferences differ from those of teachers. One can expect a certain amount of variability in how different students will judge their teachers' quality. As long as this variability is not systematically related to the student's social circumstances, this is interesting but of little practical significance. However, if the students of more humble social origins are systematically less likely to perceive their teachers as good, this is problematic. The problem is not resolved by blaming it on students, or by arguing, for example, that they are less prepared to appreciate the "true" qualities of good teaching than those whose parents are more educated, or suggesting that the different perceptions really are a reflection of how competent both groups of students are.

The implication of these findings is that there is as much, if not more, promise in examining how variations of teaching quality matter to the development of student competencies, as in examining how those competencies relate to students' backgrounds. Remembering that teaching matters is important at a time when too much of the attention of development institutions and governments in developing countries is narrowly focused on getting children to school. Absent this focus, much of the expansion in access may result in getting children to schools where they will be poorly taught and thus miss the opportunity to develop the capabilities that would expand their freedoms.

Notes

1. There are eight Millennium Development Goals: (1) eradicate extreme poverty and hunger; (2) achieve universal primary education; (3) promote gender equality and empower women; (4) reduce child mortality; (5) improve maternal health; (6) combat HIV/AIDS, malaria, and other diseases; (7) ensure environmental sustainability; and (8) develop a global partnership for development.
2. The Jomtien Conference was a global initiative to promote educational development supported by the United Nations and other development agencies and governments. The initiative was

launched at a world conference in Jomtien, Thailand, in 1990. The Dakar Conference, a decade later, took stock of the progress achieved during the decade and restated the goals of Education For All.

3. I follow here Sen's (2000) discussion of development as freedom: "In analyzing social justice, there is a strong case for judging individual advantage in terms of the capabilities that a person has, that is, the substantive freedoms he or she enjoys to lead the kind of life he or she has reason to value. In this perspective, poverty must be seen as the deprivation of basic capabilities rather than merely as lowness of incomes" (p. 87).

4. Again, I am following Sen's (2000) discussion of development as freedom: "Freedom… involves both the processes that allow freedom of actions and decisions, and the actual opportunities that people have, given their personal and social circumstances. Unfreedom can arise either through inadequate processes (such as the violation of voting privileges or other political or civil rights) or through inadequate opportunities that some people have for achieving what they minimally would like to achieve (including the absence of such elementary opportunities as the capability to escape premature mortality or preventable morbidity or involuntary starvation)" (p.17). See Sen, 2000 for further discussion of the idea of development as freedom.

5. Note that in Mexico 7 percent of students drop out of school during elementary education, an additional 16 percent drop out at the end of the primary cycle and 30 percent during secondary education (Economic Commission for Latin America and the Caribbean, 2002, p. 106). Since the dropouts are disproportionately from low-income backgrounds, these figures based on students enrolled in secondary education underestimate the number of students whose parents have low levels of education.

6. These figures are from the survey I am analyzing in this paper.

7. Admittedly by focusing on the sixth-grade teachers, I have set a stringent design to test the contributions of teaching: (1) because the role of early literacy experiences is unaccounted for, and (2) because the cumulative impact of literacy instruction in school, provided by teachers in grades K–5, is also unaccounted for. This design makes it less likely to find differences in literacy skills associated with teaching.

8. Alternative forms of direct measurement of these interactions can of course study components that can be prespecified for limited periods of time. These approaches, while valuable and useful to complement students' views, have limitations of their own if presented as valid characterizations of the relationship between teachers and students as experienced by students.

9. Because students were first given the questionnaire and then tested, it is not possible that their perception of performance on the test influenced their responses to the questionnaire.

10. I am comparing the sum of the standardized coefficients of these factors to the sum of the standardized coefficients of the factors accounting for individual differences in a multiple regression that includes parental literacy, home literacy practices, and teaching quality variables presented in Table 4.

References

Baek, S., & Choi, H. (2002). The relationship between students' perceptions of classroom environment and their academic achievement in Korea. *Asia Pacific Education Review, 3,* 125–135.

Brophy, J. (1983). Research on the self-fulfilling prophecy and teacher expectations. *Journal of Educational Psychology, 75,* 631–661.

Brophy, J. (1999). *Teaching.* Paris: International Academy of Education and International Bureau of Education.

Brophy, J., & Good, T. (1986). Teacher behavior and student achievement. In M. Wittrock (Ed.), *Handbook of research on teaching* (pp. 340–370). New York: Macmillan.

Burkam, D., Lee, V., & Smerdon, B. (1997). Gender and science learning in high school: Subject matter and laboratory experiences. *American Educational Research Journal, 34,* 297–331.

Chall, J. S. (1996). *Stages of reading development* (2nd ed.). New York: McGraw-Hill.

Cohen, D., & Hill, H. (2000). Instructional policy and classroom performance: The mathematics reforms in California. *Teachers College Record, 102*, 294–343.

Dickinson, D. K., & Tabors, P. O. (Eds.). (2001). *Beginning literacy with language: Young children learning at home and school.* Baltimore: Paul H. Brookes.

Driessen, G., & Mulder, L. (1999). The enhancement of educational opportunities of disadvantaged children. In R. Bosker, B. Creemers, & S. Stringfield (Eds.), *Enhancing educational excellence, equity and efficiency* (pp. 37–64). Dordrecht: Kluwer Academic.

Economic Commission for Latin America and the Caribbean. (2002). *Social panorama of Latin America.* Santiago, Chile: United Nations.

Fraser, B. (1986). *Classroom environment.* London: Croom Helm.

Ginsburg-Block, M., & Fantuzzo, J. (1998). An evaluation of the relative effectiveness of NCTM standards-based interventions for low achieving urban elementary students. *Journal of Educational Psychology, 90*, 560–569.

Good, T., & Brophy, J. (1987). *Looking in classrooms.* New York: Harper & Row.

Grissmer, D. (1999). Conclusions—class size effects: Assessing the evidence, its policy implication, and future research agenda. *Educational Evaluation and Policy Analysis, 21*, 231–248.

Hanushek, E. (1995). Interpreting recent research on schooling in developing countries. *World Bank Research Observer, 10*, 227–246.

Hart, B., & Risley, T. (1995). *Meaningful differences in the everyday lives of young American children.* Baltimore: Brookes.

Kremer, M. (1995). Research on Schooling: What we know and what we don't. A comment on Hanushek. *World Bank Research Observer, 10*, 247–254.

Mayer, D. (1998). Do new teaching standards undermine performance on old tests? *Educational Evaluation and Policy Analysis, 20*, 53–73.

National Center for Education Statistics. (1996). *High school seniors' instructional experiences in science and mathematics.* Washington, DC: U.S. Government Printing Office.

Nye, B., Hedges, L., & Konstantopoulos, S. (2002). Do low-achieving students benefit more from small classes? Evidence from the Tennessee Class Size Experiment. *Educational Evaluation and Policy Analysis, 24*, 201–217.

Orfield, G., & DeBray, E. H. (Eds.). (1999). *Hard work for good schools: Facts not fads in Title I reform.* Cambridge, MA: Civil Rights Project at Harvard University.

Reimers, F. (2000). Educational opportunity in Mexico. Achievements and challenges of education policies. In S. Chazaro (Ed.), *Education in Mexico: History, reality, and challenges* (pp. 249–275). Mexico: Editorial Mexico Desconocido.

Scarborough, H. S., Dorich, W., & Hager, M. (2001). Preschool literacy experience and later reading achievement. *Journal of Learning Disabilities, 24*, 508–511.

Sen, A. (2000). *Development as freedom.* New York: Knopf.

Snow, C., Burns S., & Griffin, P. (Eds.). (1998). *Preventing reading difficulties in young children.* Washington, DC: National Academy Press.

Stein, M., & Lane, S. (1996). Instructional tasks and the development of student capacity to think and reason: An analysis of the relationship between teaching and learning in a reform mathematics project. *Educational Research and Evaluation, 2*, 50–80.

Stringfield, S., & Datnow, A. (1998). Scaling up school restructuring designs in urban schools. *Education and Urban Society, 30*, 269–276.

United Nations. (2000). *Millennium development goals.* New York: Author. Retrieved November 24, 2005, from www.development.org

Von Secker, C. (2002). Effects of inquiry-based teacher practices on science excellence and equity. *Journal of Educational Research, 95*, 151–160.

Wenglinsky, H. (2002). How schools matter: The link between teacher classroom practices and student academic performance. *Education Policy Analysis Archives, 10*. Available online at http://epaa.asu.edu/epaa/v10n12/

White, C. (1982). The relation between socioeconomic status and academic achievement. *Psychological Bulletin, 91*, 461–481.

PART THREE

Community Solutions for
Educational Change

PART THREE

Introduction

Worldwide, local communities play a critical role in addressing educational challenges. In areas where armed conflict is ongoing, community-initiated schooling often provides the only site of access to education for children and adults. Communities often work to promote equity for racially, ethnically, and religiously marginalized groups when education systems do not. And in the international drive toward quality education for all children, community action is frequently an important catalyst for change.

The chapters in this section span the globe. They are all situated, however, in sites of struggle: Palestinians forbidden to educate their children during the first *intifadah* (uprising) and their resistance in the continuing search for self-rule; the class barriers that deny education to Chilean children segregated in popular sectors; the objectification of the Romà, Europe's largest ethnic minority, in educational research, which is usually done by outsiders, and the consequent lack of attention to persistent educational inequities; the HIV/AIDS epidemic in a poor urban community in Uganda and a community-based organization's use of education to combat its devastating effects on families.

In the opening essay, Khalil Mahshi and Kim Bush trace the history of the education of Palestinians since the time of the Ottoman Turks and assess the possibilities of the 1987–88 intifadah as a catalyst for educational change. Written in 1989, "The Palestinian Uprising and Education for the Future" examines different models of education that were pioneered to guarantee continued access to education at a time when schools in the Palestinian territories were forcibly shut down by the Israeli military. Examples of these pioneering solutions include the streamlining of courses through the "Crash Plan" adopted by the United Nations Relief and Works Agency schools in refugee camps in the West Bank, Gaza, Jordan, Syria, and Lebanon; private Palestinian schools training teachers to create self-study materials and develop and distribute home-learning packets; and community leaders creating "Popular Committees" that in turn organized neighborhood schools in houses, mosques, churches, and clubs. As Mahshi and Bush outline the challenges encountered by Palestinian popular educators of the time, the reader is reminded of the universal issues that must be confronted whenever education seeks to play a role in social change:

how to sustain community interest and participation in contexts of fear and suspicion, and how to build new institutions that do not replicate the inequalities of previous systems.

In a new interview, conducted in December 2005 especially for this book, the *Harvard Educational Review* talks with Khalil Mahshi about the current state of education of Palestinians. With the establishment of the Palestinian Ministry of Education and Higher Education in August 1994, Palestinians achieved control over the education of their children. By 2001–02, according to UNICEF, access to primary education within the Palestinian territory had reached 94 percent. Autonomy in curriculum and textbook development has produced exciting results, Mahshi explains, but a general satisfaction with the education system has also bred complacency. In this context, much work remains to be done to promote quality education, which, for Mahshi, centers on student-centered approaches to learning.

In "Transference and Appropriation in Popular Education Interventions: A Framework for Analysis," Liliana Vaccaro explores the role of popular education in contexts of poverty. She details the processes through which Chilean popular educators take control of educational projects often initiated in their communities by outsiders: nongovernmental organizations and/or professionals such as social workers, teachers, and researchers. With a consistent lack of state support for education in the poorest sections of Chile, Vaccaro argues that community transference and appropriation of projects that seek to promote access and quality are critical. Through a case study of the Learning Workshops program, she responds to the question, "How and under what conditions are the participants of the program able to attain autonomy of action, whereby they can take over a project and manage it themselves? She identifies two types of appropriation that communities exhibit: selective, whereby community members operate within the bounds of the initial project, and creative, whereby community members use the skills learned through one project in other actions or programs. The lessons of this chapter, particularly relating to the possibilities for community control when professionals withdraw from a program, remain relevant today.

The focus shifts from practice to research in "Why Romà Do Not Like Mainstream Schools: Voices of a People without Territory," in which Julio Vargas Clavería and Jesús Gómez Alonso address the role educational research can play in the search for equity in education. They present a theory of "communicative research," a new approach to educational research related to the Romà that emphasizes the incorporation of the voice of the community in the definition of programs and strategies for school transformation. This approach is relevant not only to the Romà but to all research related to disenfranchised groups of people. The authors describe the experience of the Romà over the past several centuries and trace the history of research on their experiences in school. They identify the objectification of the Romà, the application of deficit theory, and the lack of a Romaní perspective on research teams as the critical challenges to effective research.

This section closes with "Education in the Fight against HIV/AIDS: Caring for Ourselves, Our Families, and Our Community in Kampala, Uganda." Through vivid photos of the daily life of their programs, Joanita Nambi, Stella Alamo Talisuna, Margrethe Juncker, and a team of volunteers from the community-based organization Reach Out details their approach to caring for people living with HIV/AIDS. The volunteers demonstrate that this holistic model has at its core a belief in the power and importance of community education. They explain, for example, that Reach Out provides continuous training for its more than 1,000 clients and 150 volunteers, most of whom are also living with HIV/AIDS. They argue that the training and the ongoing support of this close-knit community help clients care for their bodies through medicine and nutrition; their minds through counseling, yoga, and prayers; and their families through skills development, microlending, and school fee assistance. The photos provide an example of how community-based organizations can use education as a tool to act on complex social problems, especially in places where there are no formal structures to access life-saving medicines, for example, or the social and economic skills that help rebuild lives.

The chapters in this section share a common stance toward struggle. Each presents forward-looking strategies that communities have adopted to harness opportunities created by adversity. In particular, they provide concrete examples of community-driven initiatives that both fill gaps in the provision of education by the state and create alternative structures for learning. Although community solutions are often ignored or underplayed in discussions of international education, the lessons they invoke are widely applicable in the search for access, equity, and quality that preoccupies the field.

The Palestinian Uprising and Education for the Future

KHALIL MAHSHI AND KIM BUSH

A popular uprising against colonial rule presents both a threat and a challenge to educators. They must abandon their traditional curricula and approaches to learning and respond to a community insistent upon meaningful change and relevance in the education of its children. The *intifadah* — the Palestinian uprising against twenty years of Israeli military occupation — now in its second year, poses this challenge to educators who live in the West Bank and Gaza. They are currently working against tremendous odds to offer alternative forms of schooling (henceforth referred to as alternative, neighborhood, or popular schooling) while all schools are closed by military order. At the same time, they are attempting to prepare for a future when a Palestinian system of education can be developed. Whether we enthusiastically create alternative schools or change the system as a whole, the ties between school and community are strengthened. The intifadah has erased traditional lines which divide educators and citizens, creating a laboratory for dramatic changes in all areas of education.

We would like to concentrate on an analysis of education. However, in order to clarify the issues involving the relationship between alternative schooling and the intifadah, we offer a bare framework of major developments in the field before 1988. Palestinians directly involved at various levels of education are a major source of information for the analysis of the current situation. They are sometimes identified, but often the names and exact locations of popular schools must remain anonymous. Because of the nature of education in Palestine, there are no reliable statistics on popular schools and the extent of popular involvement. We must rely on conjecture in many cases, hoping that a more accurate history of the movement will be written when fear of reprisals is gone. We freely admit that more extensive research in the area is needed. This paper represents an initial analysis.

The Educational System: A Historical Overview

For nearly five hundred years, outside powers have imposed their systems of education on the Palestinian people. Under the Ottoman Turks (1517–1917), education

Harvard Educational Review   Vol. 59 No. 4 November 1989, 470–483

was limited to either practical training or religious instruction. In reaction to these limitations on public Turkish education, private Muslim and Christian schools evolved in various parts of Palestine. Schools grew up in mosques as a nationalist response to Turkish control, in one of the earliest instances of Palestinian popular education. "[A] new Arab nationalist consciousness was beginning to take root in reaction to Turkish political and cultural domination. This led to a revival of interest in Arabic language and literature and the establishment of Arab Newspapers and communal schools" (Graham-Brown, 1984, p. 16).

Under the British mandate (1917–1948), both Zionism and British imperial control threatened Palestinian culture. The British increased the number of schools for Palestinian Arabs in order to increase the number of educated Arabs in the civil service. It is generally acknowledged, however, that the schools that the British government funded for Arabs failed to meet the demand of even half of the non-Jewish population (Palestine Royal Commission, 1937, p. 337). Not only was education for Arabs underfunded, but it did not meet their specific cultural and political needs (Badran, 1969, p. 142; Tibawi, 1956, p. 205). The attitudes of most Palestinians toward schooling during this period are summed up by Dr. Khalil Totah: "The major grievance of the Arabs is . . . that they have no control over it [their education]. It would seem that Arab education is either designed to reconcile the Arabs to this policy [of establishing a Jewish homeland], or to make that education so colorless as to make it harmless and to endanger the carrying out of that policy" (Graham-Brown, 1984, p. 20). As in the era of Turkish rule, the failure of the British to provide an adequate educational system for Palestinians encouraged the growth of a nonsectarian nationalist movement. Despite the inadequate provision of government education by the British, the traditional value of education, especially formal schooling, has strengthened over time. Formal education was perceived as a means for securing a white-collar job with steady income, and to enhance social status, in a predominantly peasant society.

After 1948, the West Bank fell under the authority of Jordan, and the educational system underwent yet another change, still heavily flavored by the British. Gaza, on the other hand, was controlled by the Egyptians. Both Jordanian and Egyptian systems of education follow the British model of external examinations and an exam-based curriculum. The vast number of Palestinian refugees dispersed throughout the Arab world after 1948 have been served by the United Nations Relief and Works Agency (UNRWA), created by the U.N. in 1949. UNRWA schools were established in the West Bank, Gaza, Jordan, Syria, and Lebanon in every refugee camp, providing education from first through ninth grades. From the outset, educational advisors from the United Nations Educational, Scientific and Cultural Organization (UNESCO) helped the UNRWA system develop curriculum and train teachers. UNRWA schools generally follow the curriculum and educational system of the Arab country in which they operate.

This amalgam of local, Turkish, British, and Egyptian-Jordanian systems of education was further complicated after the Six Day War in June 1967, when Israel occupied Gaza and the West Bank. In effect, the pre-1967 curricula and educational system remained in place, but they were administered by the Israeli military authority.

In 1982, as a first step toward creating an image of legitimacy for the continued occupation of the West Bank and Gaza and imposing limited self-administration on the Palestinian population, Israeli military authorities divided the Israeli military government into two parts. The Civil Administration was in charge of services and civil matters for the Palestinians. The Israeli army was to deal with security and military matters. Army officials who headed the different service departments in the military government remained in their posts after establishment of the Civil Administration. The Israeli plan to replace them with Palestinians from the West Bank and Gaza was never implemented, due to the resistance of the Palestinian population to the scheme of self-administration as an alternative to full national independence.

Education, as a service to the Palestinian population in the West Bank and Gaza, falls under the Civil Administration. Therefore it is completely controlled and supervised by Israeli authorities — a fact of great importance when we consider the Israeli reaction to the intifadah. Thus, since 1948, three separate school systems have evolved: UNRWA, private, and government, each of which adheres to essentially alien curricula, in which Palestinian culture and history have been ignored or actively suppressed by the Israelis. Just as the Palestinians created popular institutions to preserve and transmit their culture during Turkish rule and British rule, they have also resisted integration under the Israelis. They have established educational and cultural institutions, and grassroots organizations to preserve and develop their national identity, nurture self-reliance, and resist dependence on the Israeli authorities. In a very real sense, one of the faces of the intifadah is a determination to develop a national consciousness and to resist amalgamation into Israel or any Arab non-Palestinian country.

The Intifadah: Causes and Growth of a Movement

On December 8, 1987, a car carrying four Gazans was rammed by an Israeli vehicle and all were killed. Few would have predicted that this event would spark a national uprising, now entering its second year and showing no sign of abating. Analysts have suggested many causes for the intifadah, including obstruction of economic development, unjust taxation, economic hardship, denial of self-determination and human rights, repression, confiscation of land, and increasing Israeli settlement on Palestinian land. All of these reasons can be summed up as a refusal to live under foreign occupation any longer (Tamari, 1988). One might add to these the extreme frustration of a very youthful population with few opportunities for meaningful work. The Palestinian population is overeducated for the undeveloped economic situation in the West Bank and Gaza. High school and university graduates end up in jobs that do not match their qualifications. They place blame on the occupiers, and on a system of education that is archaic and in many ways irrelevant to their needs and aspirations.

The intifadah, which literally means "shaking off" in Arabic, has taken as many forms as the Israeli occupation itself. Although street action and resulting death and injury have attracted the most publicity, other forms of nonviolent action are just as important. For example, most Palestinians in the West Bank and Gaza have refused to pay taxes on property and businesses. All shops now close their doors at noon, honoring a "national" commercial strike. A campaign to boycott Israeli products has had significant impact on the occupier's economy. In a few villages, people discarded their identity cards as a symbolic rejection of military authority. These actions and many others symbolize the spirit of resistance of the Palestinians.

In conjunction with direct daily confrontation with the military, a movement based on extensive popular organization has been created. The Unified National Leadership of the Uprising (UNLU) issues a bimonthly leaflet or directive commenting on important issues, outlining major tactical steps, and indicating dates for all-day strikes. With the exception of these directives (there have been thirty-six since the beginning of the intifadah to date), the movement is decentralized and counts heavily on local initiative for new thinking and new forms of nonviolent direct action. This movement — essentially "headless" — poses the gravest threat to the Israelis because it is uncontrollable.

Israeli Response to the Intifadah

The Israelis have responded to the more visible forms of the intifadah with direct military action, through their Border Police, active and reserve army, and the Shin Bet (local equivalent of the FBI). The record of their brutal repression is well known (see Al Haq, 1988b) but these methods have failed to stop the intifadah. In addition to the use of tear gas, a wide range of weaponry, and frequent beatings, the Israelis have resorted to various forms of collective punishment, including house demolitions and sealings; preventive (called "administrative") detention; restriction of travel, communication and movement; and censorship.

Desperate to deprive the movement of its youthful energy and leadership, the Israelis have used their control over education as a way of pressuring the Palestinian population. Since February of 1988, most of the schools in the Occupied Territories have been closed, sometimes for a month, often for much longer. The official justification for school closures has been that schools have been the centers for organizing demonstrations and other direct actions. Palestinians and many Israelis, however, believe that the authorities are well aware of Palestinian reliance on education as a solution to their many problems, and that they have exploited this vulnerability by closing schools frequently and without warning as a collective punishment (see Cohen, 1989). This has resulted in West Bank schools being closed for more than thirteen of the past sixteen months since the beginning of the intifadah. (Gaza schools have suffered from prolonged and repeated curfews, though they have not been officially closed as in the West Bank.) The matriculation exam that ninth graders take to qualify for entrance into high school was canceled in 1988–1989. Last year, the Jordanian Ministry of Education accepted a proposal by education officials in the West Bank to water down the Jordanian *Tawjihi* exam required for entrance into all Arab universities (as well as universities in the West Bank and Gaza). The students were made to sit for one session of the exam (the mid-year session) instead of two, thus covering only half of the curriculum required for the Tawjihi (or for grade twelve). The exam might not be administered at all in the West Bank in 1989. After continual harassment and arbitrary closures in previous years, all West Bank and Gaza universities have been permanently closed since 1987 (Al Haq, 1988a; Jerusalem Media and Communication Center, 1989).

The long-term results of controlling education to punish a population are too hard to measure. What happens to first and second graders who are acquiring literacy skills, then denied books and instruction? What are the sociopsychological consequences of being cut off from friends, and the socialization process that schools at all levels offer? How easily will math skills learned in the elementary grades be recovered after a year's absence? Will high school students who have used the streets as classrooms be able to return to the old style of authoritarian education? Some preliminary psychological studies have been conducted on the impact of the intifadah. Experts, some of whom were interviewed for this article, describe a loss of literacy and numeracy skills, but a growth in self-reliance and self-esteem. One educator from a West Bank university spoke about the "reawakening" of the Palestinians. She recalled widespread depression and submissiveness on the part of both the educated and uneducated Palestinians in the mid-1980s, and her fear that they had given up. The events of December 1987 sparked a new determination to resist the occupation and to develop new Palestinian institutions. Her opinion is shared by many observers and participants in education, who view the intifadah as the opportunity of a lifetime.

Intifadah Education: The Challenge

Critical analysis of the educational system in the West Bank and Gaza, and its relevance to Palestinian society, started at the beginning of this decade. Even before the intifadah, a few efforts were made to introduce relevance in the educational system. These educators were arguing against the diploma-orientation of the system. Although they have remained a minority among educators in the West Bank and Gaza, the intifadah has widened this circle and accelerated this process, as educators and laypersons are on notice that the time has come for significant changes in the entire educational system. Prolonged school closures have prodded everyone into action. This action has taken three very distinct forms. Schools have sought alternative forms of instruction as a temporary substitute for classroom-based education, which is now illegal. The pressure to provide ongoing education to the population has encouraged educators to consider different types of distance-teaching, including learning by correspondence, and the use of television and radio. Popular committees in nearly every community in the West Bank have started neighborhood schools as temporary replacements for government, UNRWA, and private institutions closed by the military. Neighborhood schools have opened the eyes of parents, educators, and especially students, to new forms of education. The intifadah has increased the need for a national curriculum that reflects the new confidence Palestinians have developed in their culture and their own institutions. Clearly, the greatest challenge of the occupation and the intifadah is to discard years of occupation education and start afresh. Long-term educational planning by a handful of Palestinians is producing some impressive alternatives, among them "Education for Awareness and Involvement," which we describe later in this article.

Alternative Modes of Instruction

At first glance, alternative modes of instruction adopted by schools in the Occupied Territories may appear to have no real impact on the system itself. After all, they are only substitutes for classroom instruction. In fact, the process of developing alternative modes of instruction has raised important issues about how students learn and how those traditional patterns might change.

The UNRWA schools adopted a Crash Plan in the spring of 1988 when it became apparent that schools were going to be closed for a long period. They attempted to streamline the curriculum by prioritizing learning objectives and cutting unnecessary materials from individual courses. Teachers prepared worksheets based on textbooks, but student participation was essentially voluntary, and the results were not very encouraging. UNRWA administrators and teachers are aware of the value of autonomous learning and cooperative effort (finding parallels with the Islamic Kuttab, in which students studied the Koran in ungraded classes and helped each other). But without at least some interaction between teacher and pupil, especially at the middle school levels, or the active intervention of parents-as-teachers, the UNRWA Crash Plans seem doomed to failure. More recently, UNRWA has proposed the development of television and radio instruction, using both Jordanian and Egyptian channels at certain hours during the day. They see this as an answer to short-term needs and a step toward long-term planning in adult education. Unfortunately, Palestinians have no control over radio and television stations in neighboring countries, and therefore little has been done with programmed instruction.

Most government schools have done little to provide self-study packets or to circumvent official closures. The Civil Administration, employer of all government schoolteachers, has tremendous leverage over them. In April 1988, all government schoolteachers in the Ramallah area were called to a meeting by the Civil Administration and reminded that any attempts to provide education to students would be considered illegal and grounds for immediate dismissal. Few teachers heeded the warning completely, but they acted very discreetly.

Private schools, with their greater freedom, have been able to experiment more with home-learning packets and have been slightly more successful. Some of these schools, like the Friends Schools in Ramallah (two Quaker schools, one hundred years old, renowned in Palestinian history and in neighboring Arab countries, and foremost among schools in the West Bank), have started by training teachers to write self-study materials. After a short training period led by an educator from one of the West Bank universities, teachers produced packets for all of their classes. These packets were based on existing student textbooks and have the following five components for each unit or chapter:

1. The learning objective of the unit measured in behavioral terms
2. The activities students must engage in to meet the standards, such as studying the contents of a chapter
3. Additional assignments for further study and practice
4. Self-evaluation tests, with answers provided

5. Exercises to be turned in to the teacher for feedback and grading

In order to motivate students to work in a consistent and organized manner, packets specify the material to be covered during a period of time, at the end of which the students turn in the exercises for feedback.

Israeli military authorities have decided that the self-study packets provided by some of the private schools violate the school closure order. In fact, the army entered the Friends Boys School in Ramallah and stopped their distribution. The headmasters of this and other schools were summoned individually to the military headquarters and ordered to stop providing the packets to their students.

The use of self-study packets as an alternative mode of instruction during the intifadah raised a number of important questions:

1. How could the packets be distributed to large number of students without attracting the attention of military authorities?
2. If, in order to avoid student gatherings, students are not required to turn in homework frequently, how can one ensure motivation, regular and steady work, and self-organization?
3. If homework is graded in order to motivate students, how does one ensure that they have done the work themselves without outside help?
4. What does one do with the grades? Are they used for credit and promotion to the next grade level? Will the educational authorities who are responsible for certifying accept these grades for official purposes, when the authorities are supervised by the Israeli Civil Administration?
5. When students are barred from school campuses by the army, how can they interact with teachers to get assistance when they encounter difficulties, especially when the use of radio, television, and newspapers is not possible?
6. How does one prepare self-study packets for students in lower elementary grades who have not yet perfected their reading and writing skills?

Experimentation with self-study packets continues. It appears that in the West Bank educational system, which is exam- and grade-oriented, students will not be motivated for self-study unless exams are given on a regular basis. Schools are trying to hold exams in areas where the closure order is not in effect, or at times and places where the authorities will not be able to stop them. Experience will enable educators to develop effective self-study programs.

West Bank and Gaza universities have been subject to greater harassment and more direct military confrontations than high schools. As a result, they have been reluctant to become actively involved in alternative modes of instruction. Nevertheless, some classes have continued to meet, especially for seniors (for many of whom graduation has been postponed up to three years). In order to cover the material, most of the professors have pared down their subject matter drastically and changed the mode of instruction from teacher-centered lectures to smaller discussion groups. Thus the universities, like the elementary, preparatory, and secondary schools, have begun the process of looking for effective forms of home or non-school-centered learning.

New Forms of Education:
Popular Education in Neighborhood Schools

By March 1988, people began to realize that the intifadah was going to last a long time. The Unified National Leadership of the Uprising issued a directive that called for a boycott of the Israeli Civil Administration and for the establishment of an independent alternative structure for the provision of services to the Palestinian population. People responded by reviving the Popular Committees first created and used in 1982, when boycotting the newly established Israeli Civil Administration. The newly established committees undertook a wider range of responsibilities and services in their neighborhoods. These included cultivating neighborhood gardens to ensure the supply of vegetables in case the Israeli army stopped supplies from entering; providing public cleaning and basic health services; centrally purchasing, storing, and distributing food supplies; setting up a guard system against the Israeli settlers, the army, and thieves; and collecting donations to provide assistance to those unemployed because of the intifadah.

Popular Committees assumed responsibility for education when it became clear that the Israeli authorities intended to use school closure as a form of collective punishment. While some schools were attempting to offer alternative modes of instruction, Popular Committees began to organize neighborhood schools. Classes were held in houses, mosques, churches, and clubs. Sometimes classes were held in gardens not easily seen from the street. They were taught by anyone in the neighborhood who was educated and able to volunteer their time. In some cases, university or high school students taught younger pupils. Most often, parents, without any formal experience in education and teaching, taught classes. This movement of neighborhood schools came to be known as Popular Education. At least in the beginning, people, including those on the Popular Committees, saw these schools as temporary, necessary only until the intifadah was "over" and life "returned to normal." As a result, popular education erupted spontaneously everywhere, and there was little, if any, central direction. Only during April and May of 1988 did neighborhood schools openly flourish.

In May 1988, the Israeli authorities outlawed Popular Committees and all their activities, including educational and cultural ones. According to this law, any person convicted of membership in the Popular Committees would face a sentence of up to ten years of imprisonment. The army started actively raiding neighborhood schools, partially sabotaging popular education. In addition to military raids, Israeli authorities reopened schools for short periods of time and then closed them again. Organizers of alternative schools were demoralized; led to expect that the educational scene would return to normal, all their efforts at creating an alternative system seemed unnecessary. The Popular Education Movement is now more clandestine, decentralized, and smaller. Since May 1988, popular education has continued underground, well directed and organized in a few areas and virtually nonexistent in others. Now neighborhood schools continue to meet in some communities, and women's committees in refugee camps have organized small classes taught by international volunteers. Even these classes, which service no more than three hundred students, are subject to constant harassment, interruption, and closure.

Because popular education lacked a central organizing body for the whole West Bank, neighborhood schools differed significantly from one another and from one geographical area to another. In some towns, a single committee would direct and supervise the neighborhood school movement as a whole. In such cases neighborhood schools would be almost identical in curriculum and in the number of lessons given per week. Teachers attended meetings for coordination and evaluation. Where there were no such supervising committees, neighborhood schools differed significantly from one another in numbers of periods per day and the number of days they operated each week. They also differed in the subjects they taught and in the curriculum they used.

The curriculum of neighborhood schools was very informal, but followed the official textbooks, the Jordanian Israeli-censored textbooks that students already had and all schools in the West Bank are required to use. These texts provided a foundation for teachers who needed them (or were accustomed to them), but were abandoned by others who wanted to strike out in new directions. Students were separated into grade levels or, in some cases, combined for practical purposes. Because classes were generally smaller, averaging ten students, students had the chance to experience new teaching methods in a radically different educational atmosphere. Neighborhood schools opened everyone's eyes to alternatives, although the curriculum remained essentially unchanged. Many teachers were forced to improvise and become more creative. For example, science teachers were forced to improvise and create "kitchen laboratories" using materials at hand of examples from the intifadah (for example, a physics teacher discussed electrical conductivity by asking students why it was dangerous to remove Palestinian flags from power lines). In some neighborhood schools new classes were added, such as Palestinian drama and music, and more time was spent talking about national and political issues. Unfortunately, because of the unpredictability of the situation, most participants saw neighborhood schools as decidedly temporary, and did not put the effort into developing a truly alternative and relevant curriculum. Many students as well had a feeling that neighborhood schools were temporary and — in the formative period (April–May 1988) — did not take them seriously. They assumed that work in neighborhood schools would not be graded or accepted for credit and for promotion in their regular schools.

A number of problems and challenges face the popular education movement. Among these are the following:

1. How to sustain interest and a high level of participation when many people are fearful of official reprisals and frustrated by intermittent opening and closing of schools.
2. How to discipline students who are used to an authoritarian method of classroom management.
3. How to sustain seriousness and motivation among students who are accustomed to working only for exams and grades.
4. How to compete with the distractions in the community, like television programs, films, playing in the streets, and working for money.
5. How to develop similar standards among neighborhood schools if they are indeed the answer to the closure of schools for months or years.

6. How to assure that grades and exam results will be accepted for legal or accred-
   itation purposes.

During the formative period of the popular education movement, many teachers
and other educators considered these questions seriously. They were especially concerned about the lack of training and experience of teachers in neighborhood schools
and the absence of uniform standards in those schools. With the help of a number of
prominent educators from West Bank universities and other educational institutions,
the General Federation of Employees in the Education Sectors in the Occupied Territories, which consists of representatives of all of the teachers' unions, organized a
conference in May 1988 to address educational alternatives. The conference had very
ambitious goals, the most important of which was to shape the enthusiasm of popular educators into an alternative school system of high quality. The organizers hoped
that as a result of the papers presented and the ensuing discussion a set of guidelines
for alternative schooling would be agreed upon and later published in a handbook for
neighborhood schools. However, the detainment of members of the executive committee, the clampdown of the Israeli authorities on neighborhood schools, and the
reopening of all schools in the West Bank hampered the efforts and efficiency of the
Federation. This conference was the first, and possibly the only, step taken toward organizing the popular education movement. Now, almost a year later, those who attended the conference see it as a historic moment: for the first time, members from all
levels of the educational community met together to determine the future course of
education in the West Bank and Gaza. If one looks carefully, one will see that some of
the lofty goals of that conference are being realized, slowly and subversively, in some
schools and among some innovative educational thinkers.

New Forms: Education for the Future

The concerns raised by many Palestinian educators at the conference (and by thousands who participated in the popular education movement) have been addressed by
a few isolated but exemplary programs. Most of these started before the outbreak of
the intifadah, but the intifadah has reinforced their vision and educational philosophy. All of these programs have a common desire to create genuine alternatives to the
existing educational system. All of them seek to develop a new system relevant to Palestinian society and centering on the development of well-rounded human beings.
These programs cover a wide spectrum of educational levels, from preschool through
high school.

At the preschool level, educational psychologists and teachers are introducing ac-
tivity-oriented programs and discarding passive content orientation. The intifadah
has catalyzed these basic changes, both because teachers have had to look for alternative forms to circumvent closures and intervention, and because the uprising encourages innovation. At Bethlehem University, Jacqueline Sfeir and the teacher trainees
are developing programs that emphasize a "gadget-free" learning environment that
will work equally well in small villages and in middle-class suburban communities.
Villages have received these pilot programs in play-centered learning enthusiastically,

but the middle-class communities, which are conditioned to view learning in terms of measurable results, have been more reluctant to embrace them. Dr. Sfeir noted how village women watched their children learning while playing and said, "This makes sense; maybe we can learn this way." Later they applied that lesson to their literacy classes. The preschoolers in the Bethlehem University program are the children of the intifadah. The cornerstone of their education in preschool is problem solving and investigation. The rest of the educational system should follow this philosophy.

The Early Childhood Resource Center (ECRC) in East Jerusalem is building on the aforementioned ideas, but in a different setting. Recognizing the intifadah as a rare opportunity to introduce meaningful change into the ways children are taught, the ECRC is developing a series of self-help booklets. One booklet helps parents to recognize and respond effectively to psychological problems that have grown out of the climate of violence of the intifadah. As part of a community mental health program, it combines self-reliance with professional and paraprofessional help. Another, pitched to elementary school students, teachers, and parents in any educational milieu, encourages problem solving, cooperative learning, and reducing reliance on the teachers. This booklet resulted from the experience of many popular schoolteachers, incorporating their ideas for use of local resources and reduced reliance on formal schools.

These programs advocate comprehensive curriculum change, as well as a major transformation in teaching methodology on all levels. More important, they stress the need for the integration of school and community, and insist on education that is relevant to the current needs of the community. Only one pioneering project has responded to this challenge — "Education for Awareness and Involvement" (EAI) — the pilot project of a few private schools in the West Bank. It merits careful study because it contains the beginnings of a new Palestinian curriculum. The originators of EAI took a critical look at education in the West Bank and concluded that "it has become infected with the 'diploma disease': higher degree awarding has become the most important function of school education while the needs of about 90% of the students who never make it to university are not met" (EAI Brochure, 1988). In order to make education more relevant, they focus on five key areas:

1. Transforming teaching methods from lecturing to learning by doing
2. Making education more relevant to the world of work and production by including vocational training alongside academics
3. Introducing career counseling and internship programs to students in upper secondary grades
4. Including classes and activities more pertinent to the situation and developmental needs of the Occupied Palestinian Territories as well as increasing awareness of their unique environment and culture
5. Strengthening the ties between school and community through increased involvement in community service, the establishment of parents' committees, and parent involvement in the implementation of components of EAI

A pilot program was initiated in 1985 in the five Evangelical Lutheran Schools, and a year later in the Friends Boys School. These six schools have a total student body of about three thousand boys and girls from a wide range of socioeconomic backgrounds, from working to upper middle class. Now, nearly five years after the originators of EAI put the ideas together, the program has moved considerably toward implementing the five major goals identified above.

Teachers' committees were formed for each academic subject. These committees coordinated workshops on student-centered learning. They are presently developing activities to complement and enrich the official school curricula and textbooks. This whole approach is intended to help teachers develop self-confidence and become actively involved in a lifelong process of curriculum enrichment and development and to keep textbooks and curricula continuously relevant.

Vocational education workshops have been established in each of the participating schools. All seventh- through ninth-grade students are enrolled in two workshop periods each week. They also visit production and work sites to familiarize them with different careers in their community. Some of the schools participating in EAI have started student production in their workshops. The products, such as pottery and ceramics, are marketed through school fairs or in local shops. Some of the skills the students learn in vocational education classes, such as gardening and food preservation, have gained more importance during the intifadah, making it easier for the schools to convince the parents of the value of the nontraditional, nonacademic components of EAI. As a result, individual schools are currently thinking of placing greater stress on vocational education and reviewing course offerings. Preliminary assessment of the vocational education component of EAI has exposed a lack of centralized curriculum and too great a reliance on traditional manual-training methods. A number of teachers who were interested or involved in academic counseling have been trained in the area of career counseling during the past three years. They are presently involved in setting up a career counseling office in each of their schools.

Materials that have been developed to increase student awareness of Palestinian society are currently used in some classes. According to Yacoub Qumsiya, chairperson of the follow-up committee of EAI, the intifadah has done more than any formal course of study could ever have accomplished. In the words of a recent progress report, the last fifteen months have increased the "awareness of the students about their society and their readiness to participate in its development" (Azzouni-Mahshi, 1988). In addition, a two-year workshop for science teachers in Environmental Awareness and Protection has begun to study the natural environment of Palestine and to document the names of wild plants and animals. Again, the intifadah has stimulated new interest in Palestinian culture and history, which should be developed in future classes.

Has any progress been made in improving ties between schools and communities? The intifadah has interfered with progress in this area, although it has increased awareness of the importance of cooperation between the school and the community by making school education a preparation for life in the West Bank Palestinian community and, hopefully, in the future Palestinian state. EAI schools have not openly addressed the issues raised by popular education, but they have reinforced the belief that the community can and should be a very powerful force in shaping its own educational future.

Palestinian educators have rarely allowed themselves the luxury of dreaming about their own system of education, but EAI seems to be a step in that direction. It insists on basic changes in the teaching-learning process and in the curriculum. It has a program for realizing this goal. Four or five new schools will probably join the original ones, and others (all private) have shown an interest in the program. The originators still face some daunting challenges, such as giving students (especially veterans of the intifadah) a real voice in determining their educational future, providing good political and economic education for future leaders, evaluating the overall effectiveness of EAI at the end of five years, and finding ways to make it work in *all* schools in the Occupied Territories, not just a selected few. The real test of the value of this innovative program is whether it is flexible enough to provide an educational model for the future.

Some would argue that innovative educational programs like that of the EAI and others mentioned above won't work without a fundamental change of attitude on the part of the Palestinian population as a whole. Munir Fasheh, a professor of education at Birzeit University, is researching new ways of learning. His approach complements that of EAI by promoting learning in situations where it is least expected. Fasheh contends that if people come to value learning outside traditional institutions, learning will become a community-wide and "infectious" process. Once again, the intifadah has made the unexpected possible by throwing refugee camp dwellers and upper-middle-class businessmen into the same struggle. Both will have to change their attitudes about education fundamentally if they want to be prepared for the future.

Conclusion

The colonial heritage of the Palestinians has not only left them with an irrelevant system of education, but created a culturally dependent mentality. Whenever they have had the rare opportunity to decide what their children should study they copied ready-made programs from the West. The intifadah has brought about a fundamental change in this attitude: people from all sectors of Palestinian society have come to realize the strength that comes from collective action. From this newly found sense of power has grown a confidence in their ability to promote major institutional change and to achieve national independence. They have come to realize that an educational system stemming from their own culture and responding to their particular needs is essential in the foundation of a future state.

The intifadah has challenged Palestinians to change their attitudes about the process of learning and the existing system of education. But are the people of Palestine up to this challenge? In many interviews conducted for this article, one gets a contradictory sense of people wanting to return to life the way it was before this period of struggle and pain, yet also wanting to build a brand-new society. Palestinians have a similar attitude toward education. On the one hand, they want to return to school and pick up where they left off before the uprising started. On the other, they are experimenting with many new forms of learning. The uncertainties of the intifadah have made people look for a few islands of security, and the educational system, in whatever form, represents one of them. If people are unwilling to settle for the old ways of learning and schooling, will they put the effort into making the substantial changes required? It is really too soon to know, but one is tempted to say that as the intifadah continues, it will deepen the Palestinian resolve to take any risks necessary to build a new state and establish new institutions.

References

Al Haq. (1988a). *Israel's war against education in the occupied West Bank.* Ramallah: Author (Law in the Service of Man Series).

Al Haq. (1988b). *Punishing a nation.* Ramallah: Author (Law in the Service of Man Series).

Azzouni-Mahshi, S. (1988). *Education for awareness and involvement. Progress report no. 1-1988.* Jerusalem: Evangelical Lutheran Church.

Badran, N. A. (1969). *Education and modernization in Palestine: 1918–1948.* Beirut: Palestine Liberation Organization Research Center.

Cohen, J. S. (1989, May 18). Education as crime. *The Jerusalem Post.*

Graham-Brown, S. (1984). *Education, repression and liberation: Palestinians.* London: World University Services.

Jerusalem Media and Communication Center. (1989). *Palestinian education: A threat to Israel's security?* Jerusalem: Author.

Palestine Royal Commission Report. (1937). London: Palestine Royal Commission.

Tamari, S. (1988). What the uprising means. *Middle East Report, 152,* 24–30.

Tibawi, A. L. (1956). *Arab education in mandatory Palestine.* London: World University Services

Interview with Khalil Mahshi

Khalil Mahshi is a senior program specialist with the International Institute for Educational Planning at the United Nations Educational, Scientific, and Cultural Organization (UNESCO) and former director-general of international and public relations for the Palestinian Ministry of Education and Higher Education. On December 1, 2005, two members of the Editorial Board of the Harvard Educational Review *spoke with Mahshi about the legacy of the first Palestinian* intifadah *(uprising) and the current state of Palestinian education. Khalil Mahshi — who asked us to call him "Khalil" — emphasized the subjective nature of his observations and the complex role of commenting on the work of colleagues who are still engaged in the difficult work of building an education system. Khalil describes the changes that have taken place in the education of Palestinians since he and Kim Bush wrote "The Palestinian Uprising and Education for the Future" in 1989, and he outlines lessons from this development process that are applicable globally to the building and rebuilding of education systems in the face of occupation, resistance, and conflict.*

We are excited to speak with you, Khalil. We would like you to start by describing the educational situation in the West Bank and Gaza since the publication of your and Kim Bush's 1989 HER article, "The Palestinian Uprising and Education for the Future." What is the current status of the education system from preschool to higher education, including the kinds of alternative and community-based forms of education that you describe in that article?

Community-based education existed at the time we wrote the article because Palestinian schools were ordered closed by the Israeli military authorities. And so the community created alternatives to the closed schools. Since then, the situation has changed significantly. There is now a Ministry of Education and Higher Education in Palestine. There are two regions of Palestine — the West Bank and Gaza. Palestine is still not an independent state, [but] there is some sort of autonomy, self-rule. And, therefore, there is a Ministry of Education, which manages education at all levels. The system is managed by one ministry in both regions, the West Bank and Gaza, but in East Jerusalem, the Palestinian Ministry of Education doesn't have full control.

So, now is the time to develop education — it has been for a while — because there is a Ministry of Education. But you have to keep in mind that [Palestine] is not an independent state. There are [therefore] some constraints, and the constraints

235

have to do with the resources that are available to the Palestinians to develop their system of education. If it were an independent state — with a good tax collection system working and good external relations in terms of trade, export and import, and free movement within the country and across borders — maybe its revenues would improve and there would be more financial resources to develop education and more freedom to develop human resources. The constraints also relate to the Palestinians being carefully watched by the donor community and the international community at large in terms of what curriculum they develop, what textbooks they write, and what they include in the curriculum and the textbooks. This is the time to develop Palestinian education but not with total freedom.

In 1989, you wrote of "a future when a Palestinian system of education can be developed." How did the system of education that exists now, which is managed by one Ministry of Education, develop from the community-based forms you described in the article?

After the Oslo agreements between Israel and the Palestine Liberation Organization [in 1993], there was a decision to establish the Palestinian Authority.[1] Therefore, a number of ministries had to be established. In late August of 1994, a minister of education was appointed and, immediately after that, a core group of ten people were contacted to set up the ministry. I was one of them.

We started from scratch. We were lucky in the sense that the minister and the deputy minister who were appointed at that time — Yasser Amro and Naim Abu Hommos — wanted people who were professional educators and professional workers. He went for people who were professionally trained and who were experienced in their own fields, so it was appointment of people based on merit. These ten people created a number of departments within the ministry. You can guess most of these departments: teacher training, human resources, curriculum development, planning, financial matters, management of field offices, international relations, etc.

One clear relationship between popular education as we described it in our 1989 article and the [establishment of the] Ministry of Education is that the people who were appointed to lead the process were people who were known for their activity in education and education-related fields.

The other aspect that relates to popular education is that from the very beginning of the work of the Ministry of Education, a decision was made to involve "stakeholders," to involve the community in the work of the ministry, in giving opinions and in participating in decision-making related to the development of education.

What would you say is the legacy of the first intifadah, *which began in 1987, and the impact on Palestinian education of a continued Israeli presence in the West Bank and Gaza?*

There are two kinds of impacts, in my view. One is a positive impact. When you have occupation, you have resistance; and when you have resistance, you have defiance, and you have room for initiative, and you have room for creativity. You have room for being daring and defying. People may disagree with me, but I think a positive impact of occupation is the spirit of defiance by the occupied, by the people under occupation.

This is what was reflected in popular education: It was an act of defiance. Maybe we did not manage to cover the curriculum during the repeated closure of schools; maybe we did not give quality education. But it was an act of defiance that was translated through the process of popular education, which meant that *both* the teachers and the students were highly motivated. The whole community was highly motivated to be part of the education process.

In normal circumstances, the students are not as motivated to be part of the education process. They feel the process of schooling is some sort of homework, it is some sort of burden, which wasn't the case during popular education. Nobody forced anybody to go to school. The students would come because they wanted to come, because they were defying. And nobody forced teachers to come; [the popular education teachers] were not being paid, [and] it was also an act of defiance on the part of these "teachers."

This spirit is not the same any more. We're back to schooling. We're back to forcing students to come, and parents forcing their children to go, and teachers have to go because it's their job. Some go because they like it, but not the majority.

The negatives are many. As you know, Palestine is still not independent. We hope it's on its way to becoming a state. The situation on the ground since the first intifadah, in a sense, has worsened. Notably the separation wall, the Israeli separation wall, is causing many problems in terms of movement of Palestinians, whether students or teachers, and therefore is negatively impacting education.

Also, part of the negative legacy of the first intifadah is that schools were ordered closed. There was popular education, but it never could cover the same amount of work and quality of work that normally schools would cover. Therefore, academic quality in the Palestinian territories dropped. And we are still suffering, as Palestinians, from this dropping of quality. Quality became worse, and those who graduated from schools during the first intifadah are now teachers and managers and doctors; I think the quality of these people in terms of their knowledge and skills [is] worse than their predecessors. Therefore, this is affecting the whole society. And we are still suffering from that.

What is the legacy of the first intifadah for young Palestinians who did not experience this time and for their education today?

Young people now have not been directly affected by the first intifadah, but their teachers have been. Their teachers were then students, so the quality [of teaching], in my opinion, is not as good as it would have been if we didn't have the closure of schools during the first intifadah and punishment by denying the Palestinians formal schooling, not only at school level but also at university level, for long periods of time.

I think that one of the lasting effects is that during the period of the Israeli occupation — which still, in a sense, in one form exists in the Palestinian territories — Palestinians were denied [the chance] to teach about their own society and to develop a national identity. This is one of the priorities of the present system of education, which is being expressed through the kind of curriculum that is being developed, and the focus on activities related to national identity. When you're denied something that is important to you, you really work hard to get it done. This is what you see happening now in the Palestinian education system.

It is done through the curriculum, which is teaching now about Palestine, about Palestinian culture. You can see it also in extracurricular activities, which focus on folkloric dance, on Palestinian music, on Palestinian literature. You see it in many flags raised as well, which the Palestinians couldn't do before. You couldn't raise a Palestinian flag. You would be imprisoned if you did.

You describe the first intifadah as "the opportunity of a lifetime" for education and describe the changes in thinking around education that resulted from this period of struggle. Have there been other periods of intense change that have added or magnified the legacy of the first intifadah, as you have just described it?

The only intense change was the setting up of the Palestinian Authority and, therefore, the establishment of a Ministry of Education and, very importantly, the development of a Palestinian curriculum. This is the first time in history that the Palestinians have had an opportunity to develop their own curriculum and to write their own textbooks. This is very important; I cannot overemphasize it. It is something which Palestinians always craved: they wanted to be in control of what their children study in schools and not to be denied certain topics or certain subjects or certain textbooks or parts of textbooks.

How has the development of the curriculum and the textbooks taken place?

The development of a Palestinian Curriculum Development Center was a joint venture between the Palestinian Ministry of Education and UNESCO [United Nations Educational, Scientific, and Cultural Organization]. It started [in October 1995] with funding coming through UNESCO from Italy, where UNESCO would provide the technical support to set up a Palestinian Curriculum Development Center under the Ministry of Education. At the beginning of its work, the ministry involved academics from outside the ministry to lead the process of establishing the curriculum center and of reviewing the existing textbooks — the Jordanian [textbooks] in the West Bank and the Egyptian [textbooks] in Gaza — in preparation for putting together the elements of the curriculum and the syllabuses and, later, the textbooks.

How would you describe the implementation of the new curriculum and the introduction of the new textbooks in schools?

The Ministry set a time frame to develop the curriculum and to produce the textbooks.[2] This year, they are in the final stage. [The curricula and textbooks from Jordan and Egypt that were used in the West Bank and Gaza respectively] were replaced in stages by the Palestinian curriculum and Palestinian textbooks, two grades at a time each year, and this is the final year. After this year, [all of the] textbooks would have been replaced by Palestinian ones. And while the replacement is taking place, review of the new Palestinian textbooks is happening every year, and partial rewriting is also happening.

Just anecdotally, what do you hear from your friends or family or on the street in terms of sentiment about this new curriculum and new textbooks?

I think people are still thrilled that we can write our own textbooks based on our own curriculum. But, there are divergent views. If you ask a certain number of intellectuals in the Palestinian community, they would tell you that the textbooks and the curriculum are not up to their expectations. If you ask others, [they] would be elated simply by the fact that it is our own textbooks written by ourselves, not by others, and that we have full control of — almost full control of — what we have in these textbooks.

How you can create a consensus is the difficult question. How can you create agreement on what is to be changed and how it is to be changed and what is our common vision? It's a very difficult question — how do you create a common vision? This is why the ministry wanted to involve, as much as possible, the community in its own internal discussions about the curriculum. And [the Curriculum Development Center] has done so: town meetings, focus group meetings, interviews with leading figures, and consultations with academics and technicians. [There has been] a whole process of getting views on what is to be done, and how, and the content and how it is to be taught. Whether everything has been translated into an action plan by the ministry is the question. I think most of it has. Whether everybody is satisfied, I'm sure not. There are many people who are *not* satisfied. They would like to have better results. And each person defines what "better" is. So it's a big process. I don't think there is full satisfaction with what the ministry has done. You hear criticism, but this is natural.

You talk about the possibility that occupation creates for generating resistance. How would you describe the role that education plays in generating this resistance?

Education creates resistance by clarifying what the harmful effects of occupation are and by reinforcing the sense of community. Occupation is very harsh on individuals, but it is less harsh on people if they stick together. There is strength in being together even under harsh measures, like closure of schools. Take the first intifadah as an example. When [our schools] were ordered closed, if we each sat at home and taught our own children, we wouldn't have a strong sense of defiance and resistance as much as we would have when we [engaged in] the popular education movement. We got together as a community. We felt we were being collectively punished and we had to respond collectively — not individually, not within family units. And, therefore, in that sense occupation created resistance, created defiance, created elements of innovation, created elements of creativity to respond to these collective punishment measures.

You make a distinction between the kind of change that can happen at the individual or family level and the change that happens with large-scale involvement. What role do you think education currently plays in shaping Palestinians at an individual level, and what role it might play in larger-scale change?

Education is now trying to create a national sense of identity with elements I have described earlier. And I think it is also trying to attempt change at the individual level by creating ability to self-learn. In my view, [education in Palestine] has not yet succeeded in creating enough ability to have self-learning happen so, in that sense, education still has to go some way in Palestine. Education has to go a *long* way, really, before it allows the individual to [experience] self-learning, to [develop] self-confidence. Self-learning and learning by doing lead to active involvement in the learning process, to mastery of skills, and to a sense of ownership of knowledge. When involved, one feels that one has been productive and has made significant accomplishment. Production, accomplishment, mastery, and ownership are basic ingredients of self-confidence.

If there is self-confidence amongst Palestinian youth, it is not thanks to schools so far. It is more thanks to the culture of resistance that has been created within the Palestinian community and which is still taking place. The Palestinian community is still struggling to get independence, and the youth have played an important role in resistance. They have always led resistance, all through the various stages of occupation and resistance to occupation. The credit [for developing self-confidence] is not really to formal schooling, it is to the broader sense of education that happens mostly outside schools. It also happens partially within schools, but not *mainly* inside schools.

What implications does the second intifadah, that began in September 2000, have for how you think about the first intifadah, particularly related to the situation of education?

I did not live through the whole period of the second intifadah because I left a few months after it started. But from what I have witnessed first hand, the first intifadah was more of what we call "intifadah." Let me qualify this: Intifadah is an uprising. The meaning of intifadah is "shaking off." And people wanted to shake off Israeli occupation; they wanted to get rid of Israeli occupation. And what was different about the first intifadah, is that it was really popular, in the sense that everybody was involved. In the second intifadah, I felt that people were not as involved. This is a major difference: Many people felt detached from the second intifadah, in contrast to the first intifadah. The young people were involved, but not all others to the same extent.

And I think the second intifadah missed a lot of the creativity of the first intifadah, including related to education. But you have to keep in mind that during the second intifadah there *was* a Ministry of Education, there was a Palestinian system of education, a Palestinian *management* of education. So we did not have the need to have popular education because schools were not ordered closed by the military. (In certain areas they were, but not a blanket closure of all institutions like what happened during the first intifadah.) So, the second intifadah was less popular in terms of participation by the people. It was less demanding on our creative abilities. I think the first intifadah was a *real* intifadah, in the sense of popular participation; the second intifadah was marked by less participation and more use of violence and armed means of resistance.

You've stated why the kind of popular education that existed during the first intifadah doesn't exist in the current context. Are there other kinds of popular education that do need to exist today that may be slightly different in form but somewhat similar in intent?

I'm sometimes hesitant when we use [the word] "education." I clearly differentiate be-tween education in the broad sense and schooling. Although I'm interested in formal schooling and I've always worked for formal schooling, I see its limitations in terms of educating people for life after school. In that sense, popular education related better to the daily life of students, to their community. During the popular education period, daily life and issues of the community come into the teaching and learning process. Now there is more of a separation between this kind of relevant education and the kind of schooling that students get that is more formalistic, more bookish.

I think popular education does not exist any more. There are attempts at broaden-ing the education of students and even university students through some activities that the community initiates here and there, basically through NGOs [nongovern-mental organizations]. But the level of involvement by the community is not the same. The community has not pursued activity in education because it is not ex-pected to. At the time when we had popular education, schools were closed. Now schools are open and Palestinians are managing education — not the Israeli military any more. And so the community feels that education is in good hands.

You note that one of the challenges during the first intifadah was building and sustaining ties between schools and communities. Have there been efforts to create these links since that time?

Yes, the ministry tried to create better parents' associations; they have encouraged the process, but it was up to schools to do that. If you're asking me whether there are now stronger links between the school and the community as compared to the time when we didn't have any such mechanisms, yes, there *are* stronger links. If you are asking me whether I'm satisfied with the link between the school and the community, I would say, not really. I would have liked to see more participation on the part of the community in the life of the schools and the schools in the life of the community.

I've recently visited Egypt and, at the face value of it, I was impressed to see that the Egyptian Ministry of Education has decreed the creation of boards of trustees for each school, involving parents, teachers, and the principal or the director of the school himself or herself. Most importantly, this decree has given more authority to the community representatives on that board of trustees to make decisions on how the school operates, its budget, its future plans, its yearly plans. This hasn't happened in Palestine. Schools are still strongly governed by the Ministry of Education. I would like to see more school-community links in many respects, including the creation of decisionmaking governing boards. There should be a clearer direction toward giving more decisionmaking power to the community.

When you worked as director-general of international and public relations for the Pales-tinian Ministry of Education in Ramallah from August 1994 to January 2001, it was clearly a different time from when you wrote the article in 1989. When you were with the ministry, what was your vision for education of Palestinians?

Very different times, but my personal vision remained the same. You see, at the Min-istry of Education I was in charge of external relations, which meant really two things. It meant fundraising and liaising to the external world to get support for start-ing the development process of education. But since at that time we did not have a plan for the development of education, I had to inject my own vision. But also to make sure that the vision of my other colleagues who started the Ministry of Educa-tion was incorporated.

So my personal vision, as reflected in the article of 1989, is, first, to engage the stu-dents in active learning. They should be active in their own learning — if you want the jargon, student-centered approaches to teaching and learning. Second, [they should] learn about their situation, about their country. Third, [they should] strengthen their Palestinian identity because the Palestinian identity was not being reinforced by the curriculum or by formal teaching. They were denied the right to study about Palestine, and they were denied the right to reflect about the situation in Palestine. Fourth, I had as part of my vision to relate school education to the world of work — to production, to employment, to skill development for production. Fifth, my vision incorporated an element of participation in decisionmaking by students, relating to their education and their future life. Finally, my vision included an ele-ment of values—important values which would make it possible for people to live to-gether, to work together, to build a healthy society, and to be open to the world, not to be enclosed. Because when you're reinforcing a national identity sometimes you become chauvinistic, and that wasn't part of my vision.

In your article, you noted some of the challenges and some of the promises of Education for Awareness and Involvement.³ Has it been developed, changed, implemented, or studied further since 1989?

The Education for Awareness and Involvement captured most of my vision for edu-cation. But it's not only *my* vision — it's the vision of many people like me who worked in the education field in Palestine, who believed in a more progressive form of education. By more progressive, I mean more relevant, with clearer values that re-late to the development of society, and incorporating things we learn from the out-side world into our own education. Education for Awareness and Involvement en-capsulated these elements.

The crux of Education for Awareness and Involvement is the teaching process it-self, the teaching and learning process. In order to translate the philosophy of Educa-tion for Awareness and Involvement into action, you need teachers who would not lecture at students. You need teachers who would animate, who would incite, who would facilitate discussion and action on the part of students. You need to have *active learning* inside the classroom.

Active learning is the opposite of rote learning. Unfortunately, if you look at Pal-estinian schools nowadays, you see lecturing going on, based on the textbooks only. If you wanted to see active learning — in the sense of not bookish, academic, and lecturing methods — I don't think you would see many cases. And this is, I think, where the whole process of changing the system from the formal schooling/rote learning system into an active learning system centered around the child hasn't really happened.

Why? Because the teachers are not capable of doing that. They need to be equipped with better skills and they need to be freed from working toward preparing students for exams. The system of examinations is negatively impacting on our education system, most importantly what we call the *Tawjihi*, which is the matriculation exam at the end of twelve years of schooling. It still decides the future of students. As long as this is the most important aspect of schooling in Palestine, teachers and students will all work toward the same thing: passing the exam. And all other aspects of good schooling and good education will become subsidiary to that.

One of the contradictions that you noted about the first intifadah was the development of what you called a "culturally dependent mentality" and the idea of a tension between people wanting to go back to a predictable life versus an excitement about creating a new society. Does this tension continue to play itself out today?

Yes, the tension still exists. But now the tension is partially due to the fact that a new element is coming in: the Internet, globalization at large, the influence of the outside world on each community and each country. This is part of the new tension, tension brought about by external factors that are trying to create homogeneity of cultures. This is now the new tension: being part of the outside world, part of the international community, aspiring to become an independent state, and, therefore, being on equal footing with other countries and other nations, yet at the same time preserving our own culture, our own identity. This is not unique to the Palestinians.

How do the media and technology affect education of Palestinians today, especially in this era of globalization?

This is a positive development in the Palestinian schools. There have been serious attempts by the Ministry of Education to include media, very specifically, computers and the use of the Internet in schools. A few months ago they also initiated a major project together with the Ministry of Communication and the information technology businesses in the West Bank and Gaza to introduce more computers and more use of the Internet in the schools. This is very different from the popular education we were talking about, but it is a positive development in the direction of the vision that you asked me about, which is bringing knowledge about the world into the classroom.

I mentioned this opening up to the world as one of the elements of the vision that I and others had. I think this is happening through the Internet. Whether all schools would be able to have this accessibility to the Internet is still a question, but I think it is moving in that direction.

Why is it so important for education to help open up the world for Palestinians?

Palestine is very small. It doesn't have many natural resources. The best resources that Palestinians have are human beings. If our children are not knowledgeable about the world, if they cannot compete for income generation in this more globalized world, then it will be tough on the Palestinians economically. We will not have many sources of income. Our sources of income [need to be] more or less based on providing services and value addition to certain services, for instance, computer technologies, development of software. These all depend on our people and our human resources.

We have highly competitive neighbors: Israel, next door, is well advanced in terms of computer technology, information technology, and it's well advanced in terms of providing services, like tourism. Jordan is moving up in this direction. So the two most immediate neighbors are relatively advanced. We have the potential. But if we are enclosed, if we are not open to learning and to incorporating what we learn from other countries and from the world at large, we will be behind. And we cannot afford to be behind.

What do you think the role of peace education is within popular education?

The concern of the popular education movement was resistance to occupation. In resistance to foreign occupation you have an element of peace-building, because peace cannot be built by dominating and being dominated. Lasting peace is built between two equally free parties. In that sense, resistance itself was part of peace-building and peace education, since it aspired for freedom for the Palestinians on equal footing with the Israelis.

There isn't really an element in the present curriculum that is clearly called "peace education." This is one of the points of contention about the Palestinian curriculum, whether they should be teaching more clearly about Israel as a neighbor or not. That's a very sensitive issue that has always been a matter of heated debates and discussions within the Palestinian community itself, and between the Palestinian community and the Ministry of Education on the one hand and Israel and other parties on the other hand.

There isn't an element of peace education clearly defined as such within the Palestinian curriculum, and there wasn't within the popular education movement during the first intifadah. But you find many activities in Palestine, and also in Israel that relate to peace education at the level of trying to create mutual understanding and reconciliation. These activities have recently become more difficult — after the second intifadah and after the restriction of movement of Palestinians by the Israelis, with the separation wall and with putting up checkpoints. Before, Palestinians were able to move more freely between the West Bank and Gaza and Israel, and, therefore, to communicate, meet, have dialogue, debates, and joint activities with Israelis, which I would put under peace education at large. Now it has become more difficult and a little bit frustrating.

Currently, you work as a senior program specialist with the International Institute for Educational Planning at UNESCO. Has your vision for the education of Palestinians changed since you stepped out of a government role and started working for UNESCO? How do your experiences in Palestinian education shape your work around the world?

I think in all countries where I work, I aspire for the same thing. If a country needs support, we give it support. This is the role of UNESCO and the role of the UN. In my work, I focus on helping ministries of education based on my experience in Palestine, which was a very rich experience. I was lucky to be there when the Ministry of Education was created. How many people get the chance to start a Ministry of Education from scratch? I think very few around the world.

I go to areas or countries where there has been either conflict or a situation of emergency. [These are places where] a Ministry of Education didn't exist, or existed but stopped functioning — the case of Afghanistan, for instance, or places where there is civil war. I help ministries build capacity for planning and for quality improvement, which means I focus on their departments of planning, creating them, helping ministries develop them, and then helping ministries focus on what is important. After they achieve or start achieving access, what is important is the *quality* of education. Access to and quality of education are major, and a third element that is major is proper management.

I'm lucky to have been given the opportunity to keep believing in the same things I believed in, to keep having the same vision, and to be working to help countries that need assistance to realize this kind of vision.

What are some of the challenges Palestinians face now with respect to short-term and long-term educational planning?

In a short period of time, the Palestinians have managed to create a well-functioning Ministry of Education. There are people who are not satisfied with the kind of curriculum or the quality of the textbooks, but I think, in general, the creation and the functioning of the Ministry of Education in Palestine has been a success story. And this is a great achievement: to start a ministry from scratch and, in a matter of ten years, to achieve what the Ministry of Education has achieved by developing a Palestinian curriculum, by managing schools, by building more schools (many more schools are being built), by getting everybody to school, by keeping salaries going, by creating a planning department and formulating a five-year plan and finishing the implementation of this plan, and entering the process of formulation of the second five-year plan. If you compare it with what other countries that have been independent for so long are doing, it is a major, major achievement. So in that sense I feel that the Palestinians have to be congratulated, especially the Ministry of Education.

The challenge is a challenge of having quality education; it's not only a challenge of bringing students to school. [Access] has been achieved, more or less, by the Ministry of Education and by the Palestinians at large. It's not only the ministry — we have to give credit to the community at large for supporting education. People give land to build schools on; people give money to build schools; people donate money to schools for planning purposes; people volunteer their time to support schools. It's the community at large: people giving of their time and energy to offer ideas and to come to meetings. It's a vibrant process. It could have been better, all of us can aspire for better, but it's a good process.

Now, as I said, the challenge is a challenge of having quality education. And by quality education, I go back to the same point: students learn freely and with relevant education, rather than bookish education, rather than just rote learning, rather than just a process of preparation to pass exams. This is still a problem in Palestinian education. Education requires us to build confidence in students, confidence to think, confidence to create, confidence to learn by themselves, and not to be slaves to books and to exams.

How do you assess whether education is of good quality or not? It's really by affecting change inside the classroom, and this is where teachers become important. It is the challenge of transforming the teaching methodology, the teaching methods that are used nowadays by teachers. It's creating teachers who are self-confident themselves, to create, to innovate, to facilitate the learning of students. This is the basic challenge, in my view, for Palestinian education at large.

How do you see the education of Palestinians in 2015, the target year for reaching the Millennium Development Goals?

In terms of millennium goals, the Palestinians are very close to achieving comprehensive basic education: All children who should be in schools *are* more or less in schools, both male and female. So in terms of access to primary or basic education, the Palestinians don't have a problem. There are still a few children not attending or dropping out of education, but I think the record shows improvement. By 2015, I don't think the Palestinians will have a problem in terms of access to education if they go on doing what they are doing now, in terms of building schools and classrooms.

In terms of preschool, [access to which is also one of the Millennium Development Goals], it's a challenge. The percentage of the population group in preschool is around 35 percent. There is a long way before achieving comprehensive preschooling, and I don't think it's realizable by 2015. Preschool is provided not by the government; it's provided by the community, and NGOs, and I don't think they will be able to provide 100 percent preschooling.

In terms of equity, I think the Palestinians *are* achieving equity between males and females, and providing education for the poor is not a problem in Palestine. Everybody goes to school.

In terms of quality, this is the challenge — what kind of quality of education are we providing, and can we provide better quality in the way *I* defined it? Again, people may differ on definition. [By quality] I mean self-learning, I mean confidence, I mean inculcation of values that will keep the community cohesive, and opening up to the world. I think quality is the major challenge when it comes to the Millennium Development Goals.

What changes do you expect for education in the aftermath of the Israeli military withdrawal from Gaza?

I don't see any major change as a result of withdrawal from Gaza. My hope is that Gaza will sincerely be open to the outside world, which is not yet certain. Less than two weeks ago [November 2005] the border point between Gaza and Egypt was opened, seemingly under Palestinian control, with the presence of European observers and with remote observance by Israel. I'm hoping that this will be an opportunity for Gazans to lead a more normal life [with the possibility for freedom of movement] and, therefore, this would introduce some new demands on education. Otherwise, I don't see a major change happening in the education system because of the Israeli withdrawal from Gaza. I think people misinterpret the withdrawal of Israel as full independence, which is not yet the case.

What role has education — within the kind of culture of resistance that you've described — played in your life and your development as an educator and an activist?

Education, first of all, has helped me create awareness. I'm not talking only about formal schooling because I am also one of the products of schooling under occupation. I have learned through the broader networks of education: youth movements, political parties, meetings. I was one of the people who were open to and also took initiatives to meet with Israelis; this is also part of my broader education.

[These experiences] created a new sense of resistance. You resist to not only to overcome your enemy; you resist to be on equal terms with who is presently your enemy, so that you are partners to peace later on. And, therefore, you are not trying to defeat your enemy. You are trying to make your enemy come to terms with the fact that we both have to coexist and hopefully cooperate within our region. This kind of education I did not get from my schooling days, or from my university days. It came as a result of being involved in political activities, being involved in community-related activities, in voluntary work for the community, in NGOs, and also being part of the attempts of Palestinian peace activists and Israeli peace activists to get together and to work together. I think this has broadened my view of what we are trying to achieve: a two-state solution and not to defeat Israel. The purpose is not to defeat Israel. The purpose is to achieve peace.

Is there anything else you wanted to add, Khalil?

Yes. One thing. You're asking me about Palestinian education and about Palestinians maybe because I'm Palestinian and I happened to be there at that moment in time [the first intifadah], and wrote this article [in the *Harvard Educational Review*]. I was proud that the person I wrote the article with was not a Palestinian. He was an American, which brings me to my point. I believe in good education for all children, not only for Palestinian children. This is why I am really lucky to be working at the International Institute for Education Planning, which puts me in a position to be assisting other countries and other ministries of education, not only the Palestinian Ministry of Education, to realize better quality education for *all* children.

And this is what I was, in a sense, missing in Palestine. I've always worked for Palestinian education and in Palestine, but I felt that before being Palestinian and before being of a certain religion, I'm a human being. I think this is why I kept insisting on opening up to the world; this is more important than being of a certain nationality and carrying a certain flag or working in a certain country. We should insist that we are all human beings who have much more in common than we have differences. And, therefore, we should learn from each other and we should help each other. Our work in one part of the world should help us learn lessons that we can use in other parts of the world, with adaptation, of course.

Therefore, I do not want to give the impression that Palestinians are behind or ahead of others; it's a process that is happening all around the world to various degrees. It's a process of change. And it's a process of creating a common understanding of what works and what doesn't work, and a sharing of experiences. The Palestinians have contributed to this learning process by providing this model of popular education during part of their history, during the first intifadah. If this popular education experiment has ended, it has ended because it wasn't needed any more. But we have to learn from it. We have to keep remembering *why* we started it and what we aspire to have and to keep feeding that learning into formal education systems, not only the Palestinian system but other education systems as well.

Notes

1. Text of the agreement is available online at http://www.yale.edu/lawweb/avalon/mideast/ isrplo.htm.
2. See http://www.pcdc.edu.ps/clarification_III.htm for more information on this process.
3. Education for Awareness and Involvement was a pilot project initiated in 1985 in six private schools in the West Bank. It focuses on five key elements of educational transformation: active learning; vocational training; career exploration; study of the Palestinian situation; and building ties between school and community.

Transference and Appropriation in Popular Education Interventions: A Framework for Analysis

LILIANA VACCARO

In the last twenty years, popular education projects have increased in Latin America. In Chile, as in many other Latin American countries, this type of education has three basic features. First, it is defined by its relationship to poverty, because it seeks to alleviate the educational deficiencies of the poorest sectors of society, whose members either are illiterate or have very limited access to schools. Second, popular education is based on the understanding that the educational needs of the poor are not derived merely from inadequacies in schooling. Therefore, popular education must contribute to solving the vital problems of the poor: providing support strategies for survival and satisfaction of basic needs, generating employment, and incorporating the active participation of the people who live in popular sectors in society.[1] For this reason, popular education does not fit institutional frameworks, and is instead initiated through community education programs. Third, popular education is not politically neutral. It represents a cultural struggle that questions the ideology that dominant groups in society want to impose on the people of popular sectors. It is an educational activity that has developed within popular sectors in response to their problems.

Popular education projects are based in a variety of grassroots organizations, which either may have existed before the educational programs began, or were developed through them. The projects are usually supported by nongovernmental organizations (NGOs), though they may have evolved with professional help (from social workers, teachers, anthropologists, sociologists, economists, architects, or others).

A vital element of popular education projects is their liberating perspective. Popular education may be described in the following ways: 1) as a pedagogical ideology that aims at contributing to the raising of consciousness and to the participation of people in society; 2) as a pedagogical practice that emphasizes the use of participatory methods and the analysis of technical tools that are linked to solving concrete problems in participants' lives; and 3) as a political agenda for strengthening the social

Harvard Educational Review   Vol. 60 No. 1   February 1990, 62–78
Translated from the Spanish by Alan West.

identity of popular sectors, valuing and preserving their culture, and linking educational activities to the social organization and mobilization of popular sectors (García-Huidobro, 1988, p. 1).

In general, community projects have been successful in at least two ways. First, they offer concrete answers and solutions to problems affecting the quality of life of the poor and, second, the people from the communities who benefit from these programs become directly involved in a process of personal and social development. Two young people, participants in the Learning Workshops program, explain that they have grown as individuals and have committed themselves to collective work in their community through working in the Learning Workshops and other church organizations:

> Often you can see reality, even around here. I know my neighbor is hungry, but I don't become socially involved. The program helps me confront reality: church is not only for praying.

> When I was arrested they came to visit me. This motivates me and makes me want to keep on working. It has helped me personally. Otherwise I'd be hooked on marihuana or alcohol. Now I have something.[2] (Vaccaro & Sotomayor, 1987, p. 60)

Despite their success and the active participation of their members, these community projects usually died out once the team of professionals withdrew. Thus, the study of factors which facilitate or hinder the continuity of such programs is necessary. This situation is particularly serious, since one aim of the programs is to help the participants become autonomous; that is, able to run the programs and initiate the educational process themselves (by defining objectives, developing teaching methods, managing resources, and using educational materials). This article presents a particular case where autonomy has been accomplished effectively. The Learning Workshops Program has existed for twelve years now, and in some communities the program is run autonomously by community members, who develop as leaders by participating in the Workshops.

The achievement of autonomy by participants in educational interventions can be examined by analyzing the *transference-appropriation process.* The experience of the Learning Workshops defines transference as the phase in which the professional team, wanting the participants to become automonous in managing the programs, have collaborated with different groups in popular sectors in their work and shared their knowledge and information on teaching methods and techniques. In the appropriate phase of the process, participants learn concepts and knowledge and develop values and attitudes that enable them to then take control of the programs and generate new possibilities for social action.

In the transference-appropriation process an initial proposal is negotiated and developed with the beneficiaries from the community.[3] Negotiation allows participants to review and evaluate proposals drafted by the professionals, shaping the way the educational program is appropriated by the community. This is not a mechanical process, in which participants passively receive an unchanging body of knowledge and techniques. Instead, negotiations generate interaction between the professionals and members of the community who benefit from the program. Participants contribute

Boy in Pudahuel, a popular sector in the northwest of Santiago.

from their own perspectives and experiences to the construction of a project that they all value.

This article examines the transference-appropriation process in community-based projects. Starting with a description of one particular community-based educational project, the Learning Workshops Program, we will analyze the transference-appropriation process in this situation. Our discussion will then focus more closely on the appropriation phase of the process, because it takes into account the learning process of participants who have acquired competencies that generate social action, as well as their perceptions and commitment to the educational proposal of the program.

Examining the Learning Workshops experience will help us to address these questions: How and under what conditions are the participants of the program able to attain autonomy of action, whereby they can take over a project and manage it themselves? What competencies for social action enable participants to solve their problems? In what ways do developed competencies generate new possibilities for action in the communities?

Description of the Learning Workshops Program

The Learning Workshops program was initiated in 1977 by Programa Interdisciplinario de Investigaciónes en Educación (PIIE) in Santiago, Chile, with two clearly defined goals:

1. To confront an acute problem in Chile: the educational failure of children from low-income areas resulting from educational inequality;[4] and

2. To overcome this problem by using the educational potential of the community in a process of collective improvement and advancement.

The assumption underlying the development of the program is that in popular or slum areas there is a capacity to generate solutions for problems that affect daily existence.

By 1988, 10,000 children had been served in the program. In 1987 retention ranged from 65 percent in the northern part of the country to 91 percent in Curanilahue in the South. Currently, the program functions autonomously in communities in four regions of the country.

Poverty exists in each region, but the specific context in which each program functions is different. In Santiago, the program serves the people in the community of Pudahuel, one of the sectors where Learning Workshops have been functioning the longest (since 1980 without interruption). In this community the program started when three pastoral agents — workers connected to the Catholic Church who offer services to the community through educational activities and programs — discovered the existence of the Learning Workshops, and asked to start a pilot program in their sectors. Pudahuel is a poor area with a population of about 300,000. Unemployment has always been high; in 1980 it reached approximately 60 percent. Those who have stable employment, such as construction workers, street vendors, technicians who work in small shops, and vendors in fruit and vegetable markets, have incomes so low that many are unable to satisfy the minimum necessities for their families.

In Valparaiso, the program was developed in Cerro Los Placeres, a popular area located about 100 kilometers northwest of Santiago. Large families live in wooden shacks without connection to a sewage system. Dwellings are crowded, often shared by more than one family despite the small space. In the poorest sectors unemployment reaches approximately 70 percent.

In the north of the country (900 kilometers from Santiago) are three cities — Chanaral, Copiapo, and Vallenar — where the program began in 1983. Here, Learning Workshops are managed by the Instituto de Educación Popular, which is linked to the Catholic Church. The desert begins in the North, and villages are very isolated from each other. Many people work in the silver, iron, and gold mines. The *pirquineros* — miners who work using primitive methods and with insufficient resources — try to find metals in the Los Andes mountains. Men leave their families for long periods of time; women must work, but they earn very low salaries. Recently, employment has increased because of fruit exportation to the United States, but living conditions are similar to those in Cerro Los Placeres.

Another community in which Learning Workshops are developed in an autonomous way is Curanilahue (located 659 kilometers south of Santiago). This mining and forestry region is one of the poorest parts of the country. In 1987 unemployment was at 30 percent, and the majority of the people did not have stable jobs. Many miners work in the *pirquenes* (holes opened up in the hills to extract coal) without any kind of social security, and in most cases without a union contract. Curanilahue is one of many places where children must work to help their families — by gathering coal, cutting wood, and helping to carry sacks of goods to market.

In all the regions, the purpose of developing systematic work with children from slum areas is to help them overcome problems through teaching methods — which emphasize dialogue, group learning, and the participants' experiences and knowledge — that enable them to: 1) improve their self-image and self-expression, communication, and sociability through psychoeducational help; 2) overcome learning difficulties in reading, writing, and mathematics by providing encouraging learning situations and presenting attainable goals; 3) develop their own abilities and talents (critical spirit, imagination, and creativity) by using arts, crafts, and games; and 4) recognize and value the environment of their family, sector, region, and country by making these the central themes of educational materials and projects.[5] All activities (artistic, academic, and recreational) are integrated around these themes, and personal contact is encouraged through exhibits, visits by children to the neighborhood, and visits from parents and neighbors to the Learning Workshops.

From the beginning, a number of different participants have been involved in the Learning Workshops in the different communities. Children from six to twelve years old are selected according to general criteria: they are in the first four grades of school; they have dropped out because of economic or family problems; and they present learning or emotional difficulties that affect the development of their personality. The children are taught by monitors and coordinators, who work on a voluntary basis. Monitors are teenagers or adults from the neighborhood who have the personal and social motivation to work with children whose problems prevent them from having a positive experience in school.[6] At the same time, they have prepared themselves, with the assistance of the professional team, to be active members of their neighborhood (for example, belonging to cultural groups and participating in creating solutions for community problems). Coordinators, who are also teenagers or young adults, are in charge of monitors in each community. Frequently they have had previous experience as monitors.

To help the community to value and undertake the program, relationships are established between families with children and the local community — represented by different groups and organizations such as sports clubs, folklore and theater groups, mothers' clubs, children's soup kitchens, and job pools — through home visits, meetings in small and large groups, outings, and other workshop activities. The local community is represented in the program by an adult who acts as an advisor to the group of monitors, assisting them in their educational work and clarifying the way Learning Workshops function. This representative is responsible for the general administration of the program in the community: assigning resources, buying educational materials, and assigning rooms in which the program can operate. Professional staff from PIIE create and implement the educational interventions; the staff includes graduates in the field of education, psychologists, sociologists, elementary and high school teachers, and social workers.

A description of the role of the monitors will illustrate the participatory approach used in the Workshops. The young monitors live in the communities and are elected by local organizations supporting the educational endeavor (such as parishes or insti-

A group of popular educators working during a weekend preparatory session.

Children in one of the working sessions in Cerro Los Placeres.

tutions associated with the Catholic Church). They are chosen according to certain preestablished criteria: their educational level, their interest in working with children, their capacity to work as part of a team, and their sensitivity to social problems. Once they begin, the monitors work with children in two-hour sessions once a week; contact families through visits, meetings, or other activities; and attend preparatory sessions. As volunteers, monitors work eight hours a week.

The preparation of monitors is based on a participatory methodology. Monitors begin by examining personal experiences, reflecting collectively on them in order to learn from their lives in the communities. They then reinforce their collective learning and democratic relationships in a climate of personal and collective freedom, and integrate intellectual knowledge, simple craft projects, play, and artistic expression in an active learning process. Furthermore, they are able to "problematize" reality (that is, pose critical questions about the transformation of aspects of reality) by connecting it to the learning situation, in order to reinterpret the educational actions within the national context (such as the political situation, or social and economic problems). The monitors in Valparaiso, for example, have reflected on problems arising from the poverty experienced in their sectors. As a result of this reflection, in the last two years they have started to participate in a coordinating group of popular organizations (also known as an educational resource group), which was established to look for solutions to problems of the neighborhoods (such as lack of housing, running water, and job pools for the unemployed).[7]

The educational strategy for work with children is based on a set of principles. First, the most important way of learning is through practice. The Workshops are founded on the principle of "learning by doing," based on individual lives and experience. Play has a central role. Information gathered from a set of interviews given in 1987 to twenty children aged six to twelve who participated in the Learning Workshops illustrates the importance of this principle (Vaccaro & Sotomayor, 1987). Forty percent pointed out that everyone worked together (to complete activities collectively); 32 percent said that they completed the work by sharing; 16 percent, by "helping one another"; and 12 percent said it was done by going on outings, seeing things, and using learning materials.

Second, positive relationships between the children and the monitors help improve children's self-images and reinforce their sense of self-esteem. A personalized, affectionate, and motivating relationship encourages the child's creative participation in the work sessions. One of the children interviewed in 1980 said: "I would tell other kids to come to the workshop because the monitors understand you and you trust them. I treat them with affection and they treat us that way, too" (Vaccaro & Sotomayor, 1987).

Third, the monitor encourages diverse and active forms of expression (both verbal and physical) and learning through group work. Children have related well to their active participation in the teaching-learning process. Questioned about what they liked best in the programs, 48 percent indicated play, singing songs, simple crafts projects, and drawing; 42 percent chose activities similar to those at school (learning mathematics and Spanish); and 10 percent specified a general interest (to help study for the future, to learn, to be close to the monitor, to work together with other children).

Fourth, the activities reinforce values such as solidarity, respect, creativity, a critical spirit, and a sense of sharing. When interviewed about his interest in the program, one of the children said, "I have grown used to it, the workshop is wonderful, and I've made friends."

Educational materials have played an important role in replicating and disseminating the workshop experience. "Work units" help educators prepare their sessions with the children. Each unit emphasizes different aspects of child development (attitudes, cognition, perception, and values) and has a central, defining theme (the neighborhood, work, or certain Chilean people, such as fishermen, farmers, and miners). The children also use workbooks. In addition, the program's monitors and coordinators are given a series of booklets to reinforce their attempts at self-improvement. For example, the booklets suggest ways of constructing good relationships between adults and children, helping a child who is timid or aggressive, and reinforcing positive attitudes when a group of children is developing activities.

The experience, thus far, has shown this educational strategy to be successful. Periodic evaluations with monitors, interviews with families and children, reports on children's achievement in school, and a number of surveys have shown positive results that have been verified in external evaluations required by the agencies supporting the program.[8]

The Learning Workshops program is valued both as a remedial educational alternative and as a critique of the Chilean formal educational system. For the children and families of lower-income households, it represents a solution to serious problems, such as school failure. As one monitor explains:

> The work leads to a learning experience, not only from the Workshop to the family, but also from the family to the Workshop, because it works on the assumption of sharing experience and information. The Workshop can give parents an opportunity to acquire some understanding about their children (and their interests), and help them establish a relationship that will support the development of the child's personality, and recognize their own role as educators. (Vaccaro & Sotomayor, 1987, p. 87)

When the project started in 1977, a team of professionals asked schoolteachers for information about children who had problems with school attendance. Children selected by the teachers had a great variety of difficulties, including reading, writing, math, and behavioral problems. According to the teachers' perceptions, these children would probably not be promoted to the next grade. In an attempt to change that, the children participated in the Learning Workshops that year.

A series of student interviews have provided insights into the specific ways in which Learning Workshops have been useful and successful (Vaccaro & Sotomayor, 1987). At the end of the 1977 school year it was found that 84 percent of the 64 children who participated in the Workshops were promoted to the next grade. This was a notable achievement, especially considering that teachers who had previously identified difficulties in these children performed the assessment (Vaccaro & Schiefelbein, 1981). When another group of children (a total of 39 children) participating in Learning Workshops was interviewed in 1980, 57 percent said that they attended be-

Children of Estación Central, in southwest Santiago, participating in a recreational activity.

cause of problems at school. Two of them said they were enrolled in the workshop because of problems studying and reading. Of a group of 19 children interviewed in 1987, 40 percent expressed their interest in learning as a result of the Learning Workshop experience.

The workshops have been successful because participation is voluntary and no grades are used to evaluate learning. In order to assess progress and diagnose difficulties, monitors have used various testing instruments and strategies, including evaluations in Spanish and mathematics when children begin and complete the programs, follow-up records plotting behavioral changes, family visits to evaluate children's progress with their parents, and conversations with children's teachers about changes within the school setting. The monitor evaluates each session with the children, analyzing the activities performed, interest generated, and degree of motivation attained. In the monitors' preparatory sessions and activity-planning meetings, educators share the problems that arise with children and jointly seek solutions. As a coordinator from one of the communities in Santiago explains:

> The children change, and that motivates us to have the tools to work with them, and develop the knowledge to contribute to their learning. This gives us more security as monitors because we make suggestions to each other and realize that it's not an isolated case, that there are people who can help us, and that the problems are not limited to our own group of children. (Vaccaro & Sotomayor, 1987, p. 128)

The program proposes a "pedagogy of commitment," which expresses itself in a positive educational relationship between monitors and children, a social commitment to solving problems in the community, and a political commitment to coordinating efforts for a long-range process of social transformation. The opinion of one of the educators confirms this: "This year they asked me to be part of the Pastoral Council of the parish. Thanks to the Workshops we have brought certain issues to the Council for reflection. Things about humankind ... important things that make one think" (Vaccaro & Sotomayor, 1987, p. 99).

The Learning Workshops' educational proposal has been appropriated by existing communities to the extent that they function autonomously. Monitors have themselves undergone an educational process in developing and working in an educational project. They have been assisted by a team of PIIE professionals and by those in charge of the program locally, usually a pastoral agent. Professionals have taken on various roles in the different phases of the program; initially giving direction to the program and later assuming an advisory role. In those sectors in which the program has achieved a level of autonomy, they have served as advisors, supporting specific requests for training and analyzing problems that arise in daily practice.

A recent conversation with a general coordinator of a program in Santiago that has been functioning autonomously since 1984 gives a sense of the level of achievement:

> You feel proud of what you're doing. Not being a professional and yet through experience being able to transform certain things; analyzing the situation and constructing new goals. Moving from being a monitor to being a general coordinator, one learns to prepare the monitors well. This is the collective work we perform. (Vaccaro, Sotomayor, & Adduard, 1987)

A group of monitors interviewed in 1986 in one of the communities where the program is autonomous said:

> Last year we decided to break off from the team [of PIIE professionals] because we realized that we could take on the responsibility of dealing with a problem that was entirely our own. We felt the absence of the team, but it has been a learning experience to have had to assume the responsibility of preparation in order to satisfy the needs of monitors, and to carry on quality work with the children. (Vaccaro & Sotomayor, 1987, p. 124)

Transference and Appropriation in the Learning Workshops

Basically, in the Learning Workshops, transference is initiated by a team of professionals that wishes to share a set of competencies for actions such as obtaining and managing financial resources; planning activities; choosing subjects and activities for the preparatory sessions; creating tools for diagnosis and learning for the children; and creating educational materials (such as books or slides).

The mere desire to share skills is, however, not enough for the process to take place. Transference cannot be studied as an abstract or isolated phenomenon. The success or failure of transference-appropriation is directly related both to the degree to which skills are put into practice and to the permanence or retention of those skills

Popular educators in a weekend preparation session.

Children participating in a collective festival of the Talleres de Aprendizaje *[Learning Workshops] in Curanilahue.*

once the work of the professional team ceases. Therefore, transference can take place only when there is sufficient interest and activity on the part of participants to critically adapt and carry forth the professional team's proposal (Vaccaro, 1988). Transference will not take place if the participants are not motivated to act on their own.

To analyze the appropriation process and comprehend its nature, certain dimensions of the process should be examined — specifically, negotiation (interactions among the different members of the project), the specific space and time of appropriation, and the joining together of different actions.

Proposals elaborated by the team of professionals initiate the course of action, suggesting why an action is being taken and how to bring it about. If the object is collective improvement and development to generate autonomous action by participants (as in the Learning Workshops), the participants must develop the ability to maintain, adapt, and re-create the initial proposal as formulated by the professional team. Often the emerging lines of work go beyond the initial proposal. Those in charge of the project, as well as the participants, find themselves involved in new actions that require rethinking the initial proposal. This is usually achieved through a variety of negotiations.

In the Learning Workshops the initial negotiation is carried out with local organizations in charge of implementation (such as the parish, Catholic community groups, and institutions of popular education). In general, the negotiation begins in a response to a request or petition made by community leaders interested in the program. The objectives, and the way in which the work will be carried out, are analyzed, including who might work as monitors (adults or teenagers), how many times a week the workshops will meet, what type of preparatory sessions will be implemented, whether monitors will be volunteer or paid, and what educational materials will be used.

Negotiations are also held with monitors concerning the development of the curriculum used to prepare them. Coordinators and monitors suggest the incorporation of specific subjects for educating themselves and for teaching children. The preparatory sessions are structured around basic themes such as child psychology, classroom behavior, play, the teaching of mathematics and Spanish, the use of educational materials, and planning sessions with children. Monitors and coordinators can then tailor the curriculum to the specific needs and interests of each community, such as sex education for children, relationships among couples, machismo, juvenile experience, issues of national concern, popular culture, and current political issues.

An open curriculum has allowed monitors to contribute their own innovations to the project. Various communities have developed a variety of programs to meet diverse needs. For example, they have created adolescent counseling programs to address the serious problem of adolescent drug addiction. Another example would be literacy programs for women. They have also obtained donations of milk for the children from Church organizations and have organized mothers to prepare and serve the milk for their children during work sessions.

Another kind of negotiation between professionals and monitors concerns economic and material resources. In general, communities contribute whatever is necessary for the program to function within their area. Evaluating the availability of resources, they determine which educational materials will be used and how they will obtain them. Also, the local people in charge are responsible for developing awareness of the program in the community, promoting monitors' participation in local social structures, and acquainting families with the Workshops.

Effective action to transform society requires that the relationship among different members of projects be based on cooperation and mutual respect. It is challenging to use cooperation and respect between professionals and participants as a basis of work. Interactions are generally complex and at times, difficult, because of at least two dangers: the ownership and the misuse of knowledge and power. On what basis do we define cooperation between the professional team and the monitors? How do we balance their different visions in coordinating the actions of the project? What significance do the professionals and participants attribute to this shared action? How does one recognize the subtle forms of power that can lead to manipulation?

In one case, a break in relations between a team of professionals and a community occurred in 1982. A conflict grew among the PIIE team, the parish, and the popular educators of a neighborhood in Santiago over the financial managing of resources, the orientation of the program, and the role of the professional team. Conflict centered around the following questions: Who is responsible for the program? Does the program belong to the parish or to PIIE? To what extent should the professional team be involved in its financial management? Tension developed concerning problems of power and the orientation of the program, as well as in management of finances. The climate of distrust impeded work. When no agreement was reached for overcoming the problems, the team of professionals was forced to withdraw at a high human and professional cost. A subsequent analysis of the situation led the team to recognize the errors committed and the need to reinforced a climate of mutual trust; the team also acknowledged the need to define and clarify decisionmaking responsibilities and work methods in the other communities being served. A collaborative relationship should avoid the forms of domination common in society. For these reasons, respect, cooperation, and solidarity should be reinforced in a systematic way between children and monitors and between professionals and educators. Self-evaluation, analysis of conflicts and human relations, reflection about educational practice, and proposals of activities for collective work are all necessary.

Appropriation is carried out at a specific time and place. Each specific context, with its own dynamic, confers a particular quality on the intervention. In the Learning Workshops, for example, the problem that motivates youth monitors to collaborate is children's failure in school and their need for help. Over the years, however, another field of interest developed because monitors valued the program as an opportunity for participation and improvement, where they could meet other young people in a life experience invested with great meaning. Even with their different ways of viewing reality, both professionals and monitors agreed that the personal and collective growth of monitors is important and that it is necessary to attend to these young people's needs. Thus, in practice, the appropriation process allowed participants to adapt the Learning Workshop program to the particular community and the new needs that arose once the program started.

Finally, appropriation is shaped by practice, and by the systematic, joint action of the participants and the team in charge. In order for the process to come to fruition, the members of the professional team must be consistent in their actions, suggesting modes of intervention sensitive to the realities with which they are faced, and developing trust in other participants. Collaboration rather than authoritarianism has been the operating mode in this process.

Because of conditions resulting from the imposition of authoritarian rule in Chile in 1973, NGOs, churches, and social and political institutions have assumed the job of teaching young people from low-income families, taking into account their personal development and their position in society. These organizations have sought to channel the restlessness, needs, and demands of low-income youth in constructive ways. In this way, starting with a collaborative relationship between the professional staff and young people, a new possibility for action can come about.

The dimensions just described help us define appropriation as a creative process in which the sharing of skills allows participants to act on a specific reality and transform it. The development of skills requires the following approach: identification of areas where skills are necessary for the systematic exercise of the actions proposed by the project (such as management, social pedagogy, participatory methods and techniques, and evaluation and follow-up procedures); reinforcement of recurrent learning patterns so that participants can act autonomously; and creativity in confronting situations and inventing new possibilities for action.

Analyzing Appropriation in the Learning Workshops

In order to analyze the success of the appropriation process in the Learning Workshops, it is helpful to identify the two main types of appropriation — selective and creative — that can exist and the two main areas in which appropriation can occur — in the program's educational and management components.

In practice, autonomous action can be evident in two different ways:

1. In the restructuring of the initial proposal offered by the external agents. Here, participants take on specific areas according to their skills and depending on the real possibilities for action. Having acquired skills in certain areas of the initial proposal, they can easily use those competencies in the educational action. This may be described as selective appropriation, because participants operate within the boundaries delineated in the initial proposal.
2. In the invention or creation of possibilities for action in situations that call for a new type of intervention; here, we can speak of creative appropriation. In this case, the participants are prepared to respond to other spheres of action based on new or different problems that beset the community. In other words, participants will respond to the reality of the community by going beyond what was originally proposed.

The following paragraphs describe the success of the Learning Workshops using this framework. One of the most successful areas of selective appropriation in the Learning Workshops is the educational work that the monitors carry out with children. The monitors learn how to work with the children, as well as with their families, to help them understand their child's difficulties. The children have proven achievements in different dimensions of their lives, such as success in school and changes in their personalities. As one monitor put it:

> For me these children's performance improvement is important because I now feel that everyone has the ability to teach others; not just a teacher with a degree but anyone who has an interest in helping others.... We monitors are conveying a different king of education, one that isn't so mechanical; the children do not feel like machines. (Vaccaro & Sotomayor, 1987, p. 62)

Selective appropriation can be seen in the way the monitors form better educational relations with the children, organize activities in work sessions, and become more flexible in their use of materials. Monitors interact with other social agents such as teachers, educational psychologists, and vocational counselors who are involved with the same kinds of problems In addition, the young people feel a great deal of satisfaction in accomplishing these tasks, and they exhibit considerable idealism:

> I want to help children from the slums. Many of them ask why they came into this world. My task is to tell them and convince them that they are important and can become good people.... Before, I wasn't interested in kids. I never imagined a child could have so many problems. I guess I sort of woke up. (Vaccaro & Sotomayor, 1987, p. 61)

Creative appropriation in the educational component of the project has manifested itself in the creation of educational endeavors that deal with other problems in the community. For instance, a group of monitors, after working in the Learning Workshop in their community, began a program for young married couples, using a similar methodology. Other communities have created similar projects, such as the Literacy for Women program and support groups for women to help their families.

Selective appropriation of management skills has resulted in monitors' managing projects by setting up a decisionmaking structure similar to the one initially proposed by the professional team. In this manner, monitors are able to promote a variety of activities: implementing workshops to make contact with other organizations, motivating families to send their children to the program, raising funds and allocating financial resources according to an established budget, negotiating with authorities about the use of different locales, programming activities, and collecting information on the problems the children are having in school. The skills developed by monitors helped to increase efficiency in the use and distribution of resources.

Creative appropriation of management skills is evident when these skills are used proficiently in other actions, as when monitors carry out other community initiatives, such as setting up a summer camp for the children of a given locality.[9] Monitors have also been hired by the schools within their community to provide remedial assistance to children in grades one to four, to organize extracurricular activities, to work with preschoolers, and to aid in catechism or religious instruction. They have also been called on when adult or youth programs in their neighborhoods have been started, and have been put in charge of the self-improvement and training process, as well as the preparation of educational support materials.

Conclusion

In the development of the Learning Workshops we have been able to identify some processes and strategies that have influenced positively the occurrence of the appropriation process. In conclusion, we reiterate some of the processes and strategies that we have determined are very important for achieving appropriation. We suggest them as criteria to consider in the examination and further study of the transference-appropriation process in other community-based projects. First, through the Workshops, the learning process has been linked to the daily life of participants. Second, motivation has been crucial in establishing effective learning situations. Third, the methods used promote the participants' active involvement in the teaching-learning situation. Significantly, the participants have been systematically involved in resolving problems and developing alternatives. The learning experience takes place through a process of action, which is followed by collective reflection, in which recurring learning patterns are reinforced, opening up new possibilities for action. Fourth, the professional team supports this learning process, using permanent follow-up mechanisms when new practices are under way. Gradually, the team members define actions so that the participants can attain autonomy and redefine their role over time, moving from orientation leader, to consult, to critical advisor.

Fifth, a certain amount and organization of time is needed for those involved to learn how to manage the project. During the first stage, emphasis in on handling physical and material resources. Later, this task is taken on by the monitors, with support from the technical team, and the community coordinators are trained as administrators. In the last phase, complete self-management is achieved, including the administration of funds.

Sixth, explicit and systematic means of evaluation are set up to measure and understand results in different dimensions of the project and in the transition from one phase of development to another. Learning and effective preparation are assisted by their relationship to real problems. Finally, a support network beyond the external agents is established that participants can tap into for an autonomous, supportive, learning experience.

After twelve years, the Learning Workshops continue to respond to the educational needs of the children in popular sectors of Santiago and the provinces. Nevertheless, in the last year, a new and exciting development has taken place. The educational proposal of the Learning Workshops has been adopted by four schools in the formal educational system located in popular sectors. These schools have incorporated some people from the communities into their staff in order to support the learning of children with difficulties. This recent development confirms that popular education can contribute to the improvement of education in the poor sectors of Chilean society.

Notes

1. In this article the terms "popular sectors" or "slum areas" refer to urban sectors where there is poverty and destitution. The people who live in these sectors have been socially and politically excluded from the Chilean mainstream. In Chile there are more than four million people who live in

poverty, and critical sociocultural problems exist in the areas of housing, health, and unemployment. It is the understanding of some popular educators that the government has been financially subsidizing these communities rather than creating the conditions whereby these people can actively participate in the social, political, and financial structures of Chilean life. On the other hand, these educators present popular education as a type of education that recognizes the potential in these communities for generating constructive change to improve their living conditions.

2. This participant was detained by the police and arrested while attending an anti-government demonstration.

3. The terms "beneficiaries" and "participants" are used interchangeably in this article. They refer to those community members who are directly involved in developing the Learning Workshops and who participate in the teaching-learning process the program offers.

4. The program is developed in urban-popular sectors called *poblaciones.* As a result of the high concentration of poverty in the peripheral districts, or poblaciones, there is a new socio-spatial distribution in which diverse kinds of problems have arisen (such as housing, unemployment, infantile and juvenile prostitution, and drug abuse).

5. The program does not integrate children with physical handicaps (for example, deafness, blindness) or psychological problems that require special care (for example, autism).

6. Monitors are people from the community who have attended preparatory sessions and serve as facilitators in the teaching-learning process. In this article the terms "monitors," "facilitators," and "popular educators" are used interchangeably.

7. Recently, educational resource groups have emerged in response to the need for developing groups of popular educators able to unite the efforts and coordinate the actions of individual programs in the particular communities.

8. Usually NGOs deal with an external (foreign) development agency for funding. In this case, the Learning Workshops dealt with Nederlandse Organisatie Voor Internationale Ontddikkeingssamendderking (NOVIB) from Holland. There are several documents which narrate this experience. There are also two evaluations, done by Facultad Latino Americana de Ciencias Sociales (FLACSO) and NOVIB (1982, 1984). There is also a research paper by PIIE (Vaccaro, 1988).

9. The *colonias,* or camps, are community-organized activities set up for low-income children so that they may have times of rest and relaxation during the summer.

References

Facultad Latino Americana de Ciencias Sociales (FLACSO) and Nederlandse Organisatie Voor Internationale Ontddikkeingssamendderking (NOVIB) (1982). *Informe de evaluación del proyecto: Consolidación y extención de la experiencia piloto de formación colectiva ejecutado por PIIE y el Decanato Estación Central* [Project evaluation report: Consolidation and extension of the collective formation pilot experience performed by PIIE and Decanato Estación Central]. Santiago: FLACSO.

Facultad Latino Americana de Ciencias Sociales (FLACSO) and Nederlanse Organisatie Voor Internationale Ontddikkeingssamendderking (NOVIB). (1984). *Informe de evaluación del proyecto: Difución y estrategias de transferencia de talleres de aprendisajes a comunidades populares realizado por el PIIE* [Project evaluation report: Diffusion ad transference strategies in the Learning Workshops of popular sectors performed by PIIE]. Santiago: FLACSO.

García-Huidobro, J. E. (1988). *Aprender a vivir. Agentes educativos comunitarios* [Learning skills for living: Community educational agents]. Lima: Instituto de Technologias Apropiadas para Sectores Marginales (ITACAB).

Vaccaro, L. (1988). Participación de profesionales en el desarrollo de programas comunitarios de educación popular [Professional participation in developing programs for popular education]. In S. Martinic & H. Walker (Eds.), *Profesionales en la acción: Una mirada crítica a la educación popular* [Professionals in action: A critical look at popular education]. Santiago: Centro de Investigación y Desarrollo de la Educación (CIDE).

Vaccaro, L., & Schiefelbein, E. (1981). *Talleres de atención a ninos con problemas de aprendizaje con la participación de educadores comunitarios* [Workshops which focus on children with learning disabilities with the participation of popular educators.] Santiago: PIIE.

Vaccaro, L., & Sotomayor, C. (1987). *Análisis y evaluación de una experiencia educativa en Chile: Los Talleres de Aprendizaje* [Analysis and evaluation of an educational experience in Chile: The Learning Workshops]. Final Research Report. Santiago: PIIE

Vaccaro, L., Sotomayor, C., & Adduard, A. (1987). *Pedagogia social: ¿ Una alternativa para las escuelas urbano populares?* [Social pedagogy: An alternative for Chile's impoverished educational system?]. Santiago: PIIE.

Why Romà Do Not
Like Mainstream Schools:
Voices of a People without Territory

JULIO VARGAS CLAVERÍA
JESÚS GÓMEZ ALONSO

Classes were over in a high school in La Mina, the Romaní area on the outskirts of Barcelona. Aroa, a tenth grader, was talking with her teacher about her post-graduation plans. She excitedly shared her dream of going to college and becoming an educator for her community. In response, her teacher argued that it was silly for Aroa to enter a university since it would mean leaving the beautiful Romaní tradition of selling in informal markets and that rejection of tradition would be a shame for her family. (Personal communication, October 20, 2002)

Aroa's teacher was operating on the common belief that the Romà have a *natural* disaffection for education and for schools, a belief that has prevailed in both historical and contemporary educational research literature based largely on the performance of Romaní children in mainstream schools.[1] The story that this slim body of knowledge tells is that the Romà do not like schools and are happy to remain on the margins of society, where they remain largely invisible, unseen by politics, education, and certainly by research. It is a story that has been interpreted, reinterpreted, and used against the Romà for centuries.

Yet, Aroa's own words and actions counter that story and suggest a love of and desire for learning. As a Romaní sociologist from La Mina, a predominantly Romaní neighborhood that is one of the most deprived areas in Barcelona, and a non-Romaní professor of education who works in the area of Romaní Studies and has been involved in the Spanish Romà rights movement, we have heard many such stories in our research and involvement in the Romaní grassroots movement, stories that depict why many of the Romà, the largest European ethnic minority, do not like or trust mainstream schools. Traditionally, European educational systems have not helped the Romà to overcome their social, political, and economic marginality. Rather, schools have been sites for assimilation, reproduction of social prejudices, and the perpetuation of social exclusion. Although schools sometimes devalue or even anni-

Harvard Educational Review   Vol. 73   No. 4   Winter 2003, 559–590

hilate Romaní culture, when they include and value their culture and hear and recognize Romaní voices, Romà disaffection turns to passion.

This article is based on the conviction that research is informed by particular theoretical stands that determine methodological questions and the use of findings. It is also based on the belief that schools inevitably mirror larger social issues, such as poverty or racism, and that it is useless to talk about educational inequalities without discussing social conditions and recognizing the relations among Romaní families, culture, and the classrooms. Because the Romà have been not only silenced but also largely unseen in educational research literature, we explore a series of questions to contextualize Romaní history, focusing on the Romà in Europe. Who are Romà and where have Romà been? Where are Romà now? What do we know about education and the Romà? This article also proposes a new approach to Romaní educational research that is based on the recent communicative shift in the social sciences and has been strongly influenced by the Romà rights movement. Research from a communicative perspective implies intersubjective dialogue between researchers and researched, considers the reflections of people as agents, their motivations and interpretations, and provides greater involvement and a more egalitarian relationship among them. In this article, we ultimately argue that, if research continues to ignore the voices of Romà, it will neither solve the problems we face nor provide adequate solutions to overcome them.

Who Are the Romà?

The Romà are an ethnically differentiated group of twelve million people who live in almost all European and American countries, as well as some areas of Asia and Oceania (International Romani Union, 2001). According to the European Network Against Racism (ENAR) report, approximately one and a half million Romà live in the European Union, making them the largest ethnic minority in Europe (Machiels, 2002).

In Western Europe, Spain has the largest population of Romà, followed by France and Italy. Central and Eastern European countries also have a substantial Romà population, with Romania and Bulgaria thought to have the highest in Europe. North America has a slowly growing Romà population; nevertheless, it outnumbers the Amish and Cajuns, according to Romaní linguist Ian Hancock (King, 1999).[2]

While the Romà share origins, history, and a common culture, they are not a homogeneous group (Courthiade, 2000; de Gila Kochanowsky, 1992). As with any other ethnic group, significant intragroup differences are found among the Romà, many of which may result from geographical dispersion described above (see Table 1).[3] It is unclear how this dispersion occurred and what triggered it, but there has been much speculation on this topic in the literature and in the popular imagination. Before the late 1700s, scholars and writers speculated about the Romaní origins, but in 1780 linguists Heindrich M. Grellmann and Jacob Rudiger in Germany and Jacob Bryant in England discovered the Indian origin of the Romaní language (Sánchez Ortega, 1986). Subsequent studies confirmed the common Sanskrit roots of the Romaní dialects, and it is now generally assumed that the Romà originated in northwest India as early as the ninth century (Fraser, 1995).

TABLE 1
Estimated Romà Population

Country	Population
Australia	22,000
Brazil	800,000
Bulgaria	700,000–800,000
Denmark	2,000–3,000
France	300,000
Italy	300,000
North America	1,000,000
Norway	500–1,000
Romania	1,800,000–2,500,000
Spain	630,000

Sources cited by country consecutively: Morrow (2000); Da Costa (1996); European Commission (2002); Fernández Jiménez (1996); Machiels (2002); Machiels (2002); King (1999); Fernández Jiménez (1996); European Commission (2002); "Informe de la Subcomisión para el estudio de la problemática del pueblo gitano" (1999).

The Romaní migrations from India, for reasons not yet clear, occurred in waves spanning the ninth to fourteenth centuries. Evidence of the first wave of immigration, dating to 1068, was found in Turkey (Machiels, 2002). The second immigration wave started in the mid-eighteenth century with the abolition of slavery in Eastern Europe. Fearing that slavery would be reestablished, Romaní migration waves occurred from this eastern region to Scandinavia and southern and western Europe. Many Romà continued on to the Americas, especially Argentina, and thousands reached the United States (Fraser, 1992, 1995). Romaní immigration continues; in the late 1980s, after the fall of Communism in Eastern Europe, many Romà emigrated to Western Europe, Canada, and the United States.[4]

Throughout this dispersion across the globe, the Romà succeeded in maintaining their culture despite the absence of territorial protection of a government structure and the presence of governmental policies and strategies aimed at their assimilation and annihilation. The Romà challenge the modern concept of the nation-state that identifies territorial boundaries and socio-political rights with one ethnicity, culture, or people, for there is no single Romaní land.[5] Instead, they maintain their right to preserve their culture while living dispersed around the world as a globalized nation, able to share the territory they live in with many other groups. Their political efforts and organizations are not directed at territorial acquisition; rather, they seek to create a transnational infrastructure to defend and represent their interests internationally as a single culture even though they do not live in a specific territory. During the 2001 World Conference against Racism in Durban, the nongovernmental organization (NGO) the International Romaní Union (IRU) presented a petition, entitled "Los Gitanos somos una nación," to the United Nations to recognize the Romà as a transnational nation. At the European level, acting on a proposal by Finnish president Tarja Halonen, a European Consultative Assembly that represents Romaní interests will be established. It will guarantee Romaní representation in the European Union unification process, as well as in social and economic issues, such as education (Tsetsekou, 2002).

A History of Racism: Expulsion, *Porrajmos Romaní* (Romaní Holocaust), and Marginality

The Romà's status as outsiders in any state and their resulting invisibility make them particularly vulnerable to institutionalized and de facto racism. Since the turn of the fifteenth century, Romà have experienced systematic persecution, either via legal procedures or the lack of them, or through discriminatory personal treatment now labeled anti-gypsyism. According to Romaní linguist Ian Hancock, many factors have contributed to these various forms of discrimination, from their dark complexions, to their idiosyncratic way of life, to a generalized fear of what is perceived as an alien and therefore suspect culture (Hancock, 2002). Whatever the cause, the Romà have experienced a history of racism that includes slavery, assimilation, expulsion, and extermination.

In 1476, King Mathias of Hungary authorized the city of Harmannstad to employ Romà as slaves. Romaní slavery is also found in the hidden history of Britain, Portugal, Russia, and Spain. In Russia, Catherine the Great (1729–1796) passed laws to make Romaní slaves of the crown (Hancock, 1987). In 1538, Spain passed a decree that Romà would be enslaved for life if they wished to escape imprisonment. At that time, Spain and Portugal started to deport Romaní slaves to their colonies in North and South America, calling it *la solución Americana,* or the American solution (Hancock, 2002). From before 1300 until the mid-1800s, Romà were enslaved in Central and Eastern Europe (Hancock, 1987). When slavery was abolished in Romania in 1856, approximately 600,000 slaves were liberated without receiving any education or help to reintegrate into society. In fact, their former masters were the ones who received economic compensation (Hancock, 2002).

The Romà have experienced forms of social injustice besides slavery. Decrees outlawing or severely restricting the Romà were enacted in many European countries. According to anthropologist Teresa San Román (1998), in 1499, the Catholic Spanish king issued a decree forcing Romà to leave their itinerant life, language, and customs or to suffer the punishment of deportation or service in the galleys. In 1749, Ferdinand VI ordered the forced labor of more than 14,000 Romà in mines or other places, as well as the separation of Romaní children from their families. In 1812, the Cádiz Constitution provided some measure of stability and legal rights for the Spanish Romà by declaring everyone born in the kingdom to be Spanish. Despite this constitutional protection, the law on vagrants and criminals ordered the *Guardia Civil* (Spanish police) to consider Romà potential criminals. Moreover, Romà were obliged to carry special identification documents until the law was abolished in 1982 (Congreso de los Diputados, 1999).

Romà suffered similar exclusion and persecution in Germany and Saxony. In Germany in 1500, the Emperor Maximilian II expelled all the Romà and allowed citizens to kill them with impunity because the Romà had been accused of sorcery and child abduction on many occasions (Liégeois, 1987). More than a century later, in 1661, George II of Saxony imposed the death penalty on any Romà caught in his territory and promoted hunts to exterminate them. Finally, in 1721, Emperor Charles IV of Habsburg ordered the extermination of the Romà; men were to be executed, and women and children were to have an ear cut off before being driven out of the country at the closest border (Liégeois, 1987). The Romà in the rest of Europe, from Finland to Italy and from the United Kingdom to Eastern Europe, experienced similar institutionalized racism.

During the nineteenth century, scientific theory identified the Romà as an "inferior race," setting the philosophical foundations for the next century's Holocaust. Official discrimination was institutionalized in Germany in 1899 by the creation of a special Romaní Affairs Section within the police force in order to track and control the Romà (Novitch, 1984). After the approval of anti-Romaní measures throughout Germany, the Central Office for the Fight against the Romà was established in Munich in 1929 (Hancock, 1997).

When Hitler came to power in 1933, everything was ready for the *Porrajmos Romaní* (Romaní Holocaust). In June 1938, the "Gypsy Clean-Up Week" took place, and Romà were rounded up throughout Germany. In January 1940, 250 Romaní children were murdered while being used as guinea pigs to test the efficacy of the Zyklon-B crystals that were later used in the Nazi gas chambers. The situation worsened from 1941 until the end of World War II, and many Romà were assassinated in German-occupied Eastern Europe (Liégeois, 1987). This policy of extermination coalesced on August 1, 1944, *Zigeunernacht* (Gypsy Night), when four thousand Romà were gassed and cremated in a single action at the Gypsy Family Camp at Auschwitz-Birkenau (Hancock, 1997). Between 250,000 and 300,000 European Romà were killed during World War II (Liégeois, 1987). Despite this history, Romà have been largely excluded from compensation programs and have received little historical recognition (Mendiola, 2002).

This pattern of persecution and exclusion was apparent most recently during the Yugoslav conflict. The already vulnerable Roms were caught in the crisis and forced to choose a side, even though "there was no Romaní side and . . . neither side accepted them as ethnically their own" (Cahn & Peric, 1999, p. 1). Further, the Romà minority remained invisible in the Dayton Peace Agreements.[6] The position of the Romà reflects the dilemma of a minority caught in the middle of an open conflict (Organization for Security and Co-operation in Europe [OSCE], 2000). These circumstances enlarged the flow of Romà migrating from Eastern to Western Europe and the United States, which in turn has led to an increase in anti-Romà attacks in these countries (OSCE, 2000). In 1994, about 30,000 Romaní refugees from Bosnia and Serbia holding tourist visas sought asylum in Austria, while others tried to enter countries such as Hungary, Italy, and Germany (Arayici, 1998).

These patterns of racism throughout Europe have influenced Romaní living conditions, and despite Europe's reputation as one of the most advanced regions in the world, many Romà remain trapped in poverty (Kovats, 2002). A recent Yale University study, the first cross-country multivariate analysis looking at the Romà as an ethnic category and its associations with poverty, suggests that "conditional on being Romà, the probability of being poor is higher than that of non-Romà, irrespective of educational achievement and employment status" (Revenga, Ringold, & Tracy, 2002, p. 15). This study supports earlier small-scale studies, asserting that "Romà are both poorer than other population groups and more likely to fall into poverty and to remain poor" (p. 1). For example, according to a 2000 World Bank report, 84 percent of the Bulgarian Roms live below the poverty line while the national average is 36 percent. Similarly, in Romania 78.8 percent of Roms live below the poverty line, in comparison to 30.8 percent of the general population (Ringold, 2000, pp. 11–12).

The pernicious history of racism has constructed Romà as an invisible people largely absent from history books. It has also locked many into an ongoing and vicious cycle of poverty, marginality, and exclusion. These patterns of racism that began prior to 1300 and continue today are inevitably reflected in mainstream schools, in Romà access to education, and in what is expected from Romaní students. In many cases, these historical patterns have become so deeply engrained in the social fabric that schools, teachers, researchers, and policymakers do not see them. Looking more closely at the European educational landscape will complete the overview of the issues that the Romaní people face in the effort to secure their educational rights.

Romà in Contemporary European Educational Systems

Historically, European schools were designed to educate a homogeneous student body through an educational system built on Western White culture. Today, however, European students are increasingly diverse. This change has created a tension within European education, for the structures and ideals of the schools have not shifted and diversified in tandem with the changes in the student body. Further, teacher education programs lag behind these social changes, for they do not provide the knowledge and the special training to manage and teach in increasingly diverse classrooms. In this context, ethnic groups that differ from the mainstream White European society are often forced to adapt or fail (Flecha, 1999).

Despite international efforts to make access to education a universal reality, access still remains a challenge for Romaní families. The Romà have seen non-Romaní families rallying against their acceptance and have heard school principals say that school lists were closed to new students, especially if they were Romà (OSCE, 2000). Approximately half of the estimated three million Romaní children living in Europe have never attended school (Save the Children, 2001).

Once Romaní students are in school, the patterns of racism manifest in society are reproduced. Many Romaní students are tracked into special education programs on the basis of ethnicity and socioeconomic conditions, which are considered cultural deficits. The European Romà Rights Center (ERRC) report shows that, in the Czech Republic, 46.4 percent of Romaní children are in schools for the mentally handicapped, compared with only 3.2 percent of non-Romaní children (Cahn & Chirico,

1999). As a result, a Romaní child is approximately fifteen times more likely to be considered "intellectually deficient" than a non-Romaní child (Cahn & Chirico, 1999). An Organization for Security and Co-operation in Europe (OSCE) report denounces the assignment of excessive numbers of Romaní children to special education classes within regular schools, and notes that in the Slovak Republic and Hungary Romaní children appear to be disproportionately referred to such schools or classes (OSCE, 2000). In Romania, national statistics on the numbers of Romà in schools for children with disabilities or special educational needs are not publicly available, but local sources suggest that this tracking pattern holds. For example, the mentally handicapped school in Cluj-Napoca serves about two hundred children, of which over 70 percent are Romaní (Cahn & Petrova, 2001).

In Europe, illiteracy rates among Romaní students are high, and this figure is significantly tied to issues of quality of life, income, social participation, and the lack of other opportunities. The Save the Children Report (2001) shows that 26 percent of Romà are illiterate, compared to the European illiteracy rate of 1.3 percent (EURYDICE, 2002). In Serbia the rates range from 15 percent illiteracy among Romà age fifteen to nineteen, to 71 percent in those aged sixty-five years and over. The same report estimates that illiteracy among Greek Romaní adults reaches 80–90 percent, and approximately 80 percent among Romaní children. In Romania, a recent study found that 59 percent of all women and 44 percent of all men are illiterate (Cozma, Cucos, & Momanu, 2000). Any community that presents high illiteracy rates faces additional challenges in making their voices heard, for few enter the political or public arena.

Moreover, Romaní children demonstrate transnational patterns of low attendance/high absenteeism and elevated dropout rates that inevitably affect student performance and achievement. Romaní leaders in the former Yugoslavian Republic of Macedonia estimate that as many as 10 percent of school-aged Romaní children never enroll in the first grade, and half of those who do enroll drop out by the fifth grade, with only 30 to 40 percent finishing the eighth grade (OSCE, 2000). According to a study done in Romania,

> only 4.5 percent of the Romà population graduates from high school; forty percent of Romà children (up to the age of eight) do not go to kindergarten; and only half of the children aged seven to ten years attend primary school; only seven percent pursue a secondary education. (Cozma et al., 2000, p. 282)

In Hungary, more than 70 percent of Romaní children attend primary school, but only 33 percent go on to secondary school and most of these attend trade schools (OSCE, 2000). In Croatia, estimates show that 50 percent of Romaní children enroll in primary education. Of these, half finish primary education; that is, only 25 percent of all Romaní children. No more than 10 percent of these pupils enroll in secondary education, and only half finish (Save the Children, 2001). Figures from Western Europe suggest the same patterns of low enrollment, high absenteeism, and high dropout rates. For example, estimates from France showed that only 32.9 percent of the Romaní population under sixteen attended school (Fahier, 1993, cited in Arayici, 1998). Recent data facilitated by the E.U.-funded project OPRE ROMA[7] indicate that Romaní absenteeism reaches up to 45.1 percent versus 3.8 percent among non-Romaní children (Giménez Adelantado, Gavarri Hernández, & Gavarri Hernández, 2001).

Inevitably, these patterns result in low Romaní participation in higher education. The lack of access to professional degrees closes the social inequality circle, leaving the Romà out of most social, political, and economic decisionmaking processes. Different sources indicate that less than one percent of the European Romà population reaches higher education (Congreso de los Disputados, 1999; Save the Children, 2001). Looking at individual countries, low Romaní participation rates are confirmed. For example, only 0.46 percent of Bulgarian Roms reach higher education, versus 13.53 percent of non-Romà; 0.2 percent of Hungarian Roms in contrast to 11.99 percent of non-Romà; and 0.31 percent of Romanian Roms versus 10.44 percent of the non-Romà population in that country (Revenga et al., 2002, p. 24).

How Romà Disaffection with Schooling Has Been Traditionally Explained

Given the patterns of racism and the historical and political invisibility of Romà, educators, policymakers, researchers, and others have generated many explanations in an effort to interpret and understand Romà disaffection for schooling. For example, some might interpret the fact that only one percent of Romà take part in higher education as a mirror of the ongoing legacy of historical and current discrimination, while others would interpret it as proof that Romà are culturally uninterested in access to college. The theories that have informed explanations of Romà disaffection can be grouped in two perspectives: ethnocentrism and relativism. As part of larger philosophical traditions, each brings a series of beliefs and assumptions that define "the other" and "its" condition. Veiled under these traditions of ethnocentrism and relativism are beliefs and attitudes that perpetuate the patterns of racism in educational research, policy, and practice described in previous sections of this article.

Ethnocentric Approach: Assimilate to Succeed

Ethnocentrism is defined as the assumption that the European race is superior to other races, and it sets Western culture as the universal model that every society should adopt in order to progress (Fanon, 1975; Mills, 1997). Divergence from this pattern is interpreted as a threat to the world's unity and stability. Under this tradition, as Amartya Sen (1999) argues, "The world is invited to join the club of 'Western democracy' and to admire and endorse traditional 'Western values'" (p. 233) that are seen as universal and, as such, are assumed to be right and proper for all societies and cultures. The ethnocentric perspective leads to interpretations of Romà underachievement in education as a need for the Romà to accept Western values, shed their identity, and integrate into mainstream culture in order to succeed. It thus explains Romà disaffection for schooling as a deficit, that is, a deviation from the universal value of learning (Flecha, 1999). Educational policies that derive from such work aim at correcting this deficit through assimilation and transmission of hegemonic values that dissolve the difference that is considered to be the cause of students' failure.

Social science studies have demonstrated that many educational practices reflect this approach very subtly, as seen, for example, in teachers' beliefs or expectations regarding the academic abilities of their Romaní students (Cahn & Chirico, 1999; Calvo Buezas, 2000; Miquel, Tortajada, & Vargas, 2001). This underlying ethnocentrism is illustrated by reflections from a headmaster of a school in Dorset, England. When a group of Romaní families settled in Dorset, the headmaster listed all the difficulties that the school faced in taking in the newcomers:

1. Educational and social problems of the gypsy children themselves
2. The need for close cooperation and the building of real relationships between the school and the gypsy parents
3. The problem of integration within the school community
4. The need to ensure the minimal impact on the educational and social opportunities for the village children
5. The need to avoid any alienation between the school and the village parents (obviously the more successful we became with 4, the easier it would be to retain the good relationships we have enjoyed with our settled families) (Bateman, 1977, p. 9)

The headmaster clearly identified the "problem" as the children's culture rather than the school's inability to attend to a diversity of students. The headmaster not only foresaw the Romaní children's problems with integration but also the negative impact that presence could have on the village children, whose learning he perceived as threatened by the newcomers. He went further and denounced the lack of attention given to "the impact an alien set of values and culture could have upon the settled children of the school" (Bateman, 1977, p. 15). The headmaster was more worried about the village children's learning than the Romaní children. When Romaní culture is considered the cause of the educational failure not only for Romaní children but also the children who come in contact with them, then it becomes necessary to design measures to eliminate "the roots of the problem."

Blaming the minority culture for their disaffection is a consequence of the ethnocentric character of mainstream schools established on the basis of the Western, White, and European canon, as evidenced by a school culture, calendar, values, and curriculum. From this position of cultural superiority, a school's ethnocentric character is invisible and untouchable. The schools are already designed, and the families have to accept them as they are or forego their children's education. For example, Romaní anthropologist Ana Giménez Adelantado surveyed 261 Spanish Romaní students, of whom 48.9 percent had more than five unjustified absences in a month (Giménez Adelantado, Martínez Sancho, & Alfageme Chao, 2001). The surveys also indicated that 21.15 percent of those absences were due to the family's occupation in agricultural seasonal jobs or street sales. Traditionally, from the schools' ethnocentric perspective, teachers consider these unacceptable reasons for absence and assume that Romaní families do not care enough for their children's education. The fact that

Romaní families have no other choice than to miss school if they want to survive is not acknowledged. In any case, school structure and organization of time — that is, justification for only five days of absence, school closure for Christian holy days, and three months of summer vacation — is designed for families with stable and nearby jobs. Maybe these Romaní families would prefer to have the three months of summer vacation coincide with their seasonal work and not to miss any school, but authorities do not consult or consider them in setting school calendars.

Relativist Approach: Keep Away from Schooling to Preserve the Culture

Relativism is defined as the elimination of any fixed model or principle with which to evaluate, compare, or assess. As described by Feyerabend (1993), "There is only one principle that can be defended under all circumstances and in all stages of human development. It is the principle: *anything goes*" (p. 19). The application of this principle to the study of cultures is called cultural relativism, that is, cultures are considered neither superior nor inferior, only different.

Thus, Romà poverty and lack of access to educational opportunities are only manifestations of their cultural differences. This perspective, a pillar of the Spanish educational reform of 1990, has led some teachers, policymakers, and theorists to the conclusion that cultural preservation requires that minorities be kept away from mainstream schooling. Yet, Spanish educational research has demonstrated that the creation of separate units outside of regular classrooms has actually increased segregation and inequalities in the educational systems (Elboj, Puigdellivol, Soler, & Valls, 2002). In effect, relativist educational reforms adapt to rather than challenge inequalities and require the most disadvantaged students to accept predestined subordination in the name of cultural difference.

Romaní students face several obstacles in schools due to cultural differences. However, most obstacles are related to poverty and resulting living conditions. From the relativist perspective, respect for difference means accepting and respecting a group's poverty as a cultural factor, an effect that Ágnes Kende refers to as "the ethnicalization of poverty" (Kende, 2000). When living conditions are considered a cultural feature, members of that ethnic group are blamed for their own poverty and society is exempted from finding ways to eliminate it and reduce its impact on learning. For example, Lee and Warren (1991) argue that, since Romà have always been on the margins of educational systems, any education for Romà should maintain this outsider status by ensuring that they acquire only the basic skills required to function in contemporary societies. They argue further that the ideal Romaní formal education should only guarantee group survival and conservation of its marginal status:

> Rather than look at the provision of more and more mainstream opportunities for Romaní children — that is, to ask "What can we do for them[?]" — there is some value in looking beyond the stereotypes and asking: "What can we learn from the Romanis?" To the Romanis, mainstream schooling is demonstrably counterproductive, both for Romanis and for the Gadje.[8] (p. 320)

Although relativism and ethnocentrism differ philosophically, they share three key elements that are manifest in the policies, practices, and research findings obtained from them: the objectification of the Romaní community, the limited inclusion of Romà in the research process, and an emphasis on deficit theory. A discussion of these three elements completes our discussion of how Romà disaffection to school has been explained and sets the stage for a better understanding of the kind of research we are proposing here.

– Objectifying the Romaní Community

Objectivity, a basic principle in scientific research, implies a clear distinction between the neutral scientist and the object of study. The researcher's subjectivity, assumed to be objective, is the only one that counts, and the researcher assumes sole responsibility for interpreting any data. In both the ethnocentric and relativist perspective, the objectification of the subject of study is the consequence of an unquestioned superiority of researcher subjectivity. Educational practices, policies, and research that objectify the Romaní community are not committed to addressing the roots of Roms' marginality in order to overcome it. On the contrary, they reinforce a popular imaginary that romanticizes Romaní different traits without helping them overcome social exclusion. The process of objectification of the Romà has also shaped the kinds of studies most commonly done on the Romaní community. Kende (2000) argues that, while cultural anthropologists have focused on the exploration of Romà otherness, looking at cultural patterns and exalting exoticism, sociologists have tended to count and classify individuals as Romaní or not. Research studies about the Romaní community have presented the Romà as the strange "other" whose mysteries and secrets researchers should "discover," and few research efforts have been dedicated to eradicating their relative poverty and marginality. Instead, research has been descriptive and superficial, focusing on our culture, traditions, or biological characteristics.

As a consequence, examples of this research are more often found in anthropology or biology than in education. In 1943, upon the arrival of some families with a "great deal of gypsy-blood," the Copenhagen public authorities asked university professors at the Department of Human Genetics to find out if "the peculiarities of these families might be due to hereditarily conditioned defects" (Bartels & Brun, 1943, p. 10). The Danish researchers, after demonstrating "scientifically" that Romà have a lower than average IQ, concluded that sterilization of these families would solve the authorities' problem. Related research describing the major features of our culture is still found today. A recent Slovak study looked at physiological differences between Romà and non-Romà. They highlighted the fact that Romà have a lower weight and height average, and smaller size of the cranium (Bernasovsky & Bernasovka, 1999). Even though not directly related to education, such studies inform discriminatory measures that do not help to improve Romaní education or living conditions. On the contrary, their only purpose is to increase discriminatory actions and to generate scientific evidence to support them.

Even when research, policies, or practices are based on later comprehensivist theories that recognize social actors' subjectivity, most of those who qualify as "objects" have been barred from taking part in the interpretation process.[9] As a result, when researchers have not contrasted their interpretations with those of the participants, they risk a slanted analysis that does not take into account the methodologically relevant gap between the interpretation of reality and the reality interpreted (Habermas, 1981). This methodological oversight has left many researchers, policymakers, and teachers with only their own views and prejudices to interpret cultural behaviors.

– Non-Romaní Research Teams

The objectification of the Romà can be connected to the absence of Romaní researchers from studies of their own culture. The predominance of non-Romaní in educational research from both the ethnocentric and relativist perspective has further barred Romà representation in the creation of educational policies and suitable practices. From our experience, it is possible to say that, until a few years ago, all research about the Romaní community was carried out exclusively by non-Romaní research teams. This is due to a lack of access to the needed training, social capital, and resources to carry out research. Moreover, the complexity of the processes and structure of the scientific community has further impeded Romaní participation in research and other professional positions. For example, Toon Machiels (2002) explains that in Sweden the absence of Romaní experts prevents Romà involvement in Swedish policymaking processes. Jim Mac Laughlin denounces the same phenomena in this way:

> Debates about gypsies as the "other" in Europe today take place outside the ranks both of Gypsies themselves and Gypsy activists. They generally have little or no impact on the political consciousness or real life experiences of these groups. . . . They simply allow social theorists to appropriate the experience of "otherness" in such a way as to enhance academic discourse and allow social theorists at least to feign concern for the marginalized in European society. (Mac Laughlin, 1999, p. 57)

Certainly, few Roms have reached the high level of education usually considered a requirement in the mainstream research community, but alternative methods of cooperation with Romaní representatives from the design to the collection and interpretation of data could be found if researchers deemed them valuable and necessary to ensure validity. Recent guidelines from the European Commission in Social Sciences Research encourage such multicultural research teams (Commission of the European Communities, 1998); while inclusion is no guarantee of the total eradication of prejudices, it would be a step forward.

Deficit Theories

Deficit theories are pseudoscientific claims that support racist, ageist, sexist, or homophobic beliefs that legitimate discrimination and are commonly found in reference to the most disadvantaged social groups. Deficit theories underlie most compensatory or special education programs that target Roms and immigrants as having problems to be solved (Cahn & Chirico, 1999). These theories draw correlations between people's educational level and the degree of motivation of the learners and their culture; for example, a high rate of illiteracy among the Romaní community is interpreted as proof of their disinterest in education (Iniesta, 1981).

The influence of both ethnocentrist and relativist approaches on deficit theories is clear. Romaní families' disaffection in schools is rarely explained as a result of the education system's deficits, being cast instead as *their* problem. From our experience, despite a lack of supporting research, we can say that the explanation of Romà disaffection to schooling that blames the Romaní culture is common among teachers, policymakers, and researchers. Kende (2000) explains that these deficit theories concerning the Romà underlie the ideas and work of education experts in Hungary, who explain their dissaffection as a result of a "socialization gap." A study of the Romà in Spain states that

> the Romaní kids get to primary school, even when they have attended kindergarten, carrying deficits — different from those purely personal — that represent a handicap. These handicaps are maintained during the two following stages [grades]. During all their life, it would be impossible for them to be normal, they will remain socially marginalized forever.[10] (Iniesta, 1981, p. 179)

Data about Romaní parental involvement in mainstream schools has been interpreted as the parents' lack of interest or willingness to participate (Espinós, 2002), which fails to examine other possible reasons for parents' decisions not to participate in the school. Instead, it ascribes the issue of school failure and other common problems that emerge in Roms' education today to the shortcomings of parents, who are judged on the basis of how well they adapt to conditions identified as valuable by the school system (Center for Social and Educational Research [CREA], 2002a). Furthermore, deficit theories deny that people have the capacity to help define a better and more effective school environment.

The reproduction and perpetuation of historical racist patterns in educational research and the inability of traditional research perspectives to help the Romà, rather than merely to examine them, suggest that these approaches do not satisfy the educational needs of the Romaní community. The perspectives that have dominated the study of Roms' education have not contributed to the search for valid solutions, since they are the result of a one-sided approach to the context, the school system, and society.

How Communicative Research Explains
Romà's Disaffection to Schooling

In response to traditional research methods, we propose a communicative approach that includes the voice of the Romaní community in the definition of programs, strategies, and projects of school transformation. Research based on this perspective is grounded in intersubjective dialogue among researcher and researched, thus breaking with the traditional methodological hierarchy implicit in both the ethnocentric and relativist approaches and allowing analysis that is oriented to overcoming inequalities and social exclusion. This approach arose from the convergence of two main influences: the Spanish Romà rights movement and the communicative shift in the social sciences. In the following sections, we will discuss its origins in the Spanish Romà rights movement and the communicative shift in social science, and will then discuss some specific alternatives that have proved effective in transforming schools.

Spanish Romà Rights Movement

The Spanish Romà rights movement began in the 1960s under Franco's regime and accelerated after 1975 with the arrival of democracy. It evolved from religious beliefs such as evangelism and the theology of liberation (San Román, 1999) in highly marginalized neighborhoods where poverty and lack of opportunity were the reality and emerged from the creation of Romaní associations. These associations of women, students, families, neighbors, and youth, most of whom shared similar histories, usually arose in reaction to concrete issues such as families' expulsion from shanty towns, schools' refusals to accept Romaní kids, and mistreatment by the police. The Spanish Romà rights movement was composed of a variety of associations that offered the Roma a way to act upon shared problems that no one else, including the state, would approach. In effect, the associations transcended the extended family, the organizational center of Romaní life, to gain public visibility and voice, obtain public resources, and promote a more positive and united front (San Román, 1999).

Given the absence of a Romaní political structure per se, the associations served as a key element in the struggle for basic rights and in the survival of our culture. Although these associations have limited resources and a local or regional focus, they have been a source of representation in negotiations with the governmental agencies. For example, when, in 1985, the Spanish Parliament created the Romà Development Program (RDP), Romaní nongovernmental organizations were invited to participate as consultants to the program.[11]

The Romaní women's associations have played a leadership role in the Spanish Romà rights movement. In 1990, the first women's association, *Romí* (the Romanó word for Romaní women) was founded. In the intervening ten years, so many other Romí associations have arisen that the Spanish Romí's federation, *Kamira*, was founded in 2000 (De Botton, Puigvert, & Sánchez A., in press). Despite scarce resources, Kamira, which represented the voices of more than three thousand women, began its work with a campaign for Romí rights, including the educational rights of these women and their children (Escárraga, 1999). Kamira representatives met with the president of the congress to ask for help in securing education of quality for their children. As Rosalía Vázquez, a representative of the Romí association *Arboreá,* says, they sought "an education without ghettoes because the kind of education [our children] receive determines if they will be doctors, lawyers or politicians instead of scrap dealers" (Marcos, 2001, p. 26).[12]

The Romà rights movement mirrors many features of Romaní culture, such as dialogue and oral tradition. Our experience of sharing territories with many other cultures, including White Europeans, Arabs, Jews, Christians, and Muslims, has required the Romà to find common ground on which to interact through dialogue. This spirit is reflected in the participation of Romà and non-Romà in these associations. Traditionally, there is no distinction or exclusion, and everybody has the chance to participate. For example, the *Fundación Secretariado General Gitano* (FSGG), a Spanish nonprofit organization aimed at promoting the Romaní community, is built upon a board of management constituted by Romà and non-Romà (FSGG, n.d.).

Organization as a decentralized network is another cultural feature of the Romà that is reflected in the Romà rights movement. Romaní families are usually spread across the country and even over different states, but they maintain solidarity, another key element of our culture. Within the Romà rights movement this translates into a deeply democratic nature, since the infinite local associations spread across the state are joined in federations without a unique leading group or representatives. For example, *Union Romaní* unites its international equivalent (the International Romaní Union) and regional federations like the FAGIC (the federation of Romaní associations in Catalonia) with all the associations in Catalonia, including FAGEX (the federation of Romaní associations in Extremadura) and FAGA (the federation of Romaní associations in Aragón). The horizontal, open, and free nature of Romaní organizations perfectly suits the possibilities offered by new information technologies. These technologies, where available, have become enormously useful tools for the functioning of these horizontal structures.[13]

Contrary to the traditional perception that the Romà have a natural and cultural disinterest in education, many associations are active in securing quality education for Romaní children. At the same time, they seek to preserve Romaní culture and identity. Emilia Clavería, a respected and well-known Romí elder[14] and a leader in the movement, who has been specifically outspoken for women and children's educational rights, says,

> We want to be educated as are all the people. We want our girls to go to school, but to a good school, which should know how to give the maximum for all children.... Let's finally open the school to the Romaní Culture. (Drom Kotar Mestipen, 2001, p. 3)

Clearly, Clavería does not reject education for the Romà. Instead, she calls for schools to provide a quality education that provides Romaní children the tools and opportunities that non-Romà have, while valuing and reflecting Romaní culture. The manifesto *El Pueblo Gitano y la Educación* (Asociación Secretariado General Gitano, 2000) is another example of the Romà rights movement mobilization for education. Romaní organizations collaborated in defining the elements of this manifesto and presented a unified front that has forced the government to engage in a dialogue about Romaní concerns in education. Among other things, it proclaims the need to acknowledge and integrate Romaní culture into the Spanish educational system (ASGG, 2000).[15] For example, to guarantee equal access to education, the association demanded that the government provide the means and resources to encourage attendance, such as free lunch, free transportation, and scholarships. Also, the association requested that teachers be trained to attend to different cultural and ethnic groups. Further, they demanded the establishment of family literacy programs, to combat the high rates of literacy within the Romaní community (ASGG, 2000). The associations seek to realize this goal because they feel that the gap between Romaní culture and mainstream schooling lies behind much of the perceived Romà disaffection for schools.

In the mid-1990s, the need for these organizations to support their claims with scientific data led some Romà activists to take part in educational research. That work was punctuated by a sense of urgency born of a need to contrast and counter the racist conclusions that traditional research proposed. At the same time, some researchers interested in Romaní issues realized the need to incorporate the voices of advocacy in the academy if they were to present reliable and socially useful research. The tension between these disparate voices led to the institutionalization of this work. For example, the Spanish Romaní Studies Center, the *Centro de Estudios Gitanos* (CEG), was created at the University of Barcelona in 1997, and it has been consolidated into a network of partnerships with local, national, and international NGOs to develop their scientific activities (Vargas, Millán, & Sánchez, 2000; Vargas & Tortajada, 1998).

CEG was born from the initiative of a group of professionals at the university who are linked with research, educational practice, and various social movements. Their aim was to respond to the need for rigorous and critical scientific knowledge about the real situation of Romaní culture. The projects and initiatives that are carried out at CEG attempt to identify the specific needs of Romaní culture. The objective of CEG is to develop an alternative scientific analysis, promoting practices that create and disseminate knowledge to help overcome educational, cultural, and social inequalities that the Romaní community faces. CEG is guided by communicative theory; the organization is egalitarian in nature and built on rational argumentation.

Today this research is supported by universities and other scientific agencies that fund most European research projects. Both Romaní and European institutions are interested in studies and actions that promote educational inclusion and social cohesion. In this sense, many research projects start to require the collaboration of NGOs as consultants to bring their perspective into research (European Commission, 2002). This collaboration has opened up spaces of dialogue for Romaní and non-Romaní researchers and activists and facilitated agreements regarding the priorities of future research agendas (Drom Kotar Mestipen, 2001). The voices and proposals of the Romaní community have become essential in guiding the transformation of the school system. In addition, leaders of the Romà rights movement are bringing their voices to educational research. The theory that emerges from these collaborations is more rigorous because it includes the realities of the Romaní community (Tsetsekou, 2002; Vargas et al., 2000). These research projects have the potential of providing truly viable avenues for education.

Communicative Methodology

The research resulting from this collaboration is an example of what sociologists have termed the communicative shift taking place in both contemporary societies and in the domain of the social sciences (Beck, 1992, 1997; Beck, Giddens, & Lash, 1994; Habermas, 1998; Touraine, 2000). Ulrich Beck (1997) and Alain Touraine (2000) argue that society is currently moving toward a dialogic tendency in which people have to dialogue and come to agreements in order to coordinate their actions, solve daily problems, and make decisions about their lives. Jürgen Habermas (1981, 1987) explains this shift as recovering the original communicative essence of modernity. He argues that, after the colonization of our lives by instrumental rationality and the bureacratization of social institutions, there has been a reaction against these two processes that moves back to people's original communicative practices. This directly illuminates the process of questioning that the Romà have engaged in — a process that has challenged traditional forms of research and reconfigured research as a space where all voices are heard.

Research becomes communicative when it is designed and conducted under these dialogic circumstances, in this case making the space claimed by the Romà a reality (Elboj & Gómez, 2001). Communicative research consists of bringing together the researcher and the researched to create an egalitarian dialogue built on the common need to know. Through the intersubjective dialogue, researchers and participants jointly produce scientific knowledge and participate in the definition of actions that lead to social and educational change. Three main principles derived from contemporary philosophy and the social sciences underlie the idea of communicative research: interpretive ability, structure and agency, and the dialogic construction of knowledge.

Interpretive Ability

No subjects are superior to others or belong to a superior intellectual rank. All people are capable of language and action, that is, of interpreting and communicating about the social reality in which they live (Chomsky, 1988; Habermas, 1981). Research on the nature of communicative abilities has proved that every person possesses communicative skills, understood as the capacities developed on the basis of dialogue in different natural contexts: workplace, school, social setting, etc. This demands a new understanding of people's cognitive capacities in terms of "cultural intelligence," defined as the plurality of mental processes that assume interaction, through verbal or nonverbal means, in order to reach understanding (Flecha, 2000). Cultural intelligence includes academic and practical intelligences, as well as the multiple competencies people develop throughout their experiences. Communicative research integrates everybody's interpretations, from illiterate grandparents to Romaní girls who decide to drop out, and recognizes their reasons and rationale for making such decisions.

Structure and Agency

People are social agents who transform their environment (Freire, 1997). Contemporary social theory explains society as a dual interaction between structures and agency (Giddens, 1990) or systems and lifeworld (Habermas, 1981, 1987). The communicative approach asserts that subjects have played an important role in social change throughout history. Further, subjects' capacity for reflection has caused the transformation of social structures. When applied to Romaní studies, communicative research looks at racist and structural conditions, as well as Romaní acts of resistance against them. Due to the influence of the Romà rights movement and the resulting inclusion of first-hand testimony of Romaní associations in research, a new understanding of oppressive conditions has been constructed. At the same time, Romaní people are able to analyze and consider the processes of social transformation — the associations' initiatives to counter the structural oppression — that are already taking place in their community.

Dialogic Construction of Knowledge

Communicative research refutes the traditional assumption of an interpretative hierarchy between the researcher and the researched. Instead, all contributions and "knowledges" are equally valued and meanings are jointly built. In the communicative model, those traditionally thought of as researchers and researched now constitute a single research team. Habermas (1981) describes the dissolution of this hierarchy as breaking the methodologically relevant gap between the interpretations of the researchers and researched. In such situations, validity is based on the strength of the arguments presented in the dialogue among members of the team rather than on the individuals' position of power. This dialogue is oriented toward understanding. Within the field of research, it is grounded in communicative rationality that is characterized by the subjects' use of their experience and knowledge to reach understanding and agreement (Habermas, 1981). Notwithstanding obstacles, biases, and the unequal balance of power in social relationships, each participant is committed to the creation of this socially oriented knowledge. It is this shared commitment made to the group and to the study that holds all the participants responsible for its accomplishment. Communicative methodology becomes more than a list of research methods supported by a particular scientific paradigm. It is instead a holistic approach to research that implies a certain level of commitment to social justice and an openness to be challenged by any participant. Communicative research includes Paulo Freire's reflection on the challenges of egalitarian and democratic dialogues:

> It is truly difficult to make democracy. Democracy, like any dream, is not made with spiritual words but with reflection and practice. It is not what I say that says I am a democrat, that I am not racist or machista, but what I do. What I say must not be contradicted by what I do. It is what I do that best speaks to my faithfulness or not to what I say. (1998, p. 67)

From our experience, we are aware that the rhetoric around egalitarian and democratic spaces is not enough to make dialogue happen. As Freire says, it is not an easy journey. Certainly, communicative research requires courage and conviction from those who dare to believe that it is possible.

Communicative Methodology in Practice

What does this approach look like in action? The principles described above translate into practices relevant to Romaní research: organization, techniques, and data analysis.

Organization

The communicative organization of the research brings together the scientific community with different Romaní organizations and social agents that were once called the "target group of the study." The goals, research questions, hypothesis, application of techniques, data analysis, theoretical elaboration, and results are agreed upon by a research team that includes Romaní and non-Romaní researchers, as well as members of the Romaní community. On some occasions, collaboration with these community members is institutionalized with the creation of an advisory council that monitors the development of the study from its inception. This council is composed of representatives from Romaní associations that bring the experiences and voices of their constituency to the study. Representatives are not required to have any academic credentials or research experience, only the willingness to enter into dialogue and share their knowledge and experience toward the creation of new understandings. Advisory council members contribute their knowledge, review documents, and guide the development of the project to ensure that the Romaní experience is reflected throughout. They also evaluate the research process and the conclusions by providing input and assessment at every step in the process. Council members attend all research meetings, presenting the research at conferences and in author publications.

Multiple benefits are obtained from the experience of these mixed research teams. A situation from the *Workaló* project[16] (CREA, 2000–2003) illustrates one of the major benefits: these research teams do not take mainstream theories for granted but challenge them to really integrate the Romaní experience and make them meaningful to us. The study's first report was a theoretical literature review on what impact the transition from an industrial society to an information society has had on the Spanish labor market. However, it was not until the advisory council members of the research team joined the discussion that it became apparent that mainstream explanations did not apply to the reality of the Romaní people. Specifically, while most workers had secure lifelong employment in the industrial era, the majority of Romà had not. Thus, the decline in the number of manufacturing jobs did not affect the Romaní community as was anticipated by mainstream explanations. This recognition challenged the assumption that the shift to an information society affected everyone in Europe in the same way. This is an example of how scientific analysis can benefit from democratization.

Research Techniques

Research techniques in the communicative approach have been used in diverse European studies. These techniques are mainly, but not exclusively, qualitative. To begin, all participants know the purpose, objectives, and results of the research, so all members of the team have the same information. Further, communicative techniques do not end when an interview or a focus group ends. Instead, dialogue continues in subsequent meetings in which the transcribed data and analyzed transcripts are discussed with the subjects of the research through the revision of the conclusions, findings, and recommendations. Communicative techniques require going back to each person in the study to continue the dialogue, in order to better capture shared interpretations of reality and avoid partial and possibly inaccurate explanations of the situation and solutions for the Romà. The idea is not to seek approval but to generate knowledge together.

Among the techniques used in this process are communicative focus groups, daily life stories, and observations (CREA, 1999, 2000–2003). *Communicative focus groups* are composed of people in natural settings (like a family, a class, the staff of a restaurant, or any other worksite). In the communicative focus group the researcher is simply one more person engaged in the group's dialogue. Similarly, in the *communicative daily life stories*, a dialogue takes place between a researcher and a subject of research to analyze together the subject's reality and relationships from his or her present life, rather than discovering episodes through biography. *Communicative observation* aims at observing particular situations, people's actions and interactions, in order to open a dialogue in which the subject of research is asked to interpret their actions, rather than the researcher interpreting for them. The result is a joint assessment of what is happening.[17]

The participation of Romaní organizations in research projects facilitates the proper implementation of these techniques. Community leaders play a key role during data collection. For instance, as part of the study on Romaní community development, women from a local Romí association were the facilitators of the communicative focus groups. During one of the association's regular meetings, leaders shared the intentions and goals of the study, and then asked for the consent of all the members for the group's participation in the study. As part of the association's activities agenda, the communicative focus group was organized in order to discuss the barriers families face when getting involved in the community school and what needs to be done in order to improve it. The women invited other community members to take part in the dialogue; the room was packed and everybody was willing to share their thoughts and opinions. The fact that the communicative focus group occurred in a natural setting for the participants seemed to shape the findings in many ways. It was not an "expert" in Romaní issues who talked to them, but a Romí who was responsible for ensuring a true communicative process between the Romà and the social sciences. Validity threats to this process can arise if researchers and Romà do not maintain an egalitarian relationship. Specifically, if power claims arise, the omission of the reality of the Romà may result. Nevertheless, the communicative process, aimed at guaranteeing an egalitarian dynamic on all levels of the research, ensures that from onset to finish of the project all of the participants provide their experiences, know-how, and forms of knowledge.

Data Analysis

Communicative research is oriented to social utility and therefore must serve to draw social and educational recommendations that effect change. The process of analyzing data is thus designed toward this end. The analysis is based on the assumption that the Romà know their reality and are capable of formulating proposals to transform it. The research team codes the data by identifying the emerging themes and considering them exclusionary or transformative. An emerging theme will be considered exclusionary if it sets up barriers to Romà's social participation in education, labor market, civil society, or other social domains. To the contrary, an emerging theme will be considered transformative if it sheds light on how Romaní people overcome these barriers. For example, dimensions such as age, gender, ethnicity, culture, and socioeconomic background have often been interpreted as barriers to full participation in society. However, people's interpretations and reflections of these dimensions suggest that they can be both exclusionary and transformative.

We can take an example from a study that explores the role of the Romaní family in young Romaní women's educational success (CREA, 2002a). The Romaní family has often been interpreted as a constraint (or exclusionary element) for women in relation to the probability of their success in education (Garaizabal, 2000). However, Romí define their lives, the role of family, and the constraints they face to succeed in education differently from non-Romà women. Most of the teachers interviewed who had Romaní girls in their classrooms stated that the Romaní family is a barrier to Romaní girls' education. In a communicative daily life story, a teacher said,

> Romaní families have many prejudices about their children going to High School! I think that . . . well, gross generalizations are always bad . . . but the majority of them think that schools are places of wickedness . . . that their children will start to smoke, that who knows what will happen to their daughters. (CREA, 2002b)[18]

At the same time, a social worker explained,

> They don't want to take their daughters away from school, but they have to make this decision because their husbands sell in the markets, and women must go with them to help, and there is no childcare so they have to rely on the girls. They have no choice, it is the contingency. (CREA, 2002a, p. 56)

These two professionals interpreted the same barrier differently. While the teacher blames the Romaní family, the social worker offers a more transformative interpretation by suggesting that there is a need to provide educational options in support of these families.

The double axis of the exclusionary and transformative allows us to disclose the complexity of reality and to avoid simplistic explanations that categorize a factor as entirely exclusive or transformative. This study demonstrates that what is interpreted as oppressive from the outside is not always experienced as such from the inside. For example, the communicative daily life stories of Romí who have dropped out of school tell us that within the Romaní community the family is consistently seen as a pillar of solidarity and as providing strength to these women's personal projects, including education. One of them said, "Family is first, if anything goes wrong, we go all at once, we help each other." The same woman then explained that she found in her family the support to go back to school, because members of her extended family took care of her children during class hours. Conceived in this way, family is a transformative element for these women in getting an education.

The Romí that were interviewed in the study went beyond explaining the causes of their dropping out; they also made statements about how their decision to drop out could have been prevented. In reference to the family, one Romí said, "If family support was included in schools, more flexibility was given, then mothers would trust schools more for their girls and would continue their studies." These voices reveal transformative dimensions that emerge directly from the solutions the Romà have worked out within their communities.

Furthermore, when non-Romí researchers analyze data by themselves, it is likely that their own biases or preconceived notions — due to a lack of knowledge of the culture or concrete social situation — will permeate the research findings. The communicative methodology tries to avoid this possibility. Through this method the Romaní people can interpret reality and develop proposals that help to transfom discriminatory behavior. Thus, through reflection with the participants, researchers can identify and understand both the exclusionary and transformative elements that have been influencing the lives of the Romà.

One of the most important objectives of communicative research is to focus on describing and denouncing situations of inequality and to contribute to solutions through a dialogue among all the agents involved. It is important to create debate about social intervention through this research in such a way that what are identified as barriers to overcome and possible solutions to undertake can become programs of action oriented toward overcoming difficulties and improving the lives of Roms. Coding the data along the exclusionary/ transformative axis can help achieve this goal. What is the point of studying the Romà in education if the goal is not improving school programs to provide better possibilities for the Romaní children? Isn't it our ethical duty as researchers to seek for the social utility of our research findings?

Lessons from the Romà

Conducting research from a communicative perspective has allowed us to come closer to Romà disaffection and their needs in regard to education. We have seen how the Romaní experience exclusion and we have also identified key elements of transformation to overcome oppression. This knowledge helps us draw implications for social and educational change.

Through the communicative methodology we have learned that Romaní children and adolescents, as well as their mothers, fathers, and families, show high motivation for education. However, schools are providing "pedagogy of happiness" or "care" for the Romà — adapting curricula to basic concepts and skills, often in special education units, with the argument that these children have special social and educational needs (Elboj et al., 2002). As with the Mathew Effect (Merton, 1973), schools are offering better education and more resources to those who already have them. Results from communicative research suggest that Romaní families and children are aware of this negative discrimination (CREA, 2002a, 2002b). Rather than "adaptative" solutions like the ones mentioned above, Romaní families are asking for what they have defined as the "pedagogy of maximums" (Miquel et al., 2001).

The pedagogy of maximums was a concept developed through these families' claims gathered in a study on young Romà who had abandoned school and ended up in jail. This study, along with others also developed under this communicative approach, showed the need for a program based on the Romà's high expectations about their learning capacity (Miquel et al., 2001). Rather than implementing compensatory programs with watered-down curricula, the young Romà were more successful with learning computers, mathematics, and foreign languages. In a pedagogy of maximums, external conditions do not limit Romaní children and youth's possibilities;

rather, they get the necessary resources and support to be included in the information society.

When schools have high expectations, they match with many Romaní families' goals and often "unattainable" dreams. A Romaní mother said, in a communicative daily life story, "My dream is that my son does not need to sell in the markets; well, selling it's fine, but I would like him to study and come to be somebody." Or, as a young Romí remembered,

> When I was in high school, a teacher told me I must study because I was Romà; he used to say it was not only for me but for my people. . . . I met him later and he is very happy I made it to the university. That [his encouragement] was very important for me. (CREA, 2002b, p. 26)

Another woman argued similarly that

> the young Romí must push for an education beyond secondary school, because there is an urgent need for us to create identification models of university women who become a stimulus for the rest to continue in school. (Escárraga, 1999, p. 96)

Furthermore, through communicative fieldwork in schools, research has pointed to new educational solutions that emphasize learning interactions rather than cultural segregation or tracking. One of the pedagogical practices resulting from this research is interactive groups, which have demonstrated both improved learning among excluded minority children and increased solidarity (Aubert & Garcia, 2001; Elboj et al., 2002; Vargas & Flecha, 2000). Interactive groups consist of children from diverse groups, at different learning levels, working together in small groups with several volunteers (e.g., educators, family members, people from the community) in the same classroom. The class multiplies interactions and learning opportunities. In an environment where there is an exchange of information, positive interactions, and solidarity, excluded minority children have the opportunity to fully participate and be energized by learning, transforming their experiences, their interest, and their school achievement.

This perspective favors learning based on values that are part of one's culture. Within the Romaní culture such values include helping others and transmitting culture through elder people's experience. Interactive groups have been received by children with excitement and as a new way to open possibilities for the future.[19] For instance, in one of these schools, Manuel, a second-grade Romaní student perceived by his teachers as "disturbed" because he was inattentive, asserted that he was no longer "bored in class" because of these interactive groups. Through this approach he found a new meaning for learning in school. Teachers explain that now, when the bell rings for the playground, students are sometimes so immersed in the group that they just keep working (Aubert & Garcia, 2001).

In an interactive group session at another school, a group of third graders was working on a unit on jobs. Most said they wanted to be sellers in the marketplaces, but some pointed out that their mothers said this job has no future. One student, Rocío, said she wanted to be a teacher, and Miriam, who had been the first to talk about selling, asked with strong concern, "Are there any Romaní nurses?" The girls became silent, looked at each other, and finally concluded that they knew no Romaní nurses. Suddenly Miriam's eyes shined and she said, "So I want to be a nurse, to be able to cure the Romaní boys and girls so that they are not afraid." Educational expectations of these children changed through a dialogue that has no limits.

The Romà have been historically marginalized and made invisible in society, particularly in the educational system. Traditionally, educational research about the Romaní has not served to change or improve how Romaní children experience school. The Romà continue to have high dropout and low participation rates. Governments have not been able to provide solutions, as the data regarding the Romà in the European educational systems reported earlier in this article showed. The situation for the Romà is critical, and education is a key element for their inclusion in an information society, as well as their political, social, and economic security.

Assimilation through dissolution of Romaní identity and culture is not the answer. Such attempts have only driven the Romà further from schools and education. Instead, we need to make the Romà visible and valued in society and to recognize their contributions. When Romaní rights associations participate in research and, through research in the construction of social knowledge, we will no longer ignore the Romaní struggle and will be able to reflect further on how to overcome what oppresses the Romaní community. Communicative methodology guarantees that Romà participation and Romà voices are not just an instrument, some data, or an object for research, but a vital and valued part of a process that helps transform the barriers and improve Romà lives. Above all, our aim is to make it possible for all Romaní children — those who today enter kindergarten and those who are now struggling to finish secondary school — to have the same opportunities as other children, and to make certain that reaching the university is not an impossible dream.

Notes

1. In the 2001 Durban World Conference, Romaní NGOs made a public statement to unify and systematize the usage of the following terms: *gypsy people, romà, romanies, gitano, sinti,* and *nomads.* They stated that this terminology was misleading and caused many to consider these groups as different peoples, united only through shared problems. To remedy this the NGOs agreed to use the term *Romà* to refer to all these groups (International Romani Union, 2001). In keeping with this recommendation, we use the terms *Romà* as the plural of the nominative "the Gypsies," *Romí* for the singular feminine nominative "the gypsy women," *Rom* for the singular masculine nominative, *Romaní* as the singular genitive form that literally means "of the gypsy" or "what is characteristic of the gypsy community."

2. The data presented from here on will be estimates. The scarcity and quality of population data make comparisons across countries or with other social groups impossible. In most cases, the figures offered are based on secondary, informal, or local sources. Despite the action of the recommendations of international organizations (EU Monitoring Accession Program, 2002), there has never been an institutional effort to systematically collect data on the Romaní. For example, Romaní ethnicity is not an option on the official census or local registrars. Also, there is some reluctance among the Romà to self-identify in public registers because of fear such information will again be used to implement discriminatory, repressive policies — even expulsion (Fernández Jiménez, 1996). The situation is exacerbated by the widely held misconception that it is forbidden by law to collect ethnic or racial data (Ringold, 2000). Policymakers cite lack of data as an excuse for not funding social policies that target minority groups. However, the bottom line is that the

collection of ethnic and racial data reflects an absence of political will, rather than a legal or scientific matter (Krizsán, 2001).

3. Differences among Romaní subgroups range from varying dialects of Romanó to the names of subgroups. According to Pierre Liégeois (1987), some groups take their name from a celebrated forebear, as the Dalípides (Greece), descendants of Dalípis, or the Jonešti, descendants of Jono. Others derive their name from their livelihood: the Rom Kalderáš, boilermakers (from the Romanian *caldera*, boiler); the Èurara, sieve-makers (from the Romanian *ciura*, sieve); the Lovara, horse dealers (from the Hungarian *ló*, horse). Other subgroup names come from a place or region of origin like the Stambulía (Greece) from Istanbul or the Parizoske Romá from Paris (Liégeois, 1987).

4. Since 1989, approximately 1,200,000 people have left Eastern European countries for Western Europe or the United States. In 1991, Romà from Romania arrived in Germany; despite the German government's refusal to provide precise data, of 40,054 Romanians that asked for political asylum, approximately two-thirds were Romà (De Bresson, 1993). No data on the number of Romà immigrants in the United States or Canada exists, but Romaní experts have reported a new wave of Romà immigration (Hancock, 1999).

5. For example, in Spain at the time the Spanish Constitution was approved (1978), many regional languages like Euskera, Catalan, and Galician were officially recognized. However, there was no mention of Calo (the Spanish dialect of Romanó), since the language had no territorial link. However, in 2001 the Catalan parliament in Spain officially recognized the identity of the Romaní people and the value of its culture ("Proposició de Llei," 2001).

6. The Dayton Peace Agreements are the treaty for Peace in Bosnia-Herzegovina, formally signed in Paris on November 21, 1995.

7. For more information about this project, go to http://opre.Romà.uji.es/castellano/proyecto.

8. *Gadje* is a Romanó term used to refer to non-Romà. There are others, like *Payo* or *Gorgio*.

9. *Comprehensivist theories,* a term taken from Habermas (1981), refers to those social science theories developed in the twentieth century that recognize the need to consider how actors think and interpret their own actions, instead of relying on the researcher to construct their reality without any exchange with the actors. These theories include Symbolic Interactionism, Phenomenology, and Ethnomethodology.

10. Authors' translation. The original is: "*El gitanillo llega a la primera etapa de E.G.B, aun asistiendo a guarderías, con deficits- distintos a los propiamente personales — que constituyen handicaps mantenidos durante las dos etapas siguientes. Durante toda su vida le sera imposible llegar a la normalidad permaneciendo marginado socialmente*" (Iniesta, 1981, p. 179).

11. The Romà Development Program, created under the auspices of the Ministry of Social Affairs, was the only structured policy program addressing the Romà nation in the Spanish State. Its purpose was to improve the living conditions of and create opportunities for Romà. It sponsored projects in areas such as health, education, labor, culture, housing, antiviolence, and political participation and efforts — both governmental and nongovernmental — to promote the Romaní culture.

12. Authors' translation. The original is: "*Hemos venido a pedir educación para nuestros hijos; queremos que tengan una educación sin guetos, porque lo que se juega es que puedan ser abogados o médicos o políticos en vez de chatarreros.*"

13. For example, romnet-l (listserv@netcom.com) is an email listserv on Romaní issues and Romnews (http://www.romnews.com) disseminates news about the Romà. Individual organizations' homepages like the Patrin website (http://www.patrin.com) offer interesting information on the Romà community and include links to Romaní organizations worldwide.

14. Romaní elders are especially respected within the Romaní culture. However, age alone does not make one a "Rom of respect." To earn this term one's opinions must also be especially respected by community members. A Rom or Romí of respect is also seen as a person who carries the tradition and values of the Romaní culture to his or her family. There is not a fixed process to become a Romaní of respect; it is a spontaneous process that emerges from the community.

15. For example, to guarantee equal access to education, the association demanded the government provide the means and resources to encourage attendance, such as free lunch, free transportation, and scholarships. Also, the association requested that teachers be trained to attend to different cul-

tural and ethnic groups. Further, they demanded the establishment of family literacy programs, to combat the high rates of literacy within the Romaní community (ASGG, 2000).

16. The *Workaló* project is a study about the creation of new occupational patterns for cultural minorities in Europe sponsored by the Fifth Framework Program of Research of the European Commission. This program funds high-quality and socially useful research in Europe that informs European social policies. Given the increasing multicultural context, funded social research is required to contribute strategies and measures that reinforce social cohesion. More information is available at http//www.neskes.net/workalo.

17. For more detailed information about the communicative techniques see, CREA (1999, 2000–2003, 2002a, 2002b) and Elboj and Gomez (2001).

18. Authors' translation. The original is: *"En las familias gitanas hay muchos prejuicios que sus hijos vayan al Instituto! Piensa que . . . siempre generalizar es malo — pero la mayoría piensan que allí están todas las maldades. Que los nenes allí aprenden a fumar no sé qué . . . que las nenas yo que sé que les puede pasar."*

19. These interactive groups take place at schools that have participated in the Learning Communities project.

References

Arayici, A. (1998). The Gypsy minority in Europe: Some considerations. *International Social Science Journal, 50,* 253–262.

Asociación Secretariado General Gitano (ASGG). (2000). Dossier educación. *Gitanos Pensamiento y Cultura, 7/8,* 27–58.

Aubert, A., & Garcia, C. (2001). Interactividad en el aula. *Cuadernos de Pedagogia, 301,* 20–24.

Bartels, E. D., & Brun, G. (1943). *Gipsies in Denmark. A socio-biological study.* Copenhagen: Einar Munksgaard.

Bateman, J. (1977). Gypsy intake. *Trends, 1,* 9–15.

Beck, U. (1992). *Risk society.* New York: Sage.

Beck, U. (1997). *The reinvention of politics: Rethinking modernity in the global social order.* Cambridge, MA: Blackwell.

Beck, U., Giddens, A., & Lash, S. (1994). *Reflexive modernization: Politics, tradition, and aesthetics in the modern social order.* Stanford, CA: Stanford University Press.

Bernasovsky, I., & Bernasovka, J. (Eds.). (1999). *Anthropology of Romanies. Axiological and anthropogenetical study.* Prague, Czech Republic: Nauma & Universitas Masarykiana.

Cahn, C., & Chirico, D. (1999). *A special remedy: Roma and schools for the mentally handicapped in the Czech Republic country reports series.* Budapest: European Roma Rights Center.

Cahn, C., & Peric, T. (1999). Roma and the Kosovo conflict. *Roma Rights, 2.* Retrieved January 10, 2003, from www.errc.org

Cahn, C., & Petrova, D. (2001). *State of impunity: Human rights abuse of Roma in Romania* (Country Reports Series). Budapest: European Roma Rights Center.

Calvo Buezas, T. (2000). *España racista? Voces payas sobre los gitanos.* Barcelona: Anthropos.

Castells, M. (1996). *The information era. Economy, society and culture, Vol. 1: The social network.* Malden, MA: Blackwell.

Castells, M. (1997). *The information era. Economy, society and culture, Vol. 2: The social network.* Malden, MA: Blackwell.

Castells, M. (1999). *The information era. Economy, society and culture, Vol. 3: The social network.* Malden, MA: Blackwell.

Center for Social and Educational Research (CREA). (1999). *Teoría y metodología comunicativa: diálogo y transformación social, la alternativa dialógica.* Barcelona: Comissió Interdepartmental de Recerca Innovació.

Center for Social and Educational Research (CREA). (2000–2003). *WORKALÓ. The creation of new occupational patterns for cultural minorities: The Gypsy Case. (I+D+I). RTD, Framework Program 5th.* Retrieved January 10, 2003, from http://www.neskes.net/workalo

Center for Social and Educational Research (CREA). (2002a). *Entrevistas en profundidad: Informe final.* Barcelona: Instituto de la Mujer.

Center for Social and Educational Research (CREA). (2002b). *Informe final etapa 3: La voz de la mujer gitana.* Barcelona: Instituto de la Mujer.

Chomsky, N. (1988). *Language and politics.* New York: Black Rose Books.

Commission of the European Communities. (1998). *The Framework Program 5th.* Brussels: European Union.

Congreso de los Diputados. (1999). *Informe de la Subcomisión para el estudio de la problemática del pueblo gitano.* Retrieved January 22, 2003, from www.fsgg.org/Informe%20subcomision.htm

Courthiade, M. (2000). La lengua y la identidad gitana: Algunos datos actualizados. *I Tchatchipen, 31,* 31–34.

Cozma, T., Cucos, C., & Momanu, M. (2000). The education of Roma children in Romania: Description, difficulties, solutions. *Intercultural Education, 11,* 281–288.

Da Costa, C. (1996). Los gitanos en Brasil. *I Tchatchipen, 13,* 47–50.

De Botton, L., Puigvert, L., & Sánchez A. M. (in press). *The inclusion of other women: Dialogical learning in multicultural societies.* Dordrecht: Kluwer Academic.

De Bresson, H. (1993). Calvario de los gitanos en Europa. Acuerdo Rumanía-Alemania. *I Tchathcipen, 3,* 18–20.

de Gila Kochanowsky, V. (1992). *Romano Atmo, l'ame tsigane, Roman.* Châteauneuf: Wallâda.

Drom Kotar Mestipen. (2001, November). *Les dones gitanes de Barcelona al segle XXI.* Paper presented at the meeting of Les dones gitanes de Barcelona al segle XXI, Barcelona, Spain.

Elboj, C., & Gómez, J. (2001). El Giro dialógico de las ciencias sociales: Hacia la comprensión de una metodología dialógica. *Acciones e Investigaciones Sociales, 12,* 77–95.

Elboj, C., Puigdellívol, I., Soler, M., & Valls, R. (2002). *Comunidades de aprendizaje. Transformar la educación.* Barcelona: Editorial Graó.

Escárraga, T. (1999, October). Las Gitanas alzan la voz. *El País,* p. 96.

Espinós, D. (2002, July 26). La escolarización de los niños gitanos mejora, pero el absentismo supera el 30%. *El País,* p. 25

European Commission. (2002). *EU support for Roma communities in central and eastern Europe.* Brussels: European Commission, Directorate General for Enlargement.

EURYDICE. (2002). *Eurydice: The information network on education in Europe.* Retreived February 20, 2002, from http://www.eurydice.org/search/frameset_en.html

Fanon, F. (1975). *Peau noire, masques blancs.* Paris: Éditions du Seuil.

Fernández Jiménez, D. (1996). *Situación y perspectivas de la juventud gitana en Europa.* Barcelona: Instituto Romano.

Feyerabend, P. (1993). *Against the method.* New York: Verso.

Flecha, R. (1999). Modern and postmodern racism in Europe: Dialogic approach and anti-racist pedagogies. *Harvard Educational Review, 69,* 150–171.

Flecha, R. (2000). *Sharing words: Theory and practice of dialogic learning.* Lanham, MD: Rowman & Littlefield.

Fraser, A. (1992). The Rom migrations. *Journal of the Gypsy Lore Society, 2,* 131–145.

Fraser, A. (1995). *The Gypsies.* Cambridge, MA: Blackwell.

Freire, P. (1997). *Pedagogy of the heart.* New York: Continuum.

Freire, P. (1998). *Teachers as cultural workers: Letters to those who dare to teach.* Boulder, CO: Westview Press.

FSGG. (n.d.) *Fundación Secretariado General Gitano.* Retrieved January 22, 2003, from http://www.fsgg.org

Garaizabal, C. (2000). La femenidad Tradicional: Cambios y crisis en la identidad de las mujeres. *Gitanos Pensamiento y Cultura, 5,* 40–45.

Giddens, A. (1990). *The consequences of modernity.* Cambridge, England: Polity Press & Basil Blackwell.

Giménez Adelantado, A., Gavarri Hernández, C., & Gavarri Hernández, F. (2001). Temporerismo y ausencia escolar. *Diálogo Gitano, 19,* 14–17.

Giménez Adelantado, A., Martínez Sancho, M., & Alfageme Chao, A. (2001). *La situación escolar de la infancia gitana y el absentismo.* Paper presented at the VII Congreso Español de Sociología, Salamanca, Spain.

Habermas, J. (1981). *The theory of communicative action, vol. 1: Reasons and the rationalization of society.* Boston: Beacon Press.

Habermas, J. (1987). *The theory of communicative action, vol. 2: Lifeworld and system, A critique of functionalist reason.* Boston, MA: Beacon Press.

Habermas, J. (1998). *Between facts and norms: Contributions to a discourse theory of law and democracy.* Cambridge, MA: MIT Press.

Hancock, I. (1987). *The pariah syndrome: An account of Gypsy slavery and prosecution.* Ann Arbor, MI: Karoma.

Hancock, I. (1997). Genocide of the Roma in the Holocaust. In I. Charny (Ed.), *Encyclopedia of genocide.* Santa Barbara, CA: ABC-CLIO.

Hancock, I. (1999, May). *The schooling of Romani Americans: An overview.* Paper presented at the II International Conference on the Psycholinguistic and Sociolinguistic Problems of Roma Children's Education, Varna, Bulgaria.

Hancock, I. (2002). *We are the Romani people.* Hertfordshire, England: University of Hertfordshire Press.

Iniesta, A. (1981). *Los Gitanos: Problemas socioeducativos.* Madrid: Narcea.

International Romani Union. (2001). *About denomination of Gypsy people in official documentation of world conference against racism.* Paper presented at the World Conference against the Racism, Durban, South Africa.

Kende, A. (2000). The Hungary of otherness: The Roma (Gypsies) of Hungary. *Journal of European Area Studies, 8,* 187–201.

King, C. (1999). Invisible no more. *Teaching Tolerance, 16,* 32–39.

Kovats, M. (March 2002). *The European Roma question, new series no. 31.* London: Royal Institute of International Affairs.

Krizsán, A. (Ed.). (2001). *Ethnic monitoring and data protection: The European context.* Budapest: Central European University Press & INDOK, Human Rights Information and Documentation Center.

Lee, K. W., & Warren, W. G. (1991). Alternative education: Lessons from Gypsy thought and practice. *British Journal of Educational Studies, 39,* 311–324.

Liégeois, J. P. (1987). *Gitanos e itinerantes.* Madrid: Presencia Gitana.

Mac Laughlin, J. (1999). European Gypsies and the historical geography of loathing. *Washington Review, 22*(1), 31–59.

Machiels, T. (2002). *Keeping the distance or taking the chances: Roma and travellers in western Europe.* Brussels: European Network Against Racism (ENAR).

Marcos, P. (2001, June 16). Gitanas en el Congreso Payo. *El Pais,* p. 26.

Mendiola, A. M. (2002). El porrajmos Romaní. *Gitanos: Pensamiento y Cultura, 14,* 23–38.

Merton, R. K. (1973). *Sociology of science: Theoretical and empirical investigations.* Chicago: University of Chicago Press.

Mills, C. W. (1997). *The racial contract.* Ithaca, NY: Cornell University Press.

Miquel, V., Tortajada, I., & Vargas, J. (2001). Caló: Aprenentatge dialògic en el medi penitenciari. *Revista Catalana de Sociologia, 14,* 161–168.

Morrow, M. (2000). *Report from Australia*. Paper presented at the 5th International Romani Union Congress.

Novitch, M. (1984). *Gypsy victims of the Nazi terror*. Retrieved September 3, 2002, from http://www.geocities.com/Patrin/5121/terror.htmSeptember 3, 2002.

Organization for Security and Co-operation in Europe. (2000). *Report on the situation of the Roma and Sinti in the OSCE Area*. Geneva, Switz.: Organization for Security and Co-operation in Europe, High Commissioner on National Minorities.

Proposició de llei sobre el reconeixement de la dignitat del poble gitano i del valor de la seva cultura. (2001, July 16). *Bulleti Oficial del Parlament de Catalunya,* 41–42

Revenga, A., Ringold, D., & Martin Tracy, W. (2002). *Poverty and ethnicity: A cross-country study of Roma poverty in central Europe* (World Bank Technical Paper No. 531). Washington, DC: World Bank.

Ringold, D. (2000). *Roma and the transition in central and eastern Europe: Trends and challenges*. Washington, DC: World Bank.

San Román, T. (1998). *La diferecia inquietant: Velles i noves estrategies culturals dels gitanos.* Barcelona: Editorial Alta Fulla.

San Román, T. (1999). El desarrollo de la conciencia política de los gitanos. *Gitanos: Pensamiento y Cultura,* 36–41.

Sánchez Ortega, M. H. (1986). Evolución y contexto histórico de los gitanos españoles. In T. San Román (Ed.), *Entre la marginación y el racismo. Reflexiones sobre la vida de los gitanos*. Madrid: Alianza Editorial.

Save the Children. (2001). *Denied a future? The right to education of Roma/Gypsy and Traveller children in south-eastern and central Europe* (vol. II). London: Author.

Sen, A. (1999). *Development as freedom*. New York: Anchor Books.

Touraine, A. (2000). *Can we live together? Equality and difference*. Cambridge, Eng.: Polity Press.

Tsetsekou, E. (2002). The Roma issue: A challenge for the Council of Europe. *Lifelong Learning, 3,* 175–178.

Vargas, J., & Flecha, R. (2000). El aprendizaje dialógico como "experto"en resolución de conflictos. *Contextos Educativos: Revista de Educación, 3,* 81–88.

Vargas, J., Millán, C., & Sánchez, M. (2000). Contribución de la comunidad gitana al aumento de la calidad científica. In FACEPA (Ed.), *I jornadas de investigación en educación de personas adultas*. Barcelona: El Roure.

Vargas, J., & Tortajada, I. (1998). *CEG. Gypsy Studies Center.* Paper presented at the XVI World Sociology Congress, Montreal.

Education in the Fight against HIV/AIDS: Caring for Ourselves, Our Families, and Our Community in Kampala, Uganda

JOANITA NAMBI, STELLA ALAMO TALISUNA,
MARGRETHE JUNCKER,
AND THE VOLUNTEERS OF REACH OUT

Reach Out is a unique HIV/AIDS community initiative in a poor area on the outskirts of Kampala, Uganda. There are more than 800,000 people in Uganda living with HIV/AIDS. In Kampala, 12.3 percent of the population is infected with this disease.

Since its inception in 2001, Reach Out has grown dramatically from caring for fourteen people to caring for 1,840 people living with HIV/AIDS in our community. In the beginning, a small Christian community — together with the parish priest — visited the sick, praying for people and encouraging them. A Danish doctor soon joined them and began to provide medication and clinical care. This was the birth of Reach Out.

Reach Out's clients are mostly widows and single mothers with little education and no marketable skills. Our success in caring for these clients is a result of the exceptional network of volunteers who live in the surrounding area. Clients are never more than a few minutes walk away from a volunteer who can support and help them, day or night. A large number of our volunteers are themselves living with HIV/AIDS and have experienced the benefits of the many services that Reach Out offers. Many members of our community indeed play multiple roles: client, volunteer, teacher, and learner.

We believe that there is a need to cater to the individual as a whole. Medicine alone will not make our clients better. They need sources of livelihood and hope. Our programs address the body, the mind, the family, and the community of each client. The thread that links each of these elements of Reach Out is education. We use education to share strategies with our clients, their children, our volunteers, and our doctors about how to care for people living with HIV/AIDS, for themselves, their families, and their community.

Through the photos that follow, we provide a glimpse into the daily life of Reach Out.

Reach Out's main objective is to provide free medical care and socioeconomic, spiritual, and emotional support to those living with HIV/AIDS in Mbuya Parish. We have a special focus on those who live in the poor areas of our community, for whom such services are out of reach.

We start each clinic day with a yoga exercise, a prayer, and a song to relax the mind.

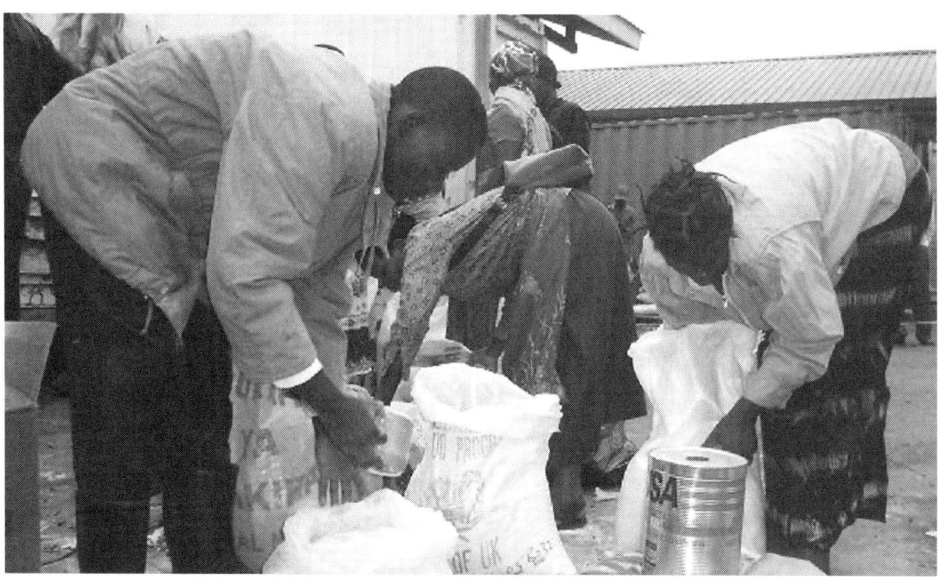

In collaboration with the World Food Programme (WFP), Reach Out provides food assistance to more than 1,000 clients and their families. Food is the first medicine, as without it, people's response to antiretrovirals (ARVs) and tuberculosis drugs is likely to be poor.

We teach our community about proper nutrition to support their medical treatment. This education takes place as they wait for their medical appointments.

We believe that expertise should be widely shared. Through biweekly medical education, we make sure that our doctors, nurses, and volunteers have current information on how to care for our clients.

Most of the care at Reach Out is not provided by doctors or nurses. Instead, clients are trained to be Community ARV and TB Treatment Supporters. They visit clients in their home neighborhood, give a weekly report on each client to one of five community supervisors, and facilitate emergency attention if needed.

The counseling section has expanded its activities beyond pre- and posttest HIV/AIDS counseling. The team also addresses other issues in the community, such as depression and alcoholism, which have devastating effects not only on our clients but also on their extended families.

Doctors, volunteers, and community supporters visit with clients in their homes when they are bedridden. In addition to providing medical care, they assist with household chores.

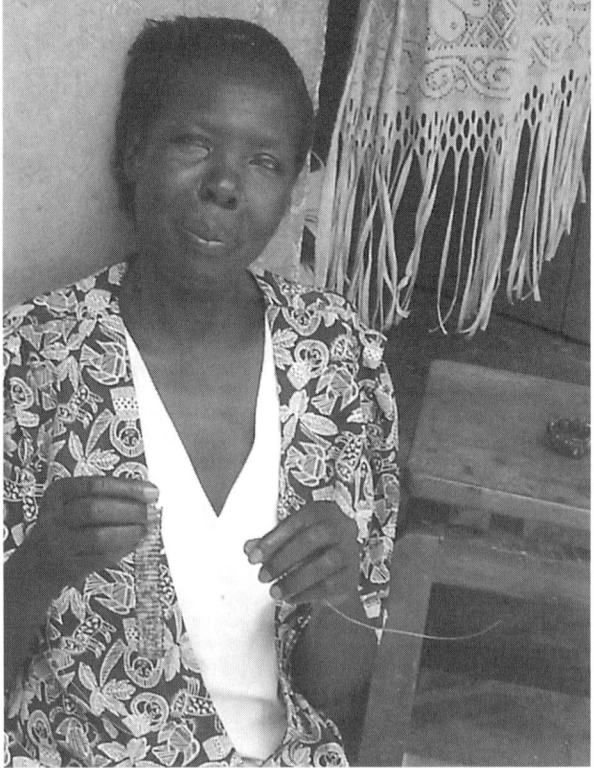

With access to ARVs, many of our clients are no longer bedridden, but they are often unemployed. Clients receive business training and loans from our micro-finance program to start small businesses so they can support their families.

Bead-making is one of the initiatives Reach Out has started as an employment alternative to the dangerous work in the local stone quarry. Our beads are made from magazine paper.

Most of our clients have no formal education. Over the long term, basic mathematics and reading and writing skills will help them not only in conducting their businesses, but also in their daily lives.

To have hope for the future, we also believe that Reach Out cannot deliver care without prevention. Our community outreach programs include community drama and role-play activities in schools and in the community, teaching skills that allow children and adults to make informed decisions on all aspects of life and to increase awareness of HIV/AIDS.

At Reach Out, every day is a day of celebration as we care for each person holistically rather than merely treating a disease.

Reach Out Mbuya Parish HIV/AIDS Initiative is a faith-based organization that runs out of Our Lady of Africa Church in Kampala, Uganda. The objective of this organization is to provide medical care and social, economic, spiritual, and emotional support to poor people living with HIV/AIDS. For more information on this organization, please see www.reachoutmbuya.org.

On Teaching for Social Change: Creating a Bridge between Academia and Practice

SUZANNE GRANT LEWIS

My purpose in teaching comparative and international education is to prepare students to be catalysts for social change. I am not interested in helping students "fit in" with the current development paradigm or maintain the status quo — the existing social and educational inequities in the world are too serious and massive. At the end of the term, I want students to think differently from when they first came into my class and be prepared to make a difference in the world. The belief in the transformative power of education held by most students coming to a graduate school of education is shared by most faculty members, including me. But this belief needs to be leavened with an understanding of the global and local forces that determine to what extent that transformative power can be exercised. Such understanding requires theoretical training on education and development. It requires the recognition that theoretical frameworks affect international, national, and local institutions, including education, and that they influence the actions of graduate students and education development professionals, consciously or not. Preparing students must involve building a bridge between academia and practice, a process by which theory is made relevant, if not essential, to the practice.

Intellectual developments in the field, as discussed by Nelly Stromquist in this volume, certainly have influenced how and what I teach. Indeed, as an active participant in recent debates on whether a comparative and international education (CIE) canon exists, where CIE courses should be located within professional schools of education (Tikly & Crossley 2001), and what constitutes a solid introductory international education course, I have changed my course syllabi accordingly.[1] Yet my practical experience and my ongoing commitment to affecting practice are what have most strongly informed my approach to teaching. Before joining the faculty at the Harvard Graduate School of Education (HGSE), I worked for over two decades with ministries of education, universities, and civil society organizations in sub-Saharan Africa. As a young college graduate teaching in a girls' boarding school in rural Kenya, I experienced the remnants of the colonial education system in that country's contemporary schools. I puzzled over the arcane mathematical principles that Form IV math students were forced to master and despaired at the loss of 10 percent of my young female students to pregnancy. Conducting dissertation research in Tanzania introduced me to the politics of policymaking and the vested interests of government bureaucracies. As a postdoctoral fellow working in the United States Agency for International Development's Africa Bureau, I eventually realized the limits of what one can really understand about a country's education system, let alone culture, in a two-week visit or a three-week sector assessment. This convinced me of the danger of pretending otherwise when millions of dollars of foreign assistance — and even the country's policy agenda — rest on the analysis of these "two-week wonders." When I worked in Namibia's newly independent ministry of education in the early 1990s, I learned how the legacy of apartheid is multigenerational, affecting not just those "educated" in the Bantu education system but also those taught by teachers trained in that system. My time in Namibia reaffirmed, however, my belief that inspired leadership can make a difference, even in bureaucratic ministries of education. My policy advising work in Malawi educated me about the adverse affects of developing countries' "donor fatigue" in the face of desperate local needs. My involvement in a capacity-building program in Namibia, that developed the research capabilities of local education leaders, taught me the power of nourishing an individual's intellectual curiosity with the types of research questions that could direct their work.

My experiences have had common elements, including the dominance of foreign aid in any discussion of education in sub-Saharan Africa and the inspiring spirit of parents, teachers, and community members making sacrifices to provide the best possible education for children given dramatic resource constraints. Each of these experiences was different in time, place, and the lessons they taught me. Together they impressed upon me the importance of both local context and global forces. They took me and my teaching back to theory to better understand this dialectic between the local and the global.

Teaching a Diverse Student Body

Master's students in the International Education Policy Program at HGSE comprise the largest group of students in my classes, but small numbers of doctoral students, a few undergraduates, and master's students from other programs who have an interest in education systems outside the United States also enroll.[2] CIE courses tend to attract a disproportionately higher number of international students, perhaps because such students seek a forum in which to make sense of their own education systems and learn from comparisons with other countries. This rich mix of international students enhances discussions in my classes because their contributions point out the varied ways that context defines educational experiences while also identifying the common intractable problems and converging policy agendas across the globe.

Students in my classes are characterized by varying depths of exposure to education outside the United States and a range of understanding regarding educational theories. Some students have limited social science backgrounds and others come with considerable fluency in critical race theory and Third World feminist theory. I poll students at the start of each semester, asking them in which countries they have worked, with which countries they are familiar, what topics they are most interested in, about their first degree, and about where they see themselves in five years. Bachelor's degrees in East Asian languages mix with business administration and international relations degrees — no field dominates. Some students come wanting to make sense of their two years in the Peace Corps or teaching English in Japan. Others come with limited work experience but having grown up in a developing society in which the wealth disparities were striking. Students express interest in a wide range of topics: how cultural and academic exchange can contribute to a country's development; how NGOs and the private sector can collaborate; the relationship between education, poverty, and inequality; and how to strengthen the dialogue between practitioners and policymakers to improve education. To address such diverse backgrounds and interests, my courses have to include mechanisms to tap into students' experiences and prior knowledge and provide space for the investigation of issues pertinent to them, as well as achieve the learning objectives of the course.

Course Content

If a CIE canon exists, it revolves around issues of equality, equity, and marginalization, rather than particular books or articles. In his reflection on the future of CIE, Anthony Welch (2003) argues, "We either take the side of the marginalized and dispossessed, or deepen their problems" (p. 40). In my introductory course, I choose materials that cover several key themes under the equality, equity, and marginalization umbrella.

As the authors in this volume indicate, there is tremendous richness and variation of issues about which to teach. The chapters by philosophers Paulo Freire and Julius Nyerere focus on the purpose of education as a tool for advancing individuals and societies. Stromquist's essay supports the bridge between academic work and practice by clearly indicating how the theoretical frameworks inform much education policy and practice in the world. Reimers's contribution reaffirms the importance of teaching, supporting my requirement that any discussion of quality must include teachers. The chapters by Vavrus, Mahshi and Bush, and Vargas Clavería and Gómez Alonso highlight the importance of local context, and how the decontextualized solution is a trap, because it denies the agency of students and communities and ignores the historical, political, economic, and cultural conditions that impinge on educational problems.

Learning Objectives, Pedagogy, and Instructional Resources

My learning objectives, pedagogy, and choices about instructional resources aim to be consistent with my understanding of appropriate and ethical behavior in contributing to the international development process. These choices are deeply personal and grow out of reflection on my own training, my search for an appropriate role as a White American woman working in sub-Saharan Africa, and from following my instincts in teaching adults and children over many years. My graduate training was strong on theory and criticism but did not prepare me to develop alternative solutions to practical problems. I was left on my own to translate theory into action. As a professor, I think I must facilitate that translation in my classes by providing opportunities for students to explore the implications of theory for action. I want to help students "to think like scholars and also make a difference," as one student wrote in a course evaluation. In addition, being a middle-class White American female, I work in countries where I am an outsider and I influence policies and practice that I do not have to live with forever. That position of privilege has troubled me, and I have reflected on how I can appropriately contribute to the improvement of education on a continent for which I have such affinity but which is not my place of origin. This reflection, combined with the model of my graduate school advisor, Joel Samoff, a professor at Stanford University, has led to my present commitment to collaboration. I collaborate with African scholars, colleagues, and students interested in Africa, and in my teaching I model that commitment to collaborative work by promoting student collaborations. I comment below on how I incorporate theory and collaboration in my courses.

Incorporating Theoretical Frameworks

I try to build students' understanding of the various theoretical frameworks used in CIE and how those theories influence policy and define practice at the local, national, and international levels. I want to reinforce Naila Kabeer's (1996) point:

> There is…an intimate relationship between ways of thinking and ways of doing. In particular, the inclusions and exclusions that characterize different ways of thinking will help to determine what is considered worth thinking about and what is considered worth doing. (p. 303)

I strive to help students understand theory as a major influence on behavior, so they see it as something they can engage with and recognize how it affects their own actions. To do this, I require students to critically read and interpret the theoretical frameworks of modernization, dependency, neo-liberalism, postmodernism, and world systems theory. Assignments then provide creative ways to strengthen the theory-practice connection.

For example, we hold a "development debate" in class in which three teams of students must each try to persuade the Guatemalan minister of education (played by me) to adopt their theoretical framework for education reform. This activity, involving twelve to fifteen students on the three teams and the rest of the class as the minister's staff in the audience, helps students understand that different theories lead to very different educational initiatives. Modernization, dependency, and postmodernism are the frameworks represented in the debate. Feedback on the debate is very positive, with students commenting on how having to represent one theory and rebut others helped to consolidate their understanding of the theories. One student requested that a second in-class debate be added to the syllabus so that all the theoretical frameworks covered in class could be debated and their implications for education reform be articulated.

Another assignment requires students to work from the other direction by reading a seemingly atheoretical education plan for a country, state, or city of their choice and identifying the dominant theoretical framework in the plan, citing evidence in the text, and referencing class readings. The student must also critique the plan using a different theoretical framework, but again, citing evidence from the plan that supports the criticism. This five-page paper requires students to review all five of the frameworks we study and then deepen their understanding of two of them. Students regularly express appreciation for being exposed to government policy documents and for having the opportunity to investigate the theoretical frameworks that underpin them.

I have found that teaching cases representing real-life dilemmas help make concrete the dilemmas faced by people and organizations working to improve educational opportunities in different parts of the world. I have supervised the writing of three such cases and would encourage other educators to develop their own or use existing cases that are published or available for purchase. One of the cases examines the dilemma facing a faith-based organization, the Mercy Center of Addis Ababa, Ethiopia, regarding whether to abandon its proselytizing church ministry work in favor of registering as a non-governmental organization and potentially receiving greater funding to support their development activities. New cases investigating the Amy Biehl Foundation in South Africa and SchoolNet Namibia will be used in the 2005–06 school year. Student response to these cases has been enthusiastic, with several assessments saying "wonderful" and "my favorite activity." Another resource is the use of audio or videoconferences to bring into the classroom practitioners who can speak to their understanding of development and the contribution of their work, even if they cannot personally be in the classroom. Among the guests I have hosted in person or virtually are the director of education at UNICEF, a National Science Foundation program officer researching women in science, and a range of doctoral students demystifying the research process and presenting the implications of their findings for practice. Exposing students to active practitioners provides role models and helps students understand their professional options. As one student reported in written feedback, the guest speaker "gave me more insight and hope that there are effective development workers out there that are genuinely committed to the local communities in which they work."

Incorporating Collaboration

A second learning objective in my classrooms is that of collaboration. To achieve this objective, I allow students to take charge of their learning and promote peer-to-peer collaborations. Very structured assignments, aimed at developing specific research or analytic skills, still allow students the choice of topic or geographical focus. Final research paper topics are open-ended as long they fit under the wide umbrella of the course. Students have taken advantage of this opportunity to explore topics as varied as nonformal education methods in the Children's Defense Fund's curriculum for Freedom Schools to the treatment of Romà ethnic minorities under self-government in Hungary.

In-class small-group activities promote collaboration among students. Some assignments can be written by pairs, which provides valuable experience applicable in a working setting while also teaching the costs and benefits of collaboration. In the required cover note about the cowriting experience, students report on how much more difficult it was to cowrite, but they often also comment on how the paper benefited from two minds working together. In a group presentation assignment, I allow students to identify organizations whose work they are interested in sharing with the class. A rich range of topics is always the result. In one class, the topics included EduVision's handheld computers in rural Kenya, distance education at Universiti Sains Malaysia, and Born Free Schools in rural India. Students must provide written feedback to peers on these presentations, which is another way to encourage the type of feedback that professionals should employ. At the start of the semester, I circulate a class list to class members with student background survey information and, toward the end of the semester, I share a list of the final research paper topics, attempting to link students with common interests and modeling the academic collaboration that often begins with sharing bibliographic resources.

Collegial behavior and creating a bridge between academia and practice can be supported by helping students identify with and draw strength from the CIE community. Career trajectories in CIE are no longer bifurcated and professionals move back and forth between academia and practice. For example, several of the authors in this volume have moved between academia and practice, including Nelly Stromquist, Richard Maclure, Paulo Freire, and Fernando Reimers. I share with students my own career path and that of some of my colleagues to help them with their own decision-making.

Encouraging Personal Reflection

Personal reflection on international development issues is another learning objective in my courses. I encourage students to identify and then question their assumptions about international development. This reflection starts on the first day of class, when I ask students to organize into small groups to discuss "what is national development?" and "what are the benchmarks of national development?" In the plenary session, groups report back and share responses, which often range from the usual macroeconomic indicators of GDP per capita to less easily measured characteristics such as respect for human rights. We come back to these personal definitions as we cover different theoretical frameworks and study China's and Tanzania's alternative development models and the changing role of international organizations. In-class discussions solicit students' reflections on their prior work and how their perspectives may have changed as a result of more critical reflection. Reinterpreting past performance in light of new perspectives can be confusing and even upsetting, as it was for a midcareer student who wondered if his previous ten years' work had been "wrongheaded" because it increased other countries' dependence on the United States. Some students despair that they have chosen the wrong field, but by the end of the course they usually emerge more cautious and thoughtful about their role in educational development, also believing that it is possible to be ethical in that role. At the end of the semester, reflecting on the theoretical frameworks and their privileged positions, I ask students to write a two-page narrative reflection about their journey over the semester. One student wrote:

> Despite having worked for the State Department and an international NGO for several years, I had no point of scholarly reference to explain the issues involved in International Education before enrolling in A-104 [my course]....Without question, my colleagues, supervisors and I could have performed our jobs more effectively and with greater autonomy had we been more informed.

Another student confessed:

> Prior to this course, I thought I would swoop into a "developing country" and heroically help advise their education systems as a policy advisor....Professor Grant Lewis's question "which one [theoretical framework] do you ascribe to?" forced me to examine my own philosophies and assumptions. This tough exercise helped me to better inform my own understanding, which will no doubt impact my future decisions and critiques of policies and proposals.

Conclusion

The mission of bridging the academic enterprise and practice has never been so critical. In her chapter, Nelly Stromquist echoes the sentiments of Anthony Welch, arguing that it is unconscionable for comparative educators to "remain indifferent to growing global inequalities in the economy, political power, and education." For Stromquist the solution rests in collective action, alliances, and going beyond research. But the most influential alliance resides in our classrooms, with our students. As educators of CIE, we have a responsibility to ensure that each cohort of our graduates, each new wave of development practitioners working in education, can recognize, understand, critique, and change the theoretical frameworks that perpetuate the gross inequalities in societies and their education systems. The future of our field rests in ensuring that students are well versed in theory, understanding education in the development process not as a technical enterprise in which theory is irrelevant, but as a complex, messy, and never fully controllable enterprise. Theoretical frameworks for understanding education's potential in addressing marginalization and inequality must be central to our preparation of researchers and practitioners.

Notes

1. The latest round of discussions started at the 1998 World Congress of Comparative Education Societies in Cape Town, in panels organized by Anne-Marie Bergh of UNISA, and continued at the 1999 annual meeting of CIES in Toronto. Subsequent CIES conferences featured panels sharing approaches to teaching introductory CIE courses. A survey on teaching CIE was conducted in 2001 by E. Epstein, G. Cook and S. Hite and a web-based resource was launched (www.luc.edu). The author participated in several of the above initiatives, including organizing a panel to debate the existence of a canon in CIE.
2. Established in 1998, the IEP Program was designed and established by Fernando Reimers, Emily Hannum, and myself. Fernando and I have each served as the program directors.

References

Kabeer, N. (1996). *Reversed realities: Gender hierarchies in development thought.* New Delhi: Kali for Women.

Tikly, L., & Crossley, M. (2001). Teaching comparative and international education: A framework for analysis. *Comparative Education Review, 45,* 561–580.

Welch, A. (2003). Technocracy, uncertainty, and ethics: Comparative education in an era of postmodernity and globalization. In R. Arnove & C. Torres (Eds.), *Comparative education: The dialectic of the global and the local* (2nd ed., pp. 24–51). Lanham, MD: Rowman & Littlefield.

About the Contributors

Kim Bush is a teacher at the Friends Boys School in Ramallah, West Bank. He is trained as a historian specializing in African history. His primary professional concern is education for refugees, both those spontaneously settled and camp dwellers. He was formerly a high school teacher in Quito, Ecuador, and in Los Olivos, California. (Editors' note: This information is from 1989, when we originally published his article. No further information is available.)

Paulo Freire, who died in 1997, was a pioneer in promoting the universal right to education and literacy. He served as Brazil's secretary of education, as a special advisor in education to the World Council of Churches in Geneva, Switzerland, and was professor of the philosophy of education at Pontifícia Universidade Cathólica de São Paulo and Universidade Estadual de Campinas, in Brazil. His published works include *Literacy: Reading the Word and the World*, coauthored with D. Macedo (1987), and his best-known work, *Pedagogy of the Oppressed* (1971).

Jesús Gómez Alonso is associate professor of educational research methods at the University of Barcelona. He was a member of the research project "Workaló — The Creation of New Occupational Patterns for Cultural Minorities: The Gypsy Case," funded by the Fifth Framework Program of the European Commission. His professional interests include communicative methodology, learning communities, and discourse on interpersonal relations and emotions in education. He is the author of *Contemporary Sociological Theory* (2003).

Jonathan David Jansen is dean of education at the University of Pretoria in South Africa. He also teaches courses on educational policy and research design. Jansen's research is broadly concerned with educational change in Third World contexts and, more recently, on studies of educational leadership in postconflict societies. He currently serves as vice president of the South African Academy of Science. His edited books include *Equal Educational Opportunities: Brown at 50 and the New South Africa at 10* (2005), *Mergers in Higher Education* (2002), and *Education Policy Implementation* (2001).

Margrethe Juncker, a medical doctor, helped initiate Reach Out in 2001, after completing two years as medical director of an HIV/AIDS project in Cambodia. Juncker has spent twenty-three years working in developing countries across Africa, Asia, and Central America, as a medical officer in refugee camps and orphanages, and as a consultant for the World Health Organization on public health programs. Juncker graduated as a Doctor of Medicine from Aarhus University in Denmark, and holds a master of public health and tropical medicine from Tulane University.

Suzanne Grant Lewis has served on the faculty at the Harvard Graduate School of Education since 1997. She codesigned Harvard's International Education Policy program and served as its director. Her research focuses on policy efforts to address educational inequalities, including gender inequalities, in sub-Saharan Africa, and she has a long-term commitment to developing educational research capacity in this region. Grant Lewis teaches courses on education and international development theory, educational policy and planning processes in developing countries, and international perspectives on addressing gender inequalities in education. Grant Lewis previously spent over five years in southern Africa, serving as an advisor to the Namibian and Malawian ministries of education. She has been awarded Fulbright fellowships for research and for teaching.

Marlaine E. Lockheed is a visiting fellow at the Center for Global Development and is teaching international education policy at the Harvard Graduate School of Education. Before retiring from the World Bank in 2004, Lockheed headed the World Bank Institute's Evaluation Group, after having served as the bank's education sector manager in the Middle East and North Africa, and as director for education, ad interim. Her research focuses on education policy and school effectiveness, with particular attention to social and cultural diversity. She has worked in over two dozen developing countries. Lockheed has served as vice president of the American Educational Research Association and associate editor of *Educational Evaluation and Policy Analysis*. She is principal author of *Primary Education in India* (1997).

Richard Maclure is an associate professor and former acting dean at the University of Ottawa Faculty of Education, where he teaches in the field of comparative and international education. His research focuses on basic education, international aid, and youth rights policies and programs in sub-Saharan Africa and Latin America. He has also worked directly with international agencies such as USAID and UNICEF. Maclure's work has appeared in journals including *Comparative Education, Journal of Latin American Studies, Third World Quarterly,* and *Journal of Youth Studies*.

Khalil Mahshi is presently program officer at UNESCO's International Institute for Educational Planning (IIEP) in Paris, where he manages education development projects and is involved in research on education in emergencies and reconstruction. At IIEP he is also involved in training educational planners from education ministries. Before joining IIEP, he was director general of international and public relations at the Palestinian ministry of education for six years, where he worked on the design and implementation of development projects. He also coordinated the production of the first five-year national education development plan. Mahshi studied science education and physics at Chelsea College in London and at the American University of Beirut.

Joanita Nambi, director of public relations for Reach Out, joined the organization as a volunteer in February 2003. She worked with the Uganda Catholic Secretariat as a graphics designer and illustrator before joining Reach Out. She holds a certificate in management sciences for health from the Virtual Leadership Development Program and is currently studying, by correspondence, for a diploma in public relations with Cambridge International College.

Julius K. Nyerere, who died in1999, was president of Tanzania from 1964, the year the country achieved independence, until his retirement in 1985. President Nyerere, otherwise known as *Mwalimu*, or teacher, was a tireless fighter for African liberation and African unity. He was a one of the founding fathers of the Organisation of African Unity, and a founding member and first president of the Tanganyika African National Union, the party that fought for and won Tanzanian independence from Great Britain. He was the first chairman of the

South-South Commission that later became the South Centre, and was also the architect and first chairman of the Frontline States, the grouping of African states that coordinated African support in the struggle for the liberation of Southern Africa and against apartheid. The Southern African Development Community evolved from the Frontline States, and Nyerere became its first chairman. Nyerere's speeches and essays appear in such books as *Freedom and Socialism, Freedom and Development, Uhuru Na Maendeleo, Ujamaa-Essays on Socialism,* and *Crusade for Liberation.* (Editors' note: Information on President Nyerere retrieved fom http://www. nyererefoundation.or.tz/)

Fernando Reimers is the Ford Foundation Professor of International Education at the Harvard Graduate School of Education, where he directs the International Education Policy Program and the Global Education Office. Reimers's research focuses on the relationship between policy reform and instructional quality, and on how teaching and policy can enhance the learning chances and opportunities of low-income students. He is currently studying how educational institutions can best prepare students to seize the opportunities created by globalization and how education can prepare students for engaged citizenship in diverse democracies. His books include *Unequal Schools, Unequal Chances: The Challenges of Educational Opportunity in the Americas* (2000), *Informed Dialogue: Using Research to Shape Education Policy Around the World* (1997), and *Hope or Despair? Primary Education in Pakistan* (1995).

Asgedet Stefanos is an assistant professor at the University of Massachusetts Boston. Her professional interests center around education and pedagogy, African studies, and women's studies. Her publications include "Angles of Vision: Teaching Multi-Disciplinary and Inclusive Courses" in *Achieving against the Odds: Teaching and Learning at the University of Massachusetts at Boston* (edited by T. Sieber and E. Kingston-Man, in press), and *An Encounter with Revolutionary Change: A Portrait of Contemporary Eritrean Women* (1997).

Nelly P. Stromquist is a professor at the University of Southern California's Rossier School of Education. She specializes in issues related to international development, education, and gender, which she analyzes from a critical sociological perspective. She is the author of numerous articles and books, including *Education in a Globalized World: The Connectivity of Economic Power, Technology, and Knowledge* (2002) and *Literacy for Citizenship: Gender and Grassroots Dynamics in Brazil* (1997). She is editor of *Women in the Third World: An Encyclopedia of Contemporary Issues* (1998). She is past president of the Comparative and International Education Society and currently a Fulbright New Century Scholar.

Stella Alamo Talisuna is a medical doctor with a focus on HIV/AIDS management and community-based disease control. She has experience in HIV/AIDS management at Mulago Hospital, Uganda's national referral hospital, as well as in outreach activities, tracing of people living with tuberculosis, and HIV sensitization in Karamoja, one of the most disadvantaged districts in Uganda. At Reach Out, Talisuna focuses on a holistic model of community-based care for people living with HIV/AIDS. She graduated from Makerere University Medical School in Kampala, and holds a masters of disease control from the Institute of Tropical Medicine, Antwerp, Belgium.

Liliana Vaccaro is a professor of educational supervision and educational administration in the Faculty of Education, Universidad Católica de Chile, and coordinator and principal investigator of the Interdisciplinary Program for Research in Education. Her publications include "Participación de Profesionales en el Desarrollo de Programas Communitarios de Educación Popular" in *Profesionales en la Acción: Una Mirada Crítica a la Educación Popular* (edited by S. Martinic and H. Walker, 1988) and "La Educación No Formal de Adultos en Sectores Populares: Jambitos de Acción para Pensar el Sistema Formal" in *Educación, Evaluación, y Perspectivas de Programas Extraescolares Formales y No Formales y su Articulación con el Sistema Educativo* (UNESCO and Oficina Regional de Educación para America Latina y El Caribe, 1988).

Julio Vargas Clavería is director of the Centre for Romà Studies at the University of Barcelona. He participated in the research project "Workaló — The Creation of New Occupational Patterns for Cultural Minorities: The Gypsy Case," sponsored by the Fifth Framework Program of the European Commission. His research work is developed in close collaboration with Romaní associations in Spain, including Romaní women's associations. He is coauthor of "Equality of Differences versus Postmodern Racism" in *Globalization of Racism* (edited by D. Macedo and P. Gounari, 2005).

Frances Vavrus is associate professor of education and associate director of the Center for African Education at Teachers College, Columbia University. She spent a year at the Harvard School of Public Health as an Andrew W. Mellon Postdoctoral Fellow in anthropological demography. Vavrus draws upon her background in education, African studies, and health in teaching her courses on international development, gender, and population change in Africa. She has also conducted extensive research on these issues in Tanzania. Her publications include "A Shadow of the Real Thing: Furrow Societies, Water User Associations, and Democratic Practices in the Kilimanjaro Region of Tanzania" in the *Journal of African American History* (2003), and "Postcoloniality and English: Exploring Language Policy and the Politics of Development in Tanzania" in *TESOL Quarterly* (2002).

About the Editors

Sarah Dryden-Peterson is an advanced doctoral student at the Harvard Graduate School of Education (HGSE) and a research associate of the Refugee Law Project in Kampala, Uganda. She has taught primary and middle school in Madagascar, South Africa, and Massachusetts; she now conducts research on migration in Uganda, the United States, and Canada, with a particular interest in the local integration of refugees in countries of first asylum and the role of schools in the reception of immigrants and refugees. She founded The Idea Truck, a mobile teacher resource center and library for students in South Africa, and directs a nonprofit that seeks to combine research, advocacy, and action in educational change in Africa. Dryden-Peterson was a Fulbright Scholar in Uganda; she is now a Presidential Fellow at Harvard and her research is funded by the Mellon Foundation. Her writing has appeared in *Refuge, Migration Information Source, New Issues in Refugee Research,* and the *International Journal of Educational Development* (in press).

Young-Suk Kim is a doctoral candidate at the Harvard Graduate School of Education. Her primary research focus is on the relationship between children's language development and literacy development for Korean and English monolingual and bilingual students. Her areas of interest include the role of phonological awareness in early literacy development in Korean, and vocabulary development, syntactic knowledge, and the role of different processing skills and their respective relationships to child's literacy development for English-speaking children. Kim is a recipient of the Spencer Research Training Grant, and her research has been funded by the HGSE Dean's Award and a National Science Foundation Dissertation Grant. Before attending Harvard, she taught primary school, high school, and community college in South Korea and the United States.

Benjamin Piper is an advanced doctoral student studying educational development in sub-Saharan Africa at the Harvard Graduate School of Education. He previously was a teacher and administrator in U.S. inner-city elementary and middle schools and worked in community youth development in the United States and Africa. Piper's current research focuses on the impact of in-service teacher education programs in sub-Saharan Africa on learner-centered instruction and student achievement. His research has been funded by the HGSE Dean's Award, the Harvey Fellowship, and the NAACP. His other research interests include improving educational and economic connections between the African diaspora and the continent, the achievement gap in the United States, and racial identity differences within the African diaspora in the United States. He is currently a cochair of the *Harvard Educational Review* Editorial Board.